DATE DUE

RITUALS
OF MANHOOD

RITUALS
OF MANHOOD
Male Initiation
in Papua New Guinea

Edited by
Gilbert H. Herdt

With an introduction by
Roger M. Keesing

University of California Press
Berkeley   Los Angeles   London

University of California Press
Berkeley and Los Angeles, California

University of California Press, Ltd.
London, England

Library of Congress Cataloging in Publication Data

Main entry under title:

Rituals of manhood.

   Includes index.
   1. Puberty rites—Papua New Guinea—Addresses,
essays, lectures. 2. Papua New Guinea—Social
life and customs—Addresses, essays, lectures.
I. Herdt, Gilbert H., 1949–
GN671.N5R55   392'.14   81-1807
AACR2

Printed in the United States of America

1 2 3 4 5 6 7 8 9

Book Designer: Linda M. Robertson

For Kenneth E. "Mick" Read,
a great ethnographer and pathfinder in New Guinea anthropology

CONTENTS

EDITOR'S PREFACE

What meanings surround the social action and cultural experience of male initiation in traditional New Guinea societies, an area long distinguished for its extraordinary ritual and secret cults? In the following set of new descriptive studies on rituals of manhood, a group of leading New Guineast anthropologists address this question. Not only do they provide a fresh body of anthropological information—the first substantial data on the general subject to appear in years—but, in addition, this is the first collection of comparative ethnography to ever appear on tribal initiation in Papua New Guinea or, more broadly, Melanesia. Following in the tradition established by the works of Gregory Bateson, Margaret Mead, Kenneth E. Read, and John W. M. Whiting, these interpretive essays provide new findings that help us understand the experience of ritual process as viewed from the interactional perspectives of society, culture, and the individual. The result combines a fine interplay of cultural theory and ethnographic praxis toward the furthering, and demythologizing of, anthropology's unfinished project.

Although this collection stems from an anthropological symposium held in 1979, its intellectual heritage reaches back in many directions over a hundred years of sustained inquiry, for the meaning of male initiation has long absorbed ethnographers and captured the imaginations of some of the great minds in the humanities and social sciences. The first scholars were armchair theorists, like Sir Edward Tylor (1873) and W. Robertson Smith (1927), who wrote about "primitive" tribal ritual and ancient Hebrew religion. After the turn of the century, other distinguished writers were spurred on by the Victorians to examine initiation rites specifically as a means to understand the creation and reproduction of sociocultural systems and individual adaptations to them: Jane Harrison, Arnold Van Gennep, Sir James Frazer, Emile Durkheim, Theodore Reik, Edward Westermarck, Sigmund Freud, and Alfred Haddon were among the most notable. Their own fieldwork experience was, of course, negligible. In the next thirty years anthropologists who had done ethnographic studies took up the subject of initiation: Robert Lowie, Bronislau Malinowski, A. R. Radcliffe-Brown, Géza Róheim, Ruth Benedict, Margaret Mead, Lloyd Warner, and others. The works of all the above are still very much with us; some have become twentieth-century classics in social and psychological theory. I cannot do justice to them here, but since the themes of those early works permeate our essays on New Guinea initiation, they should be mentioned.

The Victorians' armchair works, although profoundly influential, were telescopic and speculative. None did true fieldwork or had ever met a "primitive." Indeed, at least in the case of Sir James Frazer, they were proud of their lack of contact with their subjects.[1] Frazer's self-proclaimed ignorance of firsthand experience was especially ironic, for no early "anthropology" was as celebrated or widely read as his many-volumed *The Golden Bough* (1911–1915). No subject and no page in the archives of "human history" was overlooked in Frazer's massive, widely ranging, checkered works, which Freud and Durkheim freely cited. In large measure Frazer's *Golden Bough* carved out the territory of anthropology in twentieth-century Western thought and led untold pilgrims, colonists, and dreamy students off into ethnography's exotic service.[2]

The *Weltanschauung* and method of the Frazerians differed radically, though, from that of modern anthropology. They had no notion of culture in its present-day anthropological sense: a shared system of symbols, meanings, rules. Consequently, their works showed no idea of cultural relativism as it emerged in the American anthropology of Boas and his students, who viewed all cultural and behavioral patterns as relative and meaningful within their native context. Without fieldwork, Frazer's undeniable insights were borne from his studious reading of second-, third-, and even fourth-hand ethnographic reports made by travelers and missionaries. Tribal customs—such as initiation practices—were torn out of their native context in an offhand, historically uncritical process Evans-Pritchard (1965:10) called the "scrapbook treatment" of ethnological writing. Stripped of their local logic—language and cultural meanings—the dislocated bits of ritual action and belief were made to seem irrational when pieced back together in an alien, universalist "monstrous mosaic" (Evans-Pritchard 1965:10). That the Victorians were so comfortably cavalier in slotting the bits back

---

[1]Although Frazer "was a speculative scholar who never set foot in the field, . . . sometimes when he talked with government administrators or missionaries home from distant parts of the world, these travelers, astonished by his insight, would exclaim: 'Why, you know my blacks better than I know them after twenty years' residence among them!' Yet when the American psychologist William James asked Frazer to tell him about primitives he had met, Frazer's shocked response was: 'But God forbid!' " (Hays 1964:121).

[2]Remember that Malinowski's great work, *Argonauts of the Western Pacific*—which established him as the "father" of anthropological ethnography by setting out the principles of the participant-observant method—was prefaced by Sir James Frazer.

together into a pseudoevolutionary "hierarchy of human races" (Stocking 1968:113) shows the pervasiveness of their philosophical idealism and cultural Darwinism. Was there a "deep structure" of Western thought underlying those universalist typologies that treated the dislocated tribal customs as pieces of a great jigsaw puzzle?

The Victorians thought that they could infer experience from the random puzzle pieces of surface ritual custom and behavior. Their interpretations seemed to arise from a kind of "stratigraphy model" of the mind, in which Victorian culture was believed the most technologically "cultured," morally elaborated, least magical form of raw human nature—transparently revealed through savages as "living fossil" survivals from a ruder age (Geertz 1973:61). Their analysis was analytical and introspective: mood, feeling, motivation could be inferred from what the natives were said to do. For example, Freud, in *Totem and Taboo* (1955), beginning with Melanesian examples of widespread ritual-based maternal separation and boys' avoidance of mothers and females, strings together dislocated anecdote after anecdote from the New Hebrides and New Britain and on to Fiji, Sumatra, Africa, the Solomon Islands, the Nile, and more, to summarize thus: "I see no objection to the assumption that it is just this incestuous factor of the relationship which motivates the avoidance between son and mother-in-law among savages" (Freud 1955:23). In *The Elementary Forms of The Religious Life*, Durkheim (1965) shared in this willingness to "read" motives from ritual behavior. For instance, after questioning why examples of ineffective *Intichiuma* ceremonies among Australian aborigines do not lessen their "impulse to believe" in the rites' efficacy, he states: "It is because faith has this [psychic] origin that it is, in a sense, 'impervious to experience' " (he then cites Levy-Bruhl: Durkheim 1965: 403). These examples show the Victorians' intuitive belief in a plausible but naive set of Platonic universals, what Adolph Bastian, an employer of Boas, called the "psychic unity of mankind." Implied in their studies was a search for universal forces—biopsychic, social, geographic-historical—that had shaped the evolution of humanity from ape to savage to the preeminent colonial and spiritual place of Western man (not necessarily woman) as God's chosen.

The Victorians were thus engaged in several kinds of discourse at once. On the one hand, their fascination with ritual and totemism expressed ways of thinking about evolutionary passages: from animality to humanity, from nature to culture, and from affectivity to intellectuality (Lévi-Strauss 1963:101). On the other hand, they tended to use tribal peoples as clinical specimens of social "primitiveness" with which to compare Westerners in areas such as societal cohesiveness (Durkheim), sexual and moral development (Westermarck), and mental life and neurosis (Freud).[3] In the popular expressions of these themes, the state and church needed social controls, like stiff moral codes, to restrain the savage part of human nature hidden under a "thin veneer of civilization." The history of Western sexuality provides many illustrations of that social discourse, as Foucault (1978) has shown. That the savagery of Victorians could erupt—degenerate—when they were removed from the circumstances of normal social controls was a common theme in the popular fiction of Frazer's day, such as Joseph Conrad's *Heart of Darkness*.

The "anthropology" of Durkheim, the sociologist, and Freud, the psychoanalyst, was very much a product of this Victorian heritage, which colored their polar treatments of society, ritual, and the individual. Both *Elementary Forms* and *Totem and Taboo* were period works that drew heavily from the recent ethnography on Australian aborigines (cf. Hiatt 1975:4−5). Both books are scattered with second-hand references to Tylor, Robertson Smith, and Frazer. In crudest terms, Durkheim's project concerned the understanding of social solidarity and collective symbolic structures, whereas Freud's work stressed the phylogenetic universality of the Oedipal complex and unconscious structures of mind. For Durkheim, ritual actions expressed the social order and constituted the key functions that maintained that order; and ritual belonged "to a system of symbolic discourse, the true *referents* of which are to be found in that social order" (Skorupski 1976:24). Conversely, Freud and his followers believed that ritual actions expressed the Oedipal complex and constituted the social functions that regulated the instinctual drives of that phylogenetic complex; moreover, such ritual meanings belonged to the system of unconscious discourse, the referents of which are interpretable by the trained analyst's mind.[4] In fact, of course, the Durkheimian and Freudian paradigms both drew on social and psychological principles—for example, Durkheim's (1965) notions of the "cult," of "faith," and of "sentiments," and Freud's (1955:149, 203) ideas about a group "psyche of the mass" and of a socially organized "magic production and consumption club." And both were

---

[3]Note that *Totem and Taboo* was subtitled *Resemblances between the Psychic Lives of Savages and Neurotics*.

[4]"Thus psychoanalytic hermeneutics, unlike the cultural sciences, aims not at the understanding of symbolic structures in general. Rather, the act of understanding to which it leads is self-reflection" (Habermas 1971:228).

interested in the meaning of ritual experience, though they and their adherents stressed nonconscious and unconscious experience, without recourse to firsthand ethnographic observations. Consequently, the phenomenon of ritual was not treated as such, and its symbolic and psychological functions were not explained: its character was merely elucidated (Skorupski 1976:24; see also Evans-Pritchard 1965; Geertz 1966; Herdt 1981; Tuzin 1977).

What needs emphasis here is the point that in subsequent years no "interactionist" model of society, symbolic system, and the individual as complementary perspectives on ritual emerged in anthropology. The Durkheimian paradigm filtered through Radcliffe-Brown (1922) into the social-structural emphases of British social anthropology. "Collective representations" and ritual action were tried and tested over and again as structural-functional reflections of kinship, ancestral worship, and sociopolitical solidarity. Fired by the old Frazerian baggage and the Oedipal excesses of the Freudians, social anthropology turned away from evolutionism, universalism, culture, individualism, and the mind. Freud's direct influence was felt mainly in his followers, like Reik (1946),[5] and his too-faithful students, like Roheim (1926), who actually went to Australia to find Freud's "primal horde" (see Hiatt 1975:5 ff.). Freud's personality theory continued to exert a strong influence on American cultural anthropology, however, through the old "culture and personality" studies of Edward Sapir, Ruth Benedict, Margaret Mead, John Whiting, and others. When the Freudian paradigm faded, so did that kind of anthropology. The American school, however, always retained an interest in the individual and culture that was quite antithetic to British anthropology (Lewis 1977). It was through the influence of Benedict and Mead that Bateson (1958) interpreted Iatmul ritual and personality in New Guinea. (See Roger Keesing's Introduction below). His interactionist approach, though, was virtually ignored for decades.

In Van Gennep's (1960) essay, *Les Rites de passage*, we have a third line of work that specifically treats initiation rites and offers an interactionist model. Like his contemporaries, Durkheim and Freud, he was strongly influenced by Frazer,[6] but unlike them, his impact was

---

[5]Reik's essay, "The Puberty Rites of Savages," contains a classic Oedipal-theory formulation, and its influence was felt in both the internal discourse of psychoanalysis and in popular thought; see, for example, William Maxwell's novel *The Folded Leaf*.

[6]In an obscure paper praising Frazer's *Golden Bough*, Van Gennep writes: "I confess sincerely that . . . my *Rites de passage* is like a part of my own flesh, and was the result of a kind of inner illumination that suddenly dispelled a sort of darkness in which I had been floundering for almost ten years" (Belmont 1979:58).

almost negligible until the last twenty years. For all of its merits, the Durkheimians—in the very person of Marcel Mauss—gave poor reviews to *The Rites of Passage* (Belmont 1979:62−63). Yet its merits have not diminished. First, Van Gennep presented a formal model of ritual, based on the idea of "ceremonial sequence"—context-rooted "dramatic scenarios" that should be seen as parts of a meaningful gestalt. Social transitions of all sorts in the life cycle of individual and group were examined: pregnancy and confinement, initiation, marriage, and funerals. Initiation rites got special treatment, and Van Gennep cited some of the best-known Melanesian reports of his day. They were "very pure transitions" the life crises of which celebrated social, not physical, puberty ("it would be better to stop calling initiation rites 'puberty rites'": Van Gennep 1960:66).

Van Gennep divided transition rites into three universal phases of ceremonial sequence, as is well known. First came separation rites, removing the initiates from secular life; then followed threshold rites, marking the ambiguous movement of persons into new statuses and roles; and finally the passage was consummated in aggregation rites, which returned the actor to secular group life. Van Gennep recognized the importance of the threshold period, which ritualized the marginality of the initiate and the margins of society, so he also referred to the three transitions as preliminary, liminary, and postliminary (from the French word *limen*, "margin" ceremonies). Van Gennep's ideas have found wider currency in anthropology through Victor Turner's (1967, 1969) studies of Ndumbu ritual and the liminal process in such social phenomena as pilgrimages.

The Rites of Passage has met the test of time and cross-cultural application. Van Gennep specifically rejected simple-minded evolutionary "schemas of development" as a framework for interpreting transition rituals. Instead, and quite ahead of his time, he implicitly drew on a notion of cultural relativism by insisting that ritual meanings be understood in the "dynamic whole" of their native context (Van Gennep 1960:89) Furthermore, he emphasized the principle of "changes in social categories"—a structuralist formulation—whereby ritual becomes *the* social mechanism for relating individual life-cycle crises to group events.[7] Lastly—and here he is closer to Durkheim—Van

---

[7]"In this way, as one places oneself successively in this or that spot within the society as a whole, there is a displacement of 'magic circles'," (Van Gennep [original 1909:16], cited in Belmont [1979:61]). For a good ethnographic example of Van Gennep's structuralist treatment of initiation rites, see *The Rites of Passage* (1960:85−87) on the Masai of Kenya.

Gennep discussed the moral and educational aspects of being liminal and being trained for membership in secret societies and adult social life in general. His armchair reading, like that of Frazer, provided countless examples (many from Australian and Melanesian tribes) of how ritual initiation incorporated myth and lore, sexual experience, and military and economic training to instill social values and knowledge for profane performative life.

Later workers have modified some of Van Gennep's ideas about initiation rites in relation to the definition of adult roles. Ruth Benedict, in *Patterns of Culture* (1934), unlike Van Gennep, treated initiation rites as synonymous with "puberty institutions" (as did later writers, such as Whiting, Kluckhohn, and Anthony 1958),[8] but she argued that it was the symbolic definition of adulthood toward which they were directed: "we do not most need analyses of the necessary nature of *rites de passage*; we need rather to know what is identified in different cultures with the beginning of adulthood and their methods of admitting to the new status" (1934:25). Again, Frank Young (1965:13) generally noted that Van Gennep failed to recognize that "initiation does not confer the status of responsible adult." Chapple and Coon (1942:484 ff.) used both Van Gennep and a Durkheimian perspective: rites of passage should also be seen as a means for reequilibrating the sociocultural system. They saw a complex interaction between symbolic stress on different categories of rites—for instance, birth versus initiation—and the complexity, number, and types of social relationship involved in particular transitions within particular cultures.[9] To accommodate recurrent adult changes, Chapple and Coon added a fourth category of transition rites to Van Gennep's tripartite schema: rites of intensification, which dramatically reinforce one's social status later in life. More recently, Young has correlated initiation rites with the precise definition of sex-role dramatizations in adulthood. In his functional model, initiation works to "reinforce a boy's ability to perform his sex role in the type of society that presents him with definite and institutionalized male status. He must learn the definition of the male situation maintained by the organized adult males" (Young 1965:30). Symbolically, then, the greater the stress placed on the adult dramatization of the masculine gender role, the

---

[8]New Guinea societies offer exceptions to this equation between initiation rites and puberty, as I have argued elsewhere (see Herdt 1981:314).

[9]"These differences depend on the magnitude of the changes, on the number of individuals and institutions affected, and on the degree to which they are affected as well" (Chapple and Coon 1942:506).

greater the emphasis on male versus female initiation rites in a particular society (see also Mead 1949; Shapiro 1979).[10] In the following essays we see many examples of this social stress on male performance and adult gender differentiation structured into the symbolic environment of New Guinea initiation.

Having traced this discursive history, we can now briefly review the anthropological field studies of initiation whose impetus leads to the present volume. From the 1920s onward, it was mainly British social anthropologists who took charge of those studies. Malinowski, not long returned from his Trobriand Islands work, presided in London. Radcliffe-Brown's influence likewise grew, from professoring in South Africa and Australia to Chicago and finally Oxford. It was Malinowski (1926:126), though, who railed against the old Victorian armchair studies, the speculative and "lengthy litanies" that made the "anthropologist look silly and the savage look ridiculous." And so students were sent to Africa, Australia, and Melanesia to do fieldwork, Malinowski style, from the "native's point of view." All in all, a long and distinguished list of workers went to Africa, including M. Fortes, E. E. Evans-Pritchard, A. I. Richards, S. F. Nadel, M. Gluckman, and I. Schapera, and also to the Pacific, including R. Firth, R. Fortune, B. Blackwood, G. Bateson, P. Kaberry, I. Hogbin, H. Powdermaker, J. Layard, and others, this latter group having studied New Guinea peoples. There were few detailed treatments of initiation or male cults, although one thinks of the works of John Layard and A. Bernard Deacon on the New Hebrides, Hortense Powdermaker on New Ireland, and Camilla Wedgwood on Manam Island—exceptional studies of island Melanesia. In general these studies stressed social organization and kinship structure, and not the cultural system or native experience, but rather the social action of ritual.

The anthropological romance with initiation rites began surprisingly early in mainland New Guinea studies. No doubt this emphasis reflects the use of initiation as a powerful sociocultural organizing principle in many Melanesian groups (cf. Allen 1967). On the one hand, the New Guinea works were spared part of the trenchant formalism that for decades characterized the African ethnography. The reasons are varied, but one thing is certain: various fieldworkers of original mind and

---

[10]Various authors have also followed Freud in suggesting links between Oedipal factors (Reik 1946; Stephens 1962; Whiting, Kluckhohn, and Anthony 1958) or pre-Oedipal factors (Bettelheim 1955; Mead 1949, especially chap. 6) and the ritualized development of gender identity (see Allen 1967; Herdt 1981; partially reviewed in chap. 2).

diverse academic training had, willy-nilly, found their way to New Guinea. This group included outstanding explorer-ethnographers, such as Richard Thurnwald and Richard Parkinson (who published in German), the Swedish fieldworker Gunnar Landtman, and the Australian government anthropologist F. E. Williams, to name but a few of the colorful lot who worked from the 1900s to the 1930s. Then came the Americans, following Margaret Mead, such as Hortense Powdermaker and John Whiting; they were followed by other Australian ethnographers. On the other hand, though, the field reports from New Guinea are of quite varied sorts, textures, and tastes, some tucked away in obscure journals, some never published in English, and some representing an unusual assortment of different theories and personalities. Ironically, it was from this diverse group—working outside mainstream social anthropology—that we got our richest studies of initiation. To mention only the most significant works: Landtman, *The Kiwai Papuans* (1927); Mead, *Sex and Temperament* (1968) and *The Mountain Arapesh* (1940); Bateson, *Naven* (1958); Whiting, *Becoming a Kwoma* (1941); and, of course, the classic Papuan ethnographies of F. E. Williams, such as *Papuans of the Trans-Fly* (1936) and *Drama of Orokolo* (1940), whose riches have not been fully appreciated. These workers were remarkable in their willingness to report the actual doings and sayings of ritual behavior, not just its abstracted normative patterns of social action. And between them, Bateson and Mead left an anthropological legacy that has only recently been matched in considerations of descriptive scope, theoretical insight, and intellectual influence on New Guinea studies (cf. McDowell 1980).

By contrast, the ethnographers who followed in the 1940s and 1950s generally ignored initiation in favor of social structure and other topics. Of those few writing on the subject, most contributed only short papers that set out normative summaries of ritual action relatively devoid of real people and real events. That trend was unfortunate, for the net effect of those mid-century divertisements served to dampen, not stimulate, interest in the great questions about ritual which had intrigued early social theorists. Secret societies, body rituals, group transitions and symbolic structures, sexuality, the dynamics of personality development, and the ritual "reproduction" of society—all were virtually ignored. Even the conceptual stock and trade of Bateson and Mead's papers, the notions of ethos and sexual temperament, or alternative gender ideologies, were mostly forgotten. Undoubtedly the post–World War II opening of the Highlands as a terra incognita to intensive anthropological research contributed to this shift. The initial studies were exploratory and intensely descriptive. Some workers probably felt that initiation had already been studied and explained. Perhaps the difficulty of Highlands' non-Austronesian languages presented another field problem, since even seasoned fieldworkers questioned whether a year or two would ever prove sufficient to penetrate the insides of Highlands' exotic initiations or other complex symbolic behavior. Moreover, other anthropological interests had come along which were also important and worthy. Thus, students were sent out in pursuit of other ethnography: on social structure and big men and ceremonial exchange. On the coast, studies of social change were prominent, including several excellent studies of cargo cults (e.g., Lawrence 1964) and Mead's (1956) restudy of Manus Island. In the meantime, of course, New Guinea was being wrenchingly transformed, propelled by political and economic forces that are only partially under its control. And the dreary progress of Secularism (to use Ioan Lewis's phrase) has continued, exacting a stiff price: the general decline or demise of secret male societies and traditional initiations that F. E. Williams was already publicly lamenting some fifty years ago.

There were some exceptions to this lack of interest in ritual. K. E. Read's (1952) classic paper on the *nama* men's cult among the Eastern Highlands Gahuku-Gama, for example, established several interlocking themes of research on ritual and "sexual antagonism" (see Herdt, this volume, chap. 2). Read's (1980) later work and that of his students (see Langness 1967; Newman 1964, 1965) best exemplified these contributions. Berndt's (1962) work, though it raised powerful neglected issues, is methodologically messy and remains controversial. The popular reception of Lawrence and Meggitt's collection, *Gods, Ghosts, and Men in Melanesia* (1965), though, indicated a returning interest in symbolic and religious studies (see also Hogbin 1970; Van Baal 1966).

Over the past decade the anthropology of New Guinea initiation and symbolism has finally begun to realize the rich promise of its subject. These new studies are associated with studies of ritual and the rise of "symbolic anthroplogy" at large. The latter title is felicitous, because various kinds of paradigms are involved—structuralism and semiotics in England and France, symbolist anthropology, hermeneutics, psychological and ethnosemantic studies in America and Europe—for various sorts of researchers, scholars who are doing work on symbolic behavior, gender, cultural communication, dominant symbols, and the like. Such perspectives have recently emerged in the works of various New Guineasts: Forge (1972, 1973), Kelly (1976), Langness (1974), Lindenbaum 1972), Poole (1981), Strathern and Strathern (1971), Strathern (1978),

Tuzin (1972, 1977), Wagner (1972), and Weiner (1976). Their influence is apparent in this book (see Roger Keesing's Introduction below). Finally, a marvelous group of recent, focused, full ethnographies on male initiation and ceremonial behavior have started to capture the richness of symbolic life in New Guinea societies for which Bateson and Mead had first vouched (see Barth 1975; Gell 1975; Herdt 1981; Lewis 1980; Schieffelin 1976; Tuzin 1980). These developments have helped pave the way for our own volume: a new anthropology of ritual experience.

Not "experience" in its Frazerian sense—speculative and ethnocentric atributions based on secondhand impressions—but, rather, ethnographically oriented descriptions of individual and group behavior, communicative acts, feelings, moods, and the intersubjective process through which meanings get associated with such experiences and are interpreted by the actors, audiences, and ethnographer. Such was the hope that led me to convene a forum on male initiation. Quite simply, we wished to flush out fresh descriptive data, collected by younger anthropologists, who had actually observed initiation in New Guinea communities and could therefore talk about "meaning and experience."

The resulting original papers were all presented at a symposium of the Seventh Annual Meetings of the Association for Social Anthropology in Oceania, held in Clearwater, Florida, from February 28 to March 4, 1979. Each contributor in this resulting volume is a professional anthropologist of distinction at an American university and each researcher has conducted one or more major periods of fieldwork, the combined total of which represents over fifteen years' worth of actual experience in Papua New Guinea traditional societies.

It is worth mentioning how this group of ethnographers was selected. New Guinea is a vast area (the world's second largest island) of incredible cultural and linguistic diversity. It is believed that it has over 700 distinct tribal groups and possibly 2,000 different languages. It seemed not only valuable but indeed necessary to collect reports on initiation from as many different subcultural areas where anthropologists had worked as we could. The possibilities seemed great. Initiation ceremonies are traditionally widespread (though not universal: see Allen 1967) among indigenous groups, and several score anthropologists had worked in different communities since the war. Nonetheless, I was surprised by the numbers of workers who had not seen initiation while in the field, and, of that total pool, those who could not participate for one reason or another dramatically decreased the possibilities.

Fortunately, we assembled an outstanding group of contributors whose work encompasses four different major ethnographic subregions of Papua New Guinea. They are represented as follows: the East Sepik Province (Deborah B. Gewertz, on the Chambri; Donald F. Tuzin, on the Ilahita Arapesh); the West Sepik Province (Fitz John Porter Poole, on the Bimin-Kuskusmin); the Eastern Highlands Province (Terence E. Hays and Patricia H. Hays, on the Ndumba; Gilbert H. Herdt, on the Sambia; Philip L. Newman and David J. Boyd, on the Awa); and the Southern Highlands Province (Edward L. Schieffelin, on the Kaluli). (See map 1.)

The consistently high quality of these ethnographic essays attests to the outstanding fieldwork that produced them and to the fact that all the contributors have been interested in ritual, while half of them concentrated specifically on initiation and religion in their primary research. These essays are hermeneutic achievements: to condense large amounts of ethnographic material into single chapters without distorting the significance of complex human events—while still preserving the experiential flavors and multivalent meanings that constitute the interpretations—has been a difficult task whose final product is, we hope, successful. This feat is all the more worthy in view of the fact that these papers go beyond description to advance method and theory. Overall, these accomplishments were facilitated in large measure by the substantial publications of general ethnographic material the contributors have already produced on other aspects of these tribal societies.

Here, then, is a trove of anthropological riches whose success should be reckoned as much by the addition of new ethnography as by the many enlightened questions the essays raise. The product is incomplete, as I expected it would be: we urgently need new research to enable us to tackle those unanswered questions in the comparative ethnography of New Guinea's traditional and changing communities. Nevertheless, taken as a whole, these papers and their intellectual tradition underline anthropology's vitality in studying sociocultural systems as "total social facts" about human existence, as Professor Keesing sets out in the sweeping critique of his landmark Introduction.

The success of this venture is due in large part to the generous help of several individuals and institutions whose overall support I wish to acknowledge gratefully. First, we sincerely thank Professor L. L. Langness and Professor Shirley Lindenbaum, who served as formal discussants at the original symposium and who later provided many helpful comments. Second, we offer special thanks to Professor Mervyn Meggitt for his valuable, incisive comments at the symposium and later editorial assistance. For many helpful suggestions I wish to thank Fitz

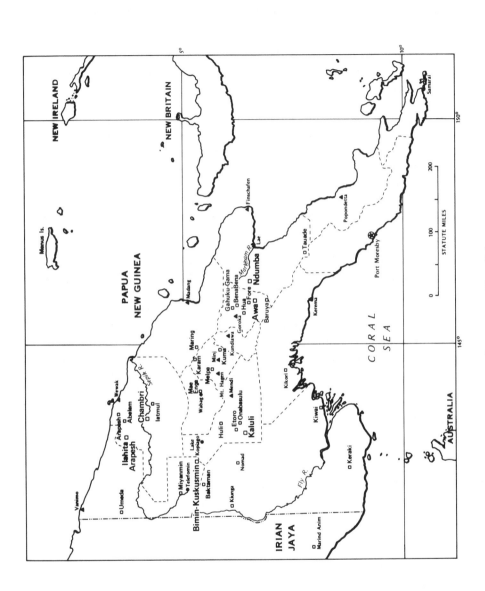

MAP 1. Papua New Guinea.

John Poole, George Spindler, and Don Tuzin. To Mac Marshall and Vern Carroll we extend our gratitude for their efforts in helping organize our symposium at the Annual Meetings of the Association for Social Anthropology in Oceania. For institutional support that facilitated the production of this volume I express my generous thanks to the Department of Psychiatry within the Neuropsychiatric Institute of the University of California, Los Angeles, where Thelma Guffan helped in typing and logistically supporting this volume while I conducted research in Papua New Guinea; and my thanks go to her again. Jim Kubeck of the University of California Press, along with Shirley Warren and Diana Rico, deserve our collective thanks for careful and patient production of this volume.

Roger Keesing found time in a crowded schedule to write the Introduction to this book, drawing on long personal and scholarly experience of Melanesia in synthesizing our essays, and I wish to extend my personal gratitude for his following *coup de maître*.

It is with special appreciation that we also acknowledge the support of the government of Papua New Guinea, which enabled us to visit and live among its peoples.

Finally, we dedicate this volume to Professor Kenneth E. Read, a great ethnographer, pathfinder, and essayist in the tradition of New Guinea studies. Some of us were his students at the University of Washington; all of us have known his writings. His triumph is *The High Valley*, a classic of modern anthropology. In it, he succeeded beyond his time in illuminating the complex realities of whole people and whole events that constitute the first studies of a Highlands group and their ritual system. Thus, the fullness of his work still engages the anthropological experience, "the essence of [which] is being able to find your way between and to live with different systems of human imagination, the one you bring to the field as a creature of your own culture and the one your subjects bring to bear on the same basic phenomena" (Read 1980:ix-x). And we have not forgotten. If this book succeeds, it will, we hope, stimulate more students, like others his work has influenced, from within and on to New Guinea, to engage in the experience of furthering anthropology's unfinished project.

GILBERT H. HERDT
Stanford, California
1981

REFERENCES

ALLEN, M. R.
1967 *Male Cults and Secret Initiations in Melanesia*. Melbourne: Melbourne University Press.

BARTH, F.
1975 *Ritual and Knowledge among the Baktaman of New Guinea*. New Haven: Yale University Press.

BATESON, G.
1958 *Naven*. 2d ed. Stanford: Stanford University Press. 1st ed. 1936.

BELMONT, N.
1979 *Arnold Van Gennep*. Trans. Derek Coltman. Chicago: University of Chicago Press.

BENEDICT, R.
1934 *Patterns of Culture*. Boston: Houghton Mifflin Co.

BERNDT, R. M.
1962 *Excess and Restraint*. Chicago: University of Chicago Press.

BETTELHEIM, B.
1955 *Symbolic Wounds, Puberty Rites, and the Envious Male*. New York: Collier Books.

CHAPPLE, E. D., and C. S. COON
1942 *Principles of Anthropology*. New York: Henry Holt and Co.

DURKHEIM, E.
1965 *The Elementary Forms of the Religious Life*. Trans. J. W. Swain. New York: Free Press. 1st ed. 1915.

EVANS, PRITCHARD, E. E.
1965 *Theories of Primitive Religion*. London: Oxford University Press.

FRAZIER, J. G.
1911–1915 *The Golden Bough: A Study in Magic and Religion*. 3d ed. 12 vols. London: Macmillan.

FORGE, ANTHONY.
1972 The golden fleece, *Man* 7:527–540.

1973 Style and meaning in Sepik art. In *Primitive Art and Society*, ed. A. Forge, pp. 169–192. London: Oxford University Press.

FOUCAULT, M.
1978 *The History of Sexuality*. Trans. R. Hurley. New York: Random House.

FREUD, S.
1955 Totem and taboo. In *The Standard Edition of the Complete Psychological Words of Sigmund Freud*, ed. and trans. J. Strachey, vols. 4–5. London: Hogarth. Orig. 1913.

GEERTZ, C.
1966 Religion as a cultural system. In *Anthropological Approaches to the Study of Religion*, ed. M. Bantam, pp. 1–46. London: Tavistock Publications.

1973 *The Interpretation of Cultures: Selected Essays by C. Geertz*. New York: Basic Books.

GELL, A.
1975 *Metamorphosis of the Cassowaries*. London: Athlone Press.

HABERMAS, J.
1971 *Knowledge and Human Interests*. Trans. Jeremy J. Shapiro. Boston: Beacon Press.

HAYS, H. R.
1964 *From Ape to Angel*. New York: Capricorn Books.

HERDT, G. H.
1981 *Guardians of the Flutes: Idioms of Masculinity*. New York: McGraw-Hill.

HIATT, L. R.
1975 *Australian Aboriginal Mythology*. Canberra: Australian Institute of Aboriginal Studies.

HOGBIN, I.
1970 *The Island of Menstruating Men: Religion in Wogeo, New Guinea*. Scranton, Pa.: Chandler Publishing Co.

KELLY, R. C.
1976 Witchcraft and sexual relations: an exploration in the social and semantic implications of a structure of belief. In *Man and Woman in the New Guinea Highlands*, ed. P. Brown and G. Buchbinder, pp. 36–53. Washington, D.C.: American Anthropological Association.

LANDTMAN, G.
1927 *The Kiwai Papuans of British New Guinea*. London: Macmillan.

LANGNESS, L. L.
1967 Sexual antagonism in the New Guinea Highlands: a Bena Bena example. *Oceania* 37 (3):161–177.

1974. Ritual power and male domination in the New Guinea Highlands. *Ethos* 2:189–212.

LAWRENCE, P.
1964 *Road Belong Cargo*. Melbourne: Melbourne University Press.

LAWRENCE, P. and M. J. MEGGITT
1965 *Gods, Ghosts, and Men in Melanesia*. Melbourne: Melbourne University Press.

LÉVI-STRAUSS, C.
1963 *Totemism*. Trans. R. Needham. Boston: Beacon Press.

LEWIS, G.
1980 *Days of Shining Red: An Essay on Understanding Ritual*. Cambridge: Cambridge University Press.

LEWIS, I.
1977 Introduction to *Symbols and Sentiments*, ed. Ioan Lewis, pp. 1–30. London: Academic Press.

LINDENBAUM, S.
1972 Sorcerers, ghosts, and polluting women: an analysis of religious belief and population control. *Ethnology* 11 (3):241–253.

MALINOWSKI, B.
1926 *Crime and Custom in Savage Society*. Totowa, N.J.: Littlefield, Adams and Co.

McDowell, N.
1980 The Oceanic ethnography of Margaret Mead. *American Anthropologist* 82:278—303.

Mead, M.
1968 *Sex and Temperament in Three Primitive Societies*. New York: William Morrow and Co. 1st ed. 1935.

1940 The Mountain Arapesh: supernaturalism. American Museum of Natural History, *Anthropological Papers* 37:319—451.

1949 *Male and Female: A Study of the Sexes in a Changing World*. New York: William Morrow and Co.

1956 *New Lives for Old, Cultural Transformation: Manus 1928-53*. New York: William Morrow and Co.

Newman, P. L.
1964. Religious belief and ritual in a New Guinea society. In *New Guinea: The Central Highlands*, ed. J. B. Watson, *American Anthropologist* 66, pt. 2 (4):257—272.

1965. *Knowing the Gururumba*. New York: Holt, Rinehart and Winston.

Poole, F. J. P.
1981 Transforming "natural" woman: Female ritual leaders and gender ideology among Bimin-Kuskusmin. In *Sexual Meanings*, ed. S. B. Ortner and H. Whitehead. New York: Cambridge University Press.

Radcliffe-Brown, A. R.
1922 *The Andaman Islanders*. Cambridge: Cambridge University Press.

Read, K. E.
1952 Nama cult of the Central Highlands, New Guinea. *Oceania* 23 (1):1—25.

1980 *The High Valley*. New York: Columbia University Press. 1st ed. 1965.

Reik, T.
1946 The puberty rites of savages. In *Ritual: Four Psycho-analytic Studies*. New York: Grove Press. Orig. essay 1916.

Roheim, G.
1926 *Social Anthropology, A Psycho-Analytic Study in Anthropology and a History of Australian Totemism*. New York: Boni and Liveright.

Schieffelin, E. L.
1976 *The Sorrow of the Lonely and the Burning of the Dancers*. New York: St. Martin's Press.

Shapiro, J.
1979 Cross-cultural perspectives on sexual differentiation. In *Human Sexuality: A Comparative and Developmental Perspective*, ed. H. A. Katchadourian, pp. 269—308. Berkeley, Los Angeles, and London: University of California Press.

Skorupski, J.
1976 *Symbol and theory*. Cambridge: Cambridge University Press.

Smith, W. R.
1927 *The Religion of the Semites*. 3d ed. New York: Appleton. 1st ed. 1889.

Stephens, W. N.
1962 *The Oedipus Complex: Cross-Cultural Evidence*. New York: Free Press.

STOCKING, G.
1968 *Race, Culture, and Evolution: Essays in the History of Anthropology*. New York: Free Press.

STRATHERN, A. J., and M. STRATHERN
1971 Marsupials and magic: A study of spell symbolism among the Mbowamb. In *Dialectic in Practical Religion*, ed. E. R. Leach, pp. 179–207. Cambridge: Cambridge University Press.

STRATHERN, M.
1978 The achievement of sex: Paradoxes in Hagen gender-thinking. In *The Yearbook of Symbolic Anthroplogy*, ed. E. G. Schwimmer, 1:171–202. London: C. Hurst.

TURNER, V.
1967 *The Forest of Symbols*. Ithaca: Cornell University Press.

1969 *The Ritual Process*. Chicago: Aldine Publishing Co.

TUZIN, D. F.
1972 Yam symbolism in the Sepik: an interpretative account. *Southwestern Journal of Anthropology* 28 (3):230–254.

1977 Reflections of being in Arapesh water symbolism. *Ethos* 5 (2):195–223.

1980 *The Voice of the Tambaran: Truth and Illusion in Ilahita Arapesh Religion*. Berkeley, Los Angeles, and London: University of California Press.

TYLOR, EDWARD B.
1873 *Primitive Culture: Researches into the Development of Mythology, Philosophy, Religion, Language, Art, and Custom*. 2d ed. 2 vols. London: John Murray.

VAN BAAL, J.
1966 *Dema*. The Hague: Martinous Nijhoff.

VAN GENNEP, A.
1960 *The Rites of Passage*. Trans. M. K. Vizedom and G. L. Caffee. Chicago: University of Chicago Press. 1st ed. 1909.

WAGNER, R.
1972 *Habu: The Innovation of Meaning in Daribi Religion*. Chicago: University of Chicago Press.

WEINER, A.
1976 *Women of Value, Men of Renown: New Perspectives in Trobriand Exchange*. Austin: University of Texas Press.

WHITING, J. W. M.
1941 *Becoming a Kwoma: Teaching and Learning in a New Guinea Tribe*. New Haven: Yale University Press.

WHITING, J. W. M., R. KLUCKHOHN, and J. ANTHONY
1958 The function of male initiation ceremonies at puberty. In *Readings in Social Psychology*, ed. E. E. Maccoby, T. M. Newcomb, and E. L. Hartley, pp. 359–370. New York: Henry Holt and Co.

WILLIAMS, F. E.
1936 *Papuans of the Trans-Fly*. Oxford: Oxford University Press.

1940 *Drama of Orokolo*. Oxford: Oxford University Press.

YOUNG, F.
1965 *Initiation Ceremonies: A Cross-Cultured Study of Status Dramatization*. Indianapolis: Bobbs-Merrill Co.

1 INTRODUCTION

Roger M. Keesing

The Author

Roger M. Keesing is Professor and Head of the Department of Anthropology, Research School of Pacific Studies, Australian National University. His primary fieldwork, which has focused on social structure, cognition, and religion, has been done among the Kwaio, a pagan people of insular Malaita, Solomon Islands, in 1962–1964, 1966, 1969–1970, 1977 and 1979. He was trained at Harvard University, where he received his Ph.D. in 1965. Born in Hawaii, Keesing is the son of Felix Keesing, whom specialists will know as a pioneering student of Pacific social anthropology. Professor Keesing directed the Center for South Pacific Studies at the University of California, Santa Cruz, after which he moved to Australia. Since then, he has been actively engaged in his Kwaio research and has authored numerous articles and a major textbook, *Cultural Anthropology: A Contemporary Perspective* (1976, 1980), as well as several Kwaio studies: *'Elota's Story* (1978), *Kwaio Dictionary* (1975), and a new book, soon to appear, *Kwaio Religion: The Living and the Dead in a Solomon Islands Society*. More recently, he has begun a new field project in village India.

Professor Keesing's long and deep interest in Melanesia provides him with a unique vantage point in synthesizing the essays in this volume with a wider comparative ethnography of male cults and initiations in island New Guinea. He addresses what he calls "Bateson's problem"—the analytic explanation of multidimensional perspectives on ritual, culture, and mind needed for understanding complex ceremonial behaviors, like the *naven* custom Gregory Bateson set out some forty-five years ago. With meaning he is thus concerned; and there could be no better starting point than this timely reconsideration of the great problems that Bateson raised and that are presented again here, in the essays below.

PROLOGUE: TOWARD A MULTIDIMENSIONAL UNDERSTANDING OF MALE INITIATION

Systems of male initiation in New Guinea, in their diverse local forms, challenge anthropological powers of interpretation and the adequacy of prevailing paradigms.[1] As quintessential social facts, they confront us the way the Iatmul *naven* rite confronted Gregory Bateson fifty years ago—for many of the same reasons.

Bateson had perceived, in characteristically visionary fashion, that to comprehend the ritualized subordination of classificatory mother's brother to sister's son would require not only functionalist analysis of Iatmul social structure: it would require a then-nonexistent theory of *cultural* structure, the cognitive patterns of opposition and axial symmetry which pervaded Iatmul culture; and it would require a scarcely imagined anthropology of personality and emotion (Bateson 1958).

In the intervening half century, anthropology has closed part of the gulf Bateson perceived when he compared the received truths and practices of what was at that time a young discipline with the complexities of Iatmul reality. Various species of cognitive, structuralist, and symbolist anthropology have given us greater powers to analyze cultural structure; and a belated attention to worlds of women and a cultural conceptualization of gender give new perspectives on the dramatic polarization of male and female realms by which Bateson and Mead were struck in their studies of the Sepik. A gulf remains, however, not least of all in the realm of personality and emotion: as ethnographers, most of us still deal with the dynamics of personality and subjective

---

[1]The task of introducing these papers was passed onto me long after the Association for Social Anthropology in Oceania conference where they were presented and discussed by Lew Langness and Shirley Lindenbaum. I accepted the challenge even though heavily burdened with other writing projects that could not be set aside; and I was acutely conscious of the limitations of my knowledge of and experience in New Guinea. To those who have helped me in this task, notably Anthony Forge, Don Gardner, Maurice Godelier, Gil Herdt, Martha Macintyre, Jadran Mimica, Marie Reay, Inge Riebe, Buck Schieffelin, Shelley Schreiner, Andrew Strathern, and Don Tuzin, I owe special thanks. My debts to those who have elsewhere attempted to draw together this comparative material, notably Michael Allen, Mike Donaldson, Lew Langness, Mervyn Meggitt, Nick Modjeska, Andrew Strathern, Jim Watson, and Robert Murphy, are substantial. Finally, I hope that this essay will constitute a preliminary expression of my deep debt to Gregory Bateson, teacher and friend for a quarter century, whose passing takes from anthropology a brilliant explorer who always pushed beyond the frontiers and from humankind one of the great minds of our times.

experience by ignoring them, just as the young Bateson's contemporaries did.

Perhaps most seriously, although we can analyze a set of customary practices as adaptations to ecological circumstances, or as manifestations of *la pensée sauvage*, or as functionally interlocking elements of social structure, or nowadays as mystifications whereby someone's surplus labor is appropriated, we still have not succeeded in putting these powerful but partial modes of interpretation together. Bateson, struggling to fit Iatmul ethos and eidos into a coherent framework,[2] was confronting problems of the structure of *explanation* which we have yet to solve.

The New Guinea men's cults and initiatory rites described in these chapters—dramatic in performance, incredible in complexity and symbolic elaboration—provide ample challenge to anthropology's growing interpretive powers. The male initiation systems and the cultural premises about humans and the cosmos which infuse them with meaning are, like naven, total social facts in a Maussian sense; but they are more global in scale, more total in cultural salience and social consequences, than the Iatmul naven rite—or, indeed, than most ritual systems of the tribal world. The New Guinea initiation rites enact a philosophy of growth, of human and cultural nature; they define the separation of men and women as a biological and religious as well as social imperative; and they transform gentle boys into warriors capable of killing rage, stealthy murder, and bravery. Global, encompassing, and transformative, the initiation systems described in these chapters demand more complex and multiple modes of explanation than Bateson assayed for naven. In the sections to follow, I shall pull from the rich materials set out for us and from the interpretations advanced by the

---

[2]Bateson retraces in the 1936 epilogue to *Naven* "the steps which have led . . . to the isolation of five major points of view for the study of human beings in society—structural [by this he means cultural structure, or eidos], emotional [by this he means ethos, or emotional orientation and expression], economic, developmental and sociological" (1958:266). In this book he examined the naven rite, in its wider social and cultural context, from three "points of view," focusing on ethos, eidos, and sociology. In this process "the orthodox 'subdivision' of culture into such institutions as marriage, kinship, initiation, religion, etc., has entirely disappeared" (1958:268). In his 1958 epilogue, he more explicitly confronted the problems of epistemology, explanation, and the fitting together of "points of view" which I characterize in this essay as "Bateson's problem": "*Naven* was a study of the nature of explanation. The book . . . is not primarily an ethnographic study. . . . Rather, it is an attempt at synthesis, a study of the ways in which data can be fitted together. . . . I was trying not only to explain by fitting data together but also to use this explanatory process as an example within which the principles of explanation could be seen and studied" (1958:280−281).

3

ethnographers some elements of a comparative analysis and some suggestions about how multiple modes of interpretation might fit together.

CONCEPTUAL ISSUES

First, there are some conceptual, theoretical, and ethnographic questions that need to be considered.

What is the class of phenomena with which we are dealing? What is the rationale for delimiting male initiation rites from other aspects of culture and society among such peoples as the Ilahita Arapesh, the Chambri, the Sambia, and the Bimin-Kuskusmin? (See map 1 for the locations of the New Guinea groups mentioned in this volume.)

Can we understand male cultism without analyzing the lives and perspectives of women? Is our primary focus to be on men's cults or on initiation—and how is this choice to be justified? And how is *initiation* to be defined? Moreover, as comparative sociologists, should we focus on such phenomena on a single island, however vast and diverse in its human ways, or should we freely draw comparisons with male cults in other parts of Melanesia, such as the Banks Islands and New Hebrides?[3] In lowland South America?

Space allows me to deal only briefly with these questions. First, none of the authors represented here would argue that the initiation rituals described could be understood except within the wider context of social structure, male-female relationships, and economy. Each is producing a series of papers (and in some cases books) that provide this wider context of ethnographic understanding (see, for example, Herdt 1981; Tuzin 1976, 1980). While some papers in this volume, notably those by Gewertz and Hays and Hays, make this wider contextualization more explicit than others, an embedding within social and cultural systems is taken as assumed background to this special highlighting of initiation.

There are important reasons why New Guinea constitutes a particularly useful setting for social anthropological analysis, why focusing on male initiation and men's cults is worthwhile even if it gives only a partial view of male-female relationships, and why bringing this material together now is especially urgent.

---

[3]I use the latter term to distinguish the New Hebrides archipelago from the Banks Islands and other peripheral groups politically included within the new nation of Vanatu.

4

The justification for looking at male initiation in New Guinea lies partly in the nature of these systems. Specific themes come up over and over again in different New Guinea societies—sacred flutes, revelation of cult secrets and esoteric meanings, systematic deception, philosophies of growth and maleness, nosebleeding and nettles, the association of male liminality with hunting. The New Guinea male cults, and the ritual processes whereby boys are inducted into them, appear to comprise species of a genus distinctive in important ways from those in other parts of Melanesia and other regions of the tribal world: in their special emphasis on growth, on male gender as a created rather than a natural consequence of maturation, in their definitions of pollution. In the next section, I will seek to characterize these recurrent themes and hence pull together common threads that run through the chapters.

The dangers of comparison on the basis of formal features have become clear to me in the course of studying, in another part of Melanesia (among the Kwaio of the Solomon Islands), a social and cosmological system of sexual polarity and pollution superficially similar to those of New Guinea, but radically different in the texture of male-female relations, in philosophy, in political and economic entailments, and in consequences for individual psychological experience. There is obvious merit in a comparative social anthropology that moves beyond strictly regional phenomena. We may hope that more systematic and theoretically motivated comparisons of data from New Guinea and Amazonia will emerge: the chapters of this volume, several of which answer Robert Murphy's (1959) call for interpretations that are at once sociological, cultural, and psychological, should provide both valuable data and theoretical models for that next step.

If we are dealing with a single genus of male cultism, its subvarieties need to be sorted out, sociologically and conceptually and culture-historically. The distinction drawn by Allen (1967) between *initiation*, which inducts individuals into a defined social group (or, in many New Guinea cases, a graded series of groups), and *puberty* rites, which mark individuals' entry into a new status, is useful in demarcating the phenomena with which we are concerned. So is his further distinction between rites of initiation, which entail secrecy vis-à-vis nonmembers, and rites of *induction*, which incorporate the inductee into a defined social group but are not characterized by cult secrecy. The increasingly rich ethnographic data from New Guinea raise further conceptual issues, however. It is important to distinguish male (and female) *cultism*—ritual practices and other activities carried on within sexually segregated groups—from initiation, despite their substantial ethnographic overlap.

5

Thus the Huli have bachelor cults without rituals of formal initiation; the Melpa have both men's and women's cults, similarly without formal rites of initiation. The Enga bachelor cults, focusing on purification, also are probably best not viewed as constituted by initiation, although they represent a sort of analogue of it. On the other hand, given the complexity of ways in which themes of sexual segregation, ritual secrecy, cult activity, and ritual marking of induction and status change are developed among New Guinea peoples, we cannot expect narrowly prescriptive definitions to fit the data comfortably, nor can we avoid borderline cases. It will suffice for our purposes to characterize initiations as *rites de passage* that introduce initiates collectively into a social group, or a series of them, through submission (Turner 1967:103) and liminality, in a climate of secrecy: the initiates are reborn both into a new status and into a group closed to, and from, those who do not (or by virtue of their sex cannot) belong.

In these terms, Schieffelin (this volume, chap. 4), may be correct in distinguishing the remarkable Kaluli *bau a* as a sequence of intensification, liminality, and (temporary) *societal* transformation from initiation as a process of collective rebirth; but this is a borderline case.

Taking male initiation rites as a focus brings comparable materials from different societies into clear relief. In doing so, however, not only is there a danger of pulling rites out of their institutional and economic context and out of the wider system of male-female relations of which they are a part; there is also a danger of taking a slice of social reality out of its context in a way that distorts its own cultural coherence. Thus Newman and Boyd (this volume, chap. 6) correctly note that to understand, in Awa terms, the cycle of initiation which turns boys into men ready for marriage, we must look at marriage as another phase of the same cycle. And as Tuzin (this volume, chap. 8) notes, the transformation of initiates in all these systems can perhaps be understood only if we focus as well on the role and behavior of these boys when, years later, it is they who do the initiating. In trying to carve out comparable slices of social reality from different societies, there is always a danger of making the slices too uniformly narrow.

NEW GUINEA MALE INITIATION: A COMPARATIVE VIEW

If New Guinea male cults and rites of initiation into them indeed comprise varieties of a single genus which contrast with forms of male cultism in seaboard Melanesia, Aboriginal Australia, Amazonia, and other parts of the tribal world, it will be useful to characterize its distinctive features (particularly as they emerge in the chapters to follow) and to sketch some of the important axes of variation. A first pervasive theme is that males and females are radically different in their physical and psychological being and that the fluids, essences, and powers of women are dangerous and inimical to those of men. This premise renders cosmic and natural the terms of men's social separation from women, men's domination of religion and ritual, and the limited coparticipation of men and women in domestic life.

Physiological conceptualizations of gender are set out particularly vividly by Poole for the Bimin-Kuskusmin, by Newman and Boyd for the Awa, by Hays and Hays for the Ndumba, and by Herdt for the Sambia. There are several recurrent themes that are expressions of this physiological opposition between male and female powers and essences. One is restriction of men's contact with the emanations of women's generative powers, and most particularly menstrual blood. Because taboos against menstrual pollution are widely spread around the world, we could be led here to spurious comparison. In the New Guinea societies where the complex of male cultism and initiation is fully developed, rules regarding menstrual pollution fit into a wider pattern in which menstrual blood may acquire positive magical potency (Meigs 1978), in which men may pollute women and one another (Faithorn 1975), and in which other bodily substances and processes are seen as manifestations of immaterial powers and dangers. A second concomitant is that with gender contrast posed in physiological terms, male power and substance and female power and substance are symbolically portrayed as parallel as well as antithetical. One manifestation is belief in parts of the Eastern Highlands in the dangerous possibility of male pregnancy, as noted for the Awa by Newman and Boyd (this volume) and for other peoples such as the Hua (Meigs 1976). Another is the widespread pattern of male bleeding for purification, whether of the nose or of the penis, and whether explicitly or covertly in emulation of menstruation. Among the Sambia and Baruya, women's nurturant roles are, as it were, appropriated by male initiators vis-à-vis the initiates who fellate them and ingest their semen, which is equated with breast-milk (Herdt, this volume, chap. 2; Godelier 1976). Among the Iatmul (Bateson 1958:282), ''male initiators are identified as 'mothers' of the novices,'' and ''the crocodile jaw which is the gate to the initiatory enclosure is called in Iatmul . . . literally 'clitoris gate' ''—one of the many striking examples in the New Guinea initiation systems of what Hiatt (1971) calls ''pseudo-procreative'' symbolism. These male inversions and emulations of women's reproductive and nurturant powers,

7

highly complex in their symbolism and underlying psychodynamics, would seem among other things to represent a covert theme of male envy, as Mead (1949) noted so long ago. As Hays and Hays (this volume, chap. 5) and Langness (1974) point out, though, the covert theme of envy is cast in an idiom of control: what men create is a cultural order; women's sexuality and reproductive powers are natural, uncontrolled, and threatening to this order. A further expression of the radical contrast between male and female, cast in physical-cosmological terms, is the dogma that boys become men, not through a natural process of maturation, but through a cultural process of creation: growth and physical strength, bravery and manliness, are achieved through sequences of isolation and ordeal, instruction and revelation. (In this abrogation by men of the powers to create men out of boys, we have once more a distinctive New Guinea form of politicized male emulation of women's reproductive powers; Sambia men [Herdt, this volume] refer to their actions as "growing a boy.")

Unless boys undergo the rigors of initiation, they will remain soft and weak. The physical mutilations and traumas—genital mutilation and piercing of the nasal septum as depicted in these chapters, scarification among such Sepik peoples as Iatmul and Chambri (Gewertz, this volume, chap. 7), and nosebleeding—are described in this volume with a directness and attention to the emotional experience of initiates seldom found in the existing literature.

An essential element in this ideology of the creation of men is the challenge of physical growth. Boys, so the dogmas have it, will be stunted and weak if they do not follow a prescribed regimen, both positive (in eating enjoined foods, in ingesting semen through mouth or anus) and negative (in avoiding tabooed foods and debilitating contacts).[4] The cosmologies of New Guinea, perhaps most strikingly in these societies where male cults are fully developed, employ elaborate systems of symbols drawn from the natural world. In the chapters of this volume, particularly those by Newman and Boyd and by Poole, we glimpse richly elaborated systems of food taboos, use of plants such as pitpit and pandanus and of fauna such as marsupials and cassowaries. Symbolic codes contrast wild plants with cultigens, wild and feral

---

[4]Growth may indeed be problematic for those New Guinea peoples living near the margins of nutritional adequacy. The cultural construction of physiology (see Rosaldo 1974:20 ff.), however, overshadows the biological here, as witness the data on delayed menarche, irregular menstrual cycles, and low fertility in populations where the maturation of girls is culturally cast as nonproblematic.

animals with domestic ones; they use the juices and saps of plants and trees, the forms and colors, as vehicles for iconic symbolism. In such systems, blood and other bodily substances are woven into wider symbolic codes; the natural world provides symbols of the body physical and the body politic (see Lindenbaum 1976).

Initiation into male cults entails both secrecy from those who are excluded and the revelation of esoteric knowledge to initiates. The New Guinea cults develop this pattern in characteristic ways. First, because the path to manhood is a gradual process of creation, there is not simply a circle of the initiated into which novices are ritually inducted. Rather, the process typically covers a span of many months, often a number of years, as a boy is made into a man. The revelation of esoteric knowledge, induction into the mysteries, takes place step by step. This sequence is not, as with the graded societies of the Banks Islands and New Hebrides, a matter of status hierarchy: the New Guineans who emerge in these chapters are fiercely egalitarian.[5] Instead, it is a graded progression to the manhood that must be created by acts of nurturance, ordeal, purification, and instruction. Initiates learn how to be men, how to protect themselves from dangers of pollution. Learning the exegetic keys to ritual symbolism becomes (as among the Baktaman [Barth 1975] or Bimin-Kuskusmin [Poole, this volume, chap. 3], not an end in itself, but a key to understanding—hence to being able to live—a male life. The ultimate revelations of mystery, the unmasking of the deception of sacred flute or bull-roarer, serve to underline the collective responsibilities, and hence solidarity, of men. One of the striking parallels between men's cults in Amazonia and those in New Guinea is the use of sacred flutes and bull-roarers as symbols of male power (including, of course, phallic power; see Van Baal 1963 and Dundes 1976, as well as Herdt, this volume). Not only are the cult objects strikingly similar: the uses to which they are put, the threat of gang rape or death to women who see the deception, and the myths in which men gain control of objects first controlled by women (Murphy 1959) show close parallels. The symbology of the cult objects is explored in several of the chapters that follow, most deeply by Herdt for the Sambia. As Herdt's analysis suggests, to pull flutes or bull-roarers out of a particular cultural context for the purpose of exemplifying recurrent themes in male cultism around the world and their psychological meanings exacts considerable cost of

---

[5]Although of course they distinguish men as more or less "big" on the basis of achievement and performance.

understanding. The Sambia equation flute=penis carries a very different meaning from that carried by the same equation where penes are bled but not fellated. And one must probe deeply into a people's symbolic system to understand why in one Eastern Highlands society (e.g., Gahuku; see Read 1952) the flutes are sacred *as objects* and carefully preserved for years, while in another (e.g., Sambia; see Herdt, this volume) the flutes as objects are of evanescent value, casually discarded and replaced. Through these variations, the flutes and bull-roarers emerge as powerful symbols of male power and solidarity: the unmasking of this deception to initiates, as the ultimate mystery, lays on them a compelling sense of their separation from women and of their responsibility, at the risk of death, to one another.

Another recurrent theme, though one less pervasively distinctive of the genus we are examining, demands attention. The incidence of institutionalized homosexual behavior in New Guinea men's cults is still far from clear. For years we had ethnographic accounts only for the Papuan coast, notably for the Keraki (Williams 1936), Kiwai (Landtman 1927), and Marind-Anim (Van Baal 1966). Subsequent evidence has extended the incidence of institutionalized male homosexual behavior through the Great Papuan Plateau (Etoro, Kaluli, Onabasulu) and into the Anga-speaking areas of the southernmost Eastern Highlands, including Baruya (Godelier 1976; cf. Sambia, Herdt, this volume). In all these areas, the ingestion of semen through fellatio or anal intercourse is depicted as essential to the growth of boys.

There are some reasons to suspect that the distribution of institutionalized male homosexual behavior is in actuality much wider than this but that it has been hidden from or by ethnographers in contexts where missionaries or administration could take repressive measures. I know of several cases where the reporting of male homosexual practices has been a matter of much soul-searching by ethnographers; in one clear case in the Eastern Highlands, the anthropologist has chosen not to disclose such practices in a community that could be placed at risk. I am led to wonder how many covert homosexual cults may exist (or may have existed) in areas where they are unreported in the literature. (I am also led to wonder whether female homosexual behavior may be practiced, even institutionalized, in some parts of New Guinea, perhaps in secrecy from men; among the Kalam of the Baiyer River, at least, adolescent girls engage in homosexual relations.)*

*Inge Riebe: personal communication.

The zone of male cult homosexual behavior, extending from the Papuan coast through the plateau and into the Southern and apparently Eastern Highlands, suggests at least that this is a widespread elaboration—perhaps even the original core—of the ideology of sexual separation, female danger, the growth of boys, and the creation of men (see Herdt 1981:318—320).[6]

New Guinea male cultism and initiation systems display other subsidiary themes. Some of them will be touched on when I deal in the next section with distributional questions, and others will be noted in subsequent sections. I have gone far enough, I think, in characterizing the New Guinea initiation systems to underline the point that as a total complex the New Guinea pattern is a genus distinct from the initiation systems and male cults elsewhere in the tribal world. I have also pointed to some of the striking parallels with male cultism in Amazonia. The men's houses and dance grounds of the Brazilian Mundurucu or Mehinacu, the pseudoprocreative themes in Australian aboriginal (Hiatt 1971) and Amazonian (Murphy 1959) ritual and myth, and the political uses of secrecy and mummery could be arrayed with bull-roarers and flutes to underline similarities between convergent genera of male cultism and initiation.

At this point it will be useful to look at some axes of variation in New Guinea male initiation. A number of the variations are sociological. The definition of female being as inimical to male growth and physical powers rationalizes, and indeed demands, a residential separation of adult men and women and the existence of a center of men's activities apart from dwelling houses. Within this general framework is much room for variation. In some New Guinea societies the dwelling houses that are primarily the province of women are nonetheless the focus of a married couple's daily life, as among the Sambia (Herdt, this volume): they may eat, talk, have sexual relations there; men may regularly or sporadically sleep in their dwelling house. The men's cult house (as with the Ilahita Arapesh; see Tuzin, this volume) becomes a center for men's *ritual* life, for political debate and male-related activities. At the other

---

[6]I know of no clear cases of institutionalized precolonial homosexual behavior in the Sepik, but that may well reflect my limited command of the literature. Anthony Forge tells me that Abelam view anal intercourse as a part of plantation culture: "Who would want to screw a boy if they could screw a girl?" Nonetheless, they do, he reports, associate semen with breast milk and growth. I am not fully convinced that institutionalized fellatio among men is absent in the Sepik; the Bimin-Kuskusmin practice (see Poole, this volume) of collective male masturbation and collection of semen to ensure the growth of crops is an interesting variant.

end of a comparative spectrum are those Eastern Highlands societies (e.g., Awa [see Newman and Boyd, this volume] and Ndumba [see Hays and Hays, this volume]) where initiated men spend most of their time in men's houses or men's company, where there is little conjugal life, where men are strictly segregated when they enter a woman's house, and where marital sexual relations in the house are prohibited (Awa) or rare (Ndumba).

The idioms of separation can be "lived in" in quite different ways: in mundane realms such as subsistence labor (where men and women may labor together daily or where work may normally take place in single-sex adult groups), sexual relations (compare the Ilahita Arapesh [Tuzin, this volume], where men regard cunnilingus as an enjoyable diversion, with the Ndumba, where marital sexual relations are strained, fraught with danger of contact with bodily substances, and infrequent), and cult ritual (where women may be essential participants in staging, performing, or observing rites or may be almost totally excluded).

What is the community that initiates its boys together? Is it an autonomous nucleated village, internally differentiated by descent, as among the Awa of the Eastern Highlands (Newman and Boyd, this volume)? Among the Chambri of the Sepik (Gewertz, this volume), each of the three large and mainly endogamous villages initiates boys separately; but unlike the Awa, the Chambri use an intricate system of kinship and initiatory moieties that crosscuts clans and villages to organize initiation. Is the initiating group a dispersed confederacy of clan hamlets, as among the Sambia (Herdt, this volume)? Moreover, given the great range in the size of the local groups described in these chapters (from communities of some 60 people among the Ndumba to the sprawling village of Ilahita, whose 1,500 or so inhabitants stage initiations together across ward and clan lines), the scale and consequences of community-wide initiation may vary considerably.

The incredible complexities of initiatory grades and partnerships interwoven with systems of kinship, descent, and alliance found in Iatmul (Bateson 1958) or Ilahita Arapesh (Tuzin, this volume), are possible only where communities and populations are relatively large; yet the staggering ritual complexity and considerable sociological intricacy of the remote Bimin-Kuskusmin (Poole, this volume) should make us wary of assuming that scale and complexity will be neatly related.

The initiatory sequences also vary considerably in terms of age span of initiation, the age variation among the novices, and the number of ritual grades to full manhood. The *am yaoor* cycle of the Bimin-Kuskusmin, in which initiates pass through ten stages over a period of ten to fifteen years, represents the fullest elaboration among the mountain peoples described here; the Awa, whose five stages of progression to manhood cover ten to eleven years, and the Ndumba, whose two stages span six to eight years, exemplify somewhat simpler progressions in the Eastern Highlands.

In the Sepik region, the structural complexity of initiatory organization is often matched by an extension of hierarchy, such that adult men, rather than forming an undifferentiated community, are graded by seniority. Thus, among the Ilahita Arapesh, "the system of cult initiations and dual structures operates in various ways to the advantage of the older men, especially those belonging to the . . . senior sub-class, [who are] believed to be the closest to the Tambaran spirits, and are able to interpret their wishes. [They command] highest authority in the village and the most potent hunting and gardening magic" (Tuzin 1976:273). Echoes of this hierarchical complexity are found on the distant margins of the Sepik in the age cycles of the Bimin-Kuskusmin.

Further sociological variations—in the organization of local groups, in patterns of marriage and relations between affines, and in intergroup politics—emerge if we compare the societies where male cults and initiatory rituals are found. It is at this conceptual level too that Highlands specialists such as Meggitt (1964), Strathern (1970), and Langness (1974) have sought explanations for different forms of sexual opposition in the Eastern Highlands and areas to the west where male initiation is characteristically absent or attenuated.

Other regional variations are economic: the societies described in these chapters range from low-production, scattered hunter-horticulturalists, through intensive sweet potato and pig producers with dense populations, to the large villages of the Sepik sustained by sago production and the protein resources of river and plains. We will return to this broad spectrum of economic variation.

The above variations, sociological and economic, suggest that a brief distributional sketch and some culture-historical speculations may be useful.

BOUNDARIES AND DISTRIBUTIONS

Having characterized New Guinea male initiation systems as comprising species of a single cultural genus, I must now qualify. First of all, a few systems, such as the bachelor cults of the Enga (Meggitt 1964), show some features of the genus I have described but nonetheless fall outside it. Second, some elements of the complex—particularly male-female separation and antagonism and pollution ideologies—have a much wider distribution than male cult initiation. Third, in some sexually polarized societies, the ideologies I have described of male and female, growth and manhood, may be substantially permuted. Thus among the Etoro (Kelly 1976) sexual intercourse is dangerous because loss of semen drains the life force, not primarily because women, their genitals, and menstrual blood are polluting.

The symbolic themes in terms of which I characterized the putative New Guinea genus are fully developed in Eastern Highlands societies, such as Awa, Ndumba, and Gahuku-Gama, and among southeasterly fringe peoples, such as Sambia; yet their economic and political entailments and sociological expression, as we have noted, vary substantially in ways that profoundly affect the lives of men and women and relations between them. These differences magnify if we look at the Sepik, where both social-economic entailments and symbolic expression depart markedly from the Eastern Highlands–centric idealized characterization of the genus.

Nor is it certain that there is a single historical complex involved. The systems of the Papuan coast—Marind-Anim, Keraki, and so forth—seem of a piece, and the peoples of the Great Papuan Plateau appear to follow this pattern in modified and attenuated ways. The systems of the Sepik again seem of a piece, with their emphasis on axial symmetry, dualism, ceremonial prominence of the initiator, and *tambaran* cultism, patterns we glimpse in Gewertz's and Tuzin's accounts of male initiation in this volume (see also Tuzin, 1976 and 1980 for Ilahita Arapesh; Bateson 1958, for Iatmul). Does the Eastern Highlands pattern represent a third and substantially independent development, or is it derivative (if so, probably up the Ramu River from the Sepik)? Fringe-area Highlands peoples, such as the Baktaman (Barth 1975), Bimin-Kuskusmin (Poole, this volume). Baruya (Godelier 1976), and Sambia (Herdt, this volume and 1981), may well have been influenced by cultural patterns coming from several directions.[7]

If these do represent separate historical complexes of male cultism and initiation, how separate? And how old? I shall leave to other better qualified scholars the challenge of trying to sort out from distributional and linguistic evidence the culture history of male cults and initiation rites in New Guinea. My own hunch, based on the New Guinea distribu-

[7]Including a seminal influence from the southwest?

tional evidence, the symbolic significance of hunting and wild plants and animals, and the comparative evidence from South America and Aboriginal Australia, is that these forms of male cultism are very old. These systems could well date back to a New Guinea population Wurm (1980) characterizes as pre-Papuan and "Australoid," represented by speakers of languages in the Sepik-Ramu linguistic phylum. If so, the hypothesized south-coast center of cult initiation, and the hypothesized Sepik center might well reflect connections in the ancient past. Such speculation may be idle; but my guess is that these systems developed under either hunting-gathering or hunting-horticultural regimens (cf. Donaldson 1980), although they have been transformed to meet new exigencies with the intensified production of cultivated sago in lowland areas of the Sepik and the south coast, and the intensified production of root crops in the Highlands.

Such speculation is not essential to my argument, except to the extent that it underlines the important task of explanation. Most of the populations we are dealing with have almost certainly not *invented* male cults, initiatory rituals, and the symbolic complexes that go with them: at some stage in their history (and in most cases probably not in their present locations) they have borrowed these systems from their neighbors and adapted and redefined them. That being the case, we cannot legitimately deal with these systems as independent social and cultural "experiments"; and we certainly cannot assume that the conditions under which such ideologies and social practices originally evolved are the same as those under which they have been borrowed (or rejected), or that these conditions can be inferred from ecological, demographic, or sociopolitical circumstances ethnographically recorded in New Guinea.

If we look at New Guinea societies in terms of broad regional systems with open boundaries through which ideas flowed and within which peoples were familiar with the customs of neighboring peoples, then we are led to see as puzzling some aspects of male cultism we might otherwise take at face value. The elaboration of cosmologies and rituals, the creation of secret knowledge, the modification of common themes in locally distinctive ways—all become processes whereby populations differentiate themselves from their neighbors, as well as processes whereby senior men set themselves apart from women and uninitiated boys. In such a universe, the ideologies of the people on this side of the mountain may not have the total, all-encompassing salience they would have to a people who lived in a closed and insulated world of ideas and customs.

In the chapters to follow we will confront cultural ideologies that

15

boys are soft and feminine by nature, that they will not grow and become strong, hard, and manlike without the ordeals of initiation. In a region, such as the Eastern Highlands, where neighboring peoples have variants of the same practices, the cult secrets of male initiates may be safeguarded across a wide area (see Newman and Boyd, this volume), and the belief systems may be mutually reinforcing. These continuous blocs of male cultism have edges, though, where initiation is practiced in attenuated form, or practiced for some boys and not for all (as with Meyanmin* and Kuma [Reay 1959]), or not practiced at all; and warfare and trade go on across these edges. In such settings the all-encompassing nature of the ideology must be opened up considerably. How is a belief that boys will not mature physically without initiation to be sustained where one's enemies or trading partners do not initiate? We have far too little evidence from these border zones, and on intercultural communication in general, to know. Perhaps the rapid breakdown of initiatory cults in the last twenty years has come partly because these dogmas, ultimately cultural illusions, can no longer be sustained at all amid Toyotas and coffee, labor migration and towns and outsiders. The initiators may have seen holes in their ideologies all along, may have been led, at least at times, to see male cults and the religious dogmas that reinforce them as "what men do" (Tuzin, this volume) to sustain their dominance. Once the potential initiates and the young men still subordinated by the system also begin to see holes—and alternative choices— male cultism may fall apart.

There is, however, another possibility, one that is also rendered more comprehensible if we see male initiation and cultism within regional systems: the perpetuation or revival of male cultism in the face of Westernization. In precolonial times, many New Guinea peoples probably saw their cultural practices partly as statements of their own distinctiveness, expressions of their identity (rather than as timeless truths of a closed cosmos). In the face of European invasion, alien influences, and cultural destruction and subversion, one possible response is to use these symbols of ethnic distinctiveness to express commitment to continuing survival as a people, to culturally expressed identity. The persistence of cultural conservatism among such peoples as the BenaBena of the Highlands (Langness 1974) and the Chambri and Ilahita Arapesh of the Sepik (Gewertz and Tuzin, this volume), and the resurgence of traditionalism among such Highlands people as the Kuma,** can be partly

*Don Gardner: personal communication.
**Reay: personal communication.

understood in these terms. The continuance of male initiation in Sepik New Guinea, or its revival after abandonment (a process particularly striking among contemporary Aboriginal Australians), is perhaps more comprehensible if we perceive that in these areas one's own culture has *always* been, in part, a commentary on one's neighbors and their cultures.

I began by suggesting that to push further in understanding systems of New Guinea male cultism and initiation, we need to take a series of perspectives on them—as Bateson did in analyzing naven. Having looked at them in terms of ecology, economy, sociology, sexual politics, symbology, and so on, we can come back to "Bateson's problem" of how such partial modes of understanding can be fitted together in a coherent process of explanation. Be forewarned that I will have no magical solutions to "Bateson's problem," only some provisional strategies for thinking about it.

MALE INITIATION AND ECOLOGICAL ADAPTATION

I have recently (Keesing 1981) set out arguments that theories of cultures as adaptations to ecological circumstance err in seeing the symbolic creations of humans as passive—and usually accidental—responses to biological exigency; and they err in imagining that some Unseen Hand of Ecological Wisdom chooses adaptive customs and discards maladaptive ones. Traditional New Guinea constituted a vast repository of maladaptive customs, as well as adaptive and ecologically neutral ones.

We cannot afford to dismiss the power of ecological analysis because of the excesses to which it has been carried. Populations survive in ecosystems across generations and progressively change their cultures as ideational systems and their patterns of behavior. They must extract adequate subsistence, must reproduce their numbers without sharp decline or uncontrolled growth, must coexist with the plants, animals, and microorganisms of their environment without drastically disrupting ecosystemic balances—or, if they do transform their environment radically, must alter their subsistence regime. In ecological analysis we need to seek, not forces that create cultural forms as adaptive responses, but hierarchies of constraint.

One system of constraints operates in the realm of subsistence. As hunters and gatherers, small populations could extract adequate subsistence from the vast forests and swamps of New Guinea: the fairly abundant fauna, particularly marsupials, birds, and fish, provided adequate animal protein. With preipomoean horticulture, mixed economies that augmented hunting and gleaning with taro, yams, and other root crops probably led to quite dramatic population increases without widespread and irreversible destruction of forest resources; and cultivation (rather than collection) of sago supported expanded and sedentary populations that were deriving considerable animal protein from fishing and hunting. With the clearing of the vast highland valleys and the replacement of forest with grasslands, pig husbandry increasingly provided the alternative animal-protein supply for expanding populations, with its snowballing entailments for the production of fodder (see Watson 1977) and the intensification of agriculture. Although the precise interconnections of this cybernetic system are still being worked out, and the relationship of these developments to introduction of sweet potatoes is still being debated, it is clear that we are dealing with human populations in ecosystems where positive feedback and progressive transformation, not simply equilibrium and stable adaptation, prevail. These processes can, I reiterate, be understood only if we see human populations as creative forces and ecological factors as constituting a circuitry of constraint.

A second (and obviously closely related) cluster of ecological factors operates in the realm of population. Although diet provides one important set of factors in the demographic situation of a population (in affecting fertility, disease susceptibility, and so forth), other factors are directly structured by cultural practices: the frequency, conditions, and sociology of sexual intercourse, practices of child rearing and feeding, infant care, and the like. Customs such as Fore endocannibalism and Marind-Anim homosexual anal intercourse may have sharp effects on demography—as do more immediately obvious mechanisms of population thinning, including infanticide, abortion, and warfare.

Since warfare appears to be a key factor in male cultism in New Guinea, the relationship between warfare, demography, and competition for land demands comment. Although New Guinea warfare has often been attributed to population pressure and attendant land shortage—with the displacement of neighboring groups as goal (see, for example, Divale 1971, Rappaport 1968, Vayda 1971)—the evidence is complex and ambiguous. As Sillitoe (1977) notes, the relationship between population density and the scale of intensity of warfare is equivocal and points to no clear correlation in the postulated direction. Moreover, recorded cases of the displacement of vanquished groups are relatively rare, while there have been large numbers of fights and raids where no land has changed hands.

In the longer time span, through, competition for niches and the displacement of populations would seem to be an important factor in shaping the distribution of entire language groups as well as of local kin groups (see, for instance, Tuzin's [1976] lucid reconstruction of population movements on the Sepik plains). In this process, the dwindling of population undoubtedly placed groups in danger of displacement, extermination, or absorption. We cannot comfortably assume, however, that either maintaining a stable demographic balance so as to avoid land shortage and environmental degradation, or increasing population so as to engage in "predatory expansion" (Vayda 1961), has been an effective *general* adaptive strategy in New Guinea, hence that cultural practices have evolved either to limit populations or to give them competitive advantage.

The issue of population regulation raises the further question, first posed by Lindenbaum (1972), of whether male cults and associated pollution ideologies and sexual polarity are, in part, cultural means of population regulation. These belief systems and associated cultural practices, she suggests, have a consequence of preventing premarital pregnancy, delaying marriage, spacing children, and otherwise limiting fertility: pollution beliefs constitute a form of "supernatural birth control" (Lindenbaum 1972:148). There are a number of provisos we must make about the population-regulating consequences of sexual polarity and pollution ideologies. First, a people are likely to be quite conscious of the implications of these customs for population: we need not necessarily invoke the Unseen Hand of Ecological Wisdom. Lindenbaum's New Guinea evidence (1976, 1979) suggests that peoples' own perceptions of their demographic situation may shape these social institutions, though sometimes (as witness Fore endocannibalism) in a maladaptive way. Second, great variations exist in the *enactment* of customs and beliefs polarizing the sexes. What matters ultimately is not a cultural theory about male and female bodily substances and a set of rules and taboos about cohabitation, but rather the frequency and circumstances of coitus. Pollution ideologies and male cultism *may* be put into practice in ways that radically limit fertility (as among the Ndumba; see Hays and Hays, this volume); but they may not. Third, as I have suggested, it is one thing to account for the initial evolution of a complex such as New Guinea male cultism and sexual polarity, and another to account for its spread and perpetuation. On a vast island characterized by regional cultural systems and open societal boundaries, peoples may have borrowed complexes of custom from their neighbors even though they lived in material circumstances quite different from those of the people from whom these customs spread. And, as with the Mountain Arapesh, "importers" of culture (Mead 1938), they may adapt borrowed ways to local ones, enacting borrowed systems in altered ways with different consequences (see Tuzin, this volume). Peoples whose demographic situation is precarious and threatened by decline (such as the Etoro described in Kelly 1976) may persist in practicing customs that have covert consequences of limiting population and weakening the numerical strength of kin groups. Once a group is wrapped up in an all-encompassing ideology that portrays initiation and sexual polarization as necessary to the creation of warriors, the abandonment of customs that limit fertility would be the far greater risk.

Ecological adaptation will not fully account for the evolution or perpetuation of the remarkable ritual systems described in these chapters. As elaborations of symbols, as outcomes of sexual-political conflict, these systems have a life of their own, a self-generating, self-perpetuating cultural force that is disengaged to substantial degree from material circumstances. (I shudder to think of frenzied cultural materialists trying to calculate the protein value of semen to growth when ingested at the top or bottom end of the alimentary canal.) By itself, ecological adaptation does not provide either an adequate conceptual framework or a complete explanation for the emergence, efflorescence, and spread of male cults and initiation systems. The challenge, I will suggest, is to incorporate ecological perspectives into a wider framework of theory that takes into account as well the organization of production, social structure, symbolic systems, psychology, and sexual politics—a path Lindenbaum herself (1976) has brilliantly but briefly reconnoitered.

PRODUCTION AND SEXUAL POLARIZATION: AN ECONOMIC PERSPECTIVE

The ecological perspective is limited not only in viewing human response to an environment as fundamentally reactive rather than creative, in depicting constraints as if they were the shaping forces of a hidden rationality; it is limited as well in seeing the encounter of humans with their environments as biological and technological rather than social.

To push our understanding of the nexus of warfare, production, and the organization of society a step further requires, I think, an economic perspective that focuses on social relations of production as well as technology: in other words, an anthropological economics in the neo-Marxist tradition.

We are dealing with societies that span a range from low-production hunting and horticulture to intensive, high-production cultivation of root crops; and with "societies" ranging in size from a few hundred to tens of thousands. Across this range, though, extend several common themes in the organization of production: the centrality of women's labor in producing subsistence and the stuff of exchange, whether directly (pigs) or indirectly (shell valuables); substantial separation of men and women in productive tasks, although they perform complementary roles; and control over women's productive and reproductive powers by senior men, who negotiate marital exchanges or alliances and finance bridewealth. Across the spectrum from low-production hunting and horticulture to high-production, intensive cultivation, the burdens of productive labor are progressively shifted toward women. In the low-production societies, men's hunting and clearing of forest swiddens complement women's horticulture and gleaning. The shift toward intensive (and especially permanent field) cultivation, reliance on large pig populations for animal protein, and orientation of production to exchange progressively removes men from central roles in production and increases the burdens on women. Concomitant increases in social stratification concentrate control over marital alliance and exchange—hence over women's labor—in the hands of big men as leaders of lineages and local groups (Modjeska n.d.).

Across the entire spectrum of production systems, we need to see male labor as invested, not simply in production, but in *reproduction* (in the Marxist sense). First of all, under conditions of lethal warfare, men's house groups were heavily committed to guarding women, patrolling territory, and planning and staging raids (which in such a political climate could be portrayed as preemptive strikes, to use the jargon of contemporary geopolitics).[8] In protecting against the threat of war, men's house groups were defending the means of production, the group's land and resources. Under constant threat of war and concomitant destruction and dispersion, this was no idle male pastime, but a real commitment to survival.

Nonetheless, if men in their men's houses were defending terri-

---

[8]See Donaldson's summary of Eastern Highlands warfare (1980) and Tuzin's (1976) reconstruction of recent Sepik cultural history.

21

tory, they were also—through marriage, exchange, peacemaking, and regional military alliance—maintaining a wider framework of political order, however fragile and transitory. Here we must raise our view above the level of the local community: for what men reproduce, with the pigs that are the embodiments of women's labor and the shells that are an abstract mystification of material production (Modjeska n.d.), is a *political* order, of peace as well as of war. And this political order extends across regional zones, within which broadly common cultural systems—and the shared secrets of men—create a kind of super-community united by implicit commitment. Affines, enemies, allies, and coconspirators to deception sustained and reproduced a political order in which murder and ceremonial exchange, arrows and pearl shells, were the media of diplomacy.

Men's labor constructed on the foundations of women's labor reproduced not only a social order but a cosmic one: a realm of spirits and powers behind the visible. The rituals that reproduce this multiply elaborated or roughly sketched cosmos are a central theme of men's labor.[9] If men in these societies were not as central as women in the realities of material production, they had at least mystified the very nature of production itself: the production of illusion, we might say, and the illusion of production. And that brings us to the initiatory sequences vividly described in the chapters that follow: for what men produce—as women cannot—is *men*.

A SOCIOLOGICAL PERSPECTIVE

The sociology of male cultism has recently been reviewed by Langness (1974) in an admirable paper that can be read with profit as a companion piece to this volume. Langness takes as text Read's initial analysis (1952) of the Gahuku-Gama *nama* cult, the seminal work on male cultism in the Highlands. He notes that a Durkheimian paradigm, viewing ritual as reinforcing social integration and ultimately celebrating society itself, can be applied only uncomfortably (as Read himself perceived) to the male rituals of the Highlands: the rites celebrate, not the unity and power of *society*, but the unity and power of *men*. They

---

[9]Cosmologies are richly developed in the Sepik (Iatmul, Ilahita Arapesh, Abelam, etc.) and on the Papuan coast (Marind—Anim, Elema, etc.) and are surprisingly rich in their hinterlands zones (represented here by Kaluli and Bimin-Kuskusmin); they tend to be much less fully elaborated in the Highlands.

22

celebrate and reinforce male dominance in the face of women's visible power to create and sustain life, and in the face of the bonds between boys and their mothers which must be broken to sustain male solidarity and dominance. Women's physical control over reproductive processes and emotional control over their sons must be overcome by politics, secrecy, ideology, and dramatized male power.

In a pioneering paper based on his research among the Mundurucu of Amazonia, Robert Murphy (1959) sought to characterize the kinds of society where sexual polarity and sexual fantasies would be likely to crystallize in institutional form, in men's cult and initiation rites. He posited that, first, these societies are "simple and relatively undifferentiated. . . . In such groups, the primary line of sex differentiation is not criss-crossed or blurred by multiple modes of role designation," and the division of labor is mainly according to sex. Second, they are societies where the size of local groups and the nature of production make "economic cooperation . . . a stable and daily affair," but where men and women play sharply constrasting economic parts—so that members of the same sex tend to work together. In these societies "the sexes are true social groups." Third, they are characterized by unilocal residence and local exogamy, which "keeps consanguines of one sex together while sending those of the opposite away. Members of the opposite sex thus tend to be outsiders and affines."

In such settings, Murphy hypothesized, the antagonism and envy universally generated in human ontogeny and the sexual themes in human fantasy are likely to rise to the conscious surface and be given cultural content and institutional form: "If we are to seek efficient causes for the institutionalization of this unconscious material . . . we must look to social structure. That we Americans do not have bull roarers . . . could hardly be due to absence of the Oedipal experience and mutual organ-envy. . . . The symbolic behavior characteristic of the men's cult is absent because our society is not structured along the simple lines that would make such rites functional" (1959:223). At the same time, and independently, Michael Allen (1967) was exploring a parallel hypothesis in relation to Melanesia: that male initiation would be institutionalized in societies with a rule of unilineal descent and a corresponding rule of unilocal residence, so that in-marrying spouses would be aliens as well as affines, and the core of the local group would comprise unilineally related members of the same sex.

Langness (1974) builds on the basic insights of Murphy and Allen and adds to them. In a social order where male loyalty to fellow males is the foundation for warfare and the solidarity of the local group, and where male prestige quests depend on systematic appropriation of women's labor, it is ties with women that pose the greatest threat, from both within and without. The bond between mothers and sons could keep boys from becoming men: it must be broken dramatically and traumatically (see Herdt 1981). The sexual bond between young men and their wives could divide men from one another and align them individually with their affines, enemies of the group; wives are potential spies, and to take them into confidence is to betray the confidence of those with whom you must fight and die.

We have, in these systems, a complex that unites and divides along lines that are strategically crucial in a political climate characterized by the threat of warfare and regional webs of intermarriage and exchange. Virilocal residence preserves the solidarity of a local community of men. Their daughters as well as their sons are reared in a circle of collective security and intense group loyalty. On the other hand, these daughters will marry men of enemy groups. Women placed in the enemy camp through marriage are potential enemies to one another as well as to their affines: the strategy that unites local men divides the community of women, who could otherwise form a solidary counterforce. Separation of the sexes and the drastic and dramatic incorporation of boys into what Reay* calls the ''viriocracy'' preserve the military secrets, as well as the solidarity, of male warriors. At the same time men's *shared* secrets of ritual contribute to the maintenance of a supercommunity within which they conduct the politics of exchange and marriage, as well as warfare, with implicit rules.

There are, of course, variations in the degree and nature of sexual polarization—variations that, as Meggitt noted in his classic paper on male-female relations (1964), are roughly correlated with the modalities of marriage and intergroup politics. That interpersonal relations between husbands and wives are so much less polarized and anxiety ridden among the Ilahita Arapesh (Tuzin, this volume) than among the Highlanders described in these chapters is probably in substantial degree a concomitant of a pattern of intravillage marriage, where a man marries the daughter of an ally, not of an enemy (Tuzin 1976). More generally, in Ilahita and among the Abelam and Iatmul, and in other Sepik societies marked by large and substantially endogamous communities, sexual antagonism is less extreme than in most reported Eastern Highlands societies: women play a role complementary to that of men, as spectators

*Reay: personal communication.

24

and fringe participants in male-dominated ritual pageantry and politics.

Although functionalist sociological analysis gives us crucial insights, there are major limitations in an ultimately Durkheimian view of social integration in societies marked by internal conflict, sexual polarization, and subordination—limitations Bateson perceived in analyzing naven.[10] We are dealing squarely with a politics of subordination masked and mystified by a shared commitment to cultural symbols. We need to examine more closely the dynamic of sexual politics—and then come back to look at the symbolic elaborations of the ideological systems that reinforce, mystify, and render imperative and cosmic an order created by humans for human ends.

THE POLITICS OF SUBORDINATION
AND MYSTIFICATION

Langness's observations about the nama cult of BenaBena and Gahuku-Gama put the matter squarely:

> The most parsimonious explanation for the secrecy, as well as for the existence and functioning of the nama cult itself, does not involve either male envy or innate male bonding propensities but, rather, power in the most fundamental sense. . . . There are four areas in which males are not otherwise assured of power and control. These all have to do generally with female resources— fertility, childcare, labor, and periodicity. . . . The nama cult with all its ritual, symbolism, and beliefs consists most fundamentally of a magical system designed to insure male power in these areas. . . . The social solidarity [expressed in ritual] rests upon a power structure entirely in the hands of males, a power structure supported where necessary by a variety of acts that are magical, pure and simple, and designed to keep power in the hands of males. (1974:19)

If we explore these cosmological and ritual schemes as cultural structures spun out by "the human mind," as fabrics of meaning, we can too easily lose sight of their meaning as instruments of subjugation and systematic deception.

I have noted the way in which ideologies about pollution and gender serve not only to subordinate and demean women but to appro-

---

[10]See Bateson's characterization of Iatmul ethos, his depiction of Iatmul culture as substantially male created, and his model of schismogenesis (Bateson 1958).

priate their labor. We may surmise that the ideologies and ritual practices described in this volume represent primarily the creations of men; they serve the political purposes of men, despite the veils of symbolism and cosmological embroidery in which they are draped.

The ideologies about male and female, the elaborations of secret knowledge and the systematic deceptions that surround them, not only sustain and rationalize the subordination of women and the appropriation of their labor by men for male ends; these ideologies also maintain the control senior men hold over boys and young men, and they disguise its nature. Physical and psychological dominance is cast in terms of duty and cosmic necessity and is mystified in ideologies about growth. (The sexual exploitation of boys by men among the Sambia, in terms of dogmas about semen and growth, is the most striking case reported in these chapters, but the pattern is pervasive; see Herdt 1981). The control big men and other seniors exercise over the labor and fighting power of juniors is maintained by the political economy of marriage financing, exchange, and prestige feasting; but it is maintained as well by control over secret ritual knowledge and the supposed physical means to growth and maturity. There is only one way to become a man, and it is a path that can be followed only through submission and years of subordination.

We are dealing with systems in which those who are dominated share an ideological consensus with those who dominate.[11] The women whose labor is appropriated, the young warriors who risk their lives in war, are, it would seem, as much a part of "the system" as those who are in control. How is such a social order *reproduced*? In the ideologies described in these chapters, what is political, contingent on power, is depicted in an all-embracing religious ideology as cosmic, natural, and inescapable, determined as it is by the confluence of supernatural control and biological nature. This is why, as Godelier (1976) says, the idiom of sexuality in which these ideologies are cast *cannot* be taken simply at face value: "Sexuality, and the difference between the sexes, . . . are sufficient in [the] eyes [of the Baruya] to justify all the different forms of economic, political and symbolic domination over women. [But] it [seems] that sexuality in fact [acts] as a language expressing, and as a reason legitimizing, . . . male domination." The reproduction of such a system of social and productive relations depends on an ideology that

---

[11]Godelier 1976; see Keesing 1981: secs. 42, 43; and O'Laughlin 1974. I am not convinced, however, – in the absence of good data—that there are no women's counterideologies in these sexually polarized societies.

26

"celestializes" (Marx) and "naturalizes" an order which is in fact human and cultural.

Seeing ideologies of male and female, growth and danger, as mystifications that reinforce male power is an essential step in comprehending male cultism and the ritual elaborations and initiation sequences described in the chapters that follow. In uncovering the political realities these symbolic systems disguise, though, we can create another distortion. These symbolic designs are deeply meaningful to those, both male and female, who live enmeshed in them. To understand the meanings and motives of the people who collectively enact these cultural forms, we must situate ourselves in these worlds as well as outside them.

A SYMBOLIC PERSPECTIVE

Whatever else they may be, the cosmological and ritual elaborations described in the ensuing chapters are magnificent expressions of the creative powers of the human mind. Perhaps most striking in this regard are the Bimin-Kuskusmin described by Poole in chapter 3. In a brief discussion focused on theoretical issues, he can here only touch on the staggering complexities of Bimin-Kuskusmin cosmology and ritual: he documents his fleeting comment on the "great richness" of symbolism in initiation by citing pages 570−1967 of his five-volume thesis (which covers only one phase of initiation ritual). This ritual, he dryly notes (citing pages 704−1425), is "very complex"; yet these mind-boggling cumulations of human symbolic creativity and sociological elaboration have been achieved and sustained by a population of only a thousand. Some societies with elaborate male cults, such as the Baktaman (Barth 1975), comprise only a few hundred people.

These vast symbolic schemes, whether created and sustained in tiny mountain communities or in the great villages of the Sepik or southern coast, have coherent logics and formal structures that can increasingly be deciphered by symbolic anthropology in ways Bateson, characteristically visionary, had glimpsed fifty years ago. The growing anthropological power to interpret codes of symbolic meaning is brilliantly illustrated by Gell's (1975) interpretation of Umeda ritual and, in a different symbolist tradition, by Schieffelin's (1976) elegant study of the Kaluli. Several of the authors of the chapters to follow have been among the leading contributors to an emerging symbolic anthropology of New Guinea, although their primary focus here is not on the decipherment of symbolic structures.

The rituals described in these chapters pervasively use processes and objects in the world of animals and plants with which humans in New Guinea have lived on intimate terms for many millennia: wild marsupials, crocodiles, cassowaries, nettles, palms become the stuff with which *bricoleurs*, New Guinea style, fashion their cultural creations.

An anthropological symbology that takes meaning as its central concern and sees rituals and myths primarily as creations of (unconscious) human *intellective* processes, however, will find in New Guinea initiatory ritual a disquieting and inescapable preoccupation with sexual themes. The phallic flutes and bull-roarers (Dundes 1976), the genital mutilation, the nosebleeding in explicit or implicit imitation of menstruation, the transparently pseudoprocreative ritual (Hiatt 1971) should make the most hardened Lévi-Straussian turn to Freud and Bettelheim. A psychoanalytically sophisticated view of the dynamics of the unconscious and of Oedipal conflict is, I think, necessary if we are to understand the sources of the fantasy materials that in these societies are crystallized into myth and ritual (but cf. Herdt 1981).

A bald psychoanalytic interpretation alone will not do, partly for the reasons Murphy (1959) notes: all humans have parallel ontogenetic experiences and private fantasies, but most have not institutionalized them in collective rituals and cult objects. We need a theory of what draws these themes to the surface and leads to their crystallization in a culture. Murphy himself and other authors, such as Allen (1967) and Langness (1974), observe that such symbolic crystallizations make sense only within particular sociological contexts.

There is another set of reasons why a crude psychoanalytic reductionism will not suffice to explicate these symbolic themes in New Guinea men's cultism. As Turner (1966, 1967, 1978), Leach (1959), and others have forcefully argued, to identify a sexual referent for a ritual object or act—a sacred flute, head shaving, or nosebleeding—does not constitute an adequate anthropological analysis. A king's scepter can symbolize both phallus and the power of the state; copulation can symbolize the creative forces of the universe. A spectrum of meanings can, as Turner notes, connect a pole at which symbols refer to primary physical experience (including sexual organs, acts, or experiences) with a pole where the same symbols express abstract social meanings. If the meaning of primary experience is compelling in terms of the psychodynamics of the individual participant in ritual, the symbolism of the cultural and social is compelling in terms of its public enactment in a context of collective action.

As Bateson (1972) argues, it may be of the *nature* of the primary-process thinking expressed in symbolism not only that the symbols be multivocal but that their deepest meanings be abstract and relational. Let us consider the flutes. In the Sambia case convincingly analyzed in this volume by Herdt, a series of equivalences are drawn: the flutes are penes, and the flutes are mothers' breasts the initiates suck; the boys become *dependent* on the initiators the way infants are dependent on their mothers. I think, however, that another powerful relational equivalence is drawn as well. For the Sambia, as for the Awa, the Ndumba, the BenaBena, the Gahuku-Gama, and many others, the flutes would seem to symbolize *power* as well as penes (see Herdt, this volume and 1981). Or perhaps more precisely, in Batesonian terms, the flutes symbolize a relationship of dominance-submission (disguised, in at least the Sambia case, as succorance-dependence), of which penes are a sign, a physical representation, vis-à-vis women and boys. The flutes are symbols at once sexual and political; they are both penes and instruments of subordination, representations of sexual power and social power.[12]

We need to interpret New Guinea cultures as systems of meaning not simply to understand the covert symbolism of pitpit and pandanus but to understand the *values* that motivate behavior. To see initiation or warfare or exchange systems as ecologically adaptive or as serving economic and political ends may give us important insights; but it also introduces serious distortions. The quest for prestige through exchange, or glory in war, acquires a symbolic force that transcends and may in fact run counter to pragmatic ends. Hallpike's characterization of Tauade warfare is overstated, but it is a useful corrective to the search for a covert rationality to which cultural materialism or vulgar Marxism would lead us (cf. Sahlins 1976):

Tauade pig-rearing, feasts and dances, fighting and vengeance are not biologically adaptive, or even socially useful in any objective sense. . . . The traditional life of the Tauade was a prolonged fantasy of power. . . . These were no sober agriculturalists, making narrow calculations of profit and loss, . . . but . . . men in the grip of a collective obsession with blood and death. For them work in their gardens was a boring necessity, to be shifted on to the women as far as possible, valuable only as the foundation of the real business of life—the pursuit of glory. (Hallpike 1977:253)

---

[12]Similar patterns of political-sexual meanings have been well explicated by a number of feminist writers in the context of Western societies.

In the realm of initiation, making boys into men, staging elaborate rituals, and teaching esoteric knowledge, the precepts of a moral life and the rules for safety from the dangers of women are deeply meaningful to the participants. We must understand these culturally constructed meanings and motives—not simply take them as reflections or disguises of something else "more real"—if we are to interpret the systems described in these chapters and their counterparts elsewhere in New Guinea. Such a cultural perspective, whether on warfare or on initiation, does not preclude (and indeed demands) others as its complement.[13] Before we return to the challenge of fitting together these partial perspectives, we need to take one more "point of view" (Bateson 1958), for we still face questions about the psychological experience of initiation which are essential if we are to understand, first, how the institutions described in these chapters affect the human beings whose lives are caught up in them and, second, how these systems endure.

THE PSYCHOLOGICAL EXPERIENCE OF INITIATION

What is the relationship between normative constructs about the nature of boys and the proper nature of men (what Poole [this volume] calls "sociocultural *personhood*") and the personal and private orientation of individuals (their "experiential *selfhood*")? Does initiation create a radically new selfhood, as it is supposed to? If so, how? And how uniformly among different individuals? How deeply does the initiatory experience cut the psychological bond between a boy and his mother, and at what cost? And with what consequences, in his later relationship to women, to men, and to his own children?

How are systems of initiation perpetuated, when perpetuation entails men inflicting on boys experiences that in their own boyhood were psychologically traumatic and physically painful? Are the initiators motivated by a hardness and cruelty that have been created partly by their own initiatory experiences? By a sense of religious duty and moral obligation which overcomes reticence and guilt (see Tuzin, this volume)?

---

[13]Thus, for instance, Sillitoe (1980) has argued of New Guinea warfare that the symbolic values of male pride, honor, and glory which lead warriors to death on the battlefield may mask the political motivations of big men—interests quite different from those of men they send into battle.

Psychological questions were asked and answered more boldly in the American anthropology of the 1940s and 1950s than they are today. The circularities and reifications of "culture and personality" theory led to eventual discouragement and widespread disenchantment. In abandoning the simplistic paradigm that the social and cultural are *generated* by individual primary experience, though, we have, by and large, stopped asking questions that in the long run may be ,crucial to our understanding of initiation and many other customary practices.These psychological experiences and orientations *created by* "the system" may be necessary if it is to be lived in and perpetuated, even though these experiences cannot legitimately be invoked alone to explain the system's existence.

But how are we to explore individual psychological experience in the process of initiation without falling into the old traps of circularity, without conceptually confounding personhood and selfhood? How, if at all, can we separate individual experience from the cultural idioms in which it is cast?

Three of the authors represented here—Herdt, Poole, and Tuzin— have been moving beyond these traps in exploring the psychological experience of New Guinea peoples. Each, in his chapter in this volume, touches on some of the questions I have raised. Herdt in his recent book *Guardians of the Flutes* (1981) and this volume, Poole in this volume, and Tuzin in this volume and elsewhere (1975, 1977, and 1980) impressively show that with strategic interviews, projective tests, dream records, and other psychological methods, we *can* separate out the strands of individual experience from the cultural designs into which they are woven. Herdt's work shows particularly clearly that what the initiation rites are about *is* psychological experience. The dramatic separation of a boy from his mother, the surrogate "maternal" role of the homosexual initiator, and the Sambia use of trauma and ordeal to create warrior bravery emerge compellingly in his book and, more briefly, in his essay in this volume. These are sequences that entail what Herdt (1981:305) calls "radical resocialization," achieved through what he likens to "a primitive form of behavioral surgery": one that "helps instill manly pride, but . . . leaves scars." The scars, as well as the surgery, may well play a necessary role in the perpetuation of these systems (see Tuzin, this volume).

Herdt shows that this "surgery" to transform boys into men takes place after the crucial aspects of personality and identity have taken form: "What is insisted on [i.e., Sambia manliness] repudiates what is inside. By the age of seven to ten years (first-stage initiation) . . . the

31

formative years of childhood development are virtually complete: the core sense of identity is set; and so the late procedures of ritualized gender surgery must rattle the very gates of life and death'' (1981:305).

If this be so, no amount of careful sociological analysis and symbol decipherment will tell us what initiation experience is about, why the blood and pain and trauma, as well as the hidden secrets, are needed to turn boys into men.

TOWARD A SYNTHESIS

''Bateson's problem'' remains. If ecological, economic, sociological, political, symbolic, psychological, and other partial explanations of New Guinea men's cults and initiation rituals are to be mutually reinforcing and suppletive, rather than mutually exclusive, we need some framework in which they can be fitted together.

One of the deep problems in prevailing cultures of science—and especially in the social sciences, which allow so much latitude for alternative approaches—is that when we commit ourselves to a paradigm, perhaps powerful but inevitably sharply limited in scope, we try to pretend that it is global, even total.

A cultural ecologist will tell us how a sociocultural system keeps a population in stable balance with their ecosystem, without evidence that their ecosystem is in fact stable, without evidence that the population is in equilibrium, without evidence that the cultural practices purported to achieve this dynamic balance are old. The synchronic coexistence of a human population, a customary pattern of behavior, and a physical environment are, with a wave of the analytical wand, turned into a dynamic theory of process. An ardent cultural materialist will go further, trying to explain every detail of symbolic behavior in terms of some covert pragmatic consequence, as if amino acids were more real than ideas. A crucial first step toward fitting our partial theories together is to appreciate the limited domain each theoretical perspective adequately comprehends.

And that, then, leads to a second step. To recognize the limitations of a partial theory is to create openings where it logically connects to other partial theories. Again let me illustrate, this time with a Marxist view of a tribal religion as an ideology that mystifies the nature of political power by ''celestialization'' and hence perpetuates a system of productive relationships. If we overstate the partial truth of this view, we are led to imagine the senior men of a New Guinea society as if they were a ruling class in miniature, sitting in the men's houses cynically inventing lies and ordeals through which to subordinate and delude boys and women. We need to accord to the view of religion as ideology and political instrument a more limited range and power. If we see senior men as the primary custodians of religious knowledge, as the members of a society who across the generations contribute the main elaborations and permutations of ritual and secret knowledge, then we understand how and why these ideational systems *take a perspective* on the social system that is shaped by male political interests; but we need not assume that male ideologues consciously invent nonexistent spirits or false theories about growth and procreation. A theory of religion as ideology, properly formulated, requires as its complement *la pensée sauvage*, a theory of humans as weavers of symbolic designs. Conversely, an adequate theory of the symbolic process, of the cumulation of cultures as systems of meaning, requires that this process be embedded in the social and political structure of real communities with real histories.

Once we anthropologists take seriously the challenge of fitting partial explanations together, further connections come into view. Thus the male political solidarity stressed in sociological theories is fully congruent with a neo-Marxist emphasis on male appropriation of women's labor and control over their reproductive powers (as Lindenbaum and Langness have noted). Women are the creators, nurturers, and sustainers of life; yet not only must they be controlled and subordinated, but the boys they bear and nurture must be taken from them and thrust into the world of men. Here, too, the symbolic must be joined to the political: the sexual symbolism of phallic power and pseudoprocreation (Hiatt 1971, Langness 1974) becomes compelling in a society where men are created, not natural, and where they must control women, whose essential nature is dark and dangerous and beyond male regulation.

Such bridge building between partial explanations itself entails further dangers. We are likely to be left with nothing more than an ever more complex functionalist matrix of interconnection, ultimately static and circular: "the system" endlessly reinforcing and perpetuating itself.

I think we need to see two sources of pressure as providing the dynamics underlying these systems: one shaping the emergence and perpetuation of male-female polarity, with all its entailments; and the other operating to transform the nature of production and, concomitantly, of sociopolitical organization.

The first dynamic, which I take to be most fundamental in generating male-female polarization, in ways that in turn ramify through social

33

and cultural systems, is warfare—of a scale and intensity and bloodiness equalled in few parts of the tribal world (perhaps only in parts of Amazonia). I do not doubt that such warfare is related to demographic and ecological factors and ultimately is grounded in competition for territory and resources—although not in the direct and mechanical ways assumed by cultural materialists pursuing a hidden ecological rationality.[14] Endemic warfare becomes self-justifying, self-fulfilling, self-perpetuating, fueled by symbolically constructed motives as well as by the urgency of defending territorial resources.

This climate of warfare in turn creates a set of sociopolitical imperatives that shape the organization of production and ramify through a social system through self-amplifying circuits of positive feedback, which align local men's house groups against one another, polarize the sexes sociologically and psychologically, and separate male productive tasks from those of females.

In such settings, the separation and solidarity of the men's house community and the separation between male and female realms are likely to be expressed and reinforced in cultural symbols, in the form of men's rituals and cosmological formulations of gender polarity. Male rituals and the planning of war are carried on in secrecy from women and children—not least of all because wives are aliens from enemy groups. The kind of social system in miniature I have described is divided by deep stress lines and contradictions, some internal, some external. Externally, the more intense the scale and dangers of warfare, the more fragile are the political relations on which intermarriage and exchange depend. Internally, the more dangerous the climate of raiding and warfare, the wider is the gulf between boys, growing up in a world of women and shaped by female gender roles and identifications (Mead 1935 and 1949; Burton and Whiting 1961; Whiting, Kluckhohn, and Anthony 1958), and the men they must eventually join and emulate. Boys tied to their mothers, growing up in women's houses surrounded by women's activities, must become brave warriors separated forever from this world of women by fear of its dangers, responsibilities for community defense, and commitments to the glory of the battlefield.

---

[14]I see no evidence that the incidence and intensity of warfare are related directly to competition for either animal protein or women, as hypothesized by Divale and Harris (1976) for Amazonia and other areas where a "male supremacy complex" prevails. The detailed comparative evidence on demography, sex ratios, marriage patterns, diet, and distributions of game required to text such a possibility is simply not available. The complexities of the Amazonian case lead me to doubt strongly whether New Guinea warfare would *directly* reflect competition for resources or women, although in the long run populations were competing for territory and resources.

34

Initiation to the men's world by ordeal and the revelation of secrets is clearly not the only way to ritualize the transition from boyhood to manhod. It does, however, dramatize the change of status through symbolic rebirth—while at the same time operating directly and drastically, at a psychological level, on the bonds to women and their world, which the novices must leave behind. Initiation may have side benefits at the level of external politics as well: regionally shared responsibilities to stage initiation and guard male secrets may help preserve a fragile supercommunity, may help senior men maintain political networks through which they can make peace, negotiate marriages, and carry on exchange.

We need not assume that initiation rituals have been separately invented over and over again. They are part of a universe of ideas about male and female, purity and pollution, that extends across vast areas of New Guinea, from one coast to another. We can speculate that the motivation to adopt a pattern of male initiation from surrounding peoples has consistently been that it was a better way to make men out of boys—or, perhaps more precisely, that it was a way of making better men. If a people took heed of the ideology that underlies the initiations practiced by other peoples—that these rites induced physical growth as well as strength and manly virtue—they were likely to have adopted the rites to attain parity in a New Guinea equivalent of an armaments race. Where warfare was less intense, or where a people already had a developed institution (such as a bachelor cult) that provided an analogue of initiation, they would probably have been less likely to borrow a whole complex of ritual initiation, with its heavy entailments of time, labor, and resources.

The dynamic leading to the transformation of New Guinea economies and sociopolitical structures lies in population increase and the intensification of production. Experts are divided, here as elsewhere in the world, about the connection between population growth and changes in production. In the New Guinea case the issue is complicated by the introduction of the sweet potato, which occurred millennia after the earliest intensification in the Highlands but obscures our understanding of preipomoean production systems.

The intensification of root-crop production, concomitant with greatly increased population density, is apparently very old in parts of the Central and Western Highlands and relatively recent in parts of the Eastern Highlands. For the latter, the snowballing effects on women's labor, the demands for pig fodder, and the efflorescence of exchange systems and big-man politics have been discussed by Watson (1977) and

35

Modjeska (n.d.). Again in the Eastern Highlands, with increasing populations and competition for garden lands, warfare if anything escalated. The initiation complexes were adapted to (or borrowed in) these altered political-economic circumstances. In the Central and Western Highlands, the presence of functionally equivalent institutions (such as Enga bachelor cults or Hagen men's cults), and perhaps more stable political relations and a concomitant lower intensity of warfare (Strathern 1970), may have militated against widespread emergence or adoption of male initiation. In the Sepik, the process of nucleation of large villages amid a flux of warfare and invasion, probably accompanied by intensification of sago production, has apparently transformed the sociology of initiation, as well as structures of marriage and community, in ways explored by Tuzin (1976) and suggested in earlier sections.

Initiation can thus be adapted to a range of systems of production and a range of sociopolitical structures. Depicting a cosmos where gender polarity is part of the natural order of things, these ideologies seemingly have had a strong self-perpetuating, self-fulfilling power and resilience, as long as the world in which men were to operate was fraught with murderous violence and external threat.

For any particular language group or local group, however, this dynamic of social reproduction, contingent as it was on success in warfare, was vulnerable from without. The characteristic time span of New Guinea cultures as separate ideational systems may have been quite short, a few generations at most, if we can safely extrapolate back from the remembered recent past.

As I have suggested, these systems were also fraught with contradiction from within. The ideologies depict as closed, self-contained, and eternal systems that are temporary and open; and they depict as natural and cosmic patterns that are cultural and contingent. They define a body of secret knowledge whose core is partly fraud and yet require that those who are supposed to know nothing of these secrets know something of them (Langness 1974). These systems create a solitary group of males whose dominance is beyond challenge and whose separation from female danger is cosmically ordained. Nevertheless, these men depend for their physical survival on the labor of the women they exclude and demean; and they depend for their own replacement in the next generation on the reproductive powers that are sources of danger and disorder, on sons born into the world of women. By separating men's realm from women's to create male solidarity, these systems leave beyond male control the everyday lives—and minds—of women. The initiation systems require that those who submitted to pain and trauma as boys inflict these ordeals upon the succeeding generation in the service of a cult ideology whose partly fraudulent nature has been revealed to them in initiation. It should not surprise us that when the pressures of danger from without are relaxed, the pressures of contradiction from within can contribute to the swift dissolution of male cultism and initiation. It is no coincidence that the disappearance of male initiation has followed the Pax Australiana in many parts of New Guinea, even where traditional exchange systems and clan organization have survived. Where the initiatory systems have survived in *form*, senior men have no illusions that the world into which the initiates are to be reborn is the same as the one they entered: "all the initiation rituals intended to prepare young men for war have been robbed of their purpose, and the Baruya have for the most part discarded them from their initiation ceremonies" (Godelier 1976).[15]

LIBERATION FROM CULTURE?

A penultimate question is one of ethics, values, and the politics of anthropology. We may appreciate the systems described here as fantastic cumulations of symbolic creativity—and, in the colonial and post-colonial periods, as expressions of cultural autonomy. But can we ultimately take a stance of cultural relativism to systems that systematically use pain, fear, and deception to dominate boys and subordinate, demean, and oppress women by threat of rape and murder? Anthropologists will not all share my views. I, for one, find the systems described here to be expressions of cruelty, inhumanity, oppression, and error, as well as of cultural creativity. It is an unfortunate fact of the political economy of contemporary Papua New Guinea that the alternatives to traditional cultures are marginal participation in the world capitalist economy, with the frequent consequence of pauperization and exploitation, and an alien and anachronistic religious ideology of sin, fire, and brimstone. If peoples of Papua New Guinea are to liberate themselves from oppressive old ways, we may hope that it will be to create their own synthesis of old and new, in ways that will give them power to shape their own lives.

---

[15]Marie Reay (personal communication), however, reminds me that those who have abandoned warfare in the face of colonial power may have expected this to be a temporary suspension, not permanent cessation, of hostilities. It is clear that senior men are likely to have very different views and interests from those of young men, both in relation to initiation and in relation to new economic alternatives.

MALE CULTS AND CULTURAL THEORY

The male cults of New Guinea have a wide significance for prevailing anthropological theories of culture. In several traditions of symbolist anthropology, most explicitly in the work of Geertz and his students, culture is talked about as a system of "shared meanings." Meanings, we are told, are public and social, not private and cognitive. The symbolic elaborations of male cultism described in these chapters, however, acquire their salience from the differential distribution of knowledge in the community. Access to cultural meanings is a crucial aspect of the political structure. The Bimin-Kuskusmin image of a nut layered like an onion is apt. Women and uninitiated boys have access only to the public meanings of the outer skin. Through initiatory revelations, the outer layers are gradually pulled away, eventually to reveal the innermost kernel. Now it is true (except in the limiting case where only one person in each generation commands the ultimate, innermost secret knowledge) that these meanings are shared. It is the distribution of knowledge, though, that is crucial here: the salience of what you and I (privy to an inner layer of meaning) know comes from the fact that others do *not* know.

Theoretically, this view has several important implications. First, if access to meanings depends on who knows what, we cannot blithely assume that (even in a society that has no secret cults) all participants in, say, a ritual perceive the same meanings (see Lewis 1980; Keesing n.d.). Ritual symbols do not *have* meanings, we might better say: they *evoke* meanings, which depend on what individuals know. Many anthropological writings on ritual or mythic symbolism have asserted that even though no native actors can proffer exegeses of symbolism, these actors "understand" meanings unconsciously. Hence much symbolic anthropology has been cast as a sort of cryptography in which the analyst decodes covert meanings and attributes them to "the culture." The New Guinea male cults, predicated on the assumption that native actors will understand covert meanings only if they are given the exegetic "keys" to do so, give the lie to *any* simplistic assumptions that it is in the nature of the human mind to strip layers of the onion away unconsciously and hence that all culturally competent native actors will partake of "shared meanings" even though all or most may be unable to verbalize them.

There is another serious implication for glib modes of symbolist anthropology which see cultures as collective creations, cumulations of unconscious mind. The elaborations of cosmology among peoples such as the Bimin-Kuskusmin are not simply collective creations: they are, almost certainly, creations of *men*. Moreover, in any particular generation, not all men contribute equally. The creators of Bimin-Kuskusmin cosmology and initiatory rites have almost certainly been those who have had access to the innermost kernel of then-prevailing esoteric knowledge—which they modify and elaborate in ways that cumulate across generations. Reflect on what this means. In this realm of religious knowledge, at least, only men (and sometimes a few exceptional women; see Poole 1981) are important creators of culture, and only then for a segment of their mature lives. We can guess, moreover, that those who have contributed important additions to ritual procedure, myth, magic, or cosmological systematization have been those most knowledgeable and gifted intellectually—the Ogotemmelis and Muchonas of the Telefomin Mountains.[16] Both the collectiveness and the sharedness of "a culture" such as that of the Bimin-Kuskusmin are cast deeply in doubt.[17]

The Durkheimian assumptions about *conscience collective* and the Boasian assumptions about culture which pervade our discipline can well bear pondering in the light of these male cultists of remote New Guinea. In societies where information is power, we need to study much more seriously and well what I have elsewhere called the "political economy of knowledge." The essays that follow pull us in that direction. They will have served us well if we are stung by the nettles of doubt and, like the initiates, are led to deeper layers of understanding.

---

[16]Here, as elsewhere, Bateson shows penetrating insights. He addresses the question of "how the stimulation of a small number of specialists can react on the culture as a whole." He notes that "these specialists constantly set themselves up as unofficial masters of ceremonies, criticising and instructing the men who are carrying out the intricacies of the culture. . . . Thus the culture is to a great extent in the custody of men trained in erudition and dialectic and is continually set forth by them for the instruction of the majority. . . . We may be fairly certain that [these] individuals . . . contribute very much more than their fellows to the elaboration and maintenance of the culture" (1958:227).

[17]An urgent priority here is a deeper probing of the lives and experiences of women in these societies. I am not convinced that women in sexually polarized New Guinea societies could not or would not give cogent autobiographical materials or commentaries on "the system" and their place in it if sufficient effort were to be spent ethnographically in creating contexts in which this would be possible; and I anticipate we would find that women's vantage points on and stances toward warfare, sex, pollution, ritual, initiation, and work are quite different from those of men, even though in some sense women "accept" the ideology and the terms of their subordination. Almost a decade after its publication, Marilyn Strathern's *Women in Between* remains the only really substantial study of women in a New Guinea society.

REFERENCES

ALLEN, M. R.
1967 *Male Cults and Secret Initiations in Melanesia.* Melbourne: Melbourne University Press.

BARTH, F.
1975 *Ritual and Knowledge among the Baktaman of New Guinea.* New Haven: Yale University Press.

BATESON, G.
1958 *Naven.* 2d ed. Stanford: Stanford University Press. 1st ed. 1936.

1972 Style, grace, and information in primitive art. In *Steps to an Ecology of Mind,* ed. G. Bateson. Philadelphia: Intext.

BURTON, R. V., and J. W. M. WHITING
1961 The absent father and cross-sex identity. *Merrill-Palmer Quarterly of Behavior and Development* 7:85−95.

DIVALE, W. T.
1971 Kapauku warfare, calories, and population control. Paper read at the 70th Annual Meetings of the American Anthropological Association.

DIVALE, W. T., and M. HARRIS
1976 Population, warfare, and the male supremacy complex. *American Anthropologist* 78:521−538.

DONALDSON, M.
1980 Warfare, production, and sexual antagonism: the political economy of pre-capitalist societies in the Eastern Highlands of Papua New Guinea. Paper read at "Melanesia: Beyond Diversity," a seminar of the Research School of Pacific Studies, Australian National University, November 7.

DUNDES, A.
1976 A psychoanalytic study of the bullroarer. *Man* 11:220−238.

FAITHORN, E. D.
1975 The concept of pollution among the Kafe of the Papua New Guinea Highlands. In *Toward an Anthropology of Women,* ed. R. R. Reiter, pp. 127−140. New York: Monthly Review Press.

GELL, A.
1975 *Metamorphosis of the Cassowaries.* London: Athlone Press.

GODELIER, M.
1976 Sex as the ultimate foundation of the social and cosmic order of the New Guinea Baruya: Myth and reality. M.G.'s translation of paper in *Sexualité et pouvoir,* ed. A. Verdiglione, pp. 268−306. Paris: Traces Payot.

HALLPIKE, C. K.
1977 *Bloodshed and Vengeance in the Papuan Mountains: The Generation of Conflict in Tauade Society.* London: Oxford University Press.

HERDT, G., H.
1981 *Guardians of the Flutes: Idioms of Masculinity.* New York: McGraw-Hill.

HIATT, L. R.
1971 Secret pseudo-procreation rites among the Australian aborigines. In *Anthropol-*

ogy in Oceania: Essays Presented to Ian Hogbin, ed. L. R. Hiatt and C. Jayawardena, pp. 77–88. Sydney: Angus and Robertson.

HILDE, R.

1980 Seasonality and Chimbu pig husbandry. *Mankind* 12 (3).

KEESING, R. M.

1979 Anthropology in Melanesia: retrospect and prospect. In *The Politics of Anthropology*, ed. G. Huizer and B. Mannheim, chap. 9. The Hague: Mouton.

1981 *Social Anthropology: A Contemporary Perspective*. New York: Holt, Rinehart and Winston.

N.d. *Kwaio Religion: The Living and the Dead in a Solomon Islands Society*. New York: Columbia University Press, forthcoming.

KELLY, R. C.

1976 Witchcraft and sexual relations: an exploration in the social and semantic implications of the structure of belief. In *Man and Woman in the New Guinea Highlands*, ed. P. Brown and G. Buchbinder, pp. 36–53. Washington, D.C.: American Anthropological Association.

LANDTMAN, G.

1927 *The Kiwai Papuans of British New Guinea*. London: Macmillan.

LANGNESS, L. L.

1974 Ritual power and male domination in the New Guinea Highlands. *Ethos* 2 (3):189–212.

LEACH, E. R.

1959 Magical hair. *Journal of the Royal Anthropological Institute* 88:147–164.

LEWIS, G.

1980 *Day of Shining Red: An Essay on Understanding Ritual*. Cambridge: Cambridge University Press.

LINDENBAUM, S.

1972 Sorcerers, ghosts, and polluting women: an analysis of religious belief and population control. *Ethnology* 11 (3):241–253.

1976 A wife is the hand of man. In *Man and Woman in the New Guinea Highlands*, ed. P. Brown and G. Buchbinder, pp. 54–62. Washington, D.C.: American Anthropological Association.

1979 *Kuru Sorcery: Disease and Danger in the New Guinea Highlands*. Palo Alto, Calif.: Mayfield Press.

MEAD, M.

1938 The Mountain Arapesh: an importing culture. American Museum of Natural History, *Anthropological Papers* 36 (3):139–349.

1949 *Male and Female: A Study of the Sexes in a Changing World*. New York: William Morrow and Co.

1968 *Sex and Temperament in Three Primitive Societies*. Reprint. New York: Dell. 1st ed. 1935.

MEGGITT, M. J.

1964 Male-female relationships in the Highlands of Australian New Guinea. *New Guinea: The Central Highlands*, ed. J. B. Watson, *American Anthropologist* 66, pt. 2 (4):204–224.

MEIGS, A. S.
1976 Male pregnancy and the reduction of sexual opposition in a New Guinea Highlands society. *Ethnology* 15 (4):393−407.

1978 A Papuan perspective on pollution. *Man* 13:304−318.

MODJESKA, C. J. N.
1978 Production among the Duna: aspects of horticultural intensification of Central New Guinea. Ph.D. dissertation, Australian National University.

N.d. *Production and Inequality: Perspectives from Central New Guinea.* Forthcoming.

MURPHY, R. F.
1959 Social structure and sex antagonism. *Southwestern Journal of Anthropology* 15 (2):89−98.

O'LAUGHLIN, B.
1974 Why Mbum women cannot eat chicken. In *Woman, Culture, and Society*, ed. M. Z. Rosaldo and L. Lamphere, pp. 301−318. Stanford: Stanford University Press.

POOLE, F. J. P.
1981 Transforming "natural" woman: female ritual leaders and gender ideology among Bimin-Kuskusmin. In *Sexual Meanings*, ed. S. B. Ortner and H. Whitehead. New York: Cambridge University Press.

RAPPAPORT, R.
1967 Ritual regulation of environmental relations among a New Guinea people. *Ethnology* 6:17−30.

1968 *Pigs for the Ancestors: Ritual in the Ecology of a New Guinea People.* New Haven: Yale University Press.

READ, K. E.
1952 Nama cult of the Central Highlands, New Guinea. *Oceania* 23 (1):1−25.

REAY, M.
1959 *The Kuma: Freedom and Conformity in the New Guinea Highlands.* Melbourne: Melbourne University Press.

ROSALDO, M. Z.
1974 Woman, culture and society: a theoretical overview. In *Woman, Culture, and Society*, ed. M. Z. Rosaldo and L. Lamphere, pp. 17−42. Stanford: Stanford University Press.

SCHIEFFELIN, E. L.
1976 *The Sorrow of the Lonely and the Burning of the Dancers.* New York: St. Martin's Press.

SILLITOE, P.
1977 Land shortage and war in New Guinea. *Ethnology* 16 (1):71−82.

1978 Big men and war in New Guinea. *Man* 13:252−271.

STRATHERN, A. J.
1970 Male initiation in the New Guinea Highlands societies. *Ethnology* 9 (4): 373−379.

TURNER, V. W.
1966 Colour classification in Ndembu ritual. In *Anthropological Approaches to the Study of Religion*, ed. M. Benton. ASA Monographs, no. 3. London: Tavistock.

1967 *The Forest of Symbols: Studies in Ndembu Ritual.* Ithaca, N.Y.: Cornell University Press.

1978 Encounter with Freud: the making of a comparative symbolist. In *The Making of Psychological Anthropology*, ed. G. D. Spindler, pp. 558−583. Berkeley, Los Angeles, and London: University of California Press.

TUZIN, D. F.

1975 The breath of a ghost: dreams and fear of the dead. *Ethos* 3:555−578.

1976 *The Ilahita Arapesh: Dimensions of Unity.* Berkeley, Los Angeles, and London: University of California Press.

1977 Reflections of being in Arapesh water symbolism. *Ethos* 5 (2):195−223.

1980 *The Voice of the Tambaran: Truth and Illusion in Ilahita Arapesh Religion.* Berkeley, Los Angeles, and London: University of California Press.

VAN BAAL, J.

1963 The cult of the bull-roarer in Australia and southern New Guinea. *Bijdragen tot de Taal-, Land-, en Volkenkunde*, 119: 201−214.

1966 *Dema.* The Hague: Martinous Nijhoff.

VAYDA, A. P.

1961 Expansion and warfare among swidden agriculturalists. *American Anthropologist* 63:346−358.

1971 Phases in the process of war and peace among the Marings of New Guinea. *Oceania* 42:1−24.

WATSON, J. B.

1977 Pigs, fodder, and the Jones effect in Postipomoean New Guinea. *Ethnology* 16(1):57−70.

WHITING, J. W. M., R. KLUCKHOHN, and A. ANTHONY

1958 The function of male initiation ceremonies at puberty. In *Readings in Social Psychology*, ed. E. E. Maccoby, T. M. Newcomb, and E. L. Hartley, pp. 359−370. New York: Henry Holt and Co.

WILLIAMS, F. E.

1936 Papuans of the Trans-fly. London: Oxford University Press.

WURM, S. A.

1980 Languages and migrations: Papuan languages. Paper read at "Melanesia: Beyond Diversity," a seminar of the Research School of Pacific Studies, Australian National University, October 31.

2 FETISH AND FANTASY IN SAMBIA INITIATION

Gilbert H. Herdt

The Author

Gilbert H. Herdt is Assistant Professor of Anthropology at Stanford University. He was born in western Kansas in 1949 and educated in Wichita. He began his graduate work in California, including weekend research among Japanese-Americans, and later conducted a year of more intense fieldwork on psychotherapy as "ritual healing" in a large psychiatric ward. Between 1972 and 1974, he did further postgraduate work at the University of Washington, where studies with Professors L. L. Langness, K. E. Read, and J. B. Watson stimulated him to work in New Guinea. There he focused on the "discarded problems" of ritual initiation and its subjective experience among initiates. On a Fulbright scholarship he then went to the Australian National University, where he studied with Professors Derek Freeman and Roger Keesing and from which he undertook two years' fieldwork among the Sambia, a hitherto unknown people of the Eastern Highlands, Papua New Guinea. The dissertation for which he received his Ph.D. from ANU in 1978 concerned the individual in Sambia male initiation. Between 1977 and 1979 Dr. Herdt was a Postdoctoral Fellow in the Department of Psychiatry of the University of California, Los Angeles, where he studied gender-identity theory and treatment with Professor Robert J. Stoller, M.D., and did work related to psychopathology, mother-infant interactions, and child psychiatry. He has taught at Stanford since 1979.

Professor Herdt conducted research among the Sambia in 1974–1976, 1979, and 1981. He remains committed to the idea of long-term anthropological case studies as a paradigmatic discovery process in psychocultural and symbolic theory. He has taught courses on sex and gender, psychological and symbolic anthropology, ethnopsychiatry, and ritual, with emphasis on Melanesian societies. He has published articles on shamanism, gender identity,

PLATE 2.1   A shaman leads the set of initiates in a dance procession on the cult-house dance ground following the secret flute ceremony of first-stage initiation.

and other aspects of Sambia culture and is the author of *Guardians of the Flutes* (1981), a study of Sambia ritual idioms and identity. He is presently working on the second part of that study, focusing on the social action and fantasy processes of collective initiation.

All cases of Fetishism, when examined, show that the worship is paid to an intangible power or spirit incorporated in some visible form, and that the fetish is merely the link between the worshiper and the object of worship.

A. C. Haddon (1921:70)

INTRODUCTION

Central to the ethos of Sambia male initiations are secret bamboo flutes of great and mysterious power.[1] Sambia men come to ''worship'' those flutes with an ambivalent mixture of fear and affection. Perhaps we should expect this of a male cult whose ritual instruments personify a compelling need to separate boys from their mothers and reinforce masculine authority traumatically, thereby creating a hierarchy of dominators over underlings. Beyond these political facts, though, there is a paradoxical side of the flutes which is as puzzling with regard to Sambia as it is when found in other New Guinea societies: the conviction that these flutes—paramount symbols of maleness—are animated by an eroticized *female* spirit. Men's ritual attachment to this Janus-faced fetish and its relationship to a culturally constituted fantasy system is the key problem of this chapter.

A generation has passed since K. E. Read (1952) established male

[1]This chapter is based on 2½ years of fieldwork (1974–1976, 1979) among the Sambia of Papua New Guinea, funded by a Fulbright scholarship to Australia (Australian-American Educational Foundation) and the Department of Anthropology, Research School of Pacific Studies, Australian National University, whose support I gratefully acknowledge. Support for the writing of this chapter came from an Individual Post-Doctoral Fellowship of the National Institute of Mental Health held in UCLA's Neuropsychiatric Institute, and I also wish to thank those institutes. I am grateful to Derek Freeman, Michael Young, Inge Riebe, and Robert J. Stoller for commenting on an earlier version of this study. For comments on the present manuscript, my thanks go to Leonard B. Glick, Shirley Lindenbaum, Michelle Z. Rosaldo, and Marilyn Strathern; and I am particularly indebted to Joseph Carrier, Terence E. Hays, Roger M. Keesing, Fitz J. P. Poole, K. E. Read, and Donald F. Tuzin. Responsibility for the final product is, of course, mine.

Sambia is a pseudonym adopted to protect the true identities and confidences of informants, and changes have also been made in place names to ensure anonymity.

46

initiation as the primary mechanism for conscripting boys into the *nama* male cult he so skillfully sketched among the Gahuku-Gama tribe of the Eastern Highlands. Read's landmark study was the first to map out, systematically, a range of interrelated anthropological interests associated with such initiatory cults. Social organization and social structure were highlighted, but the belief system also got worked into his analysis. And from the very start he gave precedence to the sacred nama flutes as a dominant symbol of this cult.

From Read's work I evince four research interests in such cults the paradigmatic importance of which still strongly influences New Guinea studies. The first, and certainly the most timely interest in its day, was sociological: the flutes were conceptualized as a "symbol of unity" representing the "solidarity of males" as kinsmen and cult members (Read 1952:7). Here, as he granted, Read's work was frankly Durkheimian in its concern with how the social functions of the cult assisted in "the regulation, maintenance and transmission of sentiments upon which Gahuku-Gama society depends" (1952:1). From this functional viewpoint arose another, expectably political, interest: the cult's significance both as an "index of male dominance and [as] an institution serving to maintain the status quo of male hegemony" (1952:15). By means of political "deceit" and "conscious falsification" (1952:9), the flutes sanctified masculine authority. Read implicitly argued that the cult was therefore a one-sided species of Durkheim's religion: society worshiped only males.

This male hegemony opened up a third thematic interest in male cults: their rampant misogyny and resulting "antagonism" between the sexes. Here, Read served notice of a basic tension existing between men's dogmas and their rituals: "In the final analysis, the idea which men hold of themselves is based primarily on what men do rather than on what they have at birth. They recognize, indeed, that in physiological endowment men are inferior to women, and, characteristically, they have recourse to elaborate artificial means to redress the contradiction and to demonstrate its opposite" (1952:14). It was those ritual "contradictions"—and what they meant for the "idea which men hold of themselves"—that gave rise to the last, and most neglected, of Read's interests.

This theme represents the multivalent meaning of the flutes themselves: how they always appeared in the three grandest pageants of masculine life—initiation rites, pig festivals, and intermittent "fertility rites" (Read 1952:2); how they were linked to powerful, male-controlled, mystical spirits; how their sounds were meant to excite men and frighten women; and how, oddly enough, the material shell of a flute was not in itself sacred (1952:4) but was easily replaceable. Read never forgot these aspects of the nama cult, as his writings show (see 1951, 1952, 1954, 1955, 1965).

Subsequent investigators have confirmed the widespread importance of initiatory cults like those of the nama throughout the Central Highlands (cf. Berndt 1962; Glasse and Lindenbaum 1969; Langness 1967, 1974; Lawrence and Meggitt 1965; Meggitt 1964; Newman 1965; Salisbury 1965; Watson 1960, 1964). In many areas these secret societies are so central that an understanding of New Guinea social organization and culture is impossible without an understanding of the cults (see Allen 1967; Strathern 1969, 1970). Further, many workers have followed Read's Durkheimian lead in studying the cults. This approach poses difficulties, as Langness (1967, 1974) and others (cf. Koch 1974) have noted. For example, a researcher taking such a structural-functional perspective on the cult would concentrate on "the solidarity of the male community," but only by understanding that it emerges "at the expense of females" (Langness 1974:200). This theoretical inadequacy, as we shall see, is of telling importance for interpreting Sambia ritual.

A narrow sociological paradigm no longer seems adequate. Read himself was clear in stating, from the start, that there were "many other problems" associated with male cults, elements that he had "chosen to exclude" (1952:1). These earlier studies were thus restricted, in scope and selection of data, by their focus on social-structural considerations. Of course, their contribution was still substantial; their perspectives also helped scholars manage the unenviable complexities of studying symbolic behavior; and all research, we assume, adheres to accepted conventions of disciplinary focus. Nevertheless, these restrictions have resulted in a gap in our understanding of the cultural and psychological elements of New Guinea cults (see Langness 1976). (Indeed, these years later, Read's [1965:95−140] last description of the now vanished Gahuku-Gama ritual initiations and their subjective aspects remains superlative.) We now need an expanded anthropological approach that encompasses those other dimensions of ritual meaning and adds new perspectives to the structural-functional studies already at hand. This study, like those of Herdt (1981), Poole (this volume, chap. 3), Schieffelin (1976), and Tuzin (1972, 1977, 1980), is concerned with building that approach.

Of Read's "many other problems" still unstudied and unsolved, I wish to examine the symbolic behavior surrounding the ritual flutes of Sambia. In various parts of Melanesia, male secret societies apparently depended on flutes (and other sound-making instruments) as a mystical institution. Among the Gahuku, in fact, as Read showed, the term *nama* (after which he termed their male cult) came from the word for a "mystical bird-like creature," whose cries were secretly produced by flute players. Now there is much of the exotic in Highlands ritual. This symbolic pattern, though, is altogether something more: the dogma, duplicity and fantasy that powerful and fantastic beings are summoned up and brought to life through those wooden fetishes women and children hear, yet must not look upon. Through the following observations I try to extend our understanding of this symbolic pattern in a direction that Read, like Bateson (1958) and Mead (1968) before him, first explored: the ritualized development of male gender identity.

In a recent study of Sambia gender idioms (Herdt 1981), I explored gender symbolism in men's cultural and personal constructs, and the present essay carries that work into the arena of collective initiation. My contention is that the efficacy of Sambia flute symbolism derives simultaneously from subjective meanings based on individual developmental experience and from the flutes' culturally constituted patterns of significance. To explicate this relationship between individual subjectivity and flute-oriented behavior requires concomitant studies of Sambia gender identity and eroticism. There are several reasons for this emphasis on sex and gender. First, the flutes are used as a political weapon vis-à-vis the social suppression and sexual repression of both women and boys. Second, the flutes' secret embodies the greatest of all mysteries for Sambia: the origins and divergence of maleness and femaleness. Third, the Sambia initiatory cult prescribes male homosexual activities that inform the ritual developmental cycle of all males. Fourth—and the point to which this chapter is directed—Sambia men transmit to initiates a fantasy system concerning the flutes and their sounds, some of whose components are explicitly erotic. The Sambia flutes thus elucidate a pervasive symbolic complex known throughout Papua New Guinea, and one to which I shall later allude: namely, the identification of men with their masculinized ritual cults, flutes, and fantasy female beings.

If, as I suggest, such a fantasy system underlies collective flute-oriented behavior, then other psychosocial processes are no doubt deviling up the ritual process too (cf. Turner 1964). How can we know? Part of the answer, I think, hinges on how we define the above research interests and on the fact that their conceptualization assumes a slant on anthropological theory and method.

A first principle: The flutes are an imaginative and multivalent fetish. They constitute more than a material instrument, a collective

49

representation, or a cultural symbol. The flutes are man-made ritual paraphernalia capable of creating evocative effects that become adored and feared. This religious power, associated with other societal phenomena like kinship affiliation or ethnic identity, we anthropologists know well enough. Nevertheless, there is that other dimension of the Sambia flutes, too: their capacity to ritually excite, to stir erotic interest, or to signify such subjective experiences or their opposite—repression. The flutes embrace a panoply of various psychosocial domains, and yet to make this admission is tantamount to opening up that discarded Pandora's black box, the mind.

By this I mean not the "collective mind" of certain structuralists, psychoanalysts, or poets but rather the subjective processes and contents of the minds of flesh-and-blood individuals with whom I talk and interact in the routine course of each ethnographic workday. It is from such observations that we can attempt to apprehend meanings, fetishistic or otherwise. *Fetish* is an old-fashioned term nowadays fallen into disrepute. We are uneasy handling its connotations even on those rare occasions when musty museologists use it. One reason for this uneasiness, I think, is that the impassioned ritual significances of a fetish implicate more than social custom. They also imply a behavioral context with its acts, moods, and values, as much as they imply psychological frames (Bateson 1972:177–193) orienting individual affects and intentions. The meaning of a fetish requires both types of data—on customs, and on behavior or subjectivity.

It is said of the late Sir Evans-Pritchard that he always advised his students to study the grain of a culture, to concentrate on those patterns, in small details or large, which cohere to form an intuitive textural theme permeating all. This is what we ethnographers are about. To describe thusly the grain of Sambia culture requires that one attend to acts, words, and feelings of individuals—sometimes impassioned acts or erotic feelings—and the mode of interpersonal communications to which they belong, and this is what I have attempted to do below.

My presentation will have five parts. I shall begin with a brief description of Sambia society, its male initiatory cult, and the corresponding belief system.[2] Second, drawing on field notes, I shall relate actual observations of flute-oriented behavior in first-stage initiation. Third, I shall sketch some subjective fragments of these ritual experi-

---

[2]Interested readers should consult Herdt (1981) for additional background and an extended analysis of the Sambia male belief system.

ences drawn from longitudinal, clinical-type case studies of initiated boys. Fourth, we shall consider the meaning of these complementary dimensions of the flutes as constituents of an intersubjective fantasy system. Last, my findings shall be summarized and compared to reports from other New Guinea societies.

BACKGROUND

Sambia are a mountain-dwelling hunting and horticultural people who number some 2,000 persons and inhabit one of New Guinea's most rugged terrains. The population is dispersed through narrow river valleys over a widespread, thinly populated rain forest; rainfall is heavy; and even today the surrounding mountain ranges keep the area isolated. Sambia live on the fringes of the Highlands, but they trace their origins to the Papua hinterlands; their culture and economy thus reflect a mixture of influences from both of those areas. Hunting still predominates as a masculine activity through which most meat protein is acquired. As in the Highlands, though, sweet potatoes and taro are the staple crops, and their cultivation is for the most part women's work. Pigs are few, and they have no ceremonial or exchange significance; indigenous marsupials, such as possum and tree kangaroo, provide necessary meat prestations for all initiations and ceremonial feasts (cf. Meigs 1976).

Sambia settlements are small, well-defended, mountain clan hamlets. These communities comprise locally based descent groups organized through a strong agnatic idiom. Residence is patrivirilocal, and most men actually reside in their fathers' hamlets. Clans are exogamous, and one or more of them together constitute a hamlets' landowning corporate agnatic body. These men also form a localized warriorhood that is sometimes allied with other hamlets in matters of fighting, marriage, and ritual. Each hamlet contains one or two men's clubhouses, in addition to women's houses, and the men's ritual life centers on their clubhouse. Marriage is usually by sister exchange or infant betrothal, although the latter form of prearranged marriage is culturally preferred. Intrahamlet marriage is occasionally more frequent (up to 50 percent of all marriages in my own hamlet field site) than one would expect in such small segmentary groupings, an involutional pattern weakened since pacification.

Sambia male and female residential patterns differ somewhat from those of other Highlands peoples. The nuclear family is an important

51

subunit of the hamlet-based extended family of interrelated clans. A man, his wife, and their children usually cohabit within a single, small, round hut. Children are thus reared together by their parents during the early years of life, so the nuclear family is a residential unit, an institution virtually unknown to the Highlands (Meggitt 1964; Read 1954). Sometimes this unit is expanded through polygyny, in which case a man, his cowives, and their children may occupy the single dwelling. Girls continue to reside with their parents until marriage (usually near the menarche, around fifteen to seventeen years of age). Boys, however, are removed to the men's clubhouse at seven to ten years of age, following their first-stage initiation. There they reside exclusively until marriage and cohabitation years later. Despite familial cohabitation in early childhood, strict taboos based on beliefs about menstrual pollution still separate men and women in their sleeping and eating arrangements.

Warfare used to be constant and nagging among Sambia, and it conditioned the values and masculine stereotypes surrounding the male initiatory cult. Ritualized bow fights occurred among neighboring hamlets, whose members still intermarried and usually initiated their sons together. At the same time, though, hamlets also united against enemy tribes and in staging war parties against them. Hence, warfare, marriage, and initiation were interlocking institutions; the effect of this political instability was to reinforce tough, strident masculine performance in most arenas of social life. "Strength" (*jerundu*) was—and is—a pivotal idea in this male ethos. Indeed, strength, which has both ethnobiological and behavioral aspects, could be aptly translated as "maleness" and "manliness." Strength has come to be virtually synonymous with idealized conformity to male ritual routine. Before conquest and pacification by the Australians, though, strength had its chief performative significance in one's conduct on the battlefield. Even today bitter reminders of war linger on among the Sambia; and we should not forget that it is against the harsh background of the warrior's existence that Sambia initiate their boys, whose only perceived protection against the inconstant world is their own unbending masculinity.

Initiation rests solely in the hands of the men's secret society. It is this organization that brings the collective initiatory cycle into being as jointly performed by neighboring hamlets (and as constrained by their own chronic bow fighting). The necessary feast-crop gardens, ritual leadership and knowledge, dictate that a handful of elders, war leaders, and ritual experts be in full command of the actual staging of the event. Everyone and all else are secondary.

There are six intermittent initiations from the ages of seven to ten and onward. They are, however, constituted and conceptualized as two distinct cultural systems within the male life cycle. First-stage (*moku*, at seven to ten years of age), second-stage (*imbutu*, at ten to thirteen years), and third-stage (*ipmangwi*, at thirteen to sixteen years) initiations—bachelorhood rites—are collectively performed for regional groups of boys as age-mates. The initiations are held in sequence, as age-graded advancements; the entire sequel takes months to perform. The focus of all these initiations is the construction and habitation of a great cult house (*moo-angu*) on a traditional dance ground; its ceremonialized building inaugurates the whole cycle. Fourth-stage (*nuposha*: sixteen years and onward), fifth-stage (*taiketnyi*), and sixth-stage (*moondangu*) initiations are, conversely, individually centered events not associated with the confederacy of interrelated hamlets, cult house, or dance ground. Each of these initiations, like the preceding ones, does have its own ritual status, social role, and title, as noted. The triggering event for the latter three initiations, unlike that for the bachelorhood rites, is not the building of a cult house or a political agreement of hamlets to act collectively but is rather the maturing femininity and life-crisis events of the women assigned in marriage to youths (who become the initiated novices). Therefore, fourth-stage initiation is only a semipublic activity organized by the youths' clansmen (and some male affines). Its secret purificatory and other rites are followed by the formal marriage ceremony in the hamlet. Fifth-stage initiation comes at a woman's menarche, when her husband is secretly introduced to additional purification and sexual techniques. Sixth-stage initiation issues from the birth of a man's wife's first child. This event is, de jure, the attainment of manhood. (The first birth is elaborately ritualized and celebrated; the next three births are also celebrated, but in more truncated fashion.) Two children bring full adulthood (*aatmwunu*) for husband and wife alike. Birth ceremonies are suspended after the fourth birth, since there is no reason to belabor what is by now obvious: a man has proved himself competent in reproduction. This sequence of male initiations forms the basis for male development, and it underlies the antagonistic tenor of relationships between the sexes.

It needs stating only once that men's secular rhetoric and ritual practices depict women as dangerous and polluting inferiors whom men are to distrust throughout their lives. In this regard, Sambia values and relationships pit men against women even more markedly, I think, than occurs in other Highlands communities (cf. Brown and Buchbinder 1976; Meggitt 1964; Read 1954). Men hold themselves as the superiors of women in physique, personality, and social position. And this dogma of male supremacy permeates all social relationships and institutions, likewise coloring domestic behavior among the sexes (cf. Tuzin 1980 for an important contrast). Men fear not only pollution from contact with women's vaginal fluids and menstrual blood but also the depletion of their semen, the vital spark of maleness, which women (and boys, too) inevitably extract, sapping a man's substance. These are among the main themes of male belief underlying initiation.

The ritualized simulation of maleness is the result of initiation, and men believe the process to be vital for the nature and nurture of manly growth and well-being. First-stage initiation begins the process in small boys. Over the ensuing ten to fifteen years, until marriage, cumulative initiations and residence in the men's house are said to promote biological changes that firmly cement the growth from childhood to manhood. Nature provides male genitals, it is true; but nature alone does not bestow the vital spark biologically necessary for stimulating masculine growth or demonstrating cold-blooded self-preservation.

New Guinea specialists will recognize in the Sambia belief system a theme that links it to the comparative ethnography of male initiation and masculine development: the use of ritual procedures for sparking, fostering, and maintaining manliness in males (see Berndt 1962; Meigs 1976; Newman 1964, 1965; Poole 1981 and this volume; Read 1965; Salisbury 1965; Strathern 1969, 1970). Sambia themselves refer to the results of first-stage collective initiation—our main interest—as a means of "growing a boy"; and this trend of ritual belief is particularly emphatic.

Unlike ourselves, Sambia perceive no imminent, naturally driven fit between one's birthright sex and one's gender identity or role.[3] Indeed, the problem (and it is approached as a situation wanting a solution) is implicitly and explicitly understood in quite different terms. The solution is also different for the two sexes: men believe that a girl is born with all of the vital organs and fluids necessary for her to attain reproductive competence through "natural" maturation. This conviction is embodied in cultural perceptions of the girl's development beginning with the sex assignment at birth. What distinguishes a girl (*tai*) from a boy (*kwulai'u*) is obvious: "A boy has a penis, and a girl does not,"

---

[3] I follow Stoller (1968) in adhering to the following distinctions: the term *sex traits* refers to purely biological phenomena (anatomy, hormones, genetic structure, etc.), whereas *gender* refers to those psychological and cultural attributes that compel a person (consciously or unconsciously) to sense him- or herself, and other persons, as belonging to either the male or female sex. It follows that the term *gender role* (Sears 1965), rather than the imprecise term *sex role*, refers to the normative set of expectations associated with masculine and feminine social positions.

men say. Underlying men's communications is a conviction that male-ness, unlike femaleness, is not a biological given. It must be artificially induced through secret ritual; and that is a personal achievement. The visible manifestations of girls' fast-growing reproductive competence, noticed first in early motor coordination and speech and then later in the rapid attainment of height and secondary sex traits (e.g., breast development), are attributed to inner biological properties. Girls possess a menstrual-blood organ, or *tingu*, said to precipitate all those events and the menarche. Boys, on the other hand, are thought to possess an inactive tingu. They do possess, however, another organ—the *kere-ku-kereku*, or semen organ—that is thought to be the repository of semen, the very essence of maleness and masculinity; but this organ is not functional at birth, since it contains no semen naturally and can only store, never produce, any. Only oral insemination, men believe, can activate the boy's semen organ, thereby precipitating his push into adult reproductive competence. In short, femininity unfolds naturally, where-as masculinity must be achieved; and here is where the male ritual cult steps in.

Men also perceive the early socialization risks of boys and girls in quite different terms. All infants are closely bonded to their mothers. Out of a woman's contaminating, life-giving womb pours the baby, who thereafter remains tied to the woman's body, breast milk, and many ministrations. This latter contact only reinforces the femininity and female contamination in which birth involves the infant. Then, too, the father, both because of postpartum taboos and by personal choice, tends to avoid being present at the breast-feedings. Mother thus becomes the unalterable primary influence; father is a weak second. Sambia say this does not place girls at a ''risk''—they simply succumb to the drives of their ''natural'' biology. This maternal attachment and paternal distance clearly jeopardize the boys' growth, however, since nothing innate within male maturation seems to resist the inhibiting effects of mothers' femininity. Hence boys must be traumatically separated—wiped clean of their female contaminants—so that their masculinity may develop.

Homosexual fellatio inseminations can follow this separation but cannot precede it, for otherwise they would go for naught. The accumu-lating semen, injected time and again for years, is believed crucial for the formation of biological maleness and masculine comportment. This native perspective is sufficiently novel to justify our using a special concept for aiding description and analysis of the data: masculinization (Herdt 1981:205 ff.). Hence I shall refer to the overall process that involves separating a boy from his mother, initiating him, ritually treating his body, administering homosexual inseminations, his biological attainment of puberty, and his eventual reproductive competence as *masculinization*. (Precisely what role personal and cultural fantasy plays in the negotiation of this ritual process I have considered elsewhere: see Herdt 1981: chaps. 6, 7, and 8.)

A boy has female contaminants inside of him which not only retard physical development but, if not removed, debilitate him and eventually bring death. His body is male: his tingu contains no blood and will not activate. The achievement of puberty for boys requires semen. Breast milk "nurtures the boy," and sweet potatoes or other "female" foods provide "stomach nourishment," but these substances become only feces, not semen. Women's own bodies internally produce the menarche, the hallmark of reproductive maturity. There is no comparable mechanism active in a boy, nothing that can stimulate his secondary sex traits. Only semen can do that; only men have semen; boys have none. What is left to do, then, except initiate and masculinize boys into adulthood?

RITUAL BEHAVIOR

The first sign that a collective initiation is approaching comes in the guise of piercing, melodious cries that appear mysteriously as if from nowhere but that children are told come from old female hamlet spirits (*aatmwog-wambu*). First from within the men's house, later near the emerging ritual cult house, and eventually at the edges of the forest, the haunting sounds demandingly increase in tempo. This signal alerts women of the coming ritual preparations. Boys, whose consternation may turn to curiosity or fear, are comforted or teased (according to the person and situation) with remarks like "The female spirit wants to get you; she wants to kill and eat you." Mother or father may smile or laugh or fall silent—responses that underscore the mounting tension that intrudes on the household of a boy whose time has come. "The female spirit protects the clubhouse; she's aged and hidden until moku [initiation] inside an old net bag," some fathers tell their sons. Boys differ in their responses to this scenario, of course, but whether stoically indifferent or tearful, they all experience a discomfort that turns into panic at initiation. It is the sound of the flutes that creates this discomfort, signaling as it does an unalterable transition into warrior life. Let us now turn to the events marking the transition.

The great cult house goes up in a matter of weeks, and its construction is soon followed by the third-stage initiation. Two principles dictate the need that older bachelors' "puberty" rites precede the second and first-stage initiations. First, following their advancement, the bachelors are expected to help organize the ensuing ritual activities. Second, as new initiators, the youths are urged (a term that conveys too weakly the elders' sense of real urgency in these matters) to demonstrate their manly feelings and behavior in particular contexts. After years of ritual ordeals, third-stage initiation once again brings nosebleedings and other tests, so bachelors have endured a great deal. Though these ordeals are necessary to build strong warriors, elders also recognize the all-too-visible frustration and anger pent up in the youths. Thus, bachelors are counseled that it is "right" for them to "pay back" their mistreatment by helping beat and nosebleed the younger initiates. Likewise, they get the go-ahead to "relax their tight penises" (proving themselves manly) by serving as dominant fellateds—for the first time—to the initiated boys, who are also encouraged to acquire the semen of youths actively.[4]

The Flutes

In what follows, our primary interest shall be with ritual behavior focused on the flutes. This behavior encompasses two primary contexts: the penis and flute ceremony (hereafter referred to as the flute ceremony); and the new initiates' first entrance into the cult house, an event that leads to erotic encounters with the bachelors on the same evening. The ritual significance of the flutes—as symbols and signs—stems from subjective, verbal and nonverbal, and situational dimensions of meaning (cf. Turner 1964) set within the naturalistic flow of the ceremonies. This perspective requires an aside about the flutes as physical objects.

Sambia have several types of ritual flutes, but they lump them together under the category term *namboolu aambelu* ("frog female"). Each flute is made from newly cut bamboo left open at one end. The hollow tubes vary in length from one to three feet; they also vary in the thickness and species of the bamboo. Two types of flutes are blown vertically from the mouth (like a jug pipe); another type is winded horizontally through a blowhole. They are always blown in pairs. Men

---

[4]A few distinctions about ritualized homosexual behavior. Sambia cult members practice only oral sex—fellatio—and no other form of homosexual intercourse. This contact is constrained by rigid rules: bachelor-fellateds (insertors), may never reverse erotic roles with younger boys (fellators, insertees), who must always swallow the semen ejaculated into their mouths. There is thus little give and take in the relationship, and the erotic focus of encounters is centered upon the bachelor's penis and the initiate's mouth, both of which are erotically fetishized.

tell women and children that the flute sounds are the wailful cries of the old female hamlet spirit who figures prominently in folklore. The bull-roarer (*duka' yungalu*, ''bird's call''), by contrast, is far less secret than the flutes and is said to produce a sound akin to a powerful but not mystical, bird (cf. what Gahuku-Gama and BenaBena say about their flutes; see Langness 1974; Read 1952). Like the various forms of making grass sporrans or like incorporeally owned ritual customs, ritual flutes—both their size and associated tunes—are identified with phratry membership and political alliance among Sambia hamlets. The flutes are played frequently during all collective initiations; once during a club-house ceremony near the end of fourth-stage initiations; and during the funeral ceremonies of young adult men or bachelors only. (This implies that the flutes ''belong'' to the bachelors, just as the youths ''belong'' to the flutes.)

The flutes are secretly guarded but played during ritual in pairs. They are hidden from women and children, who are said by the men to fear the sound. Punishment, even possible death, awaits those who might violate this code. (Men casually discuss this possibility; they take great care to conceal the flutes, and no infractions occurred during my stay.) The bamboo tubes themselves are of little intrinsic importance; they are easily made and discarded following the rituals. They are not stored or saved; they are not rubbed with semen, pig's grease, or blood nor are they stuffed with any material, such as pork (cf. Berndt 1962: 55–70; Read 1952:7). The longer flutes are referred to as ''male'' (*aatmwul*) and metaphorically as penes. The shorter and thinner flute is called a ''female'' (*aambelu*) and is sometimes likened to the glans penis. The pairs of flutes, moreover, are said to be ''married'' and are called ''spouses'' (*kwolu-aambelu*). We shall see how these notions are drawn on later.

The Initiatory Events

At the start of initiation, boys are taken from their mothers, sometimes forcibly and sometimes not, but always in an atmosphere of great tension. They are placed in the men's house momentarily, and from there on, the boys' ritual sponsors (*nyetyangu*, also ''mother's brother'') become their primary guardians until the conclusion of initiation. The sponsor-initiate relationship is usually a close one based on kinship and/or affectional bonds; the parents choose the sponsor, but he is the boys' fathers' nonagnatic peer, and he holds no other ceremonial relationship to the father or son (cf. Gewertz, this volume, chap. 7).

The boys are abruptly and permanently separated from their mothers. As the novices are led into the forest for the first ritual, which will take place that afternoon, they leave behind their mothers, women, and playmates. On the occasion I shall describe, women set up a sorrowful wail as the lads were led away; the men responded to that maternal response with pointed shouts that the boys were soon "to be killed."

On the third day of the initiation the flutes are revealed, so boys learn of their secret significance; this revelation shall be our focus. The flutes are blown at other times, too, as I noted, starting with the cult-house-raising ceremonies. They are always, however, kept just out of sight, and this has the effect, as we shall see, of building up a mood of expectation for the context of the flute ceremony later that day.

The day opens with a male "stretching rite," so called because switches are beaten against the boys to "open the skin" and foster bodily growth (*perulyapi*). Several hours later the boys' noses are bled, a powerful and traumatic experience, according to the testimony of boys and men alike. Then follows another painful rite in which stinging nettles are employed to "cleanse" the skin and "stretch" it. Finally, some four hours later in the afternoon, men assemble the novices for ceremonial dressing and painting in warrior garb. This sets the stage for the flute ceremony; it is later followed by a ceremonial procession back to the dance ground, whereupon boys enter the cult house for the first time. I wish to concentrate here on *actual observations* of a first-stage initiation sequence observed in 1975, beginning with the novices' body decoration.[5] As the decorating proceeds, the men around me quietly begin to make lewd jokes about the boys and their sponsors. The jokes are directed at the lads' emerging homosexual-fellator status. The tempo of jesting reaches a peak at the fastening of the novices' new grass sporrans. This joking draws on the Sambia view that one's type of grass sporran (of men) or skirt (of women) signals erotic status and role. The attachment of that new sporran thus dramatically distinguishes novices from the category of "neuter" children to which they formerly belonged. The banter becomes affected, the associated feelings finding expression in public joking and horseplay, and men characterize these risqué jokes and farces as traditional. (Still, not every individual participates, and certainly not to the same extent.)

[5]Between 1974 and 1976, I observed two different sequences of the entire set of Sambia initiations. The data that follow come from field notes collected over a period of eight days and nights in the Sambia River Valley in mid-1975.

I made the following observations of the men in my party who casually reclined on the grass watching the ceremonial decoration. A married man nearby pretends to copulate with an old tree trunk. He acts as if the tree is a new novice fellator, contorting his grinning face as if to express breathless rapture. The men around roar with laughter as he repeats this mime three times. Then they crack jokes among themselves. Another man asserts that the sponsors are starting to act "funny," for, as they are attaching the novices' sporrans, our men say, the sponsors' penes are erecting. A second time they suggest that the sponsors' penes are erecting, and this bawdy insinuation elicits huge guffaws of laughter. Our men then joke about men in other groups sitting nearby on the grass: they must "smell" the new grass sporrans of the boys, for they are "smiling"; and later they will coax the lads into copulating with them. More laughter follows this remark.

Next comes the flute ceremony itself, which begins in military silence as the forty-two novices are lined up, decked out in their stunning new attire, and made to await the surprises in store for them.

Two groups, each composed of four bachelors playing flutes, arrive from the forest. They circle the boys. There is total silence but for their music. The flute players are paired; one man plays a short flute, and another blows a longer flute, their musical chords harmonizing. They continue to play for about five minutes. During this period, Karavundun, a married man, picks up a long bamboo containing a narrower flute within it. He passes down the line of novices, attempting to insert the tip of the smaller, contained flute into their mouths. Approximately half the boys refuse to suck the flute. Karavundun does not press them, and there is no angry scene such as there was at another flute ceremony, when a bachelor, Erujundei, threatened the reluctant boys with a machete.[6] When a novice refuses, Karavundun simply smiles. Indeed, he jokes about those who react with displeasure. Some men nearby openly snigger at the recalcitrant novices. On the other hand, those who take to the act, "correctly" sucking the flute, are lauded, and the surrounding spectators nod their heads in approval.

Then, in visible anger at the defiant boys, Kokwai, a bachelor, unexpectedly enters the scene and strikes the novices with a long flute. Another man shouts, "Hit them hard; it is not like you were fighting them to draw blood!"

---

[6]In a different moku initiation observed in the Yellow River Valley, earlier in 1975.

Another instructing elder, Merumei, then repeatedly intimidates the novices by drawing attention to the large assembled crowd of men: "You uninitiated boys like to make jokes. . . . Now, make some jokes for the crowd of men here, we want to hear them!" He commands the boys: "You kwulai'u—open your mouths for the flute, they will place it inside . . . to try it on you. All of you, look at the large group of men . . . this large group. . . . You novices put it [the flute] inside your mouths, try it!"

The flutes are thus used for teaching about the mechanics of homosexual fellatio, and in the first references to it, the elder draws attention to the physical proof of the elders to verify his words. He does so, however, not by allusion to semen but instead by allusion to the penis. There are two groups of elders who rhetorically lecture. Damei and Mugindanbu remain at one end of the line and the fight leader, Merumei, at the other end.

The elders now condemn the novices for their childish mimicking of the flute sounds. As they do so, the flute players again strike the boys' chests with the butts of the flutes.

Mugindanbu begins, saying, "When you were uninitiated, you all played a game of imitating this sound [i.e., of the flutes], 'Um-huh, um-huh.' Now tell us, does this sound come from your mouths?"

Damei demands, "You boys think fit to imitate the flute sounds, [so] now make this sound, show us how you produce it. Why should we elders show you how to make it!

"All of you boys look at this elder. What do you think he has done? Heard the teaching this moment and grown to be big? All of them [the men] 'ate' the penis . . . and grew big. All of them can copulate with you; all of you can eat penises. If you eat them, you will grow bigger rapidly."

The novices are enjoined to secrecy and then told of the fatal consequences of breaking this taboo: "For if you do [reveal the secrets], they [unspecified] will kill and throw your body into the river. Sambia boys, you will be thrown away into the Sambia River. . . . Moonagu [phratry] boys, you will be killed and your bodies thrown into the lower Sambia River. The big men will not help you, they will not jail us either; they will help us hide it [the murder]. This custom belongs to the Baruya and other tribes, [to] all men everywhere. . . . The sun itself brought this custom which we hold! If you speak out, the stone axe and the stone club will kill you. . . . When you were children you saw the bodies of initiates. They are like the *inumdu* [shrub], green, smooth, and not used up. They are 'nice.' Those initiates eat the penises of men, and they grow big and have nice skins too. If you do not, you will not grow quickly or be handsome. You must all ingest semen. . . ."

The elder Damei praises the novices of the earlier first-stage initiation. He reveals that the men were pleased with those novices for their acceptance of homosexual activities. He thus urges the boys to follow the example of their peers earlier at the Yellow River Valley: "There we performed the moku. Our novices 'slept' [copulated] with the men. They drank the men's semen quickly. The big men all said the same: 'Those Yellow Valley men made a good moku!' The boys understood the teaching; they will grow quickly. The bachelors were pleased with the novices' . . . they felt 'sweet' [erotically satisfied]. The Yellow Valley moku was truly good. . . . This flute we will 'try out' [penetrate the mouth] on all of you. Later the men will want to copulate with you. . . . They will do the same thing."

Two elders, Damei and Worangri, then spontaneously represent themselves as authorities, testifying and sanctifying the "truth" of the penis teaching. They related that only by ingesting semen can the lads grow truly masculine: "Do you boys see us? We have white hair. We would not trick you. You must all sleep with the men. When you were uninitiated you erected the poles for banana trees and did other things. Now we have made moku for you; you must work harder. When you climb trees, your bones will ache. For that reason you must drink semen. Suppose you do not drink semen, you will not be able to climb trees to hunt possum; you will not be able to scale the top of the pandanus trees to gather nuts. You must drink semen . . . it can 'strengthen' your bones."

In the next sequence of rhetoric, semen is likened to mother's milk. Boys are taught that they must continually consume it to grow: "Now we teach you our customary story, . . . and right now you must ingest semen in the cult house. Now there are many men here; you must sleep with them. Soon they will return to their homes. Now they are here, and you ought to drink their semen. In your own hamlets, there are only a few men. When you do sleep with men, you should not be afraid of eating their penises. You will soon enjoy eating them. . . . If you try it [semen] it is just like the milk of your mother's breast. You can ingest it all of the time and grow quickly. If you do not start to drink it now, you will not ingest much of it. Only occasionally . . . and later when you are grown you will stop. If you only drink a little semen now, you will not like the penis much. So you must start now and ingest semen. When you are bigger your own penis will become bigger, and you will not want to sleep with older men. You will then want to copulate with younger boys yourself. So you should sleep with the men now. . . .''

Another man shouts that unless the boys drink semen, they will fail to blow the flutes properly: "If you do not think of this [fellatio] you will not play the flutes well. A boy who does not sleep with men plays the flute badly, for his mouth is blocked up. . . .[7] If you sleep with men you shall play the flute well. . . .''

In the final sequence, the boys' old pubic aprons are dramatically cut with a machete by the elder Mugindanbu. The limp pubic coverings then become the focus of a castration threat aimed at the boys as a deadly warning against adultery. The flutes are played again for several minutes. Merumei then lectures and shouts at the boys: "When you are grown you cannot become sexually excited over the attractive wife of another man. You can touch your own wife, that is all right. The flute wants to kill you, for if you steal a woman, she will cry out like the flute, and her man will kill you. If you touch another man's wife you will die quickly, . . . they will kill you. We are trying you out now for the time later when you might steal another man's wife. Then we would not just cut your grass sporran. If your penis rises and you want to steal a woman, we will cut it off.'' The elder cuts the old pubic covering midway between the abdomen and the genitals. "No one will help you, we will cut off your penis and kill you.'' By this act, not only is homosexual fellatio enjoined, but premarital heterosexual activities are tabooed and condemned.

Following the flute ceremony, which lasts barely an hour, the boys are carefully lined up for a last inspection prior to their ceremonial parade back to the cult house. The large group of novices and older initiates file down the hillside to the dance ground, preceded by adult men who form phalanxes around the area, separating the boys from the throng of women and children who have assembled for a last view of them. For several minutes, led by a protecting shaman, the novices are paraded around the decorated grounds. He then conducts them inside the new cult house for the first time. (They have slept in a shabby lean-to, next to the cult house, until now.) That public display is the last occasion on which women can publicly study the boys for some years to come.

---

[7]Tali, a ritual expert, says this is a double entendre: first, that boys who do not suck the penis cannot wind the flutes; and second, that this is because without fellatio their throats stay "blocked up" with the contaminated food of women (like the throats of little boys).

A while later something striking occurs, for as the boys entered the great cult house they had heard the flutes being played within. The boys are again taunted. "You can't go inside the moo-angu," the men say. They shout, "It's the menstrual hut of women; . . . women are giving birth to babies. . . . The babies are crying." Then another man says, "Look! an aatmogwambu [female hamlet spirit] is in the ritual house. . . ." The boys are led into the cult sanctuary just the same, and not more than an hour later something even more remarkable happens.

The novices are seated on the earthen floor of the cult house. It is dusk, and after going through days of initiation, on top of this particularly long and trying day, they look pretty worn out. The women and children outside have by now been chased off. A fire has been built (for the first time), and a smattering of men sit idly beside the hearth near the lads.

Some bachelors unexpectedly tromp inside, playing flutes. There are two groups of four flute players each, as there were in the earlier flute ceremony, but they are disguised. There is silence again except for the flutes. A man says to the boys, "An old woman spirit has come; . . . she is cold, she wants to come sit by the fire. . . ." The bachelors then squat to the floor, their hands and faces disguised by bark capes: the youths are impersonating female hamlet spirits. A young man says, "She is an aatmogwambu; she has come to cry for you. . . . Go away! Not good that she swallows her spit for you.[8] You must help straighten her out . . . ;[9] if you feel sorry for her, you must help her out."[10]

The men then joke about this squeamishly. The flute players hobble around behind the tense boys, playing their flutes beneath their capes. The boys are again struck on their chests with the flutes. They are told not to reveal the flutes' secrets. An elder also comments, "If you see the flutes in [your] dreams, it means that men will soon come to attack and kill you. You must think about this image. . . ."[11] The bachelors unmask themselves, and the novices are hit on the heads with the flutes, which are then thrown into the hearth fire; the lads are made to stand near the fire, warming themselves and "strengthening" their bodies with its

---

[8]A common metaphor for erotic desire.

[9]Another common metaphor, this for sucking the bachelors' penis until ejaculation, which "slackens" the penis.

[10]An implicit statement that boys should serve as fellators to the bachelors.

[11]Little references to dream images and their cultural interpretation are commonly inserted in ritual teachings like this throughout initiation; they usually link ritual imagery to warfare vigilance.

PLATE 2.2 Men and initiates dance at dawn during Sambia cult initiation ceremonies. 1975.

heat. The "formal" ceremony is over, but something else is to follow. Several of the bachelors, including those who had cloaked themselves, now come alive. It is nightfall, and what should commence are the first erotic encounters that may result in fellatio between themselves and the novices. The bachelors begin with momentary, outlandishly (and unprecedented) exotic and erotic exhibitionism, as is customary: they lift up their arse covers, exposing their naked buttocks to the boys while engaging in childish games that imitate—and thereby mock—the uninitiated boys the novices previously were. The novices are enjoined to ceremonial silence (for the breaking of which they could be soundly thrashed with cassowary quills). The exhibitionism and masculine reversal, telltale symptoms of ritual liminality (Turner 1967), finally end with a tantalizing challenge of things to come.

What soon follows, mostly from the promptings of individual boys, is the initially awkward, insistent, sometimes frantic erotic horseplay inside the house, which finally leads to private homosexual intercourse outside on the darkened dance-ground area. Not all the initiates and bachelors join in this, but most of them take part. And before the conclusion of the initiation five days later, all but a handful of novices have served as fellators, not once, but twice and more.

RITUAL EXPERIENCE

Now I should like to glance briefly at the subjectivity of ritual, focusing on selected aspects of boys' experience regarding the above ceremonial behavior oriented around the flutes. For want of space I confine myself here to the study of the initiates, not the bachelors, emphasizing the flute ceremony and subsequent homosexual activities. That focus unavoidably ignores many other important aspects of initiation, such as the creation of personal and social ties between ritual sponsor and initiate (cf. Gewertz, this volume), the development of age-mate and affinal relationships, or support for the economic division of labor and its complementary relationships between the sexes—not to mention a much wider range of ritual scenarios and multivocal symbols. The flutes, however, are the first and most central secrets revealed in this context; and that powerful "insight" (to use Read's [1952:13] term) gets attached to the male ethos and individual male identity. It is also significant that many Sambia men and boys often refer back to this particular scenario in orienting other facets of subsequent developmental experience.

Methodological Note

The following material on the initiates' subjectivity derives from longitudinal case studies that characterize individual boy's experiences in the wake of initiation.[12] Since this type of data is unusual in reports on ritual, its inclusion merits a note concerning my methodology.

Studying Sambia ritual experience always meant living in close quarters with individuals. While this holds true for most ethnographic enterprises, it was for me an absolute necessity if I was to explore the psychological dimension of ritual initiation. Training in cultural and social anthropology helped further that study, but it still afforded few techniques for understanding what the experience of symbolic behavior—and this term surely implies more than simply the outwardly apparent—meant for individuals. The verbal "style" of Sambia everyday discourse lent itself to my endeavor, since men (and boys, among themselves) commonly discuss their experiences as an ordinary mode of sociality. (This discourse is distinct from the exegesis of elders in ritual teachings or the commentaries of ritual experts in private secular settings.) Given such a rich medium, my problem was to describe what Sambia did, said, and thought; so I tried, as an outsider, interviewer, and friend, to fit in.

The ability to "fit in," as Malinowski (1922) taught, rests on one's linguistic and cultural knowledge, as well as on the imponderables of particular informants, their personal histories, social networks, likes, and dislikes. Fitting in, however, also requires empathic "trust": trust in one's own understanding of fleeting communicative acts that occur with oneself or in one's presence; trust that one's capacity to translate the meanings behind individual expressions will improve as the amount of time spent with one's informants adds up; and vital trust in one's own sense of the interpersonal relationships to others on which this trust is built. Malinowski never taught that, but he might have, for his data also belonged to this same medium of trust. Whatever the motives behind his silence, such a pedagogical reluctance is understandable, as *trust* is too simple a catchword for summarizing the various empathies that nourish one's capacity to be inside of one's own skin while also comfortably

---

[12]These longitudinal data were collected from a number of initiates (ranging in ages from nine to fourteen years), in case studies extending from three months' to fifteen months' duration but concentrated in my second year of field research. In-depth studies served as a base line from which to evaluate other superficial interviews among boys and men, including interviews of a sample of forty-two initiates which were carried out according to a structured schedule.

sharing that moment with an outsider. Those communications—words, syntax, affects, too much silence or not enough—are still data, and their behavioral concomitants also belong in our reports. This clinical ethnography, moreover, can also be applied, mutatis mutandis, to the behavior and experience of ritual, including observations of individuals' subjective perceptions of the events after the fact (cf. Geertz 1968:107−114 and 1977:481−482; see also Le Vine 1973:249 ff.). Such research is in its hungry infancy; I see at present no other recourse for the naturalistic study of individual meaning.

Subjective Aspects of Ritual

Initiation begins with and occurs through maternal separation; the effects of this separation are visible and no doubt profound. Novices often refer to that trauma, expressing feelings of loss and sadness after the separation. That subjectivity changes as they age, however, for marriage and personal autonomy rearrange social relationships and individuals' needs. Nevertheless, even old men have spontaneously remarked of their initiations, "I felt sorry to lose my mother." That sorrow and longing permeate the mood of subsequent ritual experiences in various ways, small and large. During initiation, moreover, boys may interact only with other males—fellow novices, older bachelors, and occasionally their fathers—but not with their mothers or other women. The awareness of the finality with which boys are separated and prohibited from being with their mothers must, indeed, count as a tremendous voice in an initiate's response to these other males, to ritual and, ultimately, to himself. With this idea in mind, let us return to the flute ceremony.

Less than five hours after they have been subjected to ritual beatings and nosebleedings, novices are shown the flutes. The flute players appear, and in their presence, to the accompaniment of the wailing flutes, some powerful secrets of the male cult are revealed. The setting is deeply awesome. (*Awesome* means: a great crowd waiting in silence as the mysterious sounds are first revealed; having one's mouth physically penetrated; obediently lining up for threatening review by elders; being told that secret homosexual fellatio exists; being taught how to engage in it; and, throughout it all, hearing at close range the sounds one has associated since one's earliest years with collective masculine power and pride.) The flutes were unequivocally treated as phalli. The *ritual intent* of their revelation is clear enough. Nonetheless, there is something more than mere pedagogy in the experience and related homosexual teachings. I have observed the flute ceremony during two different initiations, and while my Western experience differs greatly from that of Sambia, one thing was intuitively striking to me: men were revealing the *erotic components* of the mouth and penis—penile erection, sexual impulses, semen, homosexual activities in particular, and genital eroticism more broadly. These revelations come as boys are enjoined to become fellators, made the sharers of ritual secrets, and threatened with death lest they tell women what they have learned.

Novices' comments indicate that they perceive several different social values bound up with the expression of homosexual instruction in the flute ceremony. Let us begin with an obvious value: childhood training regarding shame about one's genitals. Here is Kambo,[13] who reveals a construct about earlier socialization: "I thought—not good that they [elders] are lying or just playing a trick. That's [the penis] not for eating. . . . When I was a child our fathers said, 'This [penis] is not for handling; if you hold it you'll become lazy.' And because of that [at first in the cult house] I felt—it's not for sucking." Childhood experience is a contributing source of shame as regards ritual fellatio: children are taught to avoid handling their own genitals. In a wider sense, moreover, Kambo's remark pertains to the alleged sexual naiveté of children and the boys' prior lack of knowledge about their fathers' homosexual activities. (This deception and ignorance surely influences boys' early gender role behavior, since boys "know" only of their fathers' visible heterosexual actions.)

Another key subjective construct concerns the nutritive value of semen. A primary source of this idea is, as we saw, men's ritual exegetical equation of semen with mother's breast milk. Novices seem to take up this idea quickly in their own subjective orientations toward fellatio. (Pandanus nuts, too, are regarded as another equivalent of semen.) This remark by Moondi is a typical example of such semen identifications in the teachings of the flute ceremony:[14] "The 'juice' of the pandanus nuts, . . . it's the same as the 'water' of a man, the same as a man's 'juice' [semen]. And I like to eat a lot of it [because] it can give me more water, . . . for the milk of women is also the same as the milk of men. It [breast milk] is for when she carries a child—it belongs to the infant who drinks it." The association between semen and the infant's

---

[13]Kambo was, at the time of these remarks, a twelve-year-old initiate who had never been out of the Sambia River Valley..

[14]Moondi was a fifteen-year-old youth whose comments were made not long before his third-stage initiation, which I observed.

breast food is also explicit in this observation by Gaimbako, a second-stage initiate: "Semen is the same kind as that [breast milk] of women . . . it's the very same kind as theirs, . . . the same as pandanus nuts too. . . . But when milk [semen] falls into my mouth [during fellatio], I think it's the milk of women."

Another experiential construct touches on revulsion and, again, shame, regarding fellatio. This is a powerful reactive attitude: I am "eating a penis" that is quite like my own. Kambo related this thought as his immediate response to the penis teaching of the flute ceremony: "I was afraid of penis [*sic*]. It's the same as mine—why should I eat it? It's the same kind, [our penes are] only one kind. We're men, not *different* [his emphasis] kinds. . . ." This supposition is fundamental and implied in many boys' understandings. The cultural frame of this attitude is decisively important, since its underlying premise (i.e., the penes are the "same kind") is a symmetrical one. Kambo is privately asserting, then, that males are of one kind, that is, "one sex," as distinct from females. This implies tacit recognition of the complementary, sexually asymmetrical character of the homosexual dyad. Remember, too, the coercive character of the setting: the men's attempt to have boys suck the flutes is laden with overt hostility, much stronger than the latent hostility expressed in the homosexual jokes made during the preceding body decoration. The boys are placed in an erotically subordinate position, a fact that is symbolically communicated in the idiom that the novices are "married" to the flutes. (Novices suck the small flute, which resembles the mature glans penis.) Men thus place boys in an invidious state of subordination which the boys may sense as being like that of a woman and wife (cf. Bateson 1958:131–132). This evokes panicky responses of both fear and shame.

Nearly all novices perform their first act of fellatio during moku initiation, and their constructs of that experience are tremendously important to our understanding of subsequent masculine development. Let me cite several responses of Moondi to this highly traumatic act: "I was wondering what they [elders] were going to do to us. And . . . I felt afraid. What will they do to us? But they inserted the bamboo in and out of the mouth; and I thought, what are they doing? Then, when they tried out our mouths, I began to understand . . . that they were talking about the penis. Oh, that little bamboo is the penis of the men. . . . My whole body was afraid, completely afraid, . . . and I was heavy, I wanted to cry.

"At that point my thoughts went back to how I used to think it was the *aatmwogwambu* [flute spirit], but then I knew that the men did it

70

[made the sounds]. And . . . I felt a little better, for before [I thought that] the aatmwogwambu would get me. But now I saw that they [the men] did it.

"They told us the penis story. . . . Then I thought a lot, very quickly. I was afraid—not good that the men 'shoot' me [penetrate my mouth] and break my neck. Ay! Why should they put that [penis] inside our mouths! It's not a good thing. They all hide it [the penis] inside their sporrans, and it's got lots of hair too.

"'You must listen well,' they said. "'You all won't grow by yourselves; if you sleep with the men you'll become a *strong* man.' They said that; I was afraid. . . . And then they told us clearly: semen is inside—and when you hold a man's penis, you must put it inside your mouth—he can give you semen. . . . It's the same as your mother's breast milk.

"'This is no lie,' the men said; 'you can't go tell the children, your sisters.' . . . And then [later] I tried it [fellatio], and I thought: Oh, they told us about *aamoonaalyi* [breast milk; Moondi means semen]—it [semen] *is* in there."

What becomes of these sentiments in later weeks and months and years? Many things could be added. For instance, despite great social pressures, some boys evince from the start a low interest, and they seldom participate in fellatio; on the other hand, some novices feverishly join in. Those are the extremes: the great majority of Sambia boys regularly engage in fellatio for years as constrained by taboo.[15] Homosexual activities are a touchy subject among males for many reasons. They begin with ceremony, it is true, but their occurrence and meaning fan out to embrace a whole secret way of life. What matters is that boys become purveyors of this hidden tradition; and we should expect them to acquire powerful feelings about bachelors, fellatio, and semen, as indeed they do. One mundane example for many: One day, while I was talking idly with Kambo, he mentioned singing to himself as he walked in the forest. I asked him what he sang about; and from this innocuous departure point, he said this: "When I think of men's name songs then I sing them: that of a bachelor who is sweet on me; a man of another line or my own line. When I sing the song of a creek in the forest I am happy about that place. . . . Or some man who sleeps with me—when he goes

---

[15]Fellatio activities are constrained by incest taboos similar to those surrounding heterosexuality. All collateral kinsmen, age mates, and ritual sponsors are prohibited as sex partners. In fact, however, male cousins sometimes illicitly violate the rule prohibiting them from engaging in fellatio.

elsewhere, I sing his song. I think of that man who gave me a lot of semen; later, I must sleep with him. I feel like this: he gave me a lot of water [semen]; . . . later, I will have a lot of water like him.''

Here we see pinpointed the male conviction of ''accumulating semen,'' which is firmly established in Kambo's thought. Even a simple activity like singing can, for Kambo at least, trigger a mood of subjective association with past fellatio experiences and prolonged homosexual contacts. Thus, Kambo's last sentence contains a wish: that he will acquire abundant manliness, like the manliness of the man of whom he sings.

The men's flutes come to embody a whole lifetime of experiences like these. It cannot be doubted that initiation sets in motion a certain ''line of development'' (Freud 1965) with discernable consequences for a boy's sense of himself and his maleness. On the other hand, though, those ritual experiences come to clothe, like a suit of armor, an earlier experiential core that has already been firmly established: what a boy felt in his prolonged, luxuriant relationship with his mother. It is my contention that the ritual cult's imposed ''design'' for creating a warrior's adult identity rests upon a psychological frame—of merging male and female fetishistic attributes associated with the flutes, whose meaning admits of both homosexual and heterosexual erotics.

This thesis points to the last context of flute-orienting behavior, the bachelors' impersonation of the female hamlet spirits. Here we confront a very thick communicative complex of institutional ceremony, semiotics, and personal motives. (For any who doubt the third factor, consider only the obvious question: Why do only certain bachelors, and not others, volunteer for this impersonation? Self-selection is but one of several related factors we must consider if we are to find an answer to this question, which I take up elsewhere.) Another anecdote must suffice to illustrate. Gaimbako recalled that the bachelors presented themselves on that night as ''wailing old women spirits.'' He noted that the men told ''stories'' about the ''milk'' of the flutes: ''This flute isn't crying out for just anything—it wants the milk [semen] of men.[16] You must all drink the milk of men. . . .'' (This comment was unsolicited; in the stream of conversing with me, talking about bachelors and fellatio, Gaimbako spontaneously associated back to the bachelors' ritual impersonation.) The significance of the flutes is clearly multivocal and multidimensional; it touches upon a wealth of subjectivity.

---

[16]Recall the men's previous allusion to the flutes as being babies crying in the cult house. Here, novices are being identified with the ''crying'' flutes that want milk.

And this significance is suspended within a paradoxical fantasy: despite being used by bachelors as phalli with which to teach fellatio, the vessels that cry out for milk are also linked with boys' mouths.[17] The flutists prevail on the novices to serve as erotic orifices; the boys should also look to the bachelors for the semen that masculinizes. Take note, however, that it is the bachelors who put this fantasy into action: some of them present themselves with naked buttocks, while others come wrapped in capes, blowing flutes, hazing the boys, all of which communicates that the bachelors possess what boys need: biologic maleness (i.e., semen) and the culturally sanctioned power to administer it erotically. Toward this goal, bachelors take the guise of cult female spirits who are erotically excited by the boys, and not by the whole person of a novice but specifically by his mouth. Why the flute-oriented behavior subsumes this precise subjectivity is the subject of my interpretation.

FETISH AND FANTASY

Because the flutes symbolically preside over the collective initiations of the Sambia male cult, it is with the meaning of their mysterious voice that we are chiefly concerned.

Their power is enigmatic. The flutes are kept "secret" from the women, but it is the open, violent threat of men which prevents women from "knowing" about the inner sanctum of their uses. The flutes also embody the mysteries of maleness and femaleness. Lastly, the flutes are paradoxical representations of orthodoxy and subversion (Leach 1972): they imply the building of maleness and masculine behavior at the expense of the maternal bond.

I choose here to examine their earliest experiential theme, of maternal loss and sorrow, rather than their later meaning of bravado and heterosexual autonomy among men. This focus entails examining the meaning of the flutes in first-stage initiation for boys. It is essential, however, to recognize that the novices' and bachelors' dispositions toward flute-oriented behavior really represent only different phases of a single dynamic process, masculinization, comprising maternal detachment, subordination, and then sexual domination, all of which leads to a

---

[17]The use of this idiom ("to cry out for") in regard to the flutes is multivalent; not only are the flutes playing, but their sound is said to represent the female spirits' cries; a common idiom (among men) for being sexually frustrated enough that the penis secretes drops of preejaculatory seminal fluid (see Pierson and d'Antonio 1974:48–49) is that the "penis is crying out for an erotic release" (i.e., for "its food").

ritually defined sense of male gender identity and competent adjustment in the masculine role. These developmental phases do not simply mirror one another; they complement and interact (cf. Allen 1967:24—27). Indeed, the symbolic efficacy of the flutes as the men's fetishistic "vehicle of communication" (Haddon 1921:72)—with their cult of peers, spirits, and their women—derives from fundamental developmental conflicts associated with the flutes but probably never resolved.

A developmental perspective must be anchored in the power context of the men's cult, the politics of which ultimately concern social reproduction. Men and women are generally antagonistic. Boys are closer to women than to men; women are polluting and, hence, so are boys (cf. Meigs 1976:401—402). Boys are detached from women only to become the relatively helpless subordinates of men, both sociopolitically and sexually. Eventually, however, the lads must become proud warriors fully in command; otherwise, how shall these little boys achieve the masculine performatory competence expected of them by women and by their peers, in warfare and in ritual? Masculinity is thus a psychosocial dialectic (Chodorow 1974), perhaps more so among the Sambia and other Highlanders than elsewhere (cf. Herdt 1981; Lidz and Lidz 1977; Young 1965). We must not forget, then, that cultural values, socialization, and the successive stages of ritual experience all produce a feedback effect on male development. Understanding the complexity of the flutes this way helps us avoid the one-dimensional "nothing but," the useless arguments that ritual symbolism is nothing more than a product of economics, or social structure, or psychodynamics—instead of a system that is constrained by all those factors, like a true "cybernetics of self" (Bateson 1972:309—337).

One of my contentions is that we have too long ignored the subjective impact of initiation on gender differentiation, which is especially unfortunate because the symbolic focus of many New Guinea ritual cults overtly concerns masculine development. Finding a place for the flutes in the male life cycle thus invites us to reexamine the first-stage rites during which they are introduced. After analyzing the behavioral context of the flutes, I will concentrate on boys' experience of the flute ceremony and bachelors' impersonations, finally leading to an interpretation of the culturally constituted fantasies surrounding the psychodynamic origins and identity functions of the flutes.

The flutes defend the secrets of ritualized masculinization, but they harbor their own mystery for women and boys. One riddle concerns how men manage to transform puny boys into virile warriors. Other questions concern the flutes' mysticism—what the sounds are, who or what animates them, and how men control the spirit being. It is not just that the flutes are a political weapon used to frighten and mystify women and children, who are supposed to fear and hide from them. The flutes are a primordial fetish: their hollow bamboo tubes, when men blow into them, are thought to be empowered by a being, a female spirit, who is, like men, hostile to women.

We have seen how the flutes' semantic attributes pinpoint yet exaggerate, merge, and redefine the vicissitudes of masculinity and femininity. The flutes are always played in pairs; they are thought to be "married." Men say they are like phalli. The longer pipe is referred to as male and as a penis; the shorter one is female and is compared to the glans penis. The flutes become the instrument for teaching about fellatio. What boys suck, in the flute ceremony, is the tip of the shorter "female glans penis bamboo," which protrudes from outside of the longer "male bamboo." The flutes are blown in rhythmic chords of two or three notes, their vibrations a synchrony among the flutists. Those orchestrated sounds—precious lamentations of human breath—broadcast the spirits' presence to excluded women and children. (In a few years, and at third-stage initiation, the boys-become-youths will learn that the flute sounds also signify the alluring, dangerous erotic moans of a woman; so life, death, and reproduction are eventually tied into the fetish.)[18] The initiates become partners to the flutes; the bachelors are their appropriate mates. Flute players act as fellateds for the flute-sucking boys, the fellators becoming a vessel for accumulating maleness, manliness. Boys have all other erotic activity prohibited, and they must scrupulously avoid females. Hence, initiates are tabooed from blowing flutes or serving as homosexual fellateds, while bachelors become their superordinates.

Novices relate three emotions impinging on flute-oriented behavior: maternal loss, fear, and shame. As a background to that subjectivity, boys know that their fathers and sponsors—gender role models—are the instigators of initiation and that ritual treatment is said to stimulate growth and thus to masculinize them.

The phenomenology of the flute ceremony begins with the cry of the flutes, a haunting, fearful sound. It is crucial to stress that a novice,

---

[18]In spite of this extensive material on the flutes, I have touched only the surface; space will not permit examination of their uses in third-stage initiation, where they become the object of teaching about heterosexual felicity and adultery. I wish to underline again, though, the various levels of meaning surrounding the flutes, since we have seen only their first pose in a wider theater-in-the-round.

like his mother (with whom he is invidiously identified), has associated the flute sounds from his earliest years with a secret power known only to his father. The sound commences whenever men hold their rituals. The music of the flutes is awesome, and whatever else children tend to feel about it, I suggest that they also fear it. Women, of course, are physically threatened by men who guard the "secret of the flutes." This fact is itself significant; Bowlby (1973:185 ff.) has noted how children as young as two years of age come to acquire the particular fears of their mothers (reinforced by siblings or others), whether or not these fears are "reality oriented." Moreover, it is plausible to assume that a boy comes to perceive the flutes as a real danger to both his mother and himself. This dangerous mystery is no doubt a source of the fearful and fascinating ambivalence of the flutes, which are finally revealed to the boys in the initiation ceremony.

The first appearance of the flute players is an omen of the hostile behavior that follows. The flute-sucking "test" is begun in silence; like the lewd joking during the preceding body decoration, it involves aggressive, intimidating behavior. The flute sucking, a goal-directed action, tacitly communicates the intentions of the elders: they seek to dominate novices through threats and seductive pleading. Human behavior is not usually so one-dimensional (cf. Bateson 1972:387−402), but the flute-sucking act is aimed primarily at traumatizing boys, reducing them to tears. Though a lad seems to have a choice between orally submitting to and refusing the flute, his sucking behavior reduces him to being a subordinate and, eventually, a fellator, for men clearly state that the act simulates the mechanics of fellatio and indicates a boy's willingness to fulfill his erotic role later. Conversely, a novice's refusal signals his defiance of men's authority. We saw how Kokwai responded to this: he entered the ritual scene, followed by several men, all of whom pounded the boys with flutes, making them cry. This "infantile" response was the desired outcome, I think, for the aggressiveness then ceased. There, as in secular life, boys who suck the flute are lauded and praised, whereas individuals who reject "it"—authority, status subordination, or fellatio—are scorned, and their resistance tends to induce the men to behave in a hostile manner toward them.

Reducing boys to that helpless state thus creates a certain mood for the emotionally charged teaching that follows. The dominating acts of men, I suggest, excite the boy and strike panic; and such authoritarian coercion, exacerbated through careful pleas or threats of death and castration (by authority figures), may engender an awareness that personal choice (e.g., in gender behavior) is being utterly withdrawn, perhaps forever.

Extraordinary erotic information is also transmitted. These suggestions—in the powerful context of the flute ceremony—lead to information processing of hitherto unknown possibilities: about one's father, one's mother, and oneself. There is however, no immediate recourse to action or escape, an experience that stimulates hyperemotionality (Pribram 1967). In this manner, I propose, a boys' conscious experience of the flute ceremony may be infused with primary-process (unconscious) thought.

I wish here to describe that first ritual experience as a *primordial traumatic act* in relation to an individual's altered state of consciousness associated with, and released by, flute-oriented behavior.

There are three main reasons for doing so. First, this is the initial experience in which men actually reveal the flutes boys have long known from their titillating sounds. Second, novices evince traumatic responses—for instance, fear, shame, and awe—but without having recourse to their mothers as primary protective figures. Third, men make powerful erotic demands in the form of homosexual practices (and, later, fantasies), sanctioned by death threats. This experiential bedrock, I contend, becomes the base for the accumulating panic of the experience.

Further, let us think of the flute ceremony, directly followed by the bachelors' ritual impersonations and associated homosexual encounters, as engendering—and objectifying—a *primordial mood* (cf. Geertz [1966:90] on "long-lasting moods"). This mood state (or psychological frame) is emotion laden and is comprised of both conscious intentionality and elements of primary process; for, as Bateson (1972:377–378; see also Le Vine 1973:237–239) argues, information processing in deeply moving experiences, like this one, tends to create an *isomorphism* between ritual symbolism and the inner objects of fantasy. If this pseudo trance state (Lex 1979) is a goal entailment of the ritual, then its affective dimensions are as anthropologically significant as the social facts that evoked it (Needham 1967 and Sturtevant 1968). Clearly, the basis for this mood state is culturally sanctioned trauma and what is done with that trauma—how it is socially channeled, ritually reinforced, and continues to live on in a boy's sense of himself and maleness. And to unravel that developmental complexity in the male ethos, we need to explore the constellation of cultural fantasy embedded in the primordial experience of the flutes.

The flute-oriented behavior involves several interlocking fantasies of enigmatic significance in which the novices' later subjective experience is suspended. The principal drama occurs in the cult house on the evening of the flute ceremony. The flute-playing bachelors—the impersonators—present themselves to the novices as (1) old female hamlet spirits, (2) wailing for the boys, (3) having lots of ''water'' (i.e., semen), and, men asserted, (4) if boys felt ''sorry'' for those beings, (5) they ought to ''help them out'' (i.e., relax the bachelors' penes by acting as their fellators), since, to take the native idiom, (6) the flutes (like helpless infants) are ''crying out for milk'' (i.e., semen). This last point apparently concerns how the flute—as a fetish—bonds the flutist bachelor (who blows it) with the novice (who sucks it) and, specifically, links the penetrating penis with the cavity of the mouth. If this fantasy system, with its convoluted ins and outs of flute players and flute suckers, seems as baffling to the reader as it first appeared to me, then reconsider its consequences.

The ritual behavior, first of all, imaginatively effects an identification between the impersonating bachelors and the female spirits. In the cult-house context, youths are dressing up as spirits. That masquerade is more than simply a metaphoric ''cultural performance'' (Wagner 1972: 9–10); it is *also* a psychologically exciting disguise, a kind of pseudo-transvestite identity similar to that of female impersonators.[19] Why initiation motivates the impersonation of specifically female cult spirits is not hard to understand, if we bear in mind the primordial traumatic act of maternal detachment and loss.

Here is a hypothesis: The female hamlet spirits are thinly disguised surrogates for the mothers of boys, who have been ''lost'' and left behind. The impersonating flute players thus become their substitutes.

Remember, though, that it is the bachelors who dramatize and act out the figures of ''wailing spirits.'' It is they who demand attention from the displaced boys by objectifying and then transferring back to the novices hostile images of loss and care following maternal separation. The flutes are rueful, then, because their spirits have ''lost their sons.'' This is not, however, the most of what bachelors communicate; permeating that sarcastic melody is also an expression of erotic seduction: that the impersonators have ''lots of water.'' (Do the speakers mean semen or mother's milk—or is the difference, at that moment, really important?) In other words, semen is contextually equated with breast milk as the bachelors' phallus is equated with the mother's breast. The ritual

---

[19]I am, however, still developing this idea and would not care to push to erotic analogy too far.

fantasy tries to transfer boys' attachments to their mothers into homosexual fellatio activities with bachelors.

The ethnography of the flute ritual confirms that a fantasy isomorphism is created between the flute player and maternal figure and between the flute sucker and infant figure. This intersubjective fantasy postulates some kind of primary-process association linking the child's experience of suckling at his mother's breast with the novice's act of sucking the bachelor's penis. One element of this complex appears to be that the bachelor has a mature glans penis and semen; he can engage in sexual intercourse, whereas the novice cannot.

At the bedrock of this extraordinary fantasy system, I think, is a piece of deep scripting: the ultimate complementary acts (and relationships, i.e., mother-son, husband-wife) are maternal breast-feeding (see Mead 1949:88) and fellatio intercourse. In the primordial mood associated with the flutes, one suspects the men are transferring a powerful metacommunication: ''Forget your mother and wanting to be like her; you'll soon have a penis that gives milk like we do.'' To what extent is that conviction internalized among boys?

Now we are in a better position to tease apart the mechanisms by which flute-oriented behavior radically alters the novice's maternal attachment relationships (Bowlby 1969). Culturally, the flute is ritually tendered and registered as a symbolic substitute for the boy's mother. Psychodynamically, in a context of traumatic maternal separation, Sambia ritual attempts to use the flute as a detachable phallus and a substitute for the female breast (cf. Bowlby 1973:268). The bachelors' impersonation of female hamlet spirits illustrates but one of various attempts to shift the boys' core gender identity (Stoller 1968). The flute-oriented behavior, releasing feelings of helplessness and fear, supplants the mother as the preferred attachment figure by offering the culturally valued penis and homosexual relationships as sensual substitutes for the mother's breast and for the mother as a whole person (cf. Bowlby 1973:316; Bateson 1972:238, 299). In behavioral terms, ritual utilizes psychophysiological techniques of ''brain-washing'' (Sargent 1957: 92−95), such as extreme aggressive behavior, to redirect the child's attachment away from the preferred maternal figure and compel it toward male figures.

Here is, in sum, a partial intepretation of the flutes' initial effects on masculine development. The secret of the flutes becomes an unspoken understanding between a boy and his father vis-à-vis his mother. It also becomes a bond among male peers in opposition to women. With the novices living under threat of castration and death, any heterosexual tendencies are blocked for years, and ritualized homosexuality becomes the royal road to unblocking them. A shame-provoking secret of male development is obviously that masculinization occurs under the hegemony of continual asymmetrical fellatio. Ritual secrecy—defended by the fearful flutes—prevents women from "knowing" that homosexual relationships transform their fledgling sons into handsome youths (Herdt 1981). It is the flutes that become their other "mothers" and "wives."

It is likely, however, that the redirection of maternal attachment is never quite successful. Such bonds are, after all, the foundation of character structure; and while they may be modified, the underlying feelings of loss are perhaps handled as much by denial and repression as by anything else. Moreover, homosexual bonds are transient. It is essential to underline this viewpoint, for it helps to account for men's ambivalence toward the flutes and homosexual activity in general. Indeed, it is apparent that death threats are necessary for men to accomplish their task: maternal separation and ritualized masculinization are not actions that boys would themselves initiate. If the boys do resist, though, as I think occurs, then how does ritual eventually produce its desired psychological transformation?

I propose that the primordial traumatic act and mood state of the flute ceremony establish a symbolic equation (Roheim 1942:348; Segal 1957) in the thought of boys, whereby the flute is eventually *felt to be* both a penis and a female breast. We should recall the psychodynamics of a symbolic equation: the symbolic substitute is treated as if it were an "internalized object" (e.g., maternal attachment figure) *without* a change in affect (Segal 1957:392−395). Ultimately, the experiential source of this subjective state is hypothesized as arising from the early conflictual nature of the child's tie to his caretakers. Certain elements of the underlying thoughts and wishes of the child, elements that are projected toward his attachment figures, may come to be repressed. Segal (1957:395) argues that the formation of a symbolic equation issues from the "capacity to experience loss and the wish to recreate the [maternal] object within oneself." Hence, the symbolic equation subjectively grows following maternal detachment and the need to deny loss; its fantasy system helps satisfy the need to feel secure and at one with one's mother.

The origins of a symbolic equation, Segal (1957:396−397) contends, follow from a basic "disturbance in differentiation" between a person and his or her internalized objects, a fusion of a symbol and its *designata* associated with "early unresolved conflicts." We are fortunately in a position to do more than simply speculate about why Sambia males might be prone to fuse the penis and the breast in their experience of the flutes. A basic aspect of all the boys' reports about their earliest initiation experiences concerns feelings of longing for their mothers. Moreover, in the course of later development, boys become involved in significant, sometimes sustained, homosexual liaisons with bachelors— the outcomes of which can only be, of course, transientness. These relationships take on aspects of substitute maternal attachment, even as boys tend to identify consciously (including notions of literal introjection; see Kambo's remarks above) with the masculinity of bachelors.

Here I wish to stress the process whereby a symbolic representation may be subjectively converted into a symbolic equation. Segal notes that when any symbol is used as a defense mechanism (i.e., of projective identification) against depressive anxieties, it can revert back to a motivating equation (Segal 1957:396−397). This may be what occurs in the experience of homosexual contacts. Perhaps, at first, a boy moves into fellatio practices because he will be rewarded with ritual conviction and social praise and because he fears punishment; his curiosity may overcome his shame, and he also faces a strong element of coercion; mixed in with those events is the use of fellatio as a defense against maternal loss and against, sooner or later, his negative feelings of shameful subordination, exploitation, and helplessness, all understandable reactions to his situation. In various ways, then, the homosexual relationship with a bachelor partially substitutes for the whole mother: his valued penis for her breast. (The success of that adjustment in individual development remains to be seen.) What seems clear in this interpretation is the focus of initiatory symbolism on the child's tie to his mother. What shall we make of that emphasis?

To go further requires some speculation about work that is still in progress, so the following ideas ought to be regarded as orienting research and theory, not as fact. To reiterate, my view is that cultural values and institutions interact as elements in a system that includes actual behavior and subjectivity. My work differs from that of Roheim (1942), for instance, on this very point: culture cannot be reduced to unconscious processes (and vice versa); and the inferences must be drawn from observational data, not theory. I underline this point to stress that my speculations about the mother-infant bond are not suggested as the only factors precipitating Sambia masculinity or expressed by the male cult.

Perhaps we could think of the roots of flute-oriented behavior, focused upon the fantasied equation penis = breast, as resulting from a kind of prolonged "symbiosis" (Mahler 1963) between mothers and boys in the antagonistic setting of Sambia relationships between the sexes. The ethnographic data support this idea in the way boys act: they are closely attached to and identified with their mothers; and they long especially for them, not their fathers, following ritual separation. Cultural belief and ritual action also uphold the urgent need to separate mothers and boys (not girls) and to masculinize them. Initiation arises from a pervasive conviction that biological maleness is tenuous and not a "natural" product; that mother's pollution threatens it; and that ritual and homosexual insemination are the only means by which to obtain it. My perspective is that this "symbolic complex" is a culturally constituted response to the situation of most individual Sambia males' needs to sense themselves unambiguously and to perform competently as masculine men in the ways demanded by their communities. Ritualized masculinization is a necessary means toward that adult outcome.

Bettelheim's classic 1955 study, *Symbolic Wounds*, ended with a similar viewpoint that has found increasing support over the years. Concentrating on the early maternal attachment of "pregenital fixations," of envy and identification with one's mother, Bettelheim (1955:17, 124 $n.-$ 126 $n.$) sought to challenge the perspectives of Freud, Reik, and Roheim that the manly initiators merely wanted to "castrate" their sons and "create sexual anxiety . . . to make the incest taboo secure." Emphasizing boys' identity conflicts in accepting their prescribed adult gender roles, Bettelheim (1955:264) concluded that initiation rites enabled a boy to acquire "the role he wishes to play in society or which society expects him to fulfill." Here is where anthropologists need to confront the psychosocial issues of gender differentiation (Money and Ehrhardt 1972), critical-period "learning," and sex typing (Luria 1979; Maccoby 1979) in more creative ways. Mahler (1963) believes that "separation-individuation"—the critical development phase for early gender differentiation—must be established for all infants to achieve an unambiguous sense of self and body boundaries, to feel themselves distinct from their mother. The mother can help or hinder this pre-Oedipal process; and the father's role is also crucial. Gender conflict may emerge if either the mother or the infant is reluctant to separate (thereby prolonging the symbiotic relationship). For males, unlike females, there is an added difficulty (Lidz 1976): boys must not only disidentify (Greenson 1968) with their mothers (break the symbiotic union) but also identify with available masculine figures. If this dual process is blocked, males are at risk that any of several basic male gender disorders can result. (Primary male transsexualism is the most spectacular: see Stoller 1968, 1975).

The anthropological significance of these perspectives is great for core gender-identity formation in the sexually polarized societies of New Guinea. Mead (1968), Whiting et al. (1958), and Young (1965) reached some early insights. In modern clinical studies, Stoller (1973:314) has most recently noted that core identity is "fairly well formed by a year and a half or two years" and is "almost irreversible by around age five or six." Only if a boy can "grow beyond the feminine identifications that resulted from his first encounters with his mother's female body and feminine qualities" can he become a "separate masculine individual" (Stoller 1968:98). The absence—or psychological aloofness—of the father has a lasting effect on this process (see Whiting and Whiting 1975). In Melanesian communities, with their chronic warfare, exogamous patrilocal organization, antagonistic male-female relationships, postpartum sex taboos, and separate sleeping arrangements, it is not surprising to find gender concerns at the center of the social reproduction of male cult activities (Allen 1967; Strathern 1978). Sambia initiation belongs to this set of cultural traditions.

To what extent is Oedipal conflict another, developmentally later, motivational source of these culturally constituted concerns with gender formation? We need more data to know. Clearly, this factor is important; perhaps initiation is an "alternative" to the Oedipal transition (see Lidz and Lidz 1977). My own review of the New Guinea literature (Herdt 1981:303–325) indicates, however, that pre-Oedipal development seems as basic and pervasive as the status-envy and post-Oedipal conflict factors postulated by Whiting and his colleagues. The outstanding impetus of Sambia first-stage initiation concerns the generalized difficulty of the male's separation-individuation from his mother and traumatic adjustment into the highly ritualized masculine gender role.

CONCLUSION

This study has pursued a line of inquiry first envisaged by Read's early study of the nama cult but generally ignored since then. Like Read, I was led to consider the consequences of male belief and ritual for masculine solidarity, politics, and sexual antagonism. In addition, however, I have attended to the symbolic complex of the flutes as revealed through observations of behavior, subjectivity, and symbolic processes within Sambia first-stage initiation. These elements form a system; an adequate understanding would have to confront them all.

Sambia differ, of course, from Gahuku-Gama and other Highlands tribes in various respects. In both form and content, the Sambia male cult belongs to its own time and place. Its use of ritualized homosexual activities makes it special. And that tradition appears to separate the Sambia from initiatory cults elsewhere in the Eastern Highlands—at least on the surface.

In other parts of New Guinea, though, ritualized homosexuality, as implemented through initiation, has long been reported from widely scattered areas. To name only a few instances: the Trans-Fly (Williams 1936a) and Kiwai Papuans (Landtman 1927:237); the Marind-Anim tribes (Van Baal 1966:834 and passim); the Great Papuan Plateau tribes—Etoro (Kelly 1976), Kaluli (Schieffelin 1976:124–126), and Onabasulu (Kelly 1977:16); and somewhat closer to Sambia, the Baruya Anga (Godelier 1976). Schieffelin's study in this volume (chap. 4) provides an important instance of a system of ritualized homosexual practices less wedded to initiation. This listing is only a small sample; yet it cannot be doubted that these groups represent a remarkable symbolic pattern neglected in the anthropology of Melanesia. Let us again concentrate on the flutes.

The flutes are archsymbols of Sambia manhood. They are identified with the normative ritual conventions of masculine performance— what we cover by the term *ritual cult*. The flutes thus ensure a measure of behavioral continuity between the past (both individual and societal) and the present contexts their sounds signify: male initiation. The complementary dimensions of the flutes' meaning therefore embrace a whole way of life, and we can agree with Glick (1972:822), who states that they "are a key to understanding culture and society" in New Guinea.

It seems apparent, moreover, that the flutes are of tremendous significance for individual identity as well. We have seen this significance in centrality emotive rituals; seen its expression crystallized in male fantasy and beliefs; identified it in subjective expressions; and inferred it from the interactions of boys and men and women. All of that we have explored. But what we do not know from the literature and cannot discover otherwise is what experiencing the flutes means precisely for particular individuals' sense of themselves at particular moments in their lives. And here anthropologists have unfortunately foregone precious historic opportunities for describing the living meanings attached to the now disappearing flutes.

We owe to Read—this time in *The High Valley* (1965: 115–117)—the most sensitive observations of the flutes still available. I will begin with that account in surveying the comparative ethnography of the flutes.

Later, back in my house with the flutes carefully laid on the floor, the men were like contestants in a game that tested their strength and concentration to the limits of their endurance. They were almost drunk with excitement, balanced on the edge of exhaustion, their nervous energy so recently strung to its highest pitch seeking to return to its normal level through incessant talking. Hunehune's [an informant] eyes were bright with feeling. His voice trembled perceptibly, like his hand, which rested lightly on a pair of flutes, while he tried to make me understand and share the wonder of the sound we had heard. . . . Hunehune turned to Bihore and remarked that his [flute] playing had so deranged him that if he had been a woman he would have come to Bihore's house. There was no mistaking the implication of his words, the attribution of sexual qualities to the *nama*. Male sexuality was a manifestation of power, the very force of life, the basis of existence; the flutes not only symbolized power . . . but also linked it to the structure of relationships that bound each man to his fellows.

With this superb sketch as a base, let us turn to other reports and adduce some general points of comparison with Sambia flute-oriented behavior.[20]

Secrecy of the Flutes

The flutes are secret. Throughout the Eastern Highlands and in other parts of New Guinea, ritual flutes embody a "tension": they are regarded as secret, but they are semipublicly played and used. One of their "secrets" concerns the powers that animate them: men rhetorically talk as if they were mystical spirits; women and children allegedly fear such. Still, many ethnographers have qualified this secrecy: "How secret are the instruments in reality?" (Gourlay 1975:101). The answer is complex. In various groups, men clearly perceive secrecy as a means of ensuring their status quo dominance over women (and children) through the contrivance of the flutes' mysticism (see Bateson 1935:169; Godelier 1976:275; Hogbin 1970:113–114; Mead 1968:15; Nilles

---

[20]For an incisive survey of the ethnomusicology and symbolism in the Melanesian literature on sound instruments, particularly bull-roarers and flutes, see Gourlay (1975). As Gourlay (1975:1–19) shows, the function and meaning of the flutes varies in different culture areas of Melanesia; in the Eastern Highlands of Gahuku-Gama and Sambia, the flutes are by far the more important instruments, though the bull-roarer is usually present too.

1950:30; Read 1952:6,14; Salisbury 1965:71; cf. also Williams 1936*b*:41, on bull-roarers). Merely excluding others gives one a mystified "superior power" (Bettelheim 1955:228) in social control, a point emphasized by Langness (1974). Another question concerns the extent of women's knowledge about the inner core of men's secret rites. Here we are on even weaker ground because no matter what part of the mystique surrounding the flutes is fiction, they are still dangerous, not a sham: their threatening guardians are armed warriors. Not surprisingly, it has been difficult to ascertain what women actually do and do not know about the flutes (cf. Gourlay 1975:102−118).

Like Langness (1974:209−210), I am convinced that some women see through at least part of the surface facade, the contrived content, of men's dogma and activities surrounding the flute. Among Sambia, however, women "understand" that certain contexts of ritual secrecy disguise other things—which they surreptitiously avoid—but my guess is that women still remain ignorant of the inner sanctum of masculine ritual. What matters, then, are the visible, disconcerting contradictions among the private, public, and secret facets of male and female inter-actions, the "charade which is not a charade" that so fascinated Read (1952).

Our analysis must be sensitive. There is a great difference between screaming secrets and whispering secrets, and we are far from under-standing the behavioral intricacies of this pervasive contrast in Melanesian cultures. In particular, we have virtually ignored the interface of mystification (Barth 1975), duplicity, and complicity regarding what men believe women and youngsters do or do not really know, though there are scattered hints in the archives (Allen 1967:37; Bateson 1958: 169; Hogbin 1970:72; Lawrence 1965:205; Nilles 1950:30, 46; Van Baal 1966:475−478; Whiting and Reed 1938:192; Williams 1936*a*: 184). (One suspects that the preponderance of male ethnographers has contributed to the situation: see, for example, the anecdotes by Camilla Wedgwood [1938:187] and Marie Reay [1959:170].) In short, there are contrasting forms of secrecy and mystery and different ways of under-standing and communicating forbidden knowledge, the point being that we should probe more carefully than before, discriminate more finely than with the gross labels *secret* and *public*.

The Spirits of the Flutes

The flutes are animated by female spirits. The literature is stimulat-ing but sketchy on this point. The flutes are, in general, identified with ancestral spirits of uncertain sex (Allen 1967:58; Glick 1972:821−822;

Gourlay 1975:75 *n.*; Nilles 1950:46; Read 1952:8; Tuzin 1980). In certain instances, the beings focused upon are fierce or carnivorous birds (Bateson 1958:162; Reay 1959:170; Salisbury 1965:60−61) or animals—for instance, crocodiles (Wirz 1959:11−17). Read (1952:10 ff.) connected the flutes to pig feasts and communal "fertility rites" invoking ancestral blessings (cf. too Newman 1964:265−266).

Aside from Sambia, however, there are several peoples who clearly treat the spirits of the flutes as female. The Keraki (Williams 1936*a*:187, 197 ff.) are closest to Sambia in this respect: initiates are led to meet an "old woman" whose name (Ause) also represents the flutes, which are said to be the "wives of the bullroarer." (Note Williams's [1936*a*:201] link between the flutes and ritualized homosexual anal sodomy.) Berndt (1965:89) says that Eastern Highlands women refer to the flutes as a "flute woman." The neighboring Siane refer to the spirits as birds, but the key figure is called the "Mother of the Birds," which initiates have revealed to them (Salisbury 1965:60−61). Read* likewise feels that the nama creatures were female.[21] And Lindenbaum (1976:56) remarkably notes that "Fore initiation involves males playing on sacred flutes (symbolic penises) which they tell women . . .are the voices of *Kabuwei*, literally 'wild women', a word that by 1970 had also come to mean a female prostitute" (cf. Lindenbaum and Glasse 1969:169). In these cultures, at least, the flutes are empowered by female beings of supernatural dimensions (see also Strathern and Strathern 1968: 197−198).

Impersonation of Spirits

Men impersonate the spirits. Here, however, we are on thin ice because the data are not fine enough to give us a clear picture of what occurs. The ceremonial impersonation of spirit beings more generally is, of course, widespread (Epstein 1969:239−242; Mead 1963; Tuzin 1980). One suspects that more is at work in cases where initiates are secretly introduced by young men impersonating those spirits (Gourlay 1975:69; Holmes 1924:121, 164; Riley 1925:194−196). Wogeo (Hogbin 1970:72 ff.), with their *nibek* monsters, and Keraki (Williams 1936*a*:158, 187), who speak of the "old women" spirits in the context

---

*Read 1979: personal communication.

[21] I am most indebted to Professor K. E. Read for his kind reading of my paper. Part of his personal communication concerning the Gahuku-Gama nama cult and its flutes should be also appropriately cited here: "The 'carnivorous bird' is simply the 'explanation' put out for 'female consumption'. Or at least if the spirit *is* thought to be bird-like, it is also 'female' *and* 'hostile' *and* 'erotic'."

of institutionalized sodomy, more closely approximate the Sambia symbolic complex.

Hostility of the Flutes

The flutes are hostile to women. This element of the flutes seems nearly universal in New Guinea (Berndt 1962:51; Hays and Hays, this volume, p. 214; Hogbin 1970:101; Newman 1965:67; Nilles 1950:30, 46; Salisbury 1965:60 ff.; Whiting 1941:90−91). Many questions arise, such as: How do men and women experience that hostility? What does that do to relationships between the sexes? And how much of a reality are men's threats in sanctioning their secrets? For instance, in reviewing this vast literature, Gourlay (1975:102−102) points out that while everywhere women could be punished by maiming or death if they were to penetrate the flutes' secret, only one case of ultimate penalty (on hearsay at that) is actually known. This does not mean that the male cults aren't serious about defending their fetishes; it rather implies that the *psychological* significance of the flutes lies in their ominous presence, which keeps the sexes separated and distant.

Flute Categorization

The flutes are polarized into "male" and "female" types. Here is another widespread symbolic principle governing the meaning of flutes. As with Sambia, we find elsewhere a polarization of the paired flutes into both "male" and "female" categories (Berndt 1962:70; Mead 1968:76; Oosterwal 1961:228), and in certain places the more precise identification of a "male" longer flute and "female" shorter flute (Glick 1964:85; Hogbin 1970:73; Whiting and Reed 1938:190; Williams 1930:185). Once again, there are hints that the flutes are elsewhere labeled "spouses," "co-wives," or "age-mates" of initiates or bull-roarers (Bamler 1911:50; Berndt 1965:89; Williams 1936*a*:186; see also Newman and Boyd, this volume, pp. 259f.

Flute Revelation

The flutes are the key "revelation" of the initiation. This point was underlined by Read (1952:13), who felt that whatever else the initiation entailed, the revelation of the flutes was its mysterious high point. The revelation dramatically bonds initiates "together with a spiritual force"

(Lindenbaum and Glasse 1969:169). That holds equally true for Sambia (cf. Newman and Boyd, this volume, p. 263).

Erotic Elements of the Flutes

The flutes are eroticized. This notion concerns my final point, and it bears especially on the Sambia cult. Although we can go only so far in analyzing the implications of the available data, this theme invites attention, since workers have long ignored the basic psychosexual significance of the flutes.

The previous elements inferred from the literature—secrecy, female spirits, ritual impersonation and hostility, sexual polarity—add weight to the viewpoint that the flutes, and their culturally constituted fantasy system, play a major role in the ritual construction of male gender identity in various New Guinea societies. (I do not doubt that bull-roarers, either alone or in conjunction with flutes, carry a homologous symbolic "load" in still other groups; see Dundes 1976; Van Baal 1963; Williams 1936*b*.) All of this seems obvious and acceptably in line with the trend of anthropological research following Read (1952). Gender roles, sexual antagonism, gender ideology, and pollution: so much of that surface discussion leases the literature. Nevertheless, in spite of that long interest, data on erotic behavior (both for females and for males)—which sex and gender are surely also about—are not to be found. Why that gap matters, as noted, is that the flutes represent more than symbols, a male cult, bamboo objects, or spirit beings: they pinpoint an erotic relationship between bachelors and initiates, the eventual outcome of which is a particular kind of erotic excitement in heterosexual relationships.

Taken together, the above points suggest that aside from being ritual symbols, the flutes—like an erotic fetish—may bear an "assignable relation" (Freud 1962:19) to men's object choices in their erotic life. It is the nature of the flutes' fetishistic qualities and the male fantasy system that most concerns us. The flutes stand for a lifetime of developmental experiences that have the effect of energizing and channeling masculine eroticism along certain lines.

The job of the flutes is to convert small, puny boys, too attached to their mothers, into virile and aggressive warriors (Hogbin 1970:101). That in itself is no small task; but added to it is a more monumental challenge: the creation of a gender identity that makes men erotically excited first by boys and then by women; and not just any sexual excitement, but a kind built around rigid, untender rules. In certain ways, still as yet to be understood, the flutes are connected with—can evoke—early experiences and fantasies I believe to begin in infancy. The culturally constituted fantasy system of the flutes disguises all this by means of its ritual form, homosexual activities, and impersonations. Those cultural disguises are critical for understanding the entire complex. Their part concerns mainly the surface, however, while the bamboo tubes by themselves are nothing: "the fetish is merely the link between the worshiper and object of worship" (Haddon 1921:70). What then, is the nature of that underlying object?

Freud first noted that there was a close nexus between an erotic fetish and what anthropologists call a religious fetish in which it is felt that the "gods are embodied" (1962:19). The precise character of that relationship undoubtedly varies from person to person and from one cultural context to another. Without individual studies, of course, we cannot infer to what extent the meanings accorded the flutes "passes beyond the point of being merely a necessary condition" culture requires of masculine character structure and into erotic "pathological abberations" (Freud 1962:20). This is the murky borderland revealed by Read's observations of Hunehune and Bihore (see above p. 85). (One wonders about the sensual smearing of pig's grease or blood on the flutes and on oneself [Sambia do not do this], or the stuffing of bamboos with pork fat [Read 1952:10 ff.] and the like: Is this indicative of a fetishistic element linking the religious and erotic in New Guinea male cults?) Indeed, all of the formal criteria by which Stoller (1979:8) identifies the creation of an erotic fetish can be inferred from these data on the flutes, but despite that, the flute behavior of Sambia is not perverse fetishism.

A finer distinction, between fetishism and the diffusely erotic, is provided by Stoller's (1979:100–101*n*) recent work. Sambia (unlike fetishists) are not sexually aroused by the flutes irrespective of context; the flutes do not count that much. Nonetheless, after years of powerful, sensual associations, *the flutes can become erotic*: their sounds can muster the fantasied drama that women and boys—curious but traumatized by the need to hide from the tempting flutes—become excited, as men had been themselves when as boys they were in the overpowered audience hiding from the flutes (cf. Newman and Boyd, this volume, p. 251). Perhaps in this way the flutes become a sign of men's achievement of mastery over women, real-life challenges, and themselves. And, through the primordial mood assisting that sign to the self, past "frustration and trauma are converted to triumph" (Stoller 1979:9).

This developmental scenario provides a new perspective for understanding the pervasive "sexual antagonism" of New Guinea societies. Langness (1967) felt that such cultural patterns were a response to the warring conditions of Highlands communities: ritual practices had to deny men's dependency on and desire for women. On a cultural level, I agree with this model that denies dependency; but on the individual level—the level of male gender identity and its preservation—I believe that we can go further. The psychological distancing mechanisms present in Sambia ritual (e.g., female avoidance, secrecy, ritualized homosexuality), as elsewhere, imply even more about male identity and character structure. In all facets of one's existence, as the flutes reveal, the differences between maleness and femaleness are fetishized, exaggerated, and blown up. This symbol structure suggests that in male erotic life, constant hostility is often needed to create *enough* of a distance, separateness, and dehumanization of women to allow there to occur the *ritually structured* sexual excitement necessary for culturally tempered heterosexuality and the "reproduction" of a society.

The flutes provide that symbolic funnel of polarity. Melanesians, however, are not the only ones to have known that, for the magical flute is, after all, a very old human symbol.

The ancient Greeks, in their own way, also "worshiped" flutes, and the myth of the creation of their instruments seems timeless. Their maker was Pan (see Bulfinch 1967:35−36), the god of flocks and shepherds, who was fond of music but whom the Greeks nevertheless dreaded by association with the gloom and loneliness of his dark forests. He desired the beautiful and much-loved nymph Syrinx and one day intercepted her as she returned from the hunt. Pan attempted to beseech her, but she became afraid:

She ran away, without stopping to hear his compliments, and he pursued till she came to the bank of the river, where he overtook her, and she had only time to call for help on her friends the water nymphs. Pan threw his arms around what he supposed to be the form of the nymph, and found he embraced only a tuft of reeds! As he breathed a sigh, the air sounded through the reeds, and produced a plaintive melody. The god, charmed with the novelty and with the sweetness of the music, said, "Thus, then, at least, you shall be mine." And he took some of the reeds, and placing them together, of unequal lengths, side by side, made an instrument which he called the Syrinx, in honour of the nymph.

From this lovely tale the Greeks identified the origins of their flutes. Is it not oddly disconcerting, though, that among lonely travelers, "sudden fright without any visible cause was ascribed to Pan, and called a Panic terror'' (Bulfinch 1967:193)?[22]

Plaintive melody and Panic fear: even the ancient Greeks knew the Janus face of our flutes.

REFERENCES

ALLEN, M. R.
1967 *Male Cults and Secret Initiations in Melanesia.* Melbourne: Melbourne University Press.

BAMLER, G.
1911 Tami. In *Deutsch New Guinea*, ed. R. Neuhauss, vol. 3. Berlin: Reimer.

BARTH, F.
1975 *Ritual and Knowledge among the Baktaman of New Guinea.* New Haven: Yale University Press.

BATESON, G.
1935 Music in New Guinea. *The Eagle* 48:158–170.

1958 *Naven.* 2nd ed. Stanford: Stanford University Press. 1st ed. 1936.

1972 *Steps to an Ecology of Mind.* San Francisco: Chandler and Sharp.

BERNDT, R. M.
1962 *Excess and Restraint: Social Control among a New Guinea Mountain People.* Chicago: University of Chicago Press.

1965 The Kamano, Usurufa, Jate, and Fore. In *Gods, Ghosts, and Men in Melanesia*, ed. P. Lawrence and M. J. Meggitt, pp. 78–104. London: Oxford University Press.

BETTELHEIM, B.
1955 *Symbolic Wounds, Puberty Rites, and the Envious Male.* New York: Collier Books.

BOWLBY, J.
1969 *Attachment and Loss.* Vol. 1, *Attachment.* New York: Basic Books.

1973 *Attachment and Loss.* Vol. 2, *Separation: Anxiety and Anger.* New York: Basic Books.

BROWN, P., and G. BUCHBINDER (eds.)
1976 *Man and Woman in the New Guinea Highlands.* Washington, D.C.: American Anthropological Association.

BULFINCH, T.
1967 *Bulfinch's Mythology.* Abridged ed. New York: Dell Publishing Co.

BURTON, R. V., and J. W. M. WHITING
1961 The absent father and cross-sex identity. *Merrill-Palmer Quarterly of Behavior and Development* 7 (2):85–95.

---

[22]After completing this manuscript I discovered the works of Hiatt (1977) and von Felszeghy (1920), whose discussions of similar phenomena—Mozart's *The Magic Flute*, secret cults, and Pan—provide interesting contrasts with my arguments here.

CHODOROW, N.
1974 Family structure and feminine personality. In *Woman, Culture, and Society*, ed. M. Z. Rosaldo and L. Lamphere, pp. 43–66. Stanford: Stanford University Press.

DUNDES, A.
1976 A psychoanalytic study of the bull-roarer. *Man* 11:220–238.

EPSTEIN, A. L.
1969 *Matupit: Land, Politics, and Change among the Tolai of New Britain*. Berkeley and Los Angeles: University of California Press.

FREUD, A.
1965 *Normality and Pathology in Childhood*. New York: International Universities Press.

FREUD, S.
1962 *Three Essays on the Theory of Sexuality*. Trans. J. Strachey. New York: Basic Books. 1st ed. 1905.

GEERTZ, C.
1966 Religion as a cultural system. In *Anthropological Approaches to the Study of Religion*, ed. M. Banton, pp. 1–46. London: Tavistock.

1968 *Islam Observed*. New Haven: Yale University Press.

1977 From the native's point of view: on the nature of anthropological understanding. In *Symbolic Anthropology*, ed. J. L. Dolgin et al., pp. 480–492. New York: Columbia University Press.

GLICK, L. B.
1964 Foundations of a primitive medical system: the Gimi of the New Guinea Highlands. Ph.D. dissertation, University of Pennsylvania.

1972 Musical instruments in ritual. In *Encyclopaedia of Papua and New Guinea*, ed. P. Ryan, pp. 821–822. Melbourne: Melbourne University Press.

GODELIER, M.
1976 Le Sexe comme fondement ultime de l'ordre social et cosmique chez les Baruya de Nouvelle-Guinée. In *Sexualité et pouvoir*, ed. A. Verdiglione, pp. 268–306. Paris: Traces Payot.

GOURLAY, K. A.
1975 *Sound-Producing Instruments in a Traditional Society: A Study of Esoteric Instruments and Their Role in Male-Female Relationships*. New Guinea Research Bulletin no. 60. Port Moresby: Australian National University Press.

GREENSON, R.
1968 Dis-identifying from mother. *International Journal of Psychoanalysis* 49: 370–374.

HADDON, A. C.
1921 *Magic and Fetishism*. London: Constable and Co.

HERDT, G. H.
1977 The shaman's "calling" among the Sambia of New Guinea. In *Possession States, Mediumship, and Shamanism in Papua New Guinea*, ed. B. Juillerat, *Journal de la Société des Océanistes* 33 (56–57):153–167.

1981 *Guardians of the Flutes: Idioms of Masculinity*. New York: McGraw-Hill.

HIATT, L. R.
1977 Queen of night, mother-right, and secret male cults. In *Fantasy and Symbol*, ed. R. H. Hook, pp. 247–265. New York: Academic Press.

HOGBIN, I.
1970 *The Island of Menstruating Men: Religion in Wogeo, New Guinea.* Scranton, Pa.: Chandler Publishing Co.

HOLMES, J. H.
1924 *In Primitive New Guinea.* London: Seeley Service.

KELLY, R. C.
1976 Witchcraft and sexual relations: an exploration in the social and semantic implications of a structure of belief. In *Man and Woman in the New Guinea Highlands*, ed. P. Brown and G. Buchbinder, pp. 36—53. Washington, D.C.: American Anthropological Association.

1977 *Etoro Social Structure.* Ann Arbor: University of Michigan Press.

KOCH, K. F.
1974 Sociogenic and psychogenic models in anthropology: the functions of male initiation. *Man* 9:397—422.

LANDTMAN, G.
1927 *The Kiwai Papuans of British New Guinea.* London: Macmillan.

LANGNESS, L. L.
1967 Sexual antagonism in the New Guinea Highlands: a Bena Bena example. *Oceania* 37 (3):161—177.

1974 Ritual power and male domination in the New Guinea Highlands. *Ethos* 2 (3):189—212.

1976 Discussion. In *Man and Woman in the New Guinea Highlands*, ed. P. Brown and G. Buchbinder, pp. 76—106. Washington, D.C.: American Anthropological Association.

LAWRENCE, P.
1965 The Ngaing of the Rai coast. In *Gods, Ghosts, and Men in Melanesia*, ed. P. Lawrence and M. J. Meggitt, pp. 198—223. Melbourne: Melbourne University Press.

LAWRENCE, P., and M. J. MEGGITT (eds.)
1965 *Gods, Ghosts, and Men in Melanesia.* Melbourne: Melbourne University Press.

LEACH, E. R.
1972 Melchisedech and the emperor: icons of subversion and orthodoxy. Royal Anthropological Institute, *Proceedings*, pp. 5—14.

LEVINE, R. A.
1973 *Culture, Behavior, and Personality.* Chicago: Aldine Publishing Co.

LEX, B. W.
1979 The neurobiology of ritual trance. In *The Spectrum of Ritual*, ed. E. G. d'Aquili et al., pp. 117—151. New York: Columbia University Press.

LIDZ, R., and L. LIDZ
1977 Male menstruation: a ritual alternative to the Oedipal transition. *International Journal of Psychoanalysis* 58 (17):17—31.

LIDZ, T.
1976 *The Person.* Rev. ed. New York: Basic Books.

LINDENBAUM, S.
1976 A wife is the hand of man. In *Man and Woman in the New Guinea Highlands*,

ed. P. Brown and G. Buchbinder, pp. 54–62. Washington, D.C.: American Anthropological Association.

LINDENBAUM, S., and R. M. GLASSE
1969 The Fore age-mates. *Oceania* 39:165–173.

LURIA, Z.
1979 Psychosocial determinants of gender identity, role, and orientation. In *Human Sexuality: A Comparative and Developmental Perspective*, ed. H. A. Katchadourian, pp. 163–193. Berkeley, Los Angeles, and London: University of California Press.

MACCOBY, E. E.
1979 Gender identity and sex-role adoption. In *Human Sexuality: A Comparative and Developmental Perspective*, ed. H. A. Katchadourian, pp. 194–203. Berkeley, Los Angeles, and London: University of California Press.

MAHLER, M. S.
1963 Thoughts about development and individuation. *Psychoanalytic Study of the Child* 18: 307–324.

MALINOWSKI, B.
1922 *Argonauts of the Western Pacific*. New York: E. P. Dutton and Co.

MEAD, M.
1949 *Male and Female: A Study of the Sexes in a Changing World*. New York: William Morrow, and Co.

1968 *Sex and Temperament in Three Primitive Societies*. New York: Dell. 1st ed. 1935.

MEGGITT, M. J.
1964 Male-female relationships in the Highlands of Australian New Guinea. In *New Guinea: The Central Highlands*, ed. J. B. Watson, *American Anthropologist*, 66, pt. 2 (4):204–224.

MEIGS, A. S.
1976 Male pregnancy and the reduction of sexual opposition in a New Guinea Highlands society. *Ethnology* 15 (4):393–407.

MONEY, J., and A. EHRHARDT
1972 *Man, Woman, Boy, Girl*. Baltimore: Johns Hopkins Press.

NEEDHAM, R.
1967 Percussion and transition. *Man* 2:606–614.

NEWMAN, P. L.
1964 Religious belief and ritual in a New Guinea society. In *New Guinea: The Central Highlands*, ed. J. B. Watson, *American Anthropologist* 66, pt. 2 (4):257–272.

1965 *Knowing the Gururumba*. New York: Holt, Rinehart and Winston.

NILLES, J.
1950 The Kuman of the Chimbu region, Central Highlands, New Guinea. *Oceania* 21 (1):25–65.

OOSTERWAL, G.
1961 *People of the Tor*. Assen, The Netherlands: Royal Van Gorcum.

PIERSON, E. L., and W. V. D'ANTONIO
1974 *Female and Male: Dimensions of Human Sexuality*. Philadelphia: J. B. Lippincott Co.

POOLE, F. J. P.

1981 Transforming "natural" woman: female ritual leaders and gender ideology among Bimin-Kuskumin. In *Sexual Meanings*, ed. S. B. Ortner and H. Whitehead. New York: Cambridge University Press.

PRIBRAM, K. H.

1967 The new neurology and the biology of emotion: a structural approach. *American Psychologist* 22:830−838.

READ, K. E.

1951 The Gahuku-Gama of the Central Highlands. *South Pacific* 5 (8):154−164.

1952 Nama cult of the Central Highlands, New Guinea *Oceania* 23 (1):1−25.

1954 Cultures of the Central Highlands, New Guinea. *Southwestern Journal of Anthropology* 10 (1):1−43.

1955 Morality and the concept of the person among Gahuku-Gama. *Oceania* 25:233−282.

1965 *The High Valley*. London: George Allen and Unwin.

REAY, M.

1959 *The Kuma: Freedom and Conformity in the New Guinea Highlands*. Melbourne: Melbourne University Press.

RILEY, E. B.

1925 *Among Papuan Headhunters*. London: Seeley Service and Co.

ROHEIM, G.

1942 Transition rites. *Psychoanalytic Quarterly* 11:336−374.

SALISBURY, R. F.

1965 The Siane of the Eastern Highlands. In *Gods, Ghosts, and Men in Melanesia*, ed. P. Lawrence and M. J. Meggitt, pp. 50−77. Melbourne: Melbourne University Press.

SARGENT, W.

1957 *Battle for the Mind*. Melbourne: Heinemann.

SCHIEFFELIN, E. L.

1976 *The Sorrow of the Lonely and the Burning of the Dancers*. New York: St. Martin's Press.

SEARS, R. R.

1965 Development of gender role. In *Sex and Behavior*, ed. F. A. Beach, pp. 133−163. New York: John Wiley and Sons.

SEGAL, H.

1957 Notes on symbol formation. *International Journal of Psychoanalysis* 38:391−397.

STOLLER, R. J.

1968 *Sex and Gender*. New York: Science House.

1973 *Splitting: A Case of Female Masculinity*. New York: Quadrangle Books.

1975 *Sex and Gender*. Vol. 2, *The Transsexual Experiment*. New York: Jason Aronson.

1979 *Sexual Excitement: The Dynamics of Erotic Life*. New York: Pantheon Books.

STRATHERN, A. J.

1969 Descent and alliance in the New Guinea Highlands: some problems of comparison. Royal Anthropological Institute, *Proceedings*, pp. 37−52.

1970 Male initiation in the New Guinea Highlands societies. *Ethnology* 9(4): 373−379.

STRATHERN, M.
1978 The achievement of sex: paradoxes in Hagen gender-thinking. In *The Yearbook of Symbolic Anthropology*, ed. E. G. Schwimmer, 1:171−202. London: C. Hurst.

STRATHERN, A. J., and M. STRATHERN
1968 Marsupials and magic: a study of spell symbolism among the Mbowamb. In *Dialectic in Practical Religion*, ed. E. R. Leach, pp. 179−207. Cambridge: Cambridge University Press.

STURTEVANT, W. C.
1968 Categories, percussion, and physiology. *Man* 3:133−134.

TURNER, V. W.
1964 Symbols in Ndembu ritual. In *Closed Systems and Open Minds*, ed. M. Gluckman, pp. 20−51. Chicago: Aldine Publishing Co.

1967 *The Forest of Symbols*. Ithaca: Cornell University Press.

TUZIN, D. F.
1972 Yam symbolism in the Sepik: an interpretative account. *Southwestern Journal of Anthropology* 28 (3):230−254.

1977 Reflections of being in Arapesh water symbolism. *Ethos* 5 (2):195−223.

1980 *The Voice of the Tambaran: Truth and Illusion in Ilahita Arapesh Religion*. Berkeley, Los Angeles, and London: University of California Press.

VAN BAAL, J.
1963 The cult of the bull-roarer in Australia and southern New Guinea. *Bijdragen tot de Taal-, Land-, en Volkenkunde*, 119:201−214.

1966 *Dema*. The Hague: Martinous Nijhoff.

VON FELSZEGHY, B.
1920 Panik und Pan-Komplex. *Imago* 4:1−40.

WAGNER, R.
1972 *Habu: The Innovation of Meaning in Daribi Religion*. Chicago: University of Chicago Press.

WATSON, J. B.
1960 A New Guinea "opening man." In *In the Company of Man*, ed. J. B. Casagrande, pp. 127−173. New York: Harper and Row.

1964 Anthropology in the New Guinea Highlands. In *New Guinea: The Central Highlands*, ed. J. B. Watson, *American Anthropologist* 66, pt. 2 (4):1−19.

WEDGWOOD, C. H.
1937−38 Women in Manam. *Oceania* 7:401−428; 8:170−192.

WHITING, J. W. M.
1941 *Becoming a Kwoma*. New Haven: Yale University Press.

WHITING, J. W. M., R. KLUCKHOHN, and J. ANTHONY
1958 The function of male initiation ceremonies at puberty. In *Readings in Social Psychology*, ed. E. E. Maccoby, T. M. Newcomb, and E. L. Hartley, pp. 359−370. New York: Henry Holt and Co.

WHITING, J. W. M., and S. W. REED
1938 Kwoma culture. *Oceania* 9 (2):170−216.

WHITING, J. W. M., and B. B. WHITING
1975 Aloofness and intimacy of husbands and wives: a cross-cultural study. *Ethos* 3:183−207.

WILLIAMS, F. E.
1930 *Orokaiva Society*. Oxford: Oxford University Press.

1936*a Papuans of the Trans-Fly*. Oxford: Oxford University Press.

1936*b Bull-roarers in the Papuan Gulf*. Anthropological Report of the Territory of Papua, no. 17. Port Moresby: Government Printer.

WIRZ, P.
1959 *Kunst und Kult des Sepik-Gebietes (Neu-Guinea)*. Amsterdam: Koninklijk Instituut Voor de Tropen.

YOUNG, F. W.
1965 *Initiation Ceremonies: A Cross-Cultural Study of Status Dramatization*. Indianapolis: Bobbs-Merrill.

3 THE RITUAL FORGING OF IDENTITY:

Aspects of Person and Self in Bimin-Kuskusmin Male Initiation

Fitz John Porter Poole

The Author

Fitz John Porter Poole is Assistant Professor of Anthropology at the University of Rochester. Born in Chicago in 1941, he was educated in New York and Massachusetts and in Europe. His undergraduate studies focused on anthropology, biology, and philosophy. After field research on Afro-American cult groups in Harlem, New York, he began graduate studies in anthropology and in social psychology at Cornell University. After further graduate work in Melanesian studies with William Davenport and Roger Keesing at the Center for South Pacific Studies of the University of California, Santa Cruz,he began his major fieldwork among the Bimin-Kuskusmin of the high valleys of the West Sepik Province, Papua New Guinea. His two years of field research among the Bimin-Kuskusmin concerned aspects of male initiation, ritual symbolism, oral traditions, ritual experience, and an ethnosemantic analysis of indigenous concepts. He was able to witness or to reconstruct all of the elaborate stages of Bimin-Kuskusmin initiation. An analysis of the first stage of this ritual cycle led to a five-volume dissertation, which earned him the Ph.D. at Cornell in 1976.

Since 1974 Dr. Poole has taught at Rochester in many areas, such as religion and symbolism, structuralism, medical anthropology, psychological anthropology, and social anthropological theory. His publications include articles on the symbolism of gender, witchcraft, food taboos, ritual secrecy, couvade, cannibalism, and comparative analyses of religious phenomena, and all exhibit his deep interest in the interrelationship of cultural, psychological, and social aspects of ritual symbolism. His work is now appearing in several edited volumes and in such journals as *Ethos* and *Social Analysis*. In 1979−80, he was a visiting professor in the Department of Anthropology of the University of California, San Diego, where he completed the first draft of a monograph on *The Rites of Childhood*, which he is now preparing for publication. He is beginning a longer study of male initiation, and he plans to continue field research among the Bimin-Kuskusmin as well as to conduct a comparative study in the Mountain-Ok region of Papua New Guinea.

Boys receive a "female name." Then the umbilical cord is buried in the taro garden. A seed is planted. In the initiation cycle the seed is growing and changing. It has strong roots and a new body. The soft parts rot away. The skin glistens with boar fat. . . . The body becomes hard and strong. . . .

Initiator discussing the first phase of male initiation

I was alone in a cave. . . . It was dark. Water dripped from the roof. . . . Blood and pieces of flesh flowed away from my body into the water. I could see my bone. I was afraid. I cried out. No one came. I was alone. . . . I saw my reflection in the water. . . . It was like a skeleton. . . . It was like a baby, . . . like a young girl. . . .

Novice recounting a dream during the first phase of male initiation

INTRODUCTION

In this essay, I explore selected aspects of personhood and selfhood, as manifested in the "forest house" (*ais am*) stage of male initiation, among the Bimin-Kuskusmin of the West Sepik interior of Papua New Guinea.[1] In particular, I focus on dimensions of "natural" substance, body images, and male gender[2] as they are constructed, transformed and

[1]Fieldwork among the Bimin-Kuskusmin (1971 − 1973) was generously supported by the National Institutes of Health, the Cornell University Humanities and Social Sciences Program, and the Center for South Pacific Studies of the University of California at Santa Cruz. The New Guinea Research Unit of the Australian National University provided valuable assistance. To those Bimin-Kuskusmin men and boys who shared the legacy of male initiation is owed the primary debt of gratitude. For valuable comments on this essay, I thank T. E. Hays, G. H. Herdt, B. Lambert, L. L. Langness, S. Lindenbaum, G. Obeyesekere, K. E. Read, M. E. Spiro, A. M. Strathern, and D. F. Tuzin. Ultimate responsibility is, of course, my own.

[2]For an analysis of the cultural construction of female gender, see Poole 1981.

(re)presented in ritual performance and as they are experienced by novices. The analysis is founded on the conviction that an understanding of ritual (or any cultural) performances (including symbols)—their nature, meaning, and capacity to produce effect (and affect)—must ultimately be rooted in the subtle interactions of social, cultural, and psychological processes (cf. Obeyesekere n.d.).[3] In this regard, Munn notes that ritual "achieves its instrumental aims through its capacity to reorganize the actor's experience of the situation . . . symbolic forms provide external templates for inner experience, and operations within the external, symbolic sphere are aimed (implicitly or explicitly) at adjusting internal orientations. . . . Ritual symbols . . . regulate and affirm a . . . relationship between individual subjectivity and the objective societal order" (1973:605–606).

My approach is influenced by the promise of Geertz's (1973) notion of the essential interaction of ethos and world view and by Turner's (1967*a*, 1967*b*, 1975) view that the *signata* of dominant symbols cluster around both sensory and ideological poles. I assume, however, that ritual significance is also bound up with cognitive and affective processes in acts of "individual signification" (Tuzin 1977:196). Although I agree with Leach (1976:45) that "we engage in rituals in order to transmit messages to ourselves," I insist that these messages involve both cognitive and affective processes that are both individual and collective phenomena. Thus, in attending to rarely explored aspects of the "meaning" of male initiation in Papua New Guinea (see Allen 1967 and Strathern 1970; but also see Herdt, this volume, chap. 2, and 1981; Tuzin 1977, 1980), I shall consider aspects of *both* semanticity *and* affectivity, sociocultural significance *and* more subjective, experiential signification.

I proceed from a general description of an ais am performance[4] to an exploration of two interrelated perspectives on the effects of initiation, but consider the interrelationship to be problematic. First, I examine the *intended* efficacy of such ritual from the point of view of initiators. I suggest that the ais am is, in part, a relatively explicit cultural

---

[3]Several caveats should be noted here. I assume that any relationship among these processes is to be demonstrated; it is not given. I do not believe that ritual (or cultural) phenomena can be reduced to a matter of symbols and semiotic analyses (see Sperber 1975 and Spiro 1966, 1970) or of social structure. Where a concern with symbols is appropriate, I do not think that symbols are simply cognitive phenomena; and I doubt that cognitive and affective aspects of symbols can ultimately be segregated in any sensitive way.

[4]Although I reconstructed several ais am performances, I am concerned here with a witnessed performance in 1971. I was permitted to have access to both initiators and novices before, during, and after this performance.

design for effecting both diffuse and specific transformations of the novices in several dimensions. The latter must endure a ritual ordeal and thus cross a critical threshold in *becoming* ''men,'' in terms of cultural perceptions, social actions, and personal evaluations appropriate to that identity. Some of the deliberate nature of this design is revealed to the boys, but much is cloaked in secrecy.

Second, I consider the *perceived* and *covert* consequences of initiation from the perspective of novices. Here I shall be interested in the ways in which boys contextualize and interpret their experience of the ais am. I supplement the more informal data of participant observation and open-ended interview, therefore, with material from individual biographies, structured interviews, dream analyses, illness episodes, divinations, and certain projective test records (Machover's draw-a-person test, the standard Rorschach test, and a projective test story based on a traditional folktale genre).[5] Individually, these more esoteric protocols are heuristic devices used here in exploratory fashion, but collectively they do yield significant patterns. Such data may provide a way of confronting the profound problem that Geertz (1968:108) notes in suggesting that anthropologists are largely denied access to ritual *experience*.[6]

---

[5]Most extensive inquiry was focused on a sample of 24 boys (from 186 novices). They were selected because they lived nearby, their parents agreed to my probing, and they exhibited the expressed ideal in age (nine to twelve years), clan membership (original, not immigrant), age-group-core membership (the most promising boys), and birth order (including firstborn sons). Data were collected before, during, and after the performance. The structured interviews were sometimes blocked by prohibitions on novices' speculations about matters of ritual symbolism and ideology. Biographies presented no similar problems. Dream analysis was facilitated by traditional interest in dreams and by the custom of a father's divination of a son's dreams prior to the ais am. Diagnoses of illness and formal divination of boys were recorded. The Machover draw-a-person test was altered to conform to local drawing practices and materials. Both male and female figures were emphasized. The standard Rorschach test presented few problems of acceptance, since it was judged to be similar to traditional divination of shadows, reflections, and like phenomena. Dream reports seemed to promote a free-associational approach. The projective test story was based on a traditional oral genre that emphasizes a relation between moral virtue and defect (often coded in body imagery) on the one hand, and social consequences on the other. The boys were asked to specify the likely corporeal traits of the protagonist after standard conclusions to the tale were presented. Only the draw-a-person test was seen as too childish to take by some boys.

[6]Geertz's formulation of this problem seems to hinge on the idea of access to ''phenomenologically accurate descriptions.'' Of course, the problem, as Geertz stated it, must remain essentially unresolved; yet, through empathy and perhaps in other ways as I noted we *do* come to understand something of the experience of others. An analogy must suffice here. It is widely recognized that a *report* of a dream is a complex amalgam of whatever the ''actual'' dream may have been, selective factors of censorship and recall, and translation into discursive language. Although the report is *not* the dream experience itself, it can be usefully analyzed as a particular kind of experiential communication.

Throughout analysis, I shall be concerned with an analytic distinction between sociocultural *personhood* and experiential *selfhood*. First, personhood refers to those attributes, capacities, and signs of "proper" social persons which mark a moral career (and its jural entitlements) in a particular society. The construct is ideological. Such attributes, capacities, and signs may be imposed upon (or denied to), in whole or in part, not only particular human actors but also categories or collectivities of human actors or nonhuman entities.[7] In sum, personhood involves basic concepts of "human nature" and is fundamentally related to ideas of corporeal (and noncorporeal) capacity, process, and structure, and also to notions of gender. Throughout life—and thereafter in ancestor-hood—gender is a significant aspect of Bimin-Kuskusmin person-hood. Although many features of personhood are common to both males and females, it is adult men—especially elders who are prominent in ritual—who can attain complete personhood of a kind and degree which is distinct from the full personhood of women (with the partial exception of paramount female ritual leaders; see Poole 1981). The ideal of complete personhood is the adult man who has demonstrated an exemplary moral career; has shown masculine virtue in strength, bravery, cunning, and stoicism; has sired legitimate male *and* female descendants; has gained prestige in the ritual-political sphere; and finally at death has exhibited the qualifications for ancestorhood. The personhood of adult women is bound up more with a moral career that is largely circumscribed by marriage, parenthood, and exemplary behavior in the domestic domain. Despite their "natural" restrictions, however, and in their sphere of social life, women can potentially attain the full person-hood peculiar to their gender (but see Poole 1981). In the ais am, as will be seen, the novices are confronted with a complex image of masculin-ity, set against concepts of female nature, which forever remains central to their personhood.

Second, it is by means of these dimensions of personhood that the particular human actor experiences himself as, and demonstrates to others that he is, the person that he is supposed to be. Thus, Fortes (1973:311) suggests that "it is surely only by appropriating to himself his socially given personhood that he can exercise the qualities, the rights, the duties, and the capacities that are distinctive of it." This view of the self's *appropriation* of cultural constructs of personhood is quite com-

---

[7]Cf. Benoist et al. (1977); and Bisilliat and Laya (1973); Dieterlen (1973); Fortes (1973); and Mauss (1968, 1969). For Melanesia, see Leenhardt (1947) and Read (1955).

plex.[8] It may be suggested that concepts of personhood provide a cultural repertoire of personal descriptors available to individuals in their search for order and meaning in themselves and others (cf. Kelly 1955). As Hallowell (1955*a*, 1955*b*, 1958, 1960, 1976) notes, critical aspects of self-concepts are culturally constituted. Indeed, Bimin-Kuskusmin elders often observe that it is the *finiik* spirit of novices—the socially appropriate self—that must be molded and strengthened in the ais am to control the more idiosyncratic *khaapkhabuurien* spirit, which threatens the social encompassment of more individual impulses. For present purposes, I shall restrict selfhood to the subjective, experiential dimension of constructs of personhood (especially of body image [Fisher 1970] and gender) which are compellingly and forcefully inculcated in the ais am.

Van Gennep (1909) recognized long ago that initiation rites simultaneously effect a change of social identity *and* are concerned with individuals. The latter aspect has remained the less explored of the two, and this essay attempts such an exploration; for, in important ways, Bimin-Kuskusmin initiation effects "the *presentation of the self to the self*" (Harris 1978:146) in both public and private senses.[9] Thus, I proceed to examine the convergence of personhood and selfhood on body imagery with respect to male gender constructs and then to explore how the ritual images of such constructs are articulated, modified and experienced in the ais am rite.

The essay is organized as follows. After an ethnographic introduction to the Bimin-Kuskusmin and their male initiation cycle, key concepts of procreation and natural substance—which are of ritual significance—are presented. Then some general features of the ais am are outlined, after which the period of formal preparations for the rite is described. The seven phases of the ais am rite are then delineated: (1) the *kauun* pandanus rite; (2) the sweet potato rite; (3) the domestic sow rite; (4) the great ancestor cassowary/spiny anteater rite; (5) the wild boar rite; (6) the taro rite; and (7) the *bokhuur* pandanus rite. Following a description of the period of ritual closure, the focus shifts to the efficacy

---

[8]Detailed exploration of this issue is being developed elsewhere in monographic form.

[9]This distinction is entirely relative and admits of interpretative degrees. By *private*, I refer to aspects of an individual's experience that are related to body image, gender, affect, sense of self, concern with personal identity and integration, and understanding of one's milieu as it involves one's self. *Public* refers to individual behavior that is most clearly related to the more structured relationships and spheres of social life. The public and the private are interwoven in complex ways (cf. Jorgensen 1978).

of the ais am in the views of initiators and then in the experience of novices. Finally, the conclusion draws together the central aspects of the analysis.

THE BIMIN-KUSKUSMIN AND MALE INITIATION

About 1,000 Bimin-Kuskusmin occupy a rugged, ecologically diverse, mountainous area in the southeast Telefomin District of the West Sepik Province. Speaking a Mountain-Ok language, they discuss with pride their cultural traditions and regional importance and mark their complex male initiation cycle (*am yaoor*) as central to their ethnic identity. Networks of trade, alliance, warfare, intermarriage, and ritual relations, however, also bring them into contact with other groups of the Mountain-Ok region and beyond (see Barth 1971). They have known something of Europeans at least since the Kaiserin-Augusta-Fluss expedition (1912–1914) penetrated the Telefomin area to the west. First direct contact with Westerners was experienced by a very few individuals in 1957. With the opening of the Oksapmin Patrol Post to the north in 1961, patrols occasionally began to probe the periphery of their territory. On the eve of fieldwork (1971), nevertheless, such contact still remained quite limited. Thus, most of the population had not seen a European; some stone tools were in regular use; little Western paraphernalia beyond steel tools was in evidence; and familiarity with government and mission was slight.

Much of the daily round is spent in sexually segregated subsistence activities. Men do all fencing and initial clearing of gardens but then largely abandon sweet potato gardens as the realm of "people of women's houses" (*wanengamariin*). The latter may not enter the taro gardens of initiated men. All boys, prior to their initiation, are "people of women's houses." The primary cultigens are taro and nut pandanus, which are associated with male cultivation, and the female-associated sweet potato. Other indigenous and European food plants are tended by women in low sweet potato gardens on valley floors. There are grown reeds from which women's skirts are fashioned, and there, too, are buried tubes of menstrual blood that are used in the ritual fertilization of female crops. Various semicultivated crops are tended only by initiated men. Grown in high male gardens on mountain slopes, taro is the paramount cultigen in ritual significance and nutritional "strength," but the female sweet potato predominates in the diets of both men and

105

women. In taro gardens, phallocrypt gourds are also grown, and tubes of semen are placed there to strengthen the finiik spirit believed to inhabit the tubers. The ritual consumption of finiik-bearing taro, infused with semen, is thus said to strengthen the male aspects of the body in ways essential to manhood. Only paramount female ritual leaders, highly androgynous in nature, are associated with both taro and sweet potato gardens (see Poole 1981).

Domestic dogs and cassowary chicks are few, and they are owned and tended by initiated men. Pig herds are tiny by Highlands standards, and they are replenished by capture of feral piglets. Domestic boars are castrated so that women and children may eat them without fear of ritual contamination from semen and finiik spirit, but feral boars are the food only of initiated men and paramount female ritual leaders. There is extensive, regular gathering of wild foods in forest and stream by both women and children, and most of these flora and fauna are "female food" (*waneng yemen*). Initiated men, through hunting and trapping, sporadically provide considerable meat, only some of which is "male food" (*kunum yemen*).

The distinction between male and female foods refers largely to the capacity of a particular food to strengthen male or female aspects of the bodily substance of *both* men *and* women. The classification also has significant implications, though, in an elaborate system of food taboos, ritual foods, and *materia medica* (see Poole 1977, 1981, and n.d.). In fact, the cultural construction of gender contrasts is elaborated analogically not only with respect to persons of different or ambiguous gender in different circumstances (e.g., of illness or stress) and at various points in the life cycle, but also in regard to the Bimin-Kuskusmin social and natural world (see Poole 1981). Within male initiation contexts, however, these contrasts—focused on the transformation of personhood and selfhood, infused with value and sentiment, and drawn from analogic contrasts in the cultural world—are elaborated with great richness as they are ritually embodied in, and experienced by, the novices (see Poole 1976*b*:570–1967; see also Harris 1978:28).

Bimin-Kuskusmin social structure (see Poole 1976*b*:384–703) is conceived in an agnatic idiom with overt recognition of significant cognatic, uterine, and affinal links. Patrilines and cognatic kindreds are traced through shared "agnatic blood" in the procreative transmissions of men (for patrilines) and of men *and* women (for kindreds), respectively. But these social categories are not represented in male-initiation contexts. Patriclans, ritual moieties, and initiation age groups, however, are reckoned in terms of shared finiik spirit through patrilineal transmissions of semen. It is through the ritual coordination of clan cult houses, the complementarity of moiety *sacrae* and ritual activities, and the ritual formation of age groups that these social categories are recognized and articulated throughout the male initiation cycle.

Bimin-Kuskusmin devote extraordinary time and energy to male ritual activities,[10] but the most spectacular of such ritual is the am yaoor initiation cycle (see Poole 1976*b*). This cycle involves an ordered sequence of ten stages over a period of some ten to fifteen years. As a result of abnormal birth, severe moral or ritual indiscretions, incurable insanity, and other flaws of the person, some males are excluded from or forced to abandon the initiation cycle. Ideally, though, boys become novices when they reach *kaataarangiinok* age (nine to twelve years).[11] At the inception of each cycle in the ais am, the novices are abruptly removed from the female realm to undergo a long series of elaborate ritual transformations until—at about nineteen to twenty-four years of age—they have completed the final stage of the cycle (in the *en am*). Only fully initiated men may enter the ritual commissions and qualify for proper ancestorhood. Moreover, proper marriage and parenthood, as well as rights to divine, grow taro, hunt large game, engage in warfare, fend off witchcraft and sorcery, sacrifice to ancestors, and perform certain other activities, are all contingent on having entered the first ais am stage. By contrast, uninitiated men are held to be weak, irrational, vulnerable, and essentially female in character and bodily substance. The *only* passage to Bimin-Kuskusmin manhood is through the successive stages and ordeals of the male initiation cycle.

It is at the beginning of the ais am that a formal age group emerges as a relationship among coinitiands which will endure for a lifetime and be perpetuated in the reckoning of ancestral identity. There is a regular cycle of four named age groups, which reemerge in fixed order over time (see fig. 3.1). No more than three of these age groups are ever represented formally among the living. The new age group formed in the ais am is said to be identical to that of all ancestors—from the primordial ais am up to the present—who share in the same age-group name and position within the cycle of age groups. Both the deceased and the living

---

[10]See Poole (1981) for an analysis of women's ritual, including initiation.

[11]Many boys are, in fact, younger or older. In such cases, however, what has been wrought by "natural" maturation is thought to be less auspicious for desired ritual efficacy. Younger boys are still too immature in the male aspects of their anatomy for successful initiation, and older boys have developed the female aspects of their anatomy and personality too far. Decisions on when to launch an initiation cycle and when to initiate a particular boy are largely (but not entirely) based on other grounds (cf. Gewertz, this volume, chap. 7).

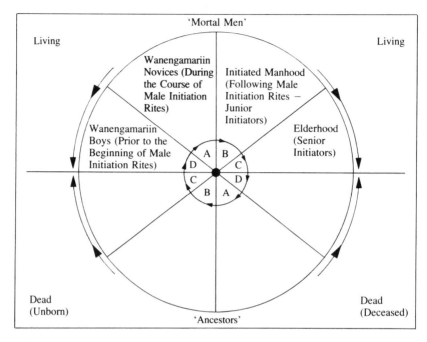

FIGURE 3.1 *The Age-Group Cycle* The cycle of age groups links "mortal men" (*kunum fiitep*) and "ancestors" (*aboyee*) through common age-group identity and partitions ritual categories of both living men and ancestors. In the present ais am performance, the novices are of the *arkhaamtakhaas* (A) age group. The junior male initiators and the male ritual elders are associated with the *abiaamtakhaas* (B) and *agorutakhaas* (C) age groups, respectively. The *gaapkhatakhaas* (D) age group, however, is not now represented among the living, but will reemerge in the next initiation cycle.

of an age group, therefore, share a significant ritual bond of identity and substance. Each age group in the cycle of four is associated with special ritual taro and taro gardens (see Poole 1977) and with particular sacrae and ais am sites. Each advanced stage of initiation is said to take place at a fixed site that does not vary from one initiation cycle to the next. The ais am of each successive initiation cycle, however, takes place at a different one of the four ais am sites—that is, at the site associated with the age group being formed at this first stage of initiation. Once the ais am rite has been performed at a particular site, no ais am will occur again on that site until the present initiation cycle and the three subsequent initiation cycles have been completed. Only then does the formal sequence of named age groups permit the "same" age group to be

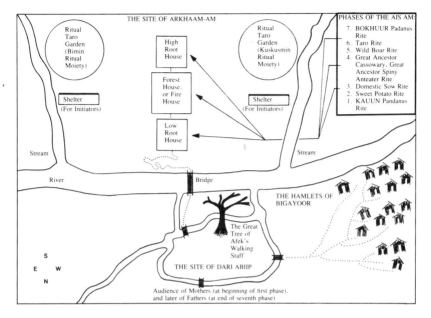

FIGURE 3.2

reconstituted. In other words, a full age-group cycle encompasses four initiation cycles.

The contemporary ais am, associated with the *arkhaamtakhaas* age group, takes place at the mountain site of Arkhaam-am (see fig. 3.2), where other men, ideally of the fourth ascending generation from the novices, also once experienced the rite and formed the last arkhaam-takhaas age group. These sacred ais am sites, detailed in mythic charters of initiation, are believed to have been created in the ancient era when the original ancestors began the first initiation cycle.

Only a few general characteristics of the complete initiation cycle can be noted here. The successive stages of the cycle exhibit a progression from a negative emphasis on the female nature of boys to an increasingly positive concern with masculinity and then to a sustained focus on male ritual control of female substance and procreative power (cf. Guideri 1975, Langness 1977, and Lindenbaum 1976). This initiation cycle is paralleled by a cycle of sacred myths, which are embedded as narratives in ritual performances and also operate as "charters" for each ritual stage. The myths reinforce the elders' view that initiation rites occur outside normal time and place and are coordinated with parallel

109

rites that occur simultaneously in the ancestral underworld. A discontinuity between ritual and ordinary experience is further emphasized through isolation, deprivation, threat, pain, shock, deception, and secrecy concerning obscure presentations of ritual sacrae cloaked in sacred language. Following the intense but naive participation in the ais am, boys' ritual involvement shifts toward a subtle fusion of experiential and canonical understanding of more esoteric matters. The nature of boys' comprehension of ritual—first experienced as unambiguous among them—becomes increasingly problematic for both advanced novices *and* initiators (see Poole 1976*a*); for when the veils of secrecy are lifted, the legacy of ancestral ritual is discovered to be, in part, the more tentative work of mortal men. Moreover, elders admit to some skepticism, guilt, and personal innovation in ritual undertakings.

Bimin-Kuskusmin elders discuss ritual understanding (both intellectual and affective) in terms of layers of meaning, as they metaphorically refer to the anatomy of a seed or nut. As one proceeds through the initiation cycle, understanding progresses from the superficial "skin meaning" toward the central "kernel meaning." Secrecy is central. Carefully controlled modes of maintaining secrecy operate through deception, deliberate opacity of messages, information control, and the metaphors that create both continuity and discontinuity when used to present successive revelations of the hidden and perhaps ultimately incomprehensible (cf. Barth 1975). Such communication evokes images and ideas of the very premises of being, personhood, and self experienced in ritual. And such revelation is a consequence not only of others' communications but also of one's participatory experience: experience cannot entirely be communicated, it must be undergone (see La Fontaine 1977). In the ais am, a myriad of verbal and nonverbal communicative acts converge to shape the novices' experience (e.g., through various ordeals) by enhancing the intensity of participation. Indeed, the intellectual opaqueness of messages only seems to reinforce the aura of mystery and power in the ais am.

There is an apparent paradox in ritual communication.[12] The elders maintain that the essentials of sacred tradition were created and formulated by primordial ancestors in terms that are difficult (if not ultimately impossible) for mortals to comprehend. Ritual performances are a means of eliciting and presenting a contemporary approximation of the ances-

[12]The elders' views presented here and later are *abstract* distillations from a massive corpus of formal exegesis, commentary, opinion, and so forth.

110

tors' definitive knowledge, which can then be understood experientially through intense participation. Although things in the world are infused with the constant ebb and flow of this ancestral knowledge, the sacred significance of the mundane is rarely obvious. Human responsibility in ritual action is like that of the bricoleur in presenting—not creating—orders of knowledge through limited and impoverished means. Initiation ritual action appears to be a way, then, of extracting and reconstructing—but always in defective form—some approximation of this ancestral knowledge in experientially compelling demonstrations, at particular moments, and for particular purposes. Nevertheless, Bimin-Kuskusmin elders express ambivalence and even cynicism about the ultimate truth of what they render ritually of such elusive (and possibly illusive) understandings of ancestral knowledge. Like the Ilahita Arapesh, they seem to recognize, at some level, that initiation ritual is perhaps little more than "what men do" (see Tuzin, this volume, chap. 8, and 1980). Since some distortion and uncertainty are inevitable, ritual innovation, skepticism, and variations in interpretation are thus acceptable, within limits, only among the elders. But in the ais am, the boys are deliberately led to assume that there is neither distortion nor ambiguity, that the elders are simply withholding fixed knowledge that could (and will) be communicated to them directly and with an assurance of truth. Being denied access to what there is of the esoterica of canonical understanding, the novices are said to experience the ais am in intense but largely subliminal ways. In other words, the experiential, rather than the intellectual, aspect of the first stage of initiation is emphasized, and little explicit commentary on what they must undergo is offered to the boys.

The ais am is the longest and most elaborate stage of initiation, although the elders insist that in many ways it is the least efficacious or significant. The elaborate symmetry of performative structure and extraordinary control over all ritual action are impressive and contrast dramatically with other initiation performances. All subsequent stages of the cycle, although far shorter and less tightly organized than this first stage, develop ais am themes in complex metaphor and symbolism. This progressive complexity poses problems for ethnographic description. Since the ais am is intended to effect fundamental changes in the identity of boys (who theretofore have been "people of women's houses"), though, even its ritual focus on body imagery and ordeals and their effects on cultural constructions of male gender are always rich and complex. To facilitate analysis, I must delineate some aspects of Bimin-Kuskusmin ideas of procreation, for it is with respect to natural substance, believed to be laid down at conception and transformed in childhood, that the critical operations of the initiation are directed.

To explicate these notions, I shall draw on an extensive corpus of exegetical commentaries. It is by now obvious that Bimin-Kuskusmin, in contrast to the neighboring Baktaman (Barth 1975:226), possess an elaborate exegetical tradition. I do not, however, restrict the term *exegesis* to meaning only the esoterica of an expert Dogon Ogotemmêli or a Ndembu Muchona, although some Bimin-Kuskusmin elders do exhibit a propensity for such elaboration. Exegesis here includes not only the complex explanations of the philosophic few but also a range of commentary from formal myth to informal gossip, speculation, and so forth. It is to *this* exegetical tradition that I turn in noting some Bimin-Kuskusmin ideas about procreation and natural substance.

A NOTE ON PROCREATION AND NATURAL SUBSTANCE

The Bimin-Kuskusmin reckoning of procreation and its morphological, psychological, and behavioral entailments is constructed in terms of the flow of natural substances *in*, *to*, and *through* persons (see Poole 1981). Agnatic blood, semen, female fertile fluids, and menstrual blood form the basic elements from which the essential nature of the person is constructed. Gender (and its potential for transformation) is an inevitable and fundamental part of this development. The natures of males and females differ in terms of not only morphological and psychological characteristics but also capacities to receive, transform, and transmit the very substances that form their identities (cf. Ellen 1977 and Meigs 1976). Furthermore, the sexes achieve distinct bodily balances among these substances.

The first key feature of Bimin-Kuskusmin models of procreation and substance is that agnatic blood is transmitted in its strongest form through males; once transmitted *through* a female, it remains viable for only three descending generations. Female substance, especially menstrual blood, weakens it. Its transmission is central to the reckoning of lineage and kindred categories. Its possession is also a characteristic of certain nonhuman entities—for instance, wild boars—that are mythically linked to humans and endowed with attributes of personhood. Weakened by contact with female substance, agnatic blood is strengthened by male ritual and by consumption of male foods, such as taro and pork. It is characterized as red in color. In the heart, agnatic blood, semen, and finiik spirit strengthen one another. In the ais am, the consumption of male foods and the application of red pigment, as well as many ritual ordeals, serve to strengthen agnatic blood, which is applied directly to novices (as is boar blood) to enhance masculine qualities.

Second, menstrual blood has a highly ambiguous nature, and it is transmitted only through uterine links. It carries the capacity for witchcraft, other kinds of mystical malevolence, and certain illnesses. It is essential for female reproduction, but it is thought to be largely under male ritual control in many contexts. Among all female substances, menstrual blood is the most antithetical to all male substances and is highly polluting to both men *and* women. In the ais am, there is much emphasis on extruding "menstrual blood" from boys' bodies—particularly from the ritually important area of the head (or skull).

Third, semen is transmitted only by males. It produces those anatomical parts of persons that are strong, hard, internal to the body, and ritually most significant. It also creates the reproductive fluids (except menstrual blood) of both sexes and the finiik spirit. It forms the forehead through which "sacred" male knowledge passes. It is manifested as fertile fluids and breast milk in females, as semen and genitalia in males, and as pus in both sexes. In the ais am, semen is ritually ingested by novices in the form of pus and of taro infused with semen (as all ritual taro is thought to be). Prior to the ais am, boys' sores are tended carefully to prevent loss of semen through pus. During the ais am, "breast milk" is ritually extruded from boys to ensure that the female manifestation of semen does not remain and continue to weaken them.

Fourth, fertile fluids are female transformations of male procreative contributions of semen. They form those anatomical parts of persons that are weak, soft, external to the body, and ritually least important. They produce the genitalia of females. In the ais am, fertile fluids per se are not extruded, since they are a manifestation of semen. Their effects, however, particularly as represented in bodily substance, are reduced through ritual enhancement of male substance, starvation, and denial of female foods.

Fifth, the forehead and the navel are male and female procreative contributions, respectively. The former permits the transmission of powerful male knowledge. The latter is associated with more mundane female knowledge. In the infancy of her offspring, the woman covers the baby's forehead with funerary mud and cleanses the navel. In the ais am, however, the forehead is shaved, cleaned, and protected with red and white pigment. In contrast, the navel is covered with funerary mud and encircled with the black pigment associated with death, illness, and menstrual blood.

Sixth, the finiik spirit, strengthened by agnatic blood, semen, and male foods and rituals, is a male procreative contribution. It represents the more social dimensions of personhood—the ordered, moral, proper aspect of personality. It is the conscience and valued intellect of the person. In the ais am, it is strengthened through all ritual enhancement of masculinity. It contrasts with the antithetical *khaapkhabuurien* spirit, which gains vigor from female substance and represents the more idiosyncratic, unmodulated personality of women.

Seventh, the male (upper body) and female (lower body) joints are distinct procreative contributions. The former permit the passage of various ritual affects that enhance masculinity. The latter, however, admit various kinds of female malevolence (e.g., black-blood illnesses, witchcraft, and other mystical attacks) that damage the male parts of the anatomy. Prior to the ais am, the fingers, wrists, elbows, shoulders, and necks of boys are covered with white pigment, which serves as protection during a period of ritual vulnerability to illness. The toes, ankles, knees, groin, and waist, however, are covered with black pigment in instances where boys are already ill.

Eighth, the body shadow/reflection is a *combined* male and female procreative contribution. It persists after death as a dangerous wraith. It is androgynous in appearance and character, as were the first ancestors. During life, it may appear in dreams, shadows, reflections, the smoke of sacrificial fires, and pools of blood or water used in divinations. It is a generalized human image, having neither distinct gender nor individual characteristics. In the ais am, some elders claim that the boys are much like body shadow/reflections during the course of the rite—being neither male nor female, nor individualized, in significant ways. The androgynous body shadow/reflection is held to be inimical to the efficacy of the rite, though, for the male-female balance of substance which it represents is thought to "block" the boys' essential transition to manhood. Thus, if a body shadow/reflection is detected in the ais am performance, special ritual procedures are used to drive it from the site. The divination of a body shadow/reflection in a boy's dream prior to the ais am may be "read" as a sign of his unreadiness to begin initiation.

These cultural elements are ritually emphasized in various combinations throughout the ais am. From an initial emphasis on the reduction of female substance through starvation, extrusion of "menstrual blood" and "breast milk," taboos on female foods, and other ritual acts,

PLATE 3.1   An uninitiated boy, wearing the topknot insignia of his status, squats in a female sweet potato garden. Upon his initiation in two months he may never again enter such female gardens, for they will have become polluting to him.

there is a transition toward a more positive emphasis on the enhancement of masculine substance. Bodily changes are also linked, however, to putative transformations of personality and behavior—all of which are merely summarized in the emergent identity of "becoming new men" which labels novices on completion of the ais am. The ritual operations of the initiation cycle in general and the ais am rite in particular are a recognition among Bimin-Kuskusmin that manhood does *not* follow naturally as a continuous development out of childhood. Instead, the personhood and selfhood of novices must be ritually disassembled and transformed in an elaborate male act of the creation of manhood. To indicate these transformations and how they are interwoven with ideas about natural substance and body imagery, I shall outline the main features of the "forest house sacred rite" (*ais am ben aiyem*).

115

THE FOREST-HOUSE STAGE OF MALE INITIATION

The ais am rite is very complex (see Poole 1976*b*:704—1425), and what is presented here must of necessity be highly selective. As an introduction, several general characteristics of the rite should be noted. First, a number of *dramatis personae* are involved, and all are identified in this context with both clan (either mythically original or historically immigrant) and ritual-moiety categories. The only exceptions are observers from other ethnic groups, who play no active role in the rite. (My own identity was clearly anomalous, but from what I could learn of the boys' attitudes toward me, I gather that I was perceived as both initiator and observer.) The boys themselves are identified as ''people of women's houses'' before, ''novices'' during, and ''becoming new men'' after the rite. The male initiators, representing each original clan, include paramount and lesser ritual leaders. It is the paramount ritual leaders of the Watiianmin and Imoranmin clans who primarily represent the Bimin and Kuskusmin ritual moieties, respectively. Other fully initiated men assist in the rite either by supplying various ritual paraphernalia or by serving as the ritual ''fathers'' and ''mothers' brothers'' of the novices. Female initiators, drawn only from the Watiianmin and Imoranmin clans, include the following: *waneng aiyem ser*—formally initiated, postmenopausal paramount ritual leaders; *waneng imok aiyem*—temporarily initiated, mature women; and *seib aiyem*—temporarily initiated, premenstruous maidens. All are responsible for supplying food, ritual net bags, pandanus roofing leaves, and hearth clay. The paramount female ritual leaders, however, are more centrally involved; and when adorned as male transvestites, they impersonate the androgynous ancestors Afek and Yomnok in the central phase of the rite.

Second, the precise social structure of the ais am is exhibited in the spatial alignments of novices and initiators, according to their ritual status, clan, and ritual-moiety identities. Here, the boys are distinguished by their identity in original or immigrant clans, by their ritual moiety, and by their inclusion in or exclusion from the core of boys deemed most promising in the age group being formed. Only during the mythic narration in the central phase of the rite is this spatial organization relaxed. The paramount male ritual leaders, representing the moieties, alternate in performing ritual tasks, narrating the sacred myth, and reciting chants that open and close each day's performance.

Third, the entire ais am, with a central focus on the mythic narration, is divided into two segments, and an elaborate performative symmetry revolves around this dual division. In the first segment, boys are negatively identified with female characteristics. They are physically controlled, harangued, and abused with respect to their female substance, food, and behavior. At night, they dwell in a "low root house," eating only sugarcane, cucumber, and raw sweet potatoes. Gradually their female substance is said to be reduced. During the central phase of the rite, they enter the forest house (ais am)—now called the "fire house" (*weng am*)—for the most critical ritual operations and the mythic narration. When they move into the second segment of the rite, they are increasingly identified with masculine substance, appearance, behavior, and other characteristics. As "becoming new men," they are less controlled and abused by initiators than they were during the first stage. At night they retreat to a "high root house," eating only sugarcane, cucumber, and cooked taro. All phases of the ais am occur during the day except the central phase, which takes place at night and parallels rites believed to occur in the ancestral underworld. Every day of the entire rite is assigned a number in the anatomically based counting system; and the correspondence between a day's number and a body part (some being sacred) is used to reckon the ritual calendar of the most critical ais am performances. The overall organization of the rite is obviously complex and precise.

Finally, the age-group site of Arkhaam-am for this performance is enveloped by a pattern of ritual dwellings and other structures (see fig. 3.2). The low root house, forest or fire house, and high root house are all constructed at the center of the ritual site in a progressive line, from the bottom to the top of a mountain slope. Near the upper perimeter are ritual-moiety taro gardens on either side. Beneath the gardens are shelters for the male initiators of each moiety. Vast supplies of materials are brought to Arkhaam-am during the several months preceding the rite. The ritual taro gardens are tended, and bamboo tubes of semen are buried in their soil. The streams that surround the ritual site are cleared of debris. These encircling streams serve as a ritual barrier; for once the novices and most initiators (except those bringing supplies) enter the site formally, they are placed in a state of ritual isolation prohibiting them from crossing the streams until the first initiation is finished. In ritual, when their agnatic blood, semen, and finiik spirit are strong, participants are said to be ritually hot and may not come into contact with cold things (such as water).

I shall now proceed to describe key features of the ais am by following the sequence of ritual phases. There are seven formal phases of the ais am, and they are bracketed by periods of formal preparation and closure. Many details must be excluded here, but this sketch is sufficient to characterize what the boys experience. The initiators intend only to convey to the boys the "skin" or "tail" meaning of sacred male knowledge, and, more importantly, also to effect in them a change of substance, gender, social personhood, and self.

Cutting the Center Time-Place

The period of formal preparations is primarily concerned with readying the ritual site and huge supplies of paraphernalia for the forthcoming rite. During this seven-day period, the initiators begin to assume special taboos as they enter ritual isolation. Materials are carefully checked, and more supplies are continually brought to the area. Ritual leaders sanctify the site, and they prepare the ritual taro gardens by sacrificing and constructing special sacrae within them. Toward the end of this period, there is a spectacular show of force and energy. Hundreds of chanting men mass and clear the area, literally with their bare hands, of all vegetation within a single day. The shelters and initiation houses are then built, but the latter are left roofless. The roofs will be added later as part of the ais am proper. One can see the massive effort required to build the initiation houses in relation to their size: this unusually large age group of boys includes 186 novices,[13] and each root house must hold all of them, while the forest house must hold not only all the boys but also almost 100 initiators!

Throughout these preparations, paramount ritual leaders carefully supervise all the frenzied activity. When all is ready on the seventh day, they bring ancestral skulls (from clan cult houses), which they have hidden in the forest, into the ritual clearing. Sacrifices are made to entice the ancestral spirits to enter the skulls. These skulls are paraded around the ritual clearing and then enshrined in the forest house. Here too are placed other important sacrae, including cassowary and spiny anteater bones associated with the early ancestors Afek and Yomnok, respectively. Finally, at dusk, the boys are led individually and in silence to the nearby hamlets of Bigayoor parish (see fig. 3.2). For the boys, the tension has been mounting: they have been advised that they are to enter

---

[13]The large number of boys is a consequence of a long delay in beginning this initiation cycle, a delay due, in part, to circumstances of severe warfare and the encroachment of European patrols. Thus, an unusually high number of boys were also beyond the ideal age range. Reconstructed evidence suggests that the normal range of an age group is about 60 to 100 boys.

PLATE 3.2   A ritual elder guards ancestral skulls that are hidden in the forest near the ritual site of Arkhaam-am. When the ais am is built, he will secretly carry them into the interior of the initiation house.

the ais am; and they have already received instruction about procreation and bodily substance. Already they have been set apart from the normal ebb and flow of community life, and their recent dreams have been divined by their fathers. For the last week, while most adult men have been conspicuously absent from hamlets and gardens, they have been forbidden to look toward the mountain site of Arkhaam-am. And they have been told little of what lies ahead.

Earlier, in the preparatory period, the Bigayoor hamlets have been readied for the coming ais am. All "people of women's houses" have been removed from the area and denied access to nearby gardens. All menstrual and birth huts have been burned. The women's houses in which the boys will temporarily remain are sanctified and adorned with secret ritual emblems that disguise the boar genitalia hidden within them. Once the novices arrive at Bigayoor, they are immediately escorted to these houses and are forbidden to leave them. They are utterly ignored by male initiators, who move silently through the hamlets, and only the female initiators issue whispered instructions to them. The boys spend

119

one sleepless night there, without fire, water, or food, before they are summoned to the kauun pandanus rite of the ais am. They engage in excited, whispered conversations about what may be expected in the morning. Their occasional outbursts are met with sharp reprimands from the female initiators.

The Kauun Pandanus Rite

The first phase of the ais am lasts for only a single day. In the predawn hours, a loud chant is suddenly heard from Arkhaam-am. As the chant builds in intensity, fires are lit throughout the ritual site; and male initiators, bearing torches, assemble along the lower perimeter of Arkhaam-am. Exploding tubes of pig fat in the fires punctuate the spectacle of light and sound that can be seen and heard for miles. This display formally opens the ais am. The chant summons the boys, and their mothers, who have spent the night in the forest near Bigayoor, to the site of Dari Abiip (see fig. 3.2), where the great ancestress Afek planted her walking staff (now a great tree) during the original ais am. This chant, like most others during the first three phases of the ais am, refers to the novices as bearers of polluted female substance and to their mothers as evil defilers of the boys. The imagery of the chant characterizes female sexual fluids and procreative aspects of the anatomy as being disgusting, dangerous, and useless essences in the novices. The tenor of the chant is taunting and humiliating, but most boys react with nervous laughter and embarrassment in the stupor of being suddenly awakened. The initiators often take almost cruel delight in this mild reaction from the boys, knowing well that it will soon be transformed into one of terror.[14]

As the chanting continues, there is a rush of activity at Bigayoor. Female initiators rouse the boys and give them cucumber and sugarcane to eat. The novices are told that they may drink no water until the rite is finished and must quench their thirst only with these substances. The boys are then stripped naked, and any regalia that they have been wearing are burned. The white pigment protecting their "male joints" is roughly removed with leaves. They are washed by female initiators, who cover the novices' heads with yellow funerary mud. Similarly, their

---

[14]I fully agree with Tuzin (this volume) that empathy, used with sensitivity, can lead to analytically useful cross-cultural labeling of behavior as, for example, "cruel," *without* doing ethnocentric violence to the data. Here, and elsewhere, such impressions are reinforced by numerous observations, as well as by delicate translations of informants' own evaluations of the tenor of particular behavior.

mothers, hidden in the forest, adorn their heads with the mud of mourning. The stripping and washing is clearly a most humiliating experience for the boys, especially since the women taunt them about their tiny genitalia. Normally, women would *never* wash boys of this age (nine to twelve years) or ridicule them in this way. Many novices try to avoid the washing of their penes or attempt to cover their genitalia. More ominously, most boys know the significance of the funerary mud from witnessing mortuary observances. If, however, they do not know, the female initiators reinforce this significance by alluding to the rumor most boys have already heard—that the men "will kill them." This female complicity in ais am ordeals will be remembered.

There is already considerable nervousness and whimpering as the novices begin to move in procession from Bigayoor to Dari Abiip with the female initiators, who reprimand such behavior. The male initiators at Arkhaam-am and the mothers in the forest also proceed to Dari Abiip. There, the initiators and boys assemble in formal ranks beneath the massive sacred tree that is believed to have been the ancestress Afek's staff. The mothers cluster on the far side of an adjacent stream, and armed guards—to prevent contact between mothers and sons—are placed on the connecting bridge. When all are assembled, the paramount male ritual leaders of the Watiaanmin and Imoranmin clans alternate in long speeches that detail how the mothers have polluted and weakened their sons over the years and why the boys must now be killed. Meanwhile, the novices, who are beginning to react strongly (crying, struggling, trying to flee) and must be restrained, are hidden behind the first row of initiators from the view of their mothers. As the speeches end, sow blood is poured over the terrified boys' heads, and the initiators intimate that the blood is human. The novices are then held up for their mothers to see. As the bloody, wailing boys come into view, the mothers stage a mock rush on the bridge, but are driven back by the guards, who fire arrows over their heads. Two young mothers become highly agitated and more determined in their assault on the bridge. One is held back by other women, but the other is hurled to the ground by the guards and thrashed with arrows. As she rises bleeding, several boys scream or try to escape and are roughly restrained by the initiators. This unexpected incident is perhaps the novices' first dramatic confrontation with the seriousness of the ais am.

As the mothers finally retreat into the forest with the characteristic sounds of the mourning wail, a long procession forms. Led by the male ritual leaders, and with the novices surrounded by female initiators in the rear, the procession turns toward Arkhaam-am. Only the paramount female ritual leaders, who remain hidden in the forest of Arkhaam-am, do not join the procession. While the boys enter the ritual site, male initiators sacrifice kauun pandanus and dapsaan marsupials (both female foods) to the ancestors. As the novices halt near the lower perimeter of the ritual site, these initiators clear a "kauun pandanus road" in the nearby forest and build a blind of boughs in the middle of the path. Then many male initiators bearing switches hide behind the blind and invite the boys to come down the path for food. As the novices approach the blind, the men leap upon them and beat them soundly with the switches. All boys show some marks from the beating, and many are bleeding and covered with welts. There is much screaming and panic, and some novices try to flee into the forest, but the men encircle them and force them back to the path with further beatings. Finally, on the kauun pandanus road, the boys are given morsels of pandanus and marsupial to eat; but they are told that they may never consume these female foods again until years later, after completing the final stage of initiation. The elders make clear that breach of this taboo will bring dire, although unspecified, consequences.

The boys are then sealed inside the low root house while the male initiators construct the roof, beginning with the "female side." Any sound from the novices is met by stern reprimand. When the roof is finished, the hidden initiators address the cowering boys from atop the roof leaves, telling them what defiled creatures they are and why they must be subjected to such discomfort and abuse. The speeches are vivid in their portrayal of the filth, putrefaction, and moral degeneracy of female substance and behavior. Many of the boys react in panic to the apparent threat that they will again be injured. The first such address was followed by abuse, and, as they will learn, this pattern is to be repeated. Surprisingly, though, here the male initiators silently descend from the roof and, after again sealing the root house, vanish into the forest. Female initiators bring sugarcane, cucumber, and raw sweet potato to the novices, who are then left alone for the night. The men remain, however, nearby in their shelters. The women will provide these same foods every evening throughout the first three phases of the ais am. The kauun pandanus rite is now at an end.

The Sweet Potato Rite

At dawn on the following day, the four-day sweet potato rite begins. Each morning and evening, male initiators speak to the boys in chants detailing their bodily defectiveness and abhorrent female nature. These chants are loud and accompanied by violent stamping. The men

122

are much concerned with creating a spectacle of anger, violence, and force, and the novices are indeed duly terrified. The effects of both female foods and female substances in the boys are emphasized, and the elders loudly observe that the novices are polluted, weak, and ugly—as is apparent by their round, fat stomachs. (With very little to eat throughout the ais am, the boys will in fact notice the increasing flatness of their stomachs, which is an admired quality of masculine physique.) The initiators are quite deliberate in their humiliation of the novices. As one notes, boys "must have 'shame' for their softness." The novices again react with anticipatory fear, since the immediate aftermath of such verbal abuse has already become somewhat unpredictable.

On the first day, a screen of boughs is built around the "women's entrance" of the root house. This screen is called the "vomit house." The boys (who remain within the root house throughout this phase) are told to thrust their heads through the boughs and to utter the female names that were bestowed on them in early childhood. To the right of the boughs, male initiators, whose foreheads are covered with red pigment, stand holding stinging nettles. To the left, female initiators, with black pigment on their foreheads, hold sweet potatoes and a special kind of ginger (both female foods).

As the boys extend their heads through the boughs, the female initiators apply black pigment to their foreheads. This pigment marks them as female, and it also blocks the forehead as the place through which male knowledge must not pass while boys' female substance is first being ritually reduced. Then the novices are forced to eat in succession five raw female foods: frog eggs, frog tadpoles, black mushrooms, frogs, and crayfish. In each instance, a boy ingests one of these foods and then eats a piece of raw sweet potato and ginger. In each instance, he is immediately thereafter rubbed harshly with nettles and then forced to vomit. A mixture of pig blood and urine is kept ready to induce vomiting if necessary. The boys cry and struggle to avoid the painful leaves, which burn into their already cut and bruised skin. (In fact, these nettles leave raised, bloody welts that are themselves quite painful.)

The trauma of vomiting and the stench of vomit cause the boys to fill the site with intermittent screams and steady sobbing. As the boys shudder in disgust and fear, the initiators clearly recognize that the novices are genuinely suffering, and many are quite ambivalent in their private views of what they are doing. Indeed, some admit that they feel bad about making young boys suffer. Others, however, seem to gain some satisfaction from the abuse, although their personal expressions of motivation are invariably couched in ritual terms.

On each of the next three days, the same procedures are followed,

123

with five new female foods being introduced on each successive day. The connotations of color, form, and other features of each female food permeate the men's speeches at each day's end. Associations of the colors red and black, which are positively and negatively valued male and female qualities, respectively, become vividly explicit. During the course of these four days, the condition of the boys, who have not been washed, becomes increasingly wretched. Their filthy bodies are covered with bleeding, scabrous sores, and many can no longer hold down the food they are offered at night. Some react in panic to any sound outside the root house, from which one hears almost constant moaning or sobbing among the boys. At the end of these four days, however, the sweet potato rite is concluded.

The Domestic Sow Rite

At dawn the following day, the domestic sow rite begins, and it lasts for two days. The numerous chants of this phase all detail the physical softness and weakness of the boys. Many analogies are drawn with respect to the unsavory characteristics of fat, stupid, domestic sows, who foul the hamlets with excrement. On the first day, male initiators begin their chants by stamping, beating on the root-house walls, and grunting like sows. There is some sardonic laughter among the initiators as the terror-stricken boys begin to shriek and cry. Female initiators bring sows into the clearing. After loudly requesting that the ancestral spirits of domestic pigs kill the novices, the male initiators shoot the sows with arrows and collect their blood in gourds. This "female blood" is smeared over the navels and breasts of the boys to weaken these areas: female knowledge must no longer pass through the navel to contaminate them. The residues of breast milk, left over from before they were weaned and now lodged in their own breasts, must also be destroyed. Flesh from the sows' genitalia is tied over the entrance of the root house. Finally, the boys are permitted to eat cold morsels of parts of the sows associated with the animals' female anatomy. As they eat, the novices are told that they may never again consume these parts of a sow. The boys are then secluded as the male initiators lecture them on their weak and failing bodies, their dying female carcasses. These speeches are punctuated by imitations of the death screams of the sows slaughtered earlier. When the female initiators bring the usual food, the boys seem slightly more relaxed, and their conversations register surprise at the lack of physical abuse. Nonetheless, they remain fearful and miserable, and many still cannot eat without vomiting.

124

The same procedures are followed on the second day. When the boys are again instructed to eat sow meat, however, there is noticeable panic, for they have also been forbidden to consume this food again; but the male initiators threaten them with further beatings and ancestral vengeance if they do not comply. Meanwhile, other initiators chant to the ancestors of domestic pigs to kill the boys in retaliation for eating their substance. Many boys seem certain that they will be beaten no matter what they do, and they begin to sob when forced to eat. Such mixed messages—exhibiting "double bind" qualities—are threaded throughout the ais am performance. They leave the novices ever fearful and always subject to the stress of their elders' unpredictability and deceptions.

When the boys are finally secluded, the sows' skulls and jaws are decorated with yellow and black funerary pigments and placed over the entrance of the root house. The novices within struggle to eat and sleep despite their considerable pain and terror about what is forthcoming. As their pathetic whimpering fades into exhausted, fitful sleep, the domestic sow rite comes to an end.

The Great Ancestor Cassowary/Spiny Anteater Rite

Within a few hours, however, the next phase begins. The great ancestor cassowary/spiny anteater rite takes place entirely at night and is presumed to parallel simultaneous ritual activities in the ancestral underworld. Since this ancestral abode is thought to be a mirror image of the world of the living, this contrast may explain why the usual analogic correspondences between male and female and high-low, right-left, and so forth in the ais am are now reversed. At the beginning of the first night, male initiators destroy the roof of the low root house, beginning with the female side, thus terrorizing the boys within. As the roof leaves are burned, chants summon the great ancestors Afek (as a cassowary) and Yomnok (as a spiny anteater) from the ancestral underworld. Other chants are directed toward the boys' still-polluted state. The men's chants produce the now expectable reaction of fear among the novices. Then fires are lit beside the female entrance of the forest house. Female initiators bring pandanus leaves, hearth clay, and firebrands to the central initiation house. After the roof is fashioned, beginning with the male side, the hearth is constructed, and a fire is made. It is at this point that the forest house becomes known as the fire house. Additional ancestral skulls, both male and female, are then brought into the fire house through the male entrance, and elaborate sacrifices begin.

The boys are led from the roofless low root house toward the female entrance of the fire house. They proceed between two moiety lines of men, who taunt and threaten them with glowing lumps of phosphorescent fungus. As the novices enter the fire house, they pass between the legs of a male initiator of their own moiety. Once inside, they are assigned a position in an elaborate spatial configuration that separates virtually all categories of participants in the rite. The remainder of the night is taken up with numerous speeches, chants, and sacrifices, but most of these are coded in a secret ritual language that is largely opaque to the boys, who must remain rigidly stationary throughout the long hours. Toward dawn they are given food and permitted to sleep. A few men remain with the fire house, tending the fire, keeping watch over the boys, and assisting those who have become quite ill from previous ritual ordeals.

On the following evening, the novices are roughly awakened by beatings with switches and are cursed as defiled, unfit creatures. After some esoteric chants, the boys resume their same spatial positions. These procedures are repeated each morning during the first segment of this phase. Then, as men of their own moiety (their "fathers") grasp them by the topknots that are the emblem of "people of women's houses," initiators of the opposite moiety (their "mothers' brothers") rub their navels with boar blood and funerary mud to "kill" this female substance. After further chants about the boys' pollution by women, the ritual mothers' brothers sever the topknots of their "sisters' sons." The novices are now no longer "people of women's houses." Incisions are made on the navel and right temple, and each cut is encircled with black pigment. The boys are told that the menstrual residues lingering near the skull must be destroyed in this way.

On the third evening, the boys' ritual fathers grasp them by the earlobes, and their ritual mothers' brothers make further incisions on the right temple and shave the novices' heads. Both head hair and topknots are placed in special net bags and deposited near the ancestral skulls. Blood from the incisions is collected and applied to the penes of boys of the opposite moiety. Although this moiety exchange of blood may be seen as an expression of a bond among age-mates, the novices are told that the blood (thought to include menstrual residues) is destroying their penes. Elders point out how the penis retracts at the touch of blood. The boys are thoroughly humiliated in this act, and they express fears that physical abuse of their penes will follow. It does not. Instead, female initiators bring special net bags decorated with the design of a red circle inside a black circle. The design is explained to the boys as another indication that their "male life"—the redness of agnatic blood—is being weakened by encompassing black menstrual residues. Although these connotations of color are here explicitly stated, they are already well known to the novices. The men place these net bags on the boys' right hips and then proceed to encircle all the incisions with black pigment. Some boys must be restrained from immediately rubbing the blood off their penes or holding the net bags away from their genitalia. Others seem too much in shock or depression to care.

On the fourth night, male initiators conduct elaborate sacrifices to summon the ancestress Afek to the fire house. Believed to be highly androgynous, but more female than male, Afek is married to her hermaphroditic sibling Yomnok, who is more male than female. Possessing a vagina in each buttock and a "penis-clitoris," Afek gave birth to the human and totemic clan ancestors. In this context, she is depicted in sacrificial chants as a giant cassowary. When the sacrifices are finished, the boys' ritual fathers grasp them by the earlobes while their mothers' brothers quickly pierce the nasal septum from the right side with a cassowary-bone dagger. The psychological and physical shock is staggering; and many boys, with blood cascading down their bodies, faint or become quite hysterical. The novices are actually told that they are now dying. Pieces of sow meat are placed in their mouths, and curative leaves are inserted in their nostrils. Finally, the nose and all other incisions are encircled with black pigment. The boys are now in a most wretched condition. Some men try to help them eat or treat their wounds. In many instances, however, the novices are understandably distrustful of this unexpected kindness, and they move away from the men with shrieks. Some initiators refuse to do the piercing, for they express concern (and, I think, guilt) over the injury and pain produced by this violent act.

On the fifth night, male initiators remove all of the boys' leaves, net bags, and bodily decorations. They then construct secret ritual bundles of sacrae near the skulls and suspend a large tree kangaroo over the fire. As some collect fat dripping from the roasting marsupial, others place curative pieces of white sago grubs in the novices' nostrils and smear the raw yolk of brush turkey eggs on their throats. Although these measures are intended to reduce female substance further, they are also seen to have a soothing effect. Next, however, hot marsupial fat and dew water are applied to the boys' inner right forearms. The novices struggle and shriek as large blisters form. Although most initiators express sadness about the pain inflicted, there are a few men who become more zealous than others in performing this act. Their motives are almost always

127

attributed to the moral or religious "necessity" of the rite; but several elders note that "some men like to cut and pierce and burn the novices." (Men who have such reputations, though, are sometimes at least discouraged from taking the lead in these ritual acts.)

The male initiators again chant, summoning the ancestress Afek to appear. Amid some commotion, two paramount female ritual leaders (unbeknownst to the boys) appear as ritual impersonators of Afek. They are dressed in both male and female ritual regalia, with exaggerated breasts, red pandanus fruit worn in the position of an erect phallus, and cassowary feathers. After these "cassowaries" (impersonators of Afek) have danced, male initiators lance the boys' blisters and collect the pus. Some of the liquid is placed on the dancers' ritual phalli. Afek is said to be "eating" this manifestation of semen. Next, the men place fat and red pigment on the chests, fat and black salt on the throats, and red pandanus juice on the jaws of the boys. The red pigment and juice are thought to strengthen their chests and skulls for receiving the critical male knowledge that is soon to be imparted. The black pigment on their throats, however, is to ensure that they will be silent during the coming sacred narrations. The novices are then told to gather informally near the fire. In fact, throughout this phase, they have been forced to move ever closer to the searing heat of the flames. They are now thoroughly cleaned with leaves and prepared to hear the sacred myth. They are told not to swallow saliva during the narration, but rather to spit on the floor (for swallowing this saliva would contaminate them). They must remain sweating and ritually "hot" (a sign of intense participation) at this critical point of the rite.

The myth is long, and it is told by paramount male ritual leaders of the Watiianmin and Imoranmin clans in alternation. It details the mythological foundations of many aspects of the ais am. The ritual transformations of bodily substances and their consequences are portrayed in detail. The basic story involves the gradual ritual ascendancy of Yomnok over his sister Afek. The narration depicts the primordial creation of the ais am by women and the ultimate acquisition of its ritual control by men. There is no complete victory, however, for it is made clear that Afek retained important ritual power of which men know very little. Both protagonists are essentially androgynous, but changes wrought ritually in the balance of their bodily substances lead to shifts in their gender, ritual status, and ritual fate. Afek and Yomnok are presented as a cassowary and a spiny anteater, both of which are said to be androgynous in nature. Through food, drink, excretion, sexual acts, experimentation, accident, and ritual operations, each loses and gains aspects of "opposite-sex" substance, while confronting the results in personality, behavior, bodily strength, and ritual power.

When the myth is finished, male initiators use leaves to wipe the sweat from the boys. As they do so, they whisper the secret male names that will be bestowed on the novices in a later phase of the ais am. The boys are told by their ritual fathers that finally they are about to "become new men." What they are not told is that some of the most severe ordeals will again be repeated. The men then make sacrifices to entice the ancestor Yomnok into the fire house. Yomnok, the spiny anteater, is much like Afek, the cassowary, in androgynous nature; but through a "penis-clitoris" that also serves as a vagina, he (the more male of the pair) gave birth to the nonhuman, totemic clan ancestors.

There is a sudden shout from the men, and Yomnok's ritual impersonators appear. They are adorned similarly to their earlier counterparts, except they wear long bamboo tubes of black salt as erect phalli and spiny anteater skins. After the impersonators have danced, the boys' ritual fathers again lance the blisters and now place the pus on the salt within the bamboo phalli. The novices are decorated as before, and each eats salt soaked with pus from the opposite moiety. New pieces of sago grubs are placed in the boys' nostrils, and cooked egg white of brush turkey eggs is smeared on their throats. Any infection in the nose is thought to be countered by the crushed grubs, and the egg white will stimulate the idealized vocal qualities of male ceremonial oratory. Then, when the boys appear relatively calm, their left forearms are suddenly seared with more hot fat. The blisters are quickly broken, and the pus is mixed with black salt. This time, the novices are forced to eat salt infused with pus from their own moiety. The very idea of eating pus, however, is most disgusting to Bimin-Kuskusmin, and many boys retch and twist away from the initiators. All are forced to swallow at least a small amount to strengthen their male substance. The male initiators then destroy the secret ritual bundles of sacrae and the tree kangaroo carcass and, with a show of deliberation, burn all the implements used in ritual surgery. Both verbally and nonverbally, the boys are led to believe that there will be no more laceration of their bodies. As they will learn, they have again been deceived.

On the sixth night, the boys (now called "becoming new men") are awakened gently with fluttering leaves. Chants refer to their growing masculinity. When all have again taken up their spatial positions, male initiators make further sacrifices to Yomnok. Suddenly, the boys' ritual fathers grasp them firmly by the earlobes, and new instruments of ritual surgery appear. Other ritual fathers pierce their nasal septa on the left side. The novices have indeed been greatly deceived, but they are told that they are now the recipients of Yomnok's strength and must be stoic. Pieces of wild boar meat are placed in their mouths, and curative leaves in their nostrils. New incisions are made on their foreheads and left temples, and all incisions are encircled with white pigment. The boys are clearly startled and terrified by this deception. Many struggle, but most are by now too weak to offer any real resistance except steady sobbing and moaning.

On the seventh evening, further incisions are made on the boys' foreheads and left temples. Their heads are covered with a ritually protective coating of white pigment and boar fat, and their penes are smeared with blood from boys of their own moiety and covered with uncured phallocrypts. These moist gourds are said to harden near the fire; to tighten around the penis; and, when finally pulled off with difficulty, to stretch the organ. Female initiators then bring the net bags, which are now decorated with a red circle inside a white circle. As an explanation of this design, the boys are told that their red agnatic blood is becoming strong but must be protected by white pigment. This pigment is used in many ritual contexts as protection when persons are especially vulnerable to stress, illness, and so on. It adorns vulnerable areas of the boys' bodies and their net bags, which are placed on their left hips. The novices are also told that they may use their secret male names, which were selected by their fathers and clan ritual leaders prior to the *ais am*. The female names of their childhood are now taboo in male ritual contexts. As a final protective measure, charcoal and marsupial fat are rubbed on the boys' navels and nipples to thwart any female influences lingering in or near their bodies, and all new incisions are encircled with red and white pigment.

On the eighth evening, the boys' ritual fathers add further protective pigments to the novices' heads, foreheads, and incisions. New incisions are made on their left temples, and blood is again smeared on their penes. But the boys are now also receiving more supportive attention from the men. There are occasional kind words and moments of gentle physical contact. The ill are tended and fed; the hysterical are occasionally comforted. Despite these gestures, however, the novices remain distrustful and fearful, and the initiators know that there is much anger beneath the surface. As one elder notes, "The novices are very angry, but they must control their anger like men." Thus, there is no expressed sympathy for those who wail and complain in the manner of "people of women's houses," and any sign of hostility is met with harsh reprimands.

On the final evening, men and boys together dismantle the fire house roof, from the female side. The roof leaves are kept. Chants now depict the boys as growing in strength and manliness, and there is no longer a hostile, taunting, humiliating thrust to these chants. Further chants bid Afek and Yomnok to return to the ancestral underworld. Novices and initiators together build the roof of the high root house, beginning with the male side, from leaves taken from the fire house. Fires are again lit by the female entrance of the fire house. The boys then pass beneath the legs of a male initiator of their own moiety and between the fires to enter a path between both moiety lines of men, who hold glowing phosphorescent fungus and cheer them. Both here and in the building of the root house roof, there are the first signs of the men's reserved respect for the boys. The latter, however, generally react impassively or with fear and avoidance. None acknowledge any sense of newfound rapport with the men, and the grisly ritual wounds on all boys are obvious to all. Some must be assisted or even carried as they proceed toward the entrance of the high root house and collapse, exhausted and in pain, within their new ritual abode. Finally, the long great ancestor cassowary/spiny anteater rite is at an end, and they are left alone for the rest of the night.

The Wild Boar Rite

Within a few hours, the wild boar rite begins; it lasts for two days. In many respects, it parallels the domestic sow rite performance, but now the emphasis is on the enhancement of masculinity. Boar blood is rubbed on the boys' foreheads and chests. Decorated boar genitalia and skulls are hung over the entrance of the high root house. The novices are given portions of hot boar meat, but they are now permitted to eat only the "female" anatomical parts of boars until they have advanced further in the initiation cycle. The boys are given larger quantities of food than before and also more time to rest. Their evening sugarcane and cucumber is now supplemented by cooked taro, although they are no longer brought raw sweet potatoes. The initiators become increasingly supportive in small ways, but most boys remain suspicious. The shouting and stamping that accompany the chants still produce panicky reactions. Otherwise, the two days of the wild boar rite pass without either verbal or physical abuse.

The Taro Rite

At dawn on the following day, the four-day taro rite begins. It is quite similar in structure to the sweet potato rite, but again the ritual focus is on the increasingly manly character of the boys. There is an

131

emphasis on male foods and substance. On the first day, the male initiators build a screen of boughs around the entrance of the low root house. This screen is called the "saliva house." To the right of the screen, male initiators, whose foreheads are covered with red pigment, hold taro and a special kind of ginger (both male foods). To the left, female initiators, with black pigment on their foreheads, hold soft cordyline leaves. As the novices step through the boughs, their ritual fathers rub red pigment on their foreheads. The boys are then told to eat in succession five cooked male foods: ground-dwelling-bird eggs, river moss or algae, red mushrooms, toads, and land crabs. In each instance, consumption of a particular male food is followed by ingestion of cooked taro and ginger. The boys are also rubbed with the soft leaves and are told to spit on the ground in recognition of the sacred power of these male foods, which they will now continue to eat. On the following three days, female initiators bring them cucumber, sugarcane, and cooked taro. The marked parallels between the wild boar and taro rites and previous phases of the ais am seem to recreate some anxiety in the boys, who still agonize over prior ordeals. Thus, some novices point at recognizable features of the present rites and scream, weep, or try to flee. Many, however, exhibit (perhaps in imitation) the stoic masks of men in pain, or sardonic grimaces.

The Bokhuur Pandanus Rite

The final phase of the ais am lasts for only a single day and exhibits some similarity to the kauun pandanus rite. A loud chant begins among the men scattered throughout Arkhaam-am and summons the "becoming new men" and their fathers to the great tree (Afek's staff) at Dari Abiip (see fig. 3.2). Fires are lit across the mountainous ritual site. Some male initiators, bearing torches, assemble along the upper perimeter of the slope. As tubes of fat explode in the fires and hundreds of men chant in unison of the bravery, strength, and manly substance of the boys, the predawn stillness is shattered by a growing intensity of light and sound. The novices are made aware that the end of the ais am is at hand. Eating quickly, they put on their new phallocrypts and decorated net bags. Men are covering their chests with white pigment and boar fat to make their skins glisten (cf. Strathern 1977). The boys' fathers, hidden in the forest near Bigayoor, are similarly adorned.

As the novices prepare to leave Arkhaam-am, they are permitted for the first time to sacrifice bokhuur pandanus and dapsaan marsupials to the ancestors. They then build a "bokhuur pandanus road" and a blind of boughs in the forest. This time the boys hold the very switches with which they were beaten in the kauun pandanus rite. As the men approach the blind, the novices fall upon them in mock attack, but finally they give them the switches. Although the boys are supposed only to feign beating the men, a few initiators show the welts of having been soundly struck. Several boys are knocked to the ground for their overt hostility, although neither they nor the initiators acknowledge that the boys' striking of men is anything more than "accidental." The novices then give the initiators morsels of pandanus and marsupial but mildly ridicule the men for accepting the latter (a female food). In turn, the men spit out the female food. They then tell the boys that they too must abandon the dapsaan marsupial but may always eat the bokhuur pandanus nuts.

The novices anoint the men with pandanus oil and seal them inside the high root house. When the boys have destroyed the root-house roof (beginning with the male side), they speak to the initiators within, telling them how strong their own bodies have become and why they had to endure the destruction of their female substance. Each novice is expected to say something, and the content of what they say gives a brief glimpse into their immediate perceptions of what has transpired in the ais am. Although these speeches are made in both seriousness and amusement, they indicate something of the boys' rudimentary understanding of ritual efficacy, and the men comment on them accordingly. When the speeches end, a long procession forms, led by the "becoming new men," with the female initiators in the rear. When the procession arrives at Dari Abiip (see fig. 3.2), the boys stand in front of all the initiators beneath the great tree (Afek's staff). The fathers assemble across the nearby river. When all are gathered in silence, the paramount male ritual leaders of the Watiianmin and Imoranmin clans alternate in long speeches explaining the fathers' procreative contribution to the boys' strong bodies, while praising the novices' endurance of the ais am ordeals. Although many are very weary, weak, and ill, the boys stand (or are held) proudly and rather self-consciously before the assembly. As the speeches end, boar blood is poured over the novices, who then break formation. As they relax on the ground, their fathers cross the bridge to congratulate them. For perhaps the first time in their lives, the boys have close physical and affectionate contact with their fathers in public. Many fathers are as misty-eyed as Bimin-Kuskusmin men are likely to become in public, and they express much pride as they caress their sons' bodies and admire their new regalia. Soon, when the fathers move back into the forest, two processions form. As the novices lead the female initiators toward the hamlets of Bigayoor, the male initiators turn back toward

Arkhaam-am. When the chants at dusk end, and the fires at Arkhaam-am are extinguished, the formal phases of the ais am (lasting over three weeks) are finally at an end.

Sealing the Center Time-Place

Following the bokhuur pandanus rite, there is a seven-day period of ritual closure. The boys are secluded in the decorated women's houses at Bigayoor, where they rest and are tended and fed by female initiators. At Arkhaam-am, the male initiators begin to disassemble the ritual paraphernalia, and gradually they are released from the taboos of ritual isolation. Small rites of desanctification of the ritual site are performed, and new fires mark such events. The ritual taro gardens are abandoned after their sacrae are destroyed. Sacrifices are made to encourage the ancestral spirits to return to the ancestral underworld. Some sacrae are removed to be enshrined elsewhere; others are destroyed. The shelters and initiation houses are burned to the ground, and the ashes are scattered in the ritual taro gardens. Soon, after this destruction has been completed, only a few ritual elders remain in the charred, smoldering clearing.

As other initiators leave the ritual isolation of Arkhaam-am for the last time, they stay at Bigayoor for a few days. It is unthinkable for them to rejoin the domain of "people of women's houses" after having been in such an intense ritual state for so long. On the sixth day of ritual closure, the boys gather up their regalia and depart for their own hamlets, where they will now live in a men's house. Although they are only "becoming new men" and must endure nine more stages of the initiation cycle, they are now "people of men's houses" and are forbidden ever to enter women's houses. When they return to their own hamlets, they are feted for about a week, and much attention is devoted to tending their ritual wounds. Their fathers will spend a good deal of time with them in the men's house, where they will begin to hear what is of concern to men; in the new taro garden, to which they have been granted rights; and in the forest, where they will learn the manly skills of trapping and bow hunting.

Once the boys have departed, there is a flurry of activity at Bigayoor. Some initiators leave for their own hamlets. Others assist in returning the Bigayoor hamlets to their normal state. The women's houses are desanctified, and the sacrae attached to them are taken away. The menstrual and birth huts are rebuilt. The entire area is searched for misplaced ritual objects. When all is ready, the initiators depart, and the "people of women's houses" are summoned back to their place of residence. At Arkhaam-am, on the final day of ritual closure, the last fires are extinguished. The paramount ritual leaders, the last to depart, carry their clan ancestral skulls secretly through the forest to their clan cult houses. For many days, they will seclude themselves in the cult houses, chanting and sacrificing to ensure the safe return of the skulls and the efficacy of the ais am for the novices of their clan. All other ritual operations of the ais am are finished. There are now "becoming new men" in the Bimin-Kuskusmin social world; another initiation cycle is in progress; and the arkhaamtakhaas age group (see fig. 3.1) is once again represented among the living.

Through the ordeals of initiation, the constellation of features that mark the personhood of "people of women's houses" has been destroyed in the boys; and new cultural elements mark the personhood of "becoming new men." Not only are the boys seen by others as possessing a new identity, but also new rights and obligations are imposed on them. They are now situated differently in their community. The tenor and the moral and jural entailments of their relations with significant social others are altered in considerable measure. The boys are now credited with many economic, political, ritual, and other social capacities that are peculiar to young men, although many boys are still too young to take many responsibilities upon themselves. They wear the ritual emblems of early manhood both on and inside of their hard, muscular, scarified bodies. The desired effect of the ais am, though, is more than these aspects of personhood; for the boys should also perceive and feel a change in themselves which is (or will soon be) manifested in behavior. To explore this dimension of the rite, I turn to the perspectives of both men and boys on the significance of what the ais am "does" to the individual.

The Force and Scope of Ais Am
Initiation: Views of Initiators

Most data on how the ais am "works," despite supplementary material from many initiated men, come from male ritual leaders, who alone have the jural and moral right to expound publicly on such matters. It is their intelligence, oratorical skill, and ritual aptitude that renders such sacred male knowledge intelligible to others, and it is their responsibility to ensure that an ais am performance is efficacious. That the ais am should have the proper beneficial effect on young boys is of genuine and profound concern to these elders. There is some consensus, however, that the desired effect is probably not achieved in novices who are much older than the ideal age range (nine to twelve years). Older boys have less malleable character (finiik and khaapkhabuurien spirit) and are prone to rebel against ritual authority "inside the heart" in ways that are inimical to ritual efficacy in its subjective dimension. Boys who are too young present a different problem. Their "natural" maturation is insufficient for the desired effects to take hold. Their substance is *too* weak and polluted, for their female qualities have recently been enhanced by breast-feeding, accompanying the mother in menstrual seclusion, and similar activities and thus cannot yet be overcome by ritual action.

Most ritual elders suggest that "people of women's houses" have no important prior knowledge of male ritual matters, for they are rigidly segregated from all liturgical concerns. What understanding occurs within the ais am is essentially experiential rather than intellectual, indexical rather than canonical (see Rappaport 1975a, 1975b, 1979). This consequence is in part attributable to a deliberate lack of explanation and to numerous intense ordeals. It should be noted, however, that Bimin-Kuskusmin distinguish only vaguely and relatively between matters of intellect and affect, cognition and emotion: these capacities are bound up together and share a locus in the heart. No terms clearly differentiate the two notions, yet contextual usage indicates some relative emphasis on "feeling" or "thinking." Each capacity, though, implicates and enhances the other in subtle ways. In ritual, all participation is said to have its own subjective efficacy, but the effects vary among different categories of participants (as well as among individuals). It is widely recognized that ritual elders command a vast corpus of esoteric knowledge, although they tend to be far less certain of its ultimate truth value than the less informed. Such knowledge, and prior experience of an entire initiation cycle (or more), however, make even their second ais am experience emotional and profound, but tempered by uncertainty, mystery, doubt, and even guilt that is thought to be unknown to the novices.

Many sacrae in the ais am are deliberately hidden from the boys. Many sacred terms and references are deliberately left opaque, and are coded in secret ritual language. Novices' inquiries beyond what is presented directly are strongly discouraged. What little is explained is deemed sufficient for the boys' masculine growth and understanding. Although the elders recognize multiple—sometimes interlinked, sometimes discontinuous—levels of understanding in initiation, they maintain that any initiation rite has a more or less self-contained efficacy that works only through participation. Ritual performances need not represent phenomena in complex detail; they can simply present them (see Harris 1976). And in the ais am, it is the experience of the isolated performance that is most emphasized.

In consequence, ritual leaders place much emphasis on the bounding, structuring, and controlling of intense experience in the ais am. They clearly recognize that this stage of the initiation cycle is unique in its duration, peculiar complexity, and brutal ordeals. All things and persons, words and acts, seem to have a prescribed place, and there is almost no opportunity for them to be out of place. Even when ritual action is temporarily halted, the boys are contained inside small structures and restrained by rigid taboos and harsh sanctions. When ritual action again begins, chants, speeches, instructions, acts, and the like, as well as prescriptions of place, time, sequence, and category of person, constantly present to boys a sense of place, identity, and self which emanates from virtually *all* significant social others in the ritual performance. Such experiential control effects a fundamental discontinuity between earlier secular and present ritual socialization. The boys, as "people of women's houses," have a great deal more freedom than young girls, since they are transient in the female domain. In the ais am, however, they are abruptly denied almost every vestige of their more carefree childhood. Moreover, such ritual control is said to produce "worry" (*sakhiik*), "fear" (*finganiinaan*), and much latent "anger" (*gaar atuur*)—most pronouncedly in the brutal ritual ordeals. These emotional reactions are thought to be potentially dangerous to both the individual and his community, for they can be symptomatic of suicidal and/or homicidal propensities. The elders seem to have some sense of how far ritual stress can proceed, and boys are watched carefully so that ritual ordeals do not exceed what they can endure. Miscalculations are always possible, of course; but coordination of precise ritual control and limited social support of individuals in the ais am is said to make stress reactions of positive value in creating masculinity—as long as the physical and psychological limits of the boys are not exceeded.

Why this emphasis on anger, fear, and worry? The anger must not be overt, for boys are beaten if they express open hostility toward initiators. Ritual authority demands respect, but *controlled* anger—in stoicism and prowess in warfare—is an esteemed quality of manhood. And it is this control of anger which is emphasized in initiation. The elders know well that the boys become tremendously angry in the ais am, but the latter are forced to suppress its overt expression in all but fleeting moments. Anxiety and fear, however, produced by real and imagined initiation ordeals, are said to make the heart beat rapidly and thus to strengthen one's male "natural" legacy of agnatic blood, semen, and finiik spirit. Worry and fear are said to "open" the heart in some obscure way that permits a heightened awareness of all influences immediately surrounding the individual—an important notion in the ais am context, where all external influences (except those of ancestral spirits) are under tight human control.

More pragmatically, however, such reactions of anxiety, fear, and anger are related to deliberately induced stress. During the ais am, boys endure severe privation, extensive degradation, extreme fatigue, constant hunger and thirst, psychological shock, enormous pain, acute illness (including nausea, diarrhea, and infection), and other trauma. They are denied the nurturant support of women, to which they have long been accustomed. Initiated men, on the other hand, have always been affectively remote and now also become brutal, deceitful, and unpredictable. The novices are largely prevented from seeking peer support, except perhaps at night in the root houses; but what I have overheard of boys' conversations at such times suggests that peers may well reinforce, rather than still, such fears and worries. The men express little, if any, sympathy. There is no escape from the ais am, and there is always the lingering threat of more suffering to come. In no instances are the boys given any warning of what is to happen. Deceptive, veiled threats often do not lead to what the boys fearfully expect. And ritual violence erupts unexpectedly. For those who must watch the agonizing piercing of the nasal septa on a hundred boys as the dagger circles ever closer, they suffer all the pain and perhaps twice the trauma of anticipation. The elders seem well aware that the ordeals produce these effects.

Male ritual leaders themselves express much concern, and even sorrow, over this inevitable stress. They claim that in the past children have died, become insane, or maimed themselves in the ais am. Although there were no specific cases of such occurrences in the performance that I described above, I have witnessed numbers of boys lapse into states of uncontrolled, pronounced physical and psychological shock, becoming unconscious or hysterical. What the boys can endure may be miscalculated. The most severe reactions aggravate the seldom-expressed guilt to which some men admit. The ritual elders still maintain, nevertheless, that such stress, as long as it is accompanied by knowledgeable control, is completely necessary to the desired efficacy of the ais am. Responsibility can always be deflected onto the ancestral ordination of stressful acts, even though there is occasional scepticism about what men actually do. Such ordeals, however—and the boys' reactions to them—are said to produce a rather special kind of awareness that seems to involve simultaneously all of the senses (i.e., of seeing, hearing, tasting, touching, and smelling) that Bimin-Kuskusmin recognize.

The idiom used to describe this diffuse awareness evokes the image of a crystal ("fire stone," or *weng tuum*), which is held to be animate and sentient. Crystals are said to reflect light or images both outwardly and inwardly. They capture their own reflections and shadows in the images of other phenomena.[15] In a sense they can reflect themselves to themselves, in the Bimin-Kuskusmin view. In some obscure way, crystals are thought to fuse all reflections and shadows from the outside into a single image on the inside, which cannot be seen or otherwise detected from the outside by mortals, except through divination. Crystals are also said to be the "eyes" of the early ancestors, who could (and can) see and understand more than living men. Because they can somehow detect and fuse impressions from everywhere, these ancestral eyes form images that are neither static nor defined only by limited dimensions of phenomena. The ancestors can grasp the "kernel meaning" of things because their eyes can absorb the totality of all phenomena. This kind of understanding takes place within the "hearts" of the early ancestors: it cannot be translated into discursive language, nor has it ever been necessary for the ancestors to do this. In consequence, the ancestors have not been able to transmit many fundamental aspects of sacred knowledge to their descendants, who lack crystalline eyes. Therefore, the legacy of initiation ritual has been given instead. Through ritual, living men must thus create the feeble lenses through which they glimpse distorted surface reflections of what the ancestors can "bring to the eye within" themselves.

There is a fundamental point to the elders' elaborate, metaphoric commentary, although real crystals—believed to be infused with the knowledge of previous ais am performances—are buried secretly beneath the fire house. The boys in the ais am are constantly made ambiguously aware of their corporeal (and noncorporeal) attributes, capacities, and sensations, but only in a rapid, bewildering, and highly stressful blur and shock of experience. The elders claim that such experience cannot be articulated sensibly during this first initiation performance, and little commentary is offered. There is thus no point to

---

[15]Reflections and shadows are focal in almost all Bimin-Kuskusmin divination, which seeks to diagnose the essential features of particular human phenomena.

PLATE 3.3   Ritual leaders hide the sacred crystals beneath the forest house. These "eyes of the ancestors" will bring understanding to the ritual participants and ensure a vital continuity with past initiation rites at which they have been present.

verbal inquiry, which is largely forbidden to the novices in any case. The ritual elders suspect that ancestral knowledge—some vague epistemological notion of more than an approximation of "truth"—is most precisely revealed in the experiential blur and intensity. Individual interpretations of this experience, rendered in ordinary language, can always be denied. There must be faith in those who have experienced the most initiation rituals—that is, the ritual elders, who, privately and among their peers, may admit to having less faith in their ritual knowledge than they lead others to believe.

The opinions of ritual leaders suggest that it is the force and scope of ritual control, as well as the more specific ritual ordeals and psychological strategies, which enhance the tremendous intensity of the experience. As one elder notes, "The boys quiver like an angry boar, like a frightened mouse. Their eyes are wide and dart around. They breathe quickly. Their hearts go fast. They tremble. Sometimes they vomit or pee." This personalized experience, in all its intensity, is central to the elders' view of what constitutes ritual efficacy. It is part of the "work" of the ais am that something must happen to boys to change their finiik spirit (that is, character) to one possessing strong, masculine qualities. Furthermore, and most explicitly, the novices must experience a shift in

140

body image and bodily sensations toward the hard, lean, muscular physique of manhood which implies the stoic ferocity of a warrior of courage and controlled anger. Both implicitly and explicitly, it seems that the critical importance of the experience of the self as transformed in the ais am is embedded in much of the elders' commentary on the rite's efficacy. In fact, they adamantly refused to discuss more intellectualized matters of ritual with me until I had undergone a special, limited version of initiation myself. Therefore, I shall now turn to some aspects of the ais am experience from the perspective of the boys who endured it.

Views of Novices

Although I spoke with some sixty boys who participated in the ais am, most data are drawn from a sample of twenty-four novices. All lived near my place of residence, were within the ideal age range (nine to twelve years), and were of the mythically original clans. Ten were of the age-group core of boys thought to be especially promising; seven were sons of ritual leaders; and six were firstborn sons (two being only sons). In all these cases, there is special social pressure placed on the boys in the expressed expectation that they will perform well (that is, with unusual stoicism) in the rite. Extensive life histories and some clinical data were taken in all cases. All interviews and projective inquiries were conducted both *before* and *after* the ais am performance. What is outlined here, however, emphasizes those features of *contrast* that follow the ritual performance and thus characterize aspects of the emergent self-experience of "becoming new men."

Two interviews conducted before the ais am (at about one month and at one week prior to it) were facilitated by the boys' familiarity with me. There is no doubt, however, that they viewed me as an adult man who had experienced some initiation and as a rather strange member of the cohort of initiators. I was thus treated with some of the deference (and later perhaps resentment) that is reserved for adult males as initiators. I was no "neutral observer" (if there ever is), and this bias should be noted.

The major difference between the two periods of preritual interviews was a marked increase in expressed (and observable) anxiety as well as exhilaration in the interviews nearest the performance. The boys clearly reveled in the public attention paid to them and in the unexpected deference of younger children. They also reacted, though, to ominous rumors of vague terrors of the ais am and to the sudden increase in whispered adult conversations that ceased at their approach. Many expressed diffuse suspiciousness and fear about some kind of bodily injury.

The general interviews indicated that eighteen boys knew that the rite had something to do with their recent instruction in matters of procreation and substance, but none expressed an opinion on the significance of the relationship. Only two provided any accurate detail of the performance itself, and both were sons of ritual leaders; but even their knowledge was slight and infused with fantasy and rumor. All boys knew that initiation meant going to a men's house, wearing a phallocrypt, being given a man's bow, and cultivating taro. Most expressed enthusiasm and pride in these forthcoming privileges of manhood. Only three acknowledged that they were unhappy to leave their mothers and sisters. Eleven, however, noted that they were reluctant to leave younger brothers, and those with younger brothers often observed that these siblings now looked up to them and that the intimacy and playfulness of the relationship had changed as a consequence. In contrast, a number of those with initiated older brothers recalled somewhat bitterly that the latter's intimacy had become aloofness abruptly after the ais am. Virtually all boys recognized the pride that their fathers (and often older brothers) took in their forthcoming participation in the rite, but four also noted their mothers' resentment and sadness. Ten said that both parents wanted them to enter the ais am, but two detected parental disagreement on the matter. All thought that parental approval (especially by mothers) indicated that initiation would be an enjoyable experience; but this positive anticipation was often tempered by vague rumors and suspicions that something about the ais am was most unpleasant. In sum, preinitiation interviews suggested that the boys held some diffuse uncertainty and anxiety about the content and tenor of the rite, but they did not relate the forthcoming experience as much to themselves as to a limited range of socially significant others. Only seven mentioned other boys undergoing the rite at the same time as important—that is, as friends with whom they would share the experience. Most readily identified, often in gloating terms, other boys of comparable age who had been excluded either from the rite or from the age-group core.

During the performance, I was able to observe extensively all boys in the sample (as well as others). I could speak with them only briefly, however, while they were secluded in the root houses at night. I could then also monitor some conversations among the novices. The most notable feature of these observations was the sharply increasing anxiety of every boy in the sample, especially during the first four phases of the ais am. Thirteen tried to escape, but none of these were of the prestigious age-group core. Three, however, were firstborn sons (including both only sons), all of whom were reputed to have been excessively pampered by their mothers. In general, those of the age-group core were notably less prominent in complaining, screaming, crying, calling for help (especially from mothers), and resisting; yet, often with tears streaming down their faces, and choking back sobs they would attempt to control their verbal outcries in a way that was itself highly emotional. This pattern was not the case with firstborn sons, who wailed with abandon in many instances. Members of the age-group core knew that they had been selected as boys exhibiting promise of higher things (ritual leadership, for example) and that much was expected of their behavior in the ais am. It is my impression, however, that with the added stress of their overt stoicism, they became both more depressed and more quickly depressed than others. By the third phase of the rite, eight of them had taken to withdrawing into corners of the root house and ignoring their peers. Later some expressed deep resentment toward boys for whom behavioral expectations were less pronounced. Virtually all of the cases of severe, prolonged diarrhea involved members of the age-group core; and they were prone to frequent vomiting even though they generally suffered in the more private realm of the root house. These boys were always the first to confront each new ordeal, and the shock of the proceedings may have been increased accordingly. They were perhaps the most pathetic cases (to me *and* to many initiators) as they struggled to show manly stoicism, suffered the added stress of the effort, and received the least sympathy for their endeavors.

Throughout the performance, I noted many times how much attention was devoted to the body, corporeal changes, and bodily effluvia when the boys were in the root houses. All lost weight rapidly, and many suffered from nausea, diarrhea, uncontrollable urination, abdominal pain, bladder infection, constant colds, and suppurating ritual wounds. Ritual stress aggravated most of these physical problems. Among their peers, boys often drew attention to their maladies and to sensitive parts of the body. Many continually touched these bodily areas. At first, forced to live with their own wastes in the root houses, they often joked about their situation. Later, some became nauseous from the stench and blamed or ridiculed others for fouling the root house. By about the third phase, most were too ill, tired, hungry, and terrified to mention what seemed to have become a relatively minor discomfort. By this time, the filth was extraordinary, and men began to remove some of the wastes. Loss of weight was a source of manly pride to many, and it concerned only those who associated it with vomiting, stomach cramps, and diarrhea. The forced vomiting of female foods was a most frightening and physically disabling experience for all boys. Many traced to this ordeal a sense of bodily weakness and constant, spontaneous vomiting that persisted throughout the performance. The piercing of the nasal septa and the burning of the forearms, however, clearly created the most trauma, producing overt signs of physical and/or psychological shock in six cases. Most boys recalled their greatest sense of terror, hopelessness, and helplessness in relation to these ordeals. Many noted an intense but diffuse rage in experiencing the shock and pain, as well as a sense of betrayal and abandonment by socially significant others. The ritual elders seemed to recognize the range of these reactions, but they limited their practical assistance and moral support to treating the very ill, calming the most hysterical, and treating infection. Clearly, then, the ais am is, both physically and psychologically, an enormously traumatic experience, and much of the trauma is focused on the body.

A good deal of the detailed data on subjective experiences of the ais am comes from contact with novices immediately after their return to their own hamlets, although I was able to speak with some boys at Bigayoor. These postinitiation interviews yielded a complex amalgam of expressed pride, continued shock, and enduring fear, depression, and resentment. The paramount ritual elders were correct in suggesting that there was no *overt* expression of hostility toward themselves; but lesser male (and female) initiators were not always exempt from the boys' anger. I have noted that the elders' ritual authority is awesome, and the boys clearly respect and very much fear them. I have also noted that great anger *is* expressed—covertly or diffusely—but often not acknowledged by the novices. This lack of expressed anger toward the elders was bound up with the aura of their great authority in ritual matters, the boys' fear of them, the ritual suppression of anger in the ais am, the cultural emphasis on masculine *control* of anger, and the boys' anxious denials of their anger toward *these* men. My own identity as a confidant of ritual elders no doubt shaped the boys' remarks to some extent. Most of their expressed resentment was either vague or deflected onto other persons—usually men, but often women.

Thirteen boys noted some hostility toward their fathers for not waiting until they were older before subjecting them to the ais am, but only two failed to rationalize their fathers' decisions in this regard. Nine expressed great anger toward their mothers for not having warned them of what to expect or for not having protected them. The complicity of female initiators was often linked to a sense of betrayal by mothers and by women in general. Seven boys singled out initiated older brothers for special hate, since the latter had betrayed a once-close fraternal trust. Most novices, however, directed their anger toward adults in general who had deceived and injured them. Nevertheless, although many were ill and weak, twenty-two wanted others (especially adults and older siblings) to see them as "becoming new men" in public, and they reveled in the adult praise they received. Many expressed a sense of triumph *despite* adult deception and injury. The remaining two continued in a state of severe depression for several weeks. The father of one feared that his son might attempt suicide—something most unusual in a boy of about ten years.

Profound concern with the body was indicated in several sets of data. First, the interviews suggested that the boys were monitoring their bodies in far more detail than they were prior to the rite. They quickly noticed minute changes and made sense of them in ways that often brought ridicule from the elders.In four cases, there was unusual anxiety over diarrhea, constipation, or both. In all cases, the burned forearms and pierced nasal septa continued to be targets of concern. Eleven boys feared that they were not healing or that their ritual wounds were suppurating excessively. Most thought that something "inside" them had been cut or had ruptured during the ais am. All bodily effluvia, both normal and abnormal, were often seen as evidence of such internal injury, as were sensations that something inside the body had become "soft" and "weak." The latter anxiety was linked to a greater proneness to accidents in four cases. Five boys thought that parts of their bodies— notably penes or noses—might fall off and that they would become deformed or die. In refocusing a rumor about the ais am, nine boys suspected that something would be done to their penes at later stages of the initiation cycle, although Bimin-Kuskusmin practice no genital mutilation.

Second, reports of dreams exhibited several patterns that differed from those obtained in other sets of dream data. There were many reports of large, misshapen men standing on high places (such as ridges or rooftops). Only two boys did not mention some image of this kind. In most cases, a diviner said that these images were *not* men, but rather ancestral or forest spirits. The boys all emphatically denied that these images could be living men or, especially, ritual elders. All novices reported large, dark animals hidden in natural formations (for example, caves or logs). Dogs (three cases), pigs (two cases), marsupials (six cases), and forest spirits (four cases) were recognized, but many boys made no other specific identification. All of these dream reports were marked by observable anxiety; and all of these recognized dream entities figured in the ais am or subsequent stages of initiation. Ten boys recalled dreams about water, usually moving water in which something was floating away. In four cases, the same theme was linked to blood. In eleven of these cases, the floating objects were identified as parts of a human body (penis, nose, or ear for instance), but only three boys said that they were parts of their own bodies. From seventeen boys there were thirty-one reports noting forty-three images of either men, women, or animals that had lost a bodily part, had an infected or discolored part of the body, had an unidentified growth or protrusion on the body, or had a weakened, hardened, or deformed bodily part. When bodily parts were identified (in seventeen cases), they tended to be protruding penes, breasts, noses, ears, stomachs, or limbs. In eight of these dream reports, five boys recognized the bodies as their own. The bodies were identified as male (twelve boys), female (three boys), or ambiguous (four boys). Of the seventeen novices who reported these dreams, eight were of the age-group core. Four of them also reported seven dreams with nine instances of severe injury to the body (such as castration or other amputation). Overall, these dream reports indicated massive anxiety regarding hidden, powerful figures and deliberate or spontaneous injury to bodily substance. In most cases, these two features were linked.

Third, the draw-a-person exercise produced some significant patterns that indicate perceptions of gender contrast. Five boys (three of the age-group core) refused to participate, noting that the task was childish. Three refused to draw a female figure but gave no explanation. The most popular color choice was red, and the most frequent combination was red and white. (Of course, these are the most auspicious colors in the imagery of the ais am.) Black was used far more frequently for female than for male figures. The more negative connotations of black in regard to menstrual blood, female substance, and the like were well known to the boys from the ais am experience. Sixteen novices drew female figures that were consistently shorter and fatter than male figures. In related comments, most of these boys noted that the women were also ''weak'' and linked this trait to their being fat—a link often expressed in the ais am. Twelve boys included the abdominal scarification that is part of female initiation. Only one female figure was said to be pregnant, but the boy noted that this condition was ''like being fat.'' All female figures were drawn with hair, but the nineteen boys who drew male figures gave them hair in only three instances. (Of course, the boys' own hair was shaved off in the ais am, but ritual elders have the longest hair among all Bimin-Kuskusmin.) All male figures were presented in profile with the pierced nasal septum; and ten male figures were also given an exaggerated navel. Perhaps this last pair of traits indicated some recognition of the retention of female substance by the boys, who knew that they would face further ordeals in later initiations. Control groups of younger children and fully initiated men rarely depicted males with any navel. The boys consistently gave the male figures an unusually distended abdomen, which was highly characteristic of female figures among control groups. Again, this feature was another recognition of persisting female traits in "becoming new men." The control groups most commonly distorted the nose—not the abdomen—in male figures, making it quite large. Two boys presented male figures with scarred forearms, and one of these figures was drawn entirely in black. Four male figures were drawn from an X-ray perspective, the drawings depicting one or more internal organs. This perspective is most unusual among Bimin-Kuskusmin, but Herdt (personal comm. 1979) notes that it might be a clinical indicator of severe psychological disturbance. In general, these drawings gave some sense of the boys' view of gender contrast in relation to ais am themes and images concerning the body and also hinted at lingering ambiguity in boys' perceptions of their own gender. Despite the praise lavished upon them as "becoming new men," they knew that later stages of initiation would deny aspects of their present tenuous masculinity and once again would reduce their female substance in ways not yet recognized.

Fourth, although seven boys refused to cooperate on the Rorschach test, this protocol aroused the most general interest. Here I focus attention on the content of Rorschach responses. Interpretation of ink blots was often seen by novices to be much like the kind of analysis of reflections, shadows, and so forth in which diviners engage. In fact, all refusals were related to the boys' admitted fear of the impropriety of emulating the work of diviners, who are also ritual elders. Fourteen boys reported seeing human or animal limbs or internal organs that were dead, rotten, infected, soft, or weak. Nine novices noted whole or broken bones (such as the skull or the pelvis). Here again, sensitivity to real and imagined injury, whether external or internal, was noted in most interviews. No female sexual organs were mentioned, but some aspect of male genitalia—often covered with blood—was reported by five boys. Ten novices observed feces inside of bodies or man-made objects or else floating in water or blood. In most cases, the interpretation of body parts dominated identification of whole bodies; but human figures tended to be judged as male, misshapen, tall, muscular, and threatening. Little human movement was reported, but three boys observed males "running away" from something hidden and unidentified. Many animals and insects were noted in thirteen interpretations, and they were judged to be dead, dying, or partially dismembered by eight boys of the age-group core. The color red stood out in all interpretations, and it was associated with blood or bloody flesh and organs. In general, the boys' Rorschach responses revealed much of the same concern with body parts and effluvia, bodily injury, fear of adult men, hidden phenomena, and escape which had been noted in other sets of data. In fact, it is the mutual confirmation of such patterns that makes these projective inquiries analytically most useful.

Finally, the projective test story added one more dimension to this study of the boys' subjective experience. I drew on a traditional oral genre in which a young man wanders into the realm of a legendary semihuman group. These creatures pretend to befriend him and then try to entice him into committing severe moral indiscretions. In one version, the young man is ideally masculine in all respects, sees through their scheme, and triumphs. In the other, he succumbs because he is subtly flawed in body, spirit, and character. I presented the boys with stereotypic conclusions to each version, asking them to reconstruct the corresponding traits of the protagonist. Twenty-one boys gave entirely stereotypic responses. They had heard many narrations of such tales, and their responses indicated that in some ways they understood adult reckoning of correspondences between bodily features (or substance) and their entailments in charcter and behavior. Thus, the flabby, weak, unscarred protagonist was always fearful, complaining, and erratic in behavior, and he was easily entrapped by the semihuman creatures. In three of the more original responses, however, there was less mention of the bodily basis than of the social foundation of character and behavior. Thus, the quality of the protagonist's relations with his parents, siblings, and others offered clues to his fate. Whether he was ''good'' or ''bad'' depended on whether or not he had been a dutiful son, supportive brother, and so on.

In summary, the boys' subjective responses to these various inquiries reveal an impression of how the ais am experience enhances their sensitivity to bodily imagery and their own bodies, often with respect to gender contrast. As ''becoming new men,'' however, their evaluations of their bodies show some ambiguities in combinations of more or less positive and negative assessments of male and female traits, respectively. On the one hand, boys take pride in their new masculinity and revel in the attention others pay to them as ''becoming new men'': as they are seen by socially significant others, so too they begin to see themselves. Many note that the ais am has made them ''better'' than females in powerful ways, and their relations with women begin to change accordingly. On the other hand, they are deliberately left with the lingering suspicion that something about themselves (and their bodies) *remains* infused with female qualities. In part, it is perhaps this diffuse doubt about their manhood which focuses so much anxiety on their bodily softness, weakness, decay, and debilitation. The ritual elders will make deliberate use of this doubt and anxiety in later initiations.

It is always hard to detect the private self more than fleetingly in this ritual context, for the public image of manhood requires rigid control of personal impulses. As months pass after the ais am, the boys become less and less willing to discuss such matters and are busily preparing for the second stage of initiation. What is wrought within must remain problematic, but the scars that marked this *rite de passage* are indelibly etched on the boys' bodies in standardized social inscription. I have shown something of the boys' subjective experience of the ais am and demonstrated that the rite's "religious ideas deal with the very guts of life, not with its bland surface" (Spiro 1970:6).

CONCLUSION

Bimin-Kuskusmin male initiation is remarkably complex, and here I have sketched only some central features of the first of ten stages of the ritual cycle. A guiding assumption of the analysis has been that the study of initiation must be informed by cultural, social, and psychological considerations. It has long been noted that initiation has something fundamental to do with forging new identities, not only in societies but also of individuals (Van Gennep 1909). The latter dimension has been much neglected, and those reductive analyses (semiotic and socio-structural) that fail to encompass actual behavior and subjectivity cannot redress the balance.

In the Papua New Guinea context, Kenneth Read (1952, 1955) has sensitively noted that his elegant ritual analyses are incomplete with regard to matters of behavior and subjectivity. He has sought to explore aspects of personhood and selfhood among Gahuku-Gama. In this volume and elsewhere, Herdt (1981), on the Sambia, and Tuzin (1975, 1977, 1980), on the Ilahita Arapesh, have directed detailed attention to some of Read's unresolved problems. This essay, in turn, has explored interrelationships among ritual ideology, performance, and subjective experience by focusing on ritually induced transformations of person, self, and body in the Bimin-Kuskusmin ais am.

149

Transformations in the constellation of attributes, capacities, and signs that define the boys' personhood are marked by the ritual transition from "people of women's houses" to "becoming new men." After long attachment to women in the domestic domain, the boys are removed from community life to endure the ordeals of the ais am, and to emerge with a new identity and new moral responsibilities, jural entitlements, and emblems of manhood. Not only are the boys now members of the social community in a different way and with new rights and obligations, but also they are increasingly seen as stoic, controlled, autonomous young men and warriors, who aggressively assert their prerogatives and actively forge what is to be made of sociopolitical relations. Much of this ritual transformation is expressed in terms of gender contrast, which, in turn, is often coded in bodily imagery and its behavioral entailments. And these entailments have their subjective dimensions.

Turner (1976a:96) suggests that initiation ritual often "gives an outward and visible form to an inward and conceptual process" (cf. Munn 1973 and Obeyesekere n.d.). Indeed, Bimin-Kuskusmin elders emphasize the experiential efficacy of the ais am, and the necessity of subjective transformation. Boys should differ in their subjective sense of self as a consequence of the ais am experience. Changes in personhood and selfhood are bound up together (cf. Fortes 1973). So that boys are separated from the realm of women and gain a lasting sense of their own masculinity, they must withstand extreme ritual ordeals that are intended to rid them of debilitating female substance (and its entailments in behavior). Both males (as initiators and fathers) and females (as initiators and mothers) conspire to betray a trusting dependence and to inflict physical and psychological trauma. The resulting ambiguity, anxiety, fear, pain, and anger have a destabilizing effect (see Kiefer and Cowan 1979); and the ais am creates a vivid personal experience that endures, for the everyday world is infused with reminders ("retrieval cues") of the rite. Eventually, after later initiations, the boys' trauma of ritual violence is ideally converted into the adult aggressive behaviors of warriors, husbands, and ultimately initiators. Now, however, immediately following the ais am, the effects have more to do with an intense sense of the separateness of one's body (and its parts and processes) and the constitution of one's masculinity as set against female substance and femininity. It is clear, moreover, that the "becoming new men" sense an ambiguity in themselves with regard to gender, and this ambiguity (and related sexual ambivalence) will be transformed again and again in other initiations, but never quite resolved. The boys' sense of self is much affected by these repeated ritual transformations and by the consequences of the transformations in their sociocultural personhood.

It is clear that individual experience (or behavior) cannot be "read off" from cultural ideology or social identity in any simple way. On the other hand, the boys' subjective ritual reactions and expressions of their sense of self can be examined in relation to their selections from the cultural repertoire of personal constructs (cf. Kelly 1955). In many contexts, Bimin-Kuskusmin draw on images of natural substance to encode and express subjective experiences in terms of "personal symbols" (Obeyesekere n.d.). If Bimin-Kuskusmin initiation rites are experiences upon which men have impressed significance of social and cultural orders, then it is also the case that they are experienced as such (see Harris 1978). The violence and trauma of the ais am facilitate this impress of sociocultural features on subjective dimensions and expressions of the ritual experience.

Finally, Geertz (1968:108) elegantly notes a difficulty in the study of ritual experience, for we cannot get "phenomenologically accurate descriptions" when persons "are really involved in worship," which is incompatible with detached analysis. In many ways, though, we *do* glimpse something important of the subjective face of ritual experience in our fieldwork, and we must try—sensitively and systematically—to take account of these observations and impressions. Through empathy, projective data, and delicate ethnography that is susceptive to behavior and subjective expression, I have demonstrated the beginning of an approach toward that end.

REFERENCES

ALLEN, M. R.
1967 *Male Cults and Secret Initiations in Melanesia.* Melbourne: Melbourne University Press.
BARTH, F.
1971 Tribes and intertribal relations in the Fly headwaters. *Oceania* 41:171–191.
1975 *Ritual and Knowledge among the Baktaman of New Guinea.* New Haven: Yale University Press.
BENOIST, J.-M., et al.
1977 *L'Identité.* Paris: Bernard Grasset.
BISILLIAT, J., and D. LAYA
1973 Représentations et connaissances du corps chez les Songhay-Zarma: analyse d'une suite d'entretiens avec une guérisseur. In *La Notion de personne en Afrique noire,* ed. G. Dieterlen, pp. 331–358. Paris: Editions du CNRS.

DIETERLEN, G.

1973 L'image du corps et les composantes de la personne chez les Dogon. In *La Notion de personne en Afrique noire*, ed. G. Dieterlen, pp. 205−229. Paris: Editions du CNRS.

ELLEN, R. F.

1977 Anatomical classification and the semiotics of the body. In *The Anthropology of the Body*, ed. J. Blacking, pp. 343−373. London: Academic Press.

FISHER, S.

1970 *Body Experience in Fantasy and Behavior*. New York: Appleton-Century-Crofts.

FORTES, M.

1973 On the concept of the person among the Tallensi. In *La Notion de personne en Afrique noire*, ed. G. Dieterlen, pp. 283−319. Paris: Editions du CNRS.

GEERTZ, C.

1968 *Islam Observed*. New Haven: Yale University Press.

1973 Ethos, world view, and the analysis of sacred symbols. *The Interpretation of Cultures*, ed. C. Geertz, pp. 126−141. New York: Basic Books.

GUIDERI, R.

1975 Note sur le rapport mâle/femelle en Mélanésie. *L'Homme* 15:103−119.

HALLOWELL, A. I.

1955a The Ojibwa self and its behavioral environment. In *Culture and Experience*, ed. A. I. Hallowell, pp. 172−182. Philadelphia: University of Pennslyvania Press.

1955b The self and its behavioral environment. In *Culture and Experience*, ed. A. I. Hallowell, pp. 75−110. Philadelphia: University of Pennsylvania Press.

1958 Ojibwa metaphysics of being and the perception of persons. In *Person Perception and Interpersonal Behavior*, ed. R.Tagiuri and L.Petrullo, pp. 63−85. Stanford: Stanford University Press.

1960 Self, society, and culture in phylogenetic perspective. In *Evolution after Darwin*, ed. S.Tax, 2:309−372. Chicago: University of Chicago Press.

1976 Ojibwa ontology, behavior, and world view. In *Contributions to Anthropology*, ed. A. I. Hallowell, pp. 357−390. Chicago: University of Chicago Press.

HARRIS, G. G

1976 Inward-looking and outward-looking symbols. In *The Realm of the Extra-Human: Ideas and Actions*, ed. A. Bharati, pp. 301−309. The Hague: Mouton.

1978 *Casting Out Anger*. London: Cambridge University Press.

HERDT, G. H.

1981 *Guardians of the Flutes: Idioms of Masculinity*. New York: McGraw-Hill.

JORGENSEN, D.

1978 The clear and the hidden: public and private aspects of self in Telefomin. Paper presented at the Annual Meeting of the Canadian Ethnological Society, London, Ontario.

KELLY, G.

1955 *The Psychology of Personal Constructs*. 2 vols. New York: W. W. Norton.

KIEFER, C. W., and J. COWAN

1979 State/context dependence and theories of ritual. *Journal of Psychological Anthropology* 2:53−83.

LA FONTAINE, J. S.
1977 The power of rights. *Man* 12:421−437.

LANGNESS, L. L.
1977 Ritual, power, and male dominance in the New Guinea Highlands. In *The Anthropology of Power*, ed. R. D. Fogelson and R. N. Adams, pp. 3−22. New York: Academic Press.

LEACH, E. R.
1976 *Culture and Communication*. London: Cambridge University Press.

LEENHARDT, M.
1947 *Do Kamo*. Paris: Gallimard.

LINDENBAUM, S.
1976 A wife is the hand of man. In *Man and Woman in the New Guinea Highlands*, ed. P. Brown and G. Buchbinder, pp. 54−62. Washington, D.C.: American Anthropological Association.

MAUSS, M.
1968 Une catégorie de l'esprit humain: la notion de personne, celle de 'moi'. In *Sociologie et anthropologie*, ed. M.Mauss, pp. 331−362. Paris: Presses Universitaires de France.

1969 L'âme, le nom, et la personne, In *Oeuvres*, M. Mauss, 2:131−135. Paris: Editions de Minuit.

MEIGS, A. S.
1976 Male pregnancy and the reduction of sexual opposition in a New Guinea Highlands society. *Ethnology* 15 (4):393−407.

MUNN, N. D.
1973 Symbolism in a ritual context: aspects of symbolic action. In *Handbook of Social and Cultural Anthropology*, ed. J. J. Honigmann, pp. 579−612. Chicago: Rand McNally.

OBEYESEKERE, G.
N.d. *Medusa's Hair*. Chicago: University of Chicago Press, forthcoming.

POOLE, F. J. P.
1976a Knowledge rests in the heart: Bimin-Kuskusmin metacommunications on meaning, tacit meaning, and field research. Paper presented at the Annual Meeting of the American Anthropological Association, Washington, D.C., November.

1976b *The Ais Am*. Ann Arbor: University Microfilms.

1977 The ethnosemantics of Yemen: food prohibitions, food transactions, and taro as cultigen, food, and symbol among the Bimin-Kuskusmin. Paper presented at the Annual Meeting of the American Anthropological Association, Houston, November.

1981 Transforming "natural" woman: female ritual leaders and gender ideology among Bimin-Kuskusmin. In *Sexual Meanings*, ed. S. B. Ortner and H. Whitehead. New York: Cambridge University Press.

N.d. "Couvade" and clinic in a New Guinea society: birth among the Bimin-Kuskusmin. In *Medicalization of Life and Patient Compliance*, ed. M. deVries and R. Berg. Cambridge: Harvard University Press, forthcoming.

RAPPAPORT, R. A.
1975a On the structure of ritual. Paper presented at the Annual Meeting of the American Anthropological Association, San Francisco.

1975*b* Ritual as communication and as state. *CoEvolution Quarterly* 6:168−183.

1979 The obvious aspects of ritual. In *Ecology, Meaning, and Religion*, ed. R. A. Rappaport, pp. 173−221. Richmond, Calif.: North Atlantic Books.

READ, K. E.

1952 Nama cult of the Central Highlands, New Guinea. *Oceania* 23:1−25.

1955 Morality and the concept of person among the Gahuku-Gama. *Oceania* 25: 233−282.

SPERBER, D.

1975 *Rethinking Symbolism*. London: Cambridge University Press.

SPIRO, M. E.

1966 Religion: problems of definition and explanation. In *Anthropological Approaches to the Study of Religion*, ed. M. Banton, pp. 85−126. London: Tavistock.

1970 *Buddhism and Society*. New York: Harper and Row.

STRATHERN, A. J.

1970 Male initiation in the New Guinea Highlands. *Ethnology* 9:373−379.

1977 Why is shame on the skin? In *The Anthropology of the Body*, ed. J. Blacking, pp. 99−110. London: Academic Press.

TURNER, V. W.

1967*a* Betwixt and between: the liminal period in *rites de passage*. In *The Forest of Symbols*, ed. V. W. Turner, pp. 93−111. Ithaca: Cornell University Press.

1967*b* Color classification in Ndembu ritual: a problem in primitive classification. In *The Forest of Symbols*, ed. V. W. Turner, pp. 59−92. Ithaca: Cornell University Press.

1967*c* Ritual symbolism, morality, and social structure among the Ndembu. In *The Forest of Symbols*, ed. V. W. Turner, pp. 48−58. Ithaca: Cornell University Press.

1975 Symbolic studies. *Annual Review of Anthropology* 4:145−161.

TUZIN, D. F.

1975 The breath of a ghost: dreams and fear of the dead. *Ethos* 3:555−578.

1977 Reflections of being in Arapesh water symbolism. *Ethos* 5:195−223.

1980 *The Voice of the Tambaran: Truth and Illusion in Ilahita Arapesh Religion*. Berkeley, Los Angeles, and London: University of California Press.

VAN GENNEP, A.

1909 *Les Rites de passage*. Paris: Émile Nourry.

4

THE *BAU A* CEREMONIAL HUNTING LODGE:
An Alternative to Initiation

Edward L. Schieffelin

The Author

Edward L. Schieffelin is a Senior Research Fellow at the Institute for the Study of Human Issues in Philadelphia. He was born in New York City in 1938. In 1960 he received his B.A. in physics and philosophy from Yale University and two years later went to the University of Chicago for graduate study in anthropology. While a doctoral student there, he did research among the East African Yao of Malawi and for his M.A. thesis wrote a Jungian analysis of Manus (Admiralty Islands) religion. From 1966 to 1968 he took up ethnographic fieldwork among the Kaluli people of the Great Papuan Plateau, Southern Highlands Province, Papua New Guinea. His dissertation, for which he was awarded a Ph.D. in 1972, was concerned with Kaluli ceremonialism and reciprocity. His research on Papua New Guinea has been published in the form of articles on social change, ecology, exchange, and spirit mediumship and in a book-length cultural analysis of the remarkable Kaluli *gisalo* ceremony, which is entitled *The Sorrow of the Lonely and the Burning of the Dancers* (1976). Professor Schieffelin returned to the Kaluli from 1975 to 1977 to study the sociocultural and symbolic changes that have come about among them under the influence of missionization. His reconstruction of the bachelorhood hunting lodge described below is based in part on that research.

Professor Schieffelin has wide-ranging anthropological interests that include symbolic systems, ritual processes, ethnohistory, and medical systems. He currently teaches at the University of Pennsylvania and is working on a book analyzing historic and symbolic change among the Kaluli from precolonial times to the evangelized present.

155

INTRODUCTION

This essay concerns the *bau a,* a bachelor men's ceremonial hunting lodge that was held periodically before European contact by the Kaluli, Onabasulu, and Etoro peoples of the Papuan Plateau in Papua New Guinea.[1] The bau a exhibited many features typical of a male initiation program, including the seclusion of the members, ritual activity aimed at promoting growth and enhancing manly qualities, and the teaching of secret lore. It also heightened the reputation of its leaders and of the sponsoring community, encouraged social integration and cessation of fighting over a wide area, and formed part of an ongoing, large-scale ceremonial cycle of food exchange. Keeping mindful of Keesing's caution (this volume, chap. 1) not to expect narrowly prescriptive definitions of initiation to fit all the data comfortably, it is nevertheless my contention that the bau a was not an initiation program but an alternative ritual institution. Despite its somewhat similar aims (gaining social acceptance for youths and young men among adults) the bau a appeared to embody a rather different ritual strategy, and a different set of fundamental attitudes, and it resulted in positing a different type of relationship between the graduating members and the rest of society than does initiation. In particular, it did not result in a social transition. In this chapter I will analyse just what the alternative strategy of this program was, assess the kind of resolution it achieved, and, finally, discuss its implications for understanding initiation as a ritual institution.

I should mention at the outset that I have never witnessed a bau a. It was discontinued as an institution by the Kaluli people themselves under the influence of European contact in 1964, two years before I arrived to begin fieldwork. Most of my detailed information, therefore, comes from extensive interviews taken in 1968 with four senior Kaluli men who had attended a bau a sponsored by clan Bona at a place called Wɔgɔle in the early 1940s. Later, in 1976, I arranged for the archaeological excavation of the Wɔgɔle site under the direction of Mary Jane Moun-

[1]This essay is based on fieldwork carried out in Papua New Guinea in 1966–1968 under a grant from the National Institutes of Health and in 1975–1977 under grants from the National Institutes of Health and the National Science Foundation. I gratefully acknowledge the support of the Research Institute for the Study of Man in New York and the Institute for the Study of Human Issues in Philadelphia, in administering these funds. Funds for archaeological excavations were provided by the Department of Prehistory of the University of Papua New Guinea.

I would also like to thank the following people for critical comments and helpful discussion of earlier drafts of this chapter: Steven Feld, Bambi Schieffelin, Steve Tobias, Steven Frankel, Jim Weiner, Donald Tuzin, Fitz John Porter Poole, Terence Hays, and Mary Jane Mountain.

tain, then senior lecturer in the Department of Prehistory, University of Papua New Guinea. Some of my original informants participated in the dig, and the many memories it reawakened for them helped clarify numerous aspects of what they had told me eight years before.

THE KALULI

The Kaluli people (numbering some 1200) live in about twenty long-house communities scattered in the tropical forest of the southern portion of the Papuan Plateau just north of Mount Bosavi. The northern part of the plateau, bordered by the Karius Range, is inhabited by the Onabasulu (population 430, Ernst n.d.) and the Etoro people (population about 400, Kelly 1977) who live to the northwest under the shadow of Mount Sisa.

The Kaluli subsist on a staple starch of sago supplemented by a variety of vegetables grown in extensive gardens cleared from the forest (Schieffelin 1975). They obtain meat by fishing and by hunting or trapping small game in the forest. Kaluli also keep domestic pigs in small numbers but kill them principally for prestations and ceremonial occasions. Relations among longhouse communities are maintained principally by ties of marriage or matrilateral affiliation (Schieffelin 1976).

FREQUENCY AND DISTRIBUTION OF THE BAU A

The bau a itself was an oval building constructed on the ground, in which the membership performed hunting magic and slept for part of the period of their ritual seclusion. The membership ranged from boys of eight or nine years old to bachelors of around twenty-eight. The period of seclusion was about fifteen months. The major criterion for admission, apart from being able to trace some kinship connection to the sponsoring community, was that the individual had never been sexually involved with a woman. The major activity of the bau a, to which most of the rituals pertained and to which all other benefits were in one way or another related, was hunting. The game, principally marsupials of moderate size, was smoked and accumulated in a smoking rack in the bau a in preparation for a large-scale distribution at the climactic ceremony that marked the young men's coming out of seclusion.

The bau a was plateau-wide in distribution. It was practiced among the Onabasulu and Etoro peoples to the north (Kelly 1976) and ranged

157

from the Sonia people on the west to the Kaluli village of Wasu on the east. From the number of ancient sites that were pointed out to me, I would judge that it was of considerable antiquity in the area. The one available originlike myth describes it as being given to the Kaluli people by *mɛmul* spirits in the central Kaluli area near clan Felisa.

The institution was not unchanging. Prior to 1930 all of the bau a sponsored by Kaluli clans from Felisa to Wasu were built in the *dobulube* style, with a particular ridge-pole configuration and two doors at one end. Some men characterized this as an Onabasulu style of bau a. In about 1934 a new style, *dokobolo*, with a different roof configuration and doors at opposite ends of the building, was introduced by the more western groups. In the next decades it was adopted from community to community eastward as the preferred style of bau a. Some informants told me that the difference in bau a house styles was accompanied by differences in magic and ritual details, but the cultural themes of hunting and ritual seclusion were unchanged. Wɔgɔle in the early 1940s was a dokobolo bau a.

A given longhouse community sponsored a bau a about once in thirty years (the shortest span I have recorded is about 14). Among the thirteen longhouse communities about which I have detailed information, between 1912 and 1964, at least one bau a was available every two to six years for youths and young men to attend. Sometimes more than one community would decide to sponsor a bau a, and, as a result, two might be in session at the same time.

The large-scale distribution of recooked smoked game at the end of a bau a formed a wide-ranging but slow-moving and much delayed system of ceremonial exchange between individuals and communities. This system of exchange centered on the bau a itself because the only appropriate return for a prestation of meat (or *mado*, as it was called to mystify its nature vis-à-vis women) from a bau a was a prestation of similar meat from another bau a.

VALUES ASSOCIATED WITH THE BAU A

In conversing about the bau a, my informants' eyes would shine; their voices would become excited or drop to low, mysterious whispers. Clearly they felt their experiences in the bau a were among the high points of their lives.

A bau a was believed to promote the growth of the young boys (about ten to fourteen years old) and to induce strength and attractively light skin color for the youths and bachelors. It was also believed to ward off sickness and death by quieting the appetites of witches in the surrounding communities. In addition, it led to a general suspension of hostilities and revenge killings among longhouse communities during the time it was in session. Finally, it represented a special relationship between men and the mɛmul spirits of Mount Bosavi.

The Bau a and the World of Spirits

The group of spirits with whom Kaluli normally interact is called *ane mama* (literally, "gone reflections"). These are the spirits of the dead, plus others just like them who have never been alive. They inhabit an invisible realm located roughly at the level of the top of the forest canopy in the vicinity of the longhouses where Kaluli live. Ane mama "show through" to the visible world, that is, manifest themselves visibly in the forms of certain varieties of birds. Another group of spirits, known as the mɛmul, live away from human habitation on the tops of hills and high places, and especially on Mount Bosavi.

Contact with the spirit world is established through spirit mediums. Ane mama often speak through mediums, since they live in the locality of the longhouse and are friendly with its inhabitants; but mɛmul spirits never do.

According to Kaluli tradition, the mɛmul are like a powerful, distant, but not hostile neighboring group. Mediums who have seen them portray them as being fierce and standoffish, keeping to an old-fashioned style of dress, and carrying bone knives and stone-headed clubs (ane mama, by contrast, are more friendly and carry steel axes and bush knives). If ane mama manifest themselves as birds and are heard as the voices of birds, the mɛmul appear as the wild pig and the cassowary, the most powerful and dangerous animals of the forest. Their voices come through as the tremendous boom and crash of tropical thunder that seems to explode from the hilltops. Though mɛmul are not unfriendly to people, they do not communicate with them directly, except in relation to the bau a. There are, however, two other ways mɛmul are involved with humankind that deserve attention.

While mɛmul appear to Kaluli in the guise of wild pigs on the visible side, Kaluli appear to mɛmul as wild pigs on the invisible side. Consequently, as Kaluli hunt and kill wild pigs, the mɛmul die, and as mɛmul hunt wild pigs, Kaluli die. (The injury or entrapment of a man's wild pig reflection is one of the causes of illness which a medium goes into the invisible world to alleviate.) There is no enmity between Kaluli and mɛmul over this killing, for, as Kaluli point out, ''when we kill a wild pig, how do we know whether it is a mɛmul or just an ordinary pig?'' It is the same for the mɛmul. For Kaluli the dilemma is just one of those tragic entailments of the scheme of things, but it evens out in the end.

Secondly, in the mythical time, it was the mɛmul spirits who came down a giant tree from their hilltop forest-canopy home and instructed Kaluli in how to live properly, cultivate gardens, make prestations of pigs, and exchange women for wealth. They didn't do a perfect job of it, Kaluli point out, but they provided what moral guidance there is before returning up their tree. Some say that it was at this time that the mɛmul showed men how to conduct the bau a. Mɛmul themselves are thought to hold bau a frequently (ane mama typically do not have bau a), and mediums sent out in seance to investigate particularly frightening thunderstorms often report that it is only the sound of the mɛmul celebrating a bau a on a nearby hill. Other people say it was through mediums that people first learned about the bau a. Long ago, the story goes, a medium entered the spirit side to investigate a particularly violent storm and discovered the mɛmul engaged in the opening ceremonies of a bau a. The mɛmul invited him to return and visit the bau a while it was in session so that he could show men how it was done. This story is based on the fact that Kaluli learn almost everything novel about the spirit world through their mediums, and unexpected information that comes up in seances is often a topic of discussion.

There is yet another tradition, which emphasizes the significance of the bau a in relation to Kaluli ideology about male and female growth.

In the ancient times ''when the world came into form,'' the mɛmul showed people how to hold a bau a and told them to send the women off to seclusion. As a result, the women hunted while the men stayed home and beat sago (a reversal of usual male-female roles). As they hunted, the women began to grow to enormous size, until finally they were taller than the trees and could look down upon the arborial marsupials from above. The men at the longhouse said, ''This is no good,'' so they called the women back and sent the bachelors out instead. All went well for a while—the men hunted and became strong, boys grew without becoming oversized. When the mɛmul saw that they had been disobeyed, however, they descended in a fury on the bau a and killed all the youths and young men, throwing their entrails into a pit and covering them with water. This place, which is on the lands of clan Felisa, is called Iwalosɔnɔ-gɔm, which means, appropriately, "high-place-killed-guts." Subsequent to this flash of anger, the mɛmul reserved the bau a for males only, and the institution spread from Felisa to other places.

The myth refers to two important themes associated with the bau a, its reputed growth-enhancing powers and the fact that it is under the auspices of the mɛmul. Kaluli believe that girls grow to womanhood and achieve maturity by themselves but that boys cannot attain manhood without assistance. They must be helped by a special growth-stimulating procedure. In the myth, women, who hold their own growth potential, grow to monstrous size when overstimulated by the growth-enhancing effects of the bau a. Youths and boys, on the other hand, are merely enabled to grow to proper maturity in the same environment, which they could not do by themselves.

The bau a was under the special tutelage of the mɛmul, who oversaw it and acted as its guardians. The way Kaluli put it, the bau a was the mɛmul's special gift to humankind, and they watched over it closely to see that everything was done properly. The members, made mindful (by the myth) of the consequences of angering the mɛmul, tried to observe closely the ritually prescribed behavior, of the bau a. The mɛmul, for their part, protected the participants from harm and responded to the bau a rituals performed every night by providing game for the hunt.

Finally, if the mɛmul were pleased with the bau a they provided its leader (wɔfu tamin kalu) with a mɛmul woman for a wife in the guise of an oddly shaped stone. This stone bride was placed next to the huge leaf oven in which the smoked game was recooked before the final distribution, and her presence was what made the meat marvelously soft and delicious. In this way mɛmul and man pledged their link to one another, though only in the context of the bau a itself.

Bau a Activities and the Development of
Manly Virtues

While relations with the mɛmul spirits provided the sanction and motivation for proper behavior within the bau a and permeated the rituals and magic formulas the members repeated each day, my informants did not particularly emphasize this mystical element of their bau a experience. Instead they stressed the hunting activities, the promotion of growth and strength, and the social harmony of surrounding communities. They attributed the creation of strength and endurance in part to the

161

fact that while they were in the bau a they ate meat every day, since all the animals that had been mangled by the dogs or were too small to smoke were theirs to eat. Bachelors and boys carried out grueling hunting expeditions from early in the morning until late in the afternoon most days. Hunting groups ranged considerable distances over the Papuan Plateau, made week-long expeditions to the forested slopes of Mount Bosavi, and traveled to the lands south of the mountain at the headwaters of the Turama river. Youths and boys thus developed extensive knowledge of the habits of animals and a familiarity with the forest geography over a wide area outside the confines of their own longhouse territories. Because of their ritual status, bau a youths always could pass through other longhouse areas safe from attack.

While the characteristics of endurance and knowledge of the forest were developed in hunting, self-control was encouraged within the bau a itself. Self-control was more than a matter of strict ritual avoidance of women (a stricture that was checked for each youth and young man periodically by divination). It also pertained to social harmony among the inmates. Argument and angry words between bau a youths were strongly censured, and if frequent, or if a fight errupted, the offenders would be expelled by the bau a leader and sent back in disgrace to their longhouses.

The growth of young boys who were around the age of puberty was encouraged specifically by pederastic homosexual intercourse with some of the older bachelors. Kaluli believe that girls attain full maturity as women by natural growth but that boys cannot do so without being given a ''boost,'' as it were, by the semen of older men. This pederasty was considered a major male secret vis-à-vis the women, and it was generally regarded with embarrassment and lascivious humor among the men themselves. Homosexual intercourse for boys also took place in everyday life beyond the bau a context whenever a boy reached the age of about ten or eleven. At that time, his father would choose a suitable partner to inseminate him, and the two would meet privately in the forest or a garden house for intercourse over a period of months or years. Less frequently a boy might choose his own inseminator, although this was risky: if the man was a witch, his semen would turn the boy into one too. In the bau a, boys were inseminated ''openly'' (that is, they were inseminated by their homosexual partner after lights out in the close, crowded, smoky darkness of the bau a while the rest of the exhausted hunters were thought to be asleep). A few of the bachelors came to the bau a specifically to act as inseminators, and fathers sometimes assigned their sons to one or the other of them. Other lads chose their own inseminators from among the older bachelors (or bachelors chose them), and formed specific liaisons for a while. Side by side with the serious business of hunting, pederastic intercourse was a marked feature of the bau a which men chuckled over self-consciously in reminiscence.

The Bau a and Male Mystique

To nonparticipants, and in particular women, the bau a was presented as a mystically powerful and dangerous institution. This came across in the tense, rather frightening and portentous secrecy with which the men cloaked the institution. Women were told that their sons had gone off to become "like wild pigs" (*iko domɛni ane*), and they were forbidden to know what went on in the bau a, to see or speak of its members, or to travel in its vicinity lest they become ill or die. Neither did they share any of the meat at the end of the seclusion period. Men used an elaborate vocabulary of esoteric code words (*bali to*) when talking about bau a activities among themselves in the longhouse, so that while women might suspect them of talking about the bau a, they did not know what was being said. The secretiveness, plus the men's dead-earnest anger and dismay at the thought that a woman might somehow transgress the bounds around the subject, conveyed a message of precarious power and danger; yet, at the same time, it was also made tantalizing. The bau a, though built at a secluded spot, was nevertheless sufficiently within earshot of the longhouse for the women to hear the whoops and animal calls of the youths in the distance (usually when they returned from a particularly successful hunt).

It is difficult to assess what women felt about the bau a. They publicly maintained the stance that it was an affair of the men and that they did not know anything about it. Actually, I discovered that many older women appeared to have a fairly good idea about what went on with regard to the more obvious hunting and homosexual activities (though not the secret ritual details). As audience to the whole performance, however, they went along with its disguises and pretended they knew nothing. The point here is that part of the importance of the bau a for the men lay in the way it was meant to frighten and mystify the women and to impress them with male mystique, a cultural ideal in which, to some extent, everyone believes. It is the same mystique and attraction that could cause a woman to lose her heart to a dancer at a public ceremony and elope by following him home (Schieffelin 1976:24).

Bau a and the Promotion of Social Harmony

Besides benefiting the membership, the bau a was thought to contribute to the general well-being of the local area. This effect stemmed in part from the belief that it warded off illness and death by calming the appetites of witches, who were charmed by its beauty and general positive excitement.

However, the bau a also fostered prosperity by implicitly encouraging a suspension of dispute and hostility and promoting social communication and interaction. The need to suspend hostilities in the area of the longhouse communities involved in a bau a was very real. It would be practically impossible to commence a bau a in a situation of warring hostility, since few people on the opposed sides would join it together. On the other hand, it was stupid and dangerous to engage in hostilities once the bau a had gone into session for the very practical reason that the members of the bau a were unarmed and vulnerable. If antagonism and violence broke out between longhouse communities, those members would be easy marks for revenge.

Although bau a members were supposed to be under the protection of the mɛmul, who would, it was thought, bring devastation upon anyone who harmed them, this consideration was effective primarily in longhouse rhetoric aimed at keeping tempers cool and avoiding unnecessary disputes; it was taken less seriously if passions got really aroused. Kaluli repeatedly emphasized the efforts made within the surrounding longhouse communities to keep the peace. Their efforts were by and large successful. During the last seventy years, no killings occurred among the participating longhouses whenever a bau a was in session, though on several occasions grievances were saved up and hostilities followed immediately after the participants came out of seclusion.

There were also more positive reasons for peaceful intercourse among communities. During the time a bau a was in session, informants recalled, the amount of visiting and social intercourse among longhouse communities markedly increased. People who otherwise would have visited infrequently or not at all came and went regularly to the sponsoring longhouse to supply their relatives in the bau a with sago and vegetable food and to participate in discussions and arrangements for ceremonies and other activities that marked the stages of the bau a. This common interest—plus the rising anticipation and excitement as the climactic distribution approached—gave a central social focus and unity of purpose to the communities that had youths in the bau a and a hungry expectation to those who were to receive a share of the mado. This commonality of purpose, though it evaporated after the bau a came out of seclusion, kept the peace on the plateau longer than any other social institution did until government control occurred.

Commenting on this state of affairs, informants told me that everyone wanted the bau a to "come up good." To "come up good" meant that the mado (recooked smoked animals) passed out at the final distribution would be so soft "that the bones fell out of it." A bau a came up badly if the meat was hard or otherwise less than delicious. Mado from a bau a, I was told, was not like ordinary recooked smoked game, but something entirely and distinctly different, superior to anything else one would ever taste.

Ritual Avoidance of Women

Whether a bau a "came up good" was believed to be largely a matter of the proper behavior of its membership. In practical terms, this meant that the bau a inmates had to perform the rituals conscientiously, observe appropriate cooperation and peaceful decorum, and especially avoid contact with women. The object lesson for failure to do this was the example of the bau a at Hondugusi (about 1918), which became legend because its mado came out burned. The bau a leader, it was subsequently discovered, had secretly seduced a young woman in the forest during the period of seclusion.

Sexual infractions involving women were particularly likely to enrage the mɛmul. If really aroused, the mɛmul were feared likely to attack the bau a personally, as in the myth, attacking in the forms of wild pigs and cassowaries, amid a violent tropical storm. Such beliefs were taken quite seriously, especially when there was a storm violent enough to shake the building and tear the thatch. After one particularly frightening storm struck Wogole in the 1940s, the leader called the membership together and performed a divination. One bachelor was revealed to have had intercourse with a woman he met secretly. He was immediately expelled from the bau a, which eventually came up well.

It was clear from the animated and emphatic way informants reminisced about the bau a they had attended more than twenty years previously that it had been a high point in their lives. The nostalgic excitement and zest in the telling expressed the extent to which, for the youths and young men especially and for their elders vicariously, the experience had been dramatic and enjoyable. The members of the bau a were the center of attention for all the surrounding communities. The continual hunting over wide ranges of forest, the growth-stimulating pederasty in the bau a, the ritual discipline and unity of purpose, the vigorous manly ethos and mystification of women—all came together under the auspices of the mɛmul spirits to form a kind of sacralized paradigm of masculine productivity and the manly life. In this sense it expressed what men liked best about themselves, what they stood for and wanted to be. This desirable and idealized image of males was confirmed, when, at the end of a "good" bau a, the mɛmul presented the leader with a mɛmul bride, in the guise of an oddly shaped stone. Or, as sometimes happened, the bride was said to have lost her heart to the bau a leader and eloped, following him home like a girl smitten by the beauty of a dancer at a ceremony.

Motivations and Conditions for Setting Up a Bau a

The motivations that impelled a community to set up a bau a were various, and they frequently differed substantially with the different people involved and with the conditions of the particular social-historical context. Older men with a concern for tradition often spoke of sponsoring a bau a because intrinsically it was a good thing, because they hadn't sponsored one in a long time, and because they wished to teach its ways to the young men so that such traditions would not be forgotten. (This indicates, of course, a rhetorical sense of responsibility, since many youths and bachelors would have already attended bau a sponsored by neighboring communities). Younger, middle-aged men tended to share this sentiment, but voiced it in terms of community reputation: "Everyone else has held a bau a recently except us." This was also bound up with a desire to make a return for the mado that they had received in previous bau a. Old and middle-aged men might also voice concern that the young boys weren't growing properly or that the youths and bachelors seemed to be looking for trouble in their restiveness and interest in women. The young men (between eighteen and twenty-eight), for their part, were at a time in life when they were trying to make their way into the adult world and claiming a place for themselves in it. This they did in the traditionally assertive and dramatic manner, building a reputation for themselves as forceful personalities by taking prominent and dramatic part in fights and raids, participating as dancers in ceremonial performances (where they could display themselves before the admiring eyes of women), or, as the mature men not inaccurately perceived, restively getting into trouble. To a youth or young man, taking part in a bau a meant prestige, excitement, attention, and—particularly if he played a leading role in it—a marvelous opportunity for the limelight. All this plus the all-male company, the hunting life, and the manly ethos involved made the bau a enormously appealing. It was not infrequently a strong-minded bachelor who first offered to lead a bau a and so persuaded the community to sponsor one.

General social conditions in the area may also have been conducive to the sponsoring of a bau a. A feeling of boredom and low social energy, a malaise about things not going well, occasionally came over a community. This might go along with talk about recent sickness and anxiety over witchcraft or deaths in the area. Men might add the gloomy observation that their youngsters weren't growing well. A medium might pass on the news that he had recently seen the mɛmul having a bau a and that one or two of the recent deaths actually represented mado for that spiritual bau a—so perhaps it was time to have a bau a of their own. Finally, a young but strong-willed bachelor might be caught trying to seduce an unmarried girl. In order to prevent the community from getting involved in a dispute, his elders might try to hustle up a bau a to keep him out of further trouble.

THE PHASES OF THE BAU A

Preliminaries and Preparations

In what follows I describe the five major phases of the bau a and their concomitant activities.

The progress of a bau a is divided into five stages:

1. *Gɔmulɔ*: Following the decision to hold a bau a and the necessary preparations, the youths who are to be the *ayasilo*, or ritual officers, open the bau a with a ceremonial event called "gɔmulɔ." The bau a itself is then constructed and closed up, and the youths and boys move to a ceremonial sago camp to prepare sago and hunt for two or three months.

2. *Sibulu*: The membership invests the bau a after the period at the sago camp. Full membership is made up. Divinations are performed. Hunting takes place in the vicinity of the bau a, and then youths split up into hunting groups to cover more distant hunting grounds.

3. *Tiane*: The youths return to reinvest the bau a; further divinations are made before youths again split up.

4. *Sogonɔ*: Final investment of the bau a takes place, as does the announcement of who is to receive mado. Full-time hunting terminates, and a period of preparations for the final ceremony and for coming out of seclusion begins.

5. *Handalaki*: The coming-out-of-seclusion ceremony is held, and the stone bride is received from the mɛmul. Then the animals are cooked, and the ceremony of distribution is conducted.

When conditions are right in a community, one begins to hear discussion of a bau a. Preparations include the selection of ritual officers (ayasilo), assessment of food availability, and some instruction of the ayasilo concerning the proper way to proceed.

As mentioned earlier, there are usually a number of precipitating circumstances that lead a community to sponsor a bau a. In the case of Wɔgɔle bau a sponsored by the community of clan Bona, in about 1943, a certain amount of subtle pressure was brought to bear on the community from outside. Bona had received a substantial amount of mado from a bau a held at a place called Asibi, sponsored by clan Waliso and supported by two other communities. Four years later Bona's people began to hear rumors that the former leader of Asibi bau a was wondering aloud to his housemates whether he would ever get some return for the mado distributed at Asibi. About the same time, a spirit medium from clan Didesa (also participants in Asibi bau a) visited Bona and held a seance. A spirit came up and suggested that Bona hold a bau a. Nothing was done, however, until a senior man of the community had a dream in which he learned that the mɛmul were preparing to bring a (stone) bride. Thus assured that the bau a would be a success, the old man secretly started discussions among the men of the community about sponsoring a bau a, and he urged the oldest bachelor in the community to act as leader and organize it.

The bachelor designated to be leader gets together with the other young men of the community, and, in consultation with the older married men (who have been to a bau a themselves or have received mado from one), they decide which communities will be designated to receive mado from their bau a, who will serve as the other ritual officers (there are seven altogether), and when to hold the gɔmulɔ, or opening rite.

The time of the gɔmulɔ for a bau a is kept secret, but it is usually staged to coincide with the celebration of some other, larger social event, such as a wedding. That way there is a large gathering of people to whom the gɔmulɔ can serve as a dramatic surprise and also, implicitly, as a public announcement that a new bau a has gone in session. In the days preceding this event, the older men of the community, particularly those who have recently participated in a bau a, instruct the prospective leader in some of the fundamentals he needs to know about bau a procedure; but they reveal none of the esoterica.

In addition to the leader, there are six other ayasilo who act as ritual and practical officers under his direction. Of the total seven ayasilo, five are adult bachelors, and the remaining two are a youth of about sixteen and a boy of twelve or thirteen years. By the time everything is ready for the gɔmulɔ, all the adult bachelor ayasilo have been settled upon, either by invitation from the leader or by volunteering on their own initiative. The "child" ayasilo are not chosen until the night of the gɔmulɔ itself.

Gɔmulɔ: Going into Seclusion and the Building of the Bau a

The word *gɔmulɔ* means "to howl" (as a dog does) and refers to the strange howling call made by the youths in the forest after they have left the longhouse to commence the bau a.

A few days before the gɔmulɔ is to take place, the two leading ayasilo locate a good-sized (about twenty-five centimeters in diameter) *fɛfɔleg* tree near the spot where the bau a is to be constructed and clear the undergrowth around it. This tree will form the center post of the bau a. A hollow runs up through the heart of the trunk and is always crawling with ants (ants crawl up and down the bark outside as well). Kaluli chose the fɛfɔleg as the center post of the bau a partly in the magical belief that the bau a will attract animals as the fɛfɔleg attracts ants. (There may also be another deeper, though unacknowledged, meaning in that the image of ants crawling down the fɛfɔleg trunk is analogous to the image of animals coming down a "tree-trunk ladder" as gifts from the mɛmul, a notion that figures prominently in bau a hunting spells.)

The gɔmulɔ ceremony takes place a few days later. In the early hours of the morning, when the ceremonial social event that has been chosen as a starting point for gɔmulɔ is at its height, the adult bachelors of the community and the ayasilo drift one by one out of the longhouse and gather in the darkness of the nearby forest. (At Wɔgɔle bau a, thirteen young men participated—the seven ayasilo and six other bachelors in their twenties.) The group creeps up on the fɛfɔleg tree like

169

a war party. The sixteen-year-old ayasilo leaps out of the darkness and grabs the trunk, yelling, "I take it!" as though grabbing a victim to be murdered. The rest of the group bursts out with loud war yells; "Bruu! Bruu! Bruu!" These climax with a rousing intonation and unified shout (*ulab*; see Schieffelin 1976:134). The leader then fells the tree with his stone adz, and the group shoulders the trunk and carries it through the forest, intoning for the first time the bau a "howl." If during the taking of the fɛfɔleg an animal is discovered and killed, it is considered an especially good omen for the success of the bau a. From this point on, almost every activity in relation to the bau a is combined with hunting.

Arrived at the spot where the bau a is to be built, the young men wait until dawn, when the married men from the longhouse show up and begin to clear the area. It is the task of the married men to clear a plaza around the bau a and build the *nage a*, an auxiliary building used for cooking, socializing, and sheltering visiting guests. The bau a itself is built only by the bachelors.

After they have raised the fɛfɔleg, the bau a members (*bau a sinɔ*: "those who sat [or stayed] in the bau a") begin a ceremonialized search for other materials with which to construct the building. Filing through the forest, they self-consciously cover long distances through adjacent longhouse territories, gathering their materials and hunting as they go. Building the bau a takes about fifteen days. During this time the members return to the longhouse in the late evening to eat and spend the night. The ordinary bachelors may still appear before the eyes of women at this point (though such is minimized by the darkness), but the ayasilo must sleep out of sight in a special sleeping enclosure at the back of the longhouse. In the morning, the bau a members quietly awaken before dawn and, gathering briefly in the central hall of the longhouse, hold a sudden, fierce, shouting and stamping ulab, to shake the whole structure and startle everybody awake. They then set off for the forest and another day of hunting, gathering materials, and house building. During this period the three senior ayasilo (the leader, the second-in-command, and the sixteen-year-old youth) do virtually no hard work. They lead the processions to hunt for animals and building materials, but when the others are busy constructing the bau a, these three, especially the leader, are instructed in the esoteric lore and ritual procedure of the bau a by visitors who have recently attended a bau a themselves and in whom its memory is fresh. For Bona clan, these instructors were relatives who had attended Asibi bau a and wanted to ensure that this Bona bau a came up well.

The bau a, when completed, is an oval building about 9 meters long and 8 meters wide, with a small door at each end. The exterior walls are about 1.7 meters high and made of split slabs of wood driven into the ground and banded together with thick strands of cane. Inside, the walls are lined with woven sago leaf to keep any light from entering through the chinks.

The roof rises from the walls to a peak 3.5 meters or 4.5 meters above the base of the center post. The post protrudes through the roof peak and is topped with a Y-shaped decoration incorporating (like other important pieces of the lodge) magical substances to ensure good hunting and the growth of strength and endurance for the inmates. The nage a, a rectangular building about 9 meters long and 4.5 meters wide, is built by the married men about 6 meters from the bau a opposite the door at the back, or "child," end of the bau a. When it is completed and ready for use (at the time of the sibulu celebration), the interior of the bau a is dug out to a depth of 15 to 18 centimeters, except for a platform at the base of the center post where the leading ayasilo has his sleeping place. The rest of the members sleep in parallel rows on either side down the length of the lodge. Logs forming head- and footrests mark the sleeping areas. The bau a members sleep on a mattress of leaves and rubbish laid on the ground. Firewood is stacked behind the sleeping areas against the wall. Fire pits and pits for cooking stones are located in the central passage toward each end of the building. The dominant feature of the interior of the bau a is an enormous rack for smoking the accumulated game, which takes up practically the whole interior of the roof.

The general impression an outsider gets of the interior of the bau a is subterranean: low, dark, close, and smoky, the ground strewn with flea-infested rubbish, and everything blackened and begrimed with soot and grease from where people have wiped their hands on the walls after eating. Traditional Kaluli, however, would not regard these features as hardships.

The interior of the bau a is a true sacred space, and definite rules govern behavior there. Inside the lodge, the members must abandon frivolous socializing and strictly observe the rules of proper conduct. As one informant told me, "In the bau a nothing is done to no purpose. Everything is done properly and for a reason." Voices are kept low, and talking is restricted to the speaking of magical spells and hunting ritual, to planning for the next day's hunt, and to joking about women and sex. Any discussion about important matters pertaining to events in the surrounding longhouse communities which might inflame excitement or argument is strictly forbidden. Those who wish to talk about such issues retire to the nage a, which is available for mundane socializing. Once the formal hunting and cooking rituals have begun in the evening, no one can leave the bau a even to relieve himself. Bamboo tubes are passed through the walls so that inmates can urinate in the middle of the night without having to go outside.

The fɛfɔleg post in the middle of the central passage marks a major ritual division in the bau a between the bachelor's end and the child's end. Of the two ends, the bachelor's is the more sacred, masculine, and "strong" (*halaido*). No one involved in homosexual activity with the youngsters in the bau a may sit or sleep at the bachelor end, nor may he share food with those who did. All ritual, hunting magic, and divination are conducted at the bachelor's end, and the game intended for the smoking rack is also cooked there. No rituals are conducted from the child's end of the bau a, and the fire and stone pit there are used only for cooking meat to be eaten by the membership. The small door at the bachelor's end of the bau a is also a kind of threshold to the spirit world at night. The stone pit at that end of the bau a is actually built partly in the doorway so that the mɛmul can come invisibly and inspect the meat being cooked.

The door at the child end of the bau a is larger than the bachelor door, as it is used for bringing in firewood and for other practical domestic necessities. Except for ceremonial processional entrances, the bau a members always enter and leave the bau a by the door corresponding to the side where they sleep.

The Ayasilo, Ritual Officers of the Bau a

While all members of the bau a are set apart from the rest of Kaluli society during their seclusion, the ayasilo are themselves set apart to some degree from the rest of the membership (*kɛgɛl*). The ayasilo, but particularly their leader, are said to "own" the bau a. (One gets a sense that in some respects the kɛgɛl, other members, are their guests.) It is the ayasilo (again with precedence given the leader) who receive the lion's share of the reputation resulting from the bau a and whose own planned prestations of meat are hunted and secured first. Ayasilo do not engage in any homosexual activity, which, though growth inducing, is ultimately profane in Kaluli belief because it is sexual. In processions, the ayasilo always march in rank order. The existence of the ayasilo hierarchy in the bau a is rather a reversal of the usual egalitarian relationships in Kaluli society, prescribing, as it does, status and authority by virtue of (ritual) office rather than by virtue of personal character. This is the only example of formally ascribed social hierarchy in Kaluli society.

The hierarchy becomes visible whenever the bau a members advance in formal ceremonial procession from the forest to the bau a, filing in order of importance. At the front of the line are the sixteen-year-old youth and the leader of the bau a. These two roles are closely associated and must be analyzed together. The leader's title, "wɔfu tamin kalu," means "stone-adz front-of-the-line man" (hereafter referred to as "adz leader"). The title refers to the ceremonial stone adz he carries at all times as a badge of office and to the fact that he leads the bau a members in procession. He organizes the bau a, knows the esoteric lore (which others in the bau a don't know), conducts the magic spells and ritual procedures, and makes the major decisions about phases in the bau a. He also expels miscreants and troublemakers. He is both ritual leader and moral authority in the bau a and represents it to the mɛmul spirits and the outside world. In the final ceremony, he receives the mɛmul bride, and his name is the one most prominently remembered in association with a bau a.

The sixteen-year-old ayasilo (who actually takes the first place in the procession) is known as "bau a *bibihɛnɛnowɔ*." The term is composed of two elements: the name of a ground pigeon (*bibi*, or *Gallicolumba rufigula*; see Feld 1979) that is known for "making a trail" in the forest groundcover, and the verb "to go." We can refer to this youthful ayasilo as the "trailbreaker." His major ritual function is to break the trail through the forest by walking first in the file of bau a hunters. He accompanies the adz leader at all times, running minor errands for him and playing second to him in the performance of bau a hunting ritual. This youth also is considered to stand for the "return bride," which symbolizes a woman to be given in sister exchange to the mɛmul in return for their giving a mɛmul bride to the adz leader. (In social imagination, that makes him analogous to the adz leader's sister.) As such, and because he is yet a youngster, he has little practical authority in the bau a vis-à-vis older (but ritually lesser) ayasilo and even older bachelor kɛgɛl of his own community, although he has considerable ritual knowledge and status. He and the adz leader do no mundane chores around the bau a, cook no food, and carry no loads. Their privileges are countered by the responsibility they have to go hunting every single day, rain or shine, sick or well, with no respite while the bau a is in session.

The adz leader and the trailbreaker are so ritually special that they may not be seen or heard either by women or by men who are not members of the bau a (except on ceremonial occasions).

The next four ayasilo serve roughly parallel functions in their

173

respective ends of the bau a. The *seli tok asifɛnowɔ*, or "closer of the bachelor door," follows third in the bau a processions after the adz leader and acts as his assistant and second-in-command in many circumstances. He also plays an important role in rituals of return from the hunt, and he closes the bachelor door to the bau a every night after the dogs have been chased out, when all inside are ready to sleep.

The bachelor-door closer is followed by the *seli tok kolalifɛnowɔ*, or "opener of the bachelor door," also an ayasilo of a certain degree of disciplinary authority, but whose ritual role was restricted largely to opening the door at the bachelor end of the bau a every morning. The bachelor-door opener is followed by the ayasilo of the child end of the bau a, the "closer of the child door" and the "opener of the child door," whose ritual functions parallel those of the analogous officers in the bachelor end of the bau a. Finally, there is the twelve-year-old boy ayasilo, the *sewa us*, or "child between," who has a few ritual functions besides following last in line of the ayasilo, before the ordinary members.

The ayasilo maintain their special separate status also in relation to socializing with visitors. Though they may converse freely with other bau a members, they have a separate section of the nage a to themselves, where they sit apart from and partly out of sight of visitors and do not speak within their earshot.

The Sago Camp; Beginning the Hunting Period

When the bau a is completed the members close it up, leaving the thatch untrimmed and the interior bare, and return one last time to the longhouse for a night. The following morning the members set off for a distant sago area chosen the night before. The women wail as they go, for this is the last time they will see their sons around the longhouse for about fifteen months.

In the forest the youths discard their netted pubic sporrans and replace them with leaves picked along the way. They will not bathe again until just before the final ceremony.

At the sago area, the sixteen-year-old youth "captures" a sago tree of a ritually important variety by grabbing it in the same way he did the fɛfɔleg, and the leading ayasilo cuts it down with due solemnity, splits it open, and scrapes the pith. The trailbreaker, performing the female role, beats the sago and collects the starch. The work at the sago camp is intended to produce sago to be passed out at the final ceremony for garden magic and also the sago to be cooked with the game in the bau a. The sago processing takes a long time because as soon as the rough bau a sago-camp shelter is constructed, the youths spend most of their time hunting, far and wide, although they always return at night. Only a few people are left in the camp to work the sago and keep hungry dogs out of the game-smoking shelter.

During the time the bau a members live at the sago camp, the ayasilo, starting with the leader and proceeding one by one, perform divination to prove to all their virginity. The regular members of the bau a do not perform their divinations until they have entered the real bau a after the time at the sago camp is over.

During the first few days at the sago camp, the ayasilo and bachelors decide among themselves upon the particular people to whom they intend to give mado and how much they will give. In this complex calculation, made in consultation with the married men, they attempt to ensure that everyone who gave mado to someone presently in the bau a or to one of his relatives somehow gets a return. Fathers urged their sons in the bau a to repay the gifts of mado that they themselves received during former bau a. Bau a members may also have gifts of their own to repay, or they may wish to make an opening gift of mado to a favorite relative or friend who is not in the present bau a but may be in a future one. Once the number of people who will receive mado has been settled upon, the total amount of game required is calculated. Hunting is then undertaken to secure the meat prestations required one by one. The animals caught while the bau a members are at the sago camp are earmarked first for the ayasilo. Hunting expeditions go out knowing exactly how many animals they are aiming to get and for whom. After enough game has been accumulated to make up a unit of thirty-five animals for the adz leader, the next unit of equal size is hunted for the second-rank ayasilo, and so on down the line, in order of rank. Only after several of the ayasilo obligations are fulfilled can the other bachelors collect animals for their own prestations.

During the month or two the bau a members are at the sago camp, younger youths and boys of the sponsoring longhouse community come to join with them. These are youngsters who did not know about the impending bau a before the gɔmulɔ but who wish (or have been urged by their fathers) to join so that they will grow big and strong. At the Wɔgɔle sago cutting, six youths and boys ranging in age from ten to fifteen years old joined up, bringing the total number of bau a members to nineteen. These newcomers were all at the age when they were ready to receive insemination from adult men, but no homosexual intercourse took place in the sago camp because everyone was from the same community and incest taboos obtained.

After enough sago has been accumulated to supply the bau a for a while, and after one standard prestation unit of game has been accumulated for each ayasilo—that is, after a period of two or three months—the bau a members are ready for the ceremonial entrance to the bau a itself. The adz leader then instructs the married men of the sponsoring community to prepare for the ceremony to celebrate the ''trimming of the thatch.''

The Sibulu Celebration; Formal Investment of the Bau a

The sibulu (trimming of the thatch) is the celebration of the formal occupation of the bau a by the membership. It is celebrated by an all-night gisaro ceremony (Schieffelin 1976) at the sponsoring longhouse and is attended by all those who lend support to the bau a or expect to receive mado from it. In the afternoon before the ceremony, the married men come to watch the procession of the bau a membership into the bau a lodge for the formal investiture. The interior of the lodge has been dug out and prepared for habitation and the thatch trimmed in preparation the previous day. The visiting married men are usually milling about in the cleared yard in front of the bau a when the membership approaches in single file through the forest. Four members burst out from the forest margin, spinning around and around and whirling tiny bull-roarers. They chase the visiting married men, who feign great fear, off the bau a plaza into the forest on either side. Then the procession of the membership files out of the forest laden with bags of smoked game from the sago camp and led by the trailbreaker, who carries a bag of sago. After a preliminary ritual, the membership descends through the bachelor's door into the lodge to deposit their bags of animals at the center post. The married men draw close again to make this ritual remark: ''They go down into the vagina in order to come out the anus.'' While the members sit quietly inside the bau a for a while, the older men peek in the door and say, ''Hey, they're screwing! I see them screwing in there!'' They rustle the thatch and rattle sticks against the walls to see if they can make the members laugh or otherwise break the demeanor of ritual sobriety and distance appropriate to sitting within the lodge. To the satisfaction of all, however, the bau a members never laugh. Presently they file out of the child door into the nage a to eat a meal prepared by the married men.

In the evening, while married men are occupied with the gisaro ceremony in the longhouse, the bau a inmates play a practical joke on the youngsters who joined the membership at the sago camp. Earlier, during the hunting rituals, the bachelors had told them a bandicoot would be cooked for each of them that night to determine if they had been having sexual relations with women (a ridiculous allegation for youths and boys under sixteen). The bachelors clandestinely remove the heart and liver of each bandicoot before cooking it and then replace it afterward so that it appears the bandicoots have come up raw inside—proof of forbidden sexual activity. "Hey!" yell the bachelors angrily. "These are raw! You have been screwing around! What is this? Out! Out! You can't stay here in the bau a. Go home!" If the boys protest, the bachelors yell, "You mean to tell us that tiny thing went up a woman? Terrible! Out! Out!" They raise enough rumpus to frighten the boys thoroughly. Some of them cry and attempt to run away before it is all revealed as a joke. Each further juncture between phases of the bau a is marked by some such practical joke on the youngsters.

The next morning all the youths, boys, and bachelors from other longhouses wanting to join the bau a appear at the nage a hut to be admitted. At the Wɔgɔle bau a about seventeen showed up, eleven of whom were adult bachelors, and six youths and boys (aged about eleven to nineteen). This addition brought the membership of the bau a up to thirty-six. (Of these, four were later expelled for disputing, another was dismissed for having had intercourse with a woman, and one little boy left because his father did not supply him with enough food.)

At this time also, those who have come specifically for the purpose of acting as homosexual inseminators for the growing youngsters announce themselves. At Wɔgɔle there were three such men. The adz leader assigns one or more individual boys to each of these men. Some of the other bachelors eventually get involved in homosexual intercourse with the boys, but without announcing themselves beforehand. Out of fourteen youths and boys at Wɔgɔle bau a, two were regarded as too small to be ready for homosexual activity, and two considered themselves too big and resisted it. Of the remaining nine, four were sexually assigned by the ayasilo to one or another of the self-announced bachelor inseminators, and five presumably had intercourse clandestinely with others.

Homosexuality and Hunting

Homosexual activity, while contributing to the general social atmosphere and configuration of growth enhancement in the bau a, seems to be considered a secular activity. Certainly there is no ritualization about the act itself. It is carried out clandestinely either in the dark of the bau a while, it is hoped, everyone is asleep, or else a bachelor takes a youngster off into the forest with him to "help cut firewood" or "draw water" or on some other pretext.

Opinions differ on the subject, but one former ayasilo told me that homosexual activity is not necessary to the bau a and that without it the bau a would not be adversely affected or necessarily come up badly. Indeed, homosexual activity seems to have a certain aura of the profane or impure about it. The ayasilo do not participate in homosexual activity, nor do they share food with anyone who has. Those involved in homosexual activity sleep in the child end of the bau a and (except for ceremonial occasions) come and go through the child door.

The cultural relationship of sexuality to hunting ability is important here and cuts deeply into Kaluli belief. Kaluli believe that virgin youths and young men are the most effective hunters; indeed, this is one stated reason why virginity is required for admission to a bau a.

This bau a requirement exists partly because Kaluli believe that women have a debilitating influence on men. A man who has too much to do with women is likely to lose his stamina, become fatigued on the trail. The reason most frequently given for why virgin young men hunt well, however, is that "the animals appear before them." This does not occur simply because the youth may have sharper eyes. The animals are always there in the undergrowth or the forest canopy, but they "come out to" or "manifest themselves to" a virgin youth more readily than to other men.

The theme is explicated in a well-known myth about "the mother of the animals." The man Dɔsali (the mythical exemplar of strong but balanced Kaluli manhood) went hunting on the slopes of Mount Bosavi. Late in the evening, he reached the top and found a house inhabited by an old woman. She offered him shelter, and he accepted, behaving modestly, like a perfect guest. After dark, he saw a strange sight: the woman called as though calling her pigs, and lo! the animals of the forest came into the house to stay the night. The next day the old woman filled several net bags with game and gave them to Dɔsali to take home. At home, Dɔsali met his cross-cousin Newelesu, a clownish figure who is always getting into trouble because he cannot control his appetites. Newelesu asked where he got so much game. Dɔsali told him, and Newelesu headed off for the hut of the mother of the animals. There he behaved with greedy bad manners, and in the night when the animals were gathered, he forced the old woman to have intercourse with him. On seeing this, all the animals fled the house (followed by the old woman) and went to live south of the mountain around the headwaters of the Turama River. Newelesu returned home empty-handed. Kaluli consider this myth to account for why there is much more game south of the mountain than in the area where they live. For our purposes, the pertinent point is that animals are not afraid of the hunter before he has sexual intercourse—but they flee, disappear from him, after he copulates with the old woman.

We have here, then, a mythical theme reminiscent of the "loss of innocence" familiar in the biblical story of the Fall. (An even better parallel is provided by the story of Enkidu in the epic of Gilgamesh. Enkidu, created by the gods to oppose Gilgamesh, lived among the animals as one of them until he was seduced by a prostitute. On seeing this, the animals deserted him, and he was forced to join human society.)

The point is that the heterosexually innocent male is somehow more attuned to the domain of the animals than are other men. For Kaluli this is less a question of moral than of social innocence: it requires, not an innocence of knowledge, but an innocence of social entanglement. Sexual intercourse with a woman automatically involves a socially unencumbered person with central social issues of marriage, alliance, dispute, and exchange; and as it draws him more deeply into these human entanglements, it simultaneously destroys his rapport with the animal world. The same is not true for homosexual behavior: heterosexual intercourse has primarily human social consequences, but homosexual intercourse is thought to have primarily "physiological" consequences (for instance, growth). The social bonds it implies are ephemeral, and it does not significantly affect one's ability to hunt. Nevertheless, pederasty is a sexual activity, occupying an intermediate position between forbidden heterosexuality and the more ideal celibacy of the ayasilo. Consequently, it is regarded as a profane activity and relegated to the child end of the bau a, away from the major focus of ritual relations to the mɛmul.

Hunting

For the week or two after the sibulu celebration, the ayasilo and bau a membership sleep in the bau a lodge and hunt in the local area. They hunt without the use of bows or traps, assisted only by a pack of dogs. (Each youth or bachelor brings one or two dogs to the bau a. A conservative estimate would put fifty or sixty dogs at Wɔgɔle.) To hunt, the bau a membership spreads out and makes a series of sweeps over a chosen system of ridges and creeks. One's hunting ability depends on having sharp eyes and quick reflexes to enable him to spot game in the undergrowth and fall upon it before it can escape. Animals that break and run are brought down by the dogs. Those that go underground are dug out. All game caught during the period of divinations goes to the ayasilo for their accumulations.

During the first week or so in the bau a, divinations are performed in the evenings by the adz leader for members of the bau a to prove that they are chaste. First, chastity is sworn over a bandicoot, which is then cooked. If it comes up raw after cooking, the man is considered a liar and is expelled from the bau a.

Once cleared by divination, regular bachelors hunt for their own prestations, organizing expeditions to Mount Bosavi or to the area south of the mountain where game is particularly abundant. Older youths join to help, since there is more meat to eat on these expeditions than back at the bau a. After several weeks of these expeditions, when all those making prestations have enough to make one, the adz leader announces it is time to "split the bau a." At Wɔgɔle, three groups of members moved out of the "mother" bau a, leaving only the five major ayasilo and a few others behind. Each group established a "side" bau a on the lands of adjacent longhouse communities under the leadership of a regular bachelor who was not engaged in pederasty, in order to widen the hunting range. Each leader took an adz and acted in the capacity of a minor adz leader, performing the same hunting rituals as in the mother bau a. While the bau a members are engaged in hunting full time, they are supplied with vegetable food and sago by their relatives in nearby communities.

The Tiane Celebration, Mid-course in the Hunting Period

The tiane (or gone-down) celebration marks the mid-course of the bau a seclusion period and celebrates the return of the members from the side bau a back to the mother lodge, where they store their accumulations of smoked game. Another round of divinations follows to ensure that everyone has kept away from women. The timing of the tiane is usually determined by the amount of game accumulated, but there may be additional circumstances involved. At Wɔgɔle, for example, when it was nearing time for the tiane, there was an exceptionally violent tropical storm that hurled branches out of the trees, tore a great boulder out of bank of the Walu River, and rolled it about half a mile downstream. The bau a members feared it was mɛmul come to attack, as in the myth, and huddled in their shelters, spitting magic bark to keep them away. Within a few days, the trailbreaker ayasilo dreamed he had encountered an angry mɛmul, who shouted at him, "You shouldn't do that! You aren't supposed to do that!" He told his dream to the adz leader, who immediately suspected that someone had been fooling with women. He called in the membership for the tiane and performed the divinations. Sure enough, one man's bandicoot turned up raw, and he was expelled.

After the tiane divination is completed, the bau a membership disperses once more to the small bau a lodges to hunt as before.

The Ambiguity of Spirit Relations

The constant hunting, rituals, and seclusion make the bau a very much a world unto itself, a world rooted in its privileged relationship with the invisible mɛmul spirits. Kaluli have little in the way of a systematic explication of the place of the bau a in relation to the spirits, but much of what my informants could tell me about the significance of bau a rituals and magic spells revealed how they perceived this relationship.

If hunting is the major activity of the bau a which is relevant to its placement in the wider social order (through prestations), the winning of the mɛmul bride is the major activity in relation to the cosmological order (that is, the relations between this world and the spirit world). The bride is expected to appear in the form of a stone during a dramatic night ceremony at a waterfall just before the bau a members come out of seclusion. Her arrival signals the final approval of the mɛmul. If she does not come, the mado will be spoiled in cooking and the bau a will fail, resulting in social embarrassment for its sponsors and members.

All through the period of seclusion, preservation of the right relationship with the mɛmul is of continuing concern, especially for the senior ayasilo. Thus the adz leader enforces proper decorum in the bau a; expels those who fight among themselves; and holds divinations to check that the members are keeping away from women.

Rites directed specifically at obtaining the bride begin while the bau a is under construction and the adz leader is receiving advice and instruction from knowledgeable bau a graduates. Shortly before the gɔmulɔ at Wɔgɔle, a spirit medium told the prospective adz leader that in a trance he had seen that the bride would be presented at a particular waterfall on the Tako Creek.

Shortly after the construction of the bau a had begun, the adz leader and bachelor-door closer went clandestinely to the Tako, supposedly to hunt but in reality to throw a chip from the bau a fɛfɔleg into the waterfall pool. Later a piece of the leaf bole from the ritually cut sago was also thrown in. My informants explained that these were like spirit bride-wealth, used "to make the bride come," the chip representing an ax to the bride's father, the sago bark a pearl shell to the mother.

The ayasilo—principally the adz leader and the trailbreaker—also received encouragement in special dreams during the period of seclusion. The former trailbreaker of Wɔgɔle told me that typically he would dream of visiting a mɛmul house on Mount Bosavi, where he would be shown a young woman and told that she was the forthcoming bride. In the morning he would confidentially communicate this favorable omen to the adz leader. These dreams maintained a continuing sense of close contact with the mɛmul, but they were usually kept secret from ordinary members—and even from some of the lesser ayasilo (as were also parts of the hunting rituals in which everyone daily participated).

The regular members, however, also had their part to play in the mɛmul marriage drama which was kept secret from the adz leader. At Wɔgɔle, while the membership was split among the small side bau a, knowledgeable relatives told some members that the bride, although usually taken at the waterfall, might not wait for the wedding but might elope and try to join the adz leader before the appointed time if the bau a was an especially good one. Therefore they should be on the lookout for a stone that moved. Shortly afterward, two bachelors returning from a hunting trip were scouting an area near a waterfall of a small creek. "We heard a loud 'plop!'" one of them later recalled to me, "as though a frog had just jumped down the waterfall. We looked and saw a stone moving along the bottom of the water. We grabbed it and took it back to our side bau a, thinking to use it in our cooking rituals. But when we showed it to Sialo [the son of the sister of the medium mentioned before], he said, 'This looks like the stone bride. My uncle said it could come this way. Put it in a tree stump, and if fireflies gather there in the evening we will know it is for the adz leader.' So we put it in a stump, and in the evening, sure enough, fireflies gathered.'' They saved the stone and hid it for the final ceremony, telling only a few bachelors and senior men of the longhouse, but not the adz leader.

Although Kaluli maintain that the stone bride nearly always appears in the waterfall at the final ceremony and that its discovery in the forest beforehand is unusual, my inquiries reveal that such is not the case. Most brides are taken by the regular members in the manner described—but few informants seem aware of it.

In addition to making efforts to maintain a harmonious relationship with the mɛmul in order to solicit the stone bride, the bau a members daily engaged in a paradoxically opposite activity—namely, the attempt to kill them.

In the evening, when the ayasilo and whatever other members are present are assembled to cook the animals caught during the day, they pronounce the major hunting spell for the next day. It runs like this:

Engiruwɔ Muliyɛ
Kekedowɔ Eningayɛ
Yodabeyɔ Wowe
Show hot, don't show cold
That in the morning I will meet animals.
Put them down before me
Put them down before the dogs
Put them down at Sandamɔ*
Put them down at Sisande*
Put them down in plain sight.

So saying, they chew a magical bark and spit it around the bau a to chase the mɛmul away.

The spell requests that game be made available to the hunters and names the area where the bau a members plan to hunt on the following day. The key to the spell, however, rests, not with the request, but with the three pairs of names that are invoked at the opening. These are names of mɛmul, husband-and-wife pairs, who are, as one informant put it, "mothers of the animals" (*nɔ ano*) who ripen the game so that it may be taken by the hunters. Sometimes an informant would say that when the hunters were on Mount Bosavi, the mɛmul would look down and, feeling sorry for them, lower net bags full of animals to them. Then the bau a hunters would catch abundant game in one area. On another level, however, these "mothers of the animals" have a more sinister aspect. They represent witches among the mɛmul people, and the animals they "ripen" are their own fellows whose bodies then fall as game to the hunters. A Kaluli medium vividly revealed how the process works in his

*Place names.

account of a hunt held by mɛmul at one of their spirit bau a. The game here, of course, are Kaluli people. In his trance journey he was accompanying some mɛmul hunters when they came upon a Kaluli woman of his acquaintance in the forest. The hunters killed her, and as they cut her up, her arms became bandicoots (*mahi*), her legs became tree kangaroos (*dunubɛ*), her head became an echidna (*sogobei*) and so on, which they stuffed as game into a net bag.

Witches (whether spirit or human) traditionally are believed to operate by dismembering the invisible aspects of their victims' bodies and taking the pieces away. The real contents of the "net bags of animals" which the mɛmul witches lower down to the hunters of the bau a are, then, the dismembered bodies of mɛmul in the visible form of animals. (This is to be distinguished from their "wild pig" manifestations, which are killed by Kaluli under other circumstances).

This bau a hunting spell is not used on Mount Bosavi lest the mɛmul who live there become infuriated and attack the hunters (or the spirit witches who helped them). It is spoken only in the bau a itself.

These activities of the bau a reveal that the members live in a paradoxical and ambivalent relation to the mɛmul. On the one hand they make every effort, by preserving ritual purity and decorum, to ensure the favor of these spirits so that they will receive the stone bride. At the same time, though, they are repeating spells every night to ensure that mɛmul die and fall to them as game in their hunts. This apparent contradiction was neither explicated by my informants nor regarded as particularly significant. Indeed, both sides of the contradiction contribute substantially to the success of the bau a. We will return to this puzzling relationship in the concluding section.

**The Sogono Celebration; the End of the
Hunting Period**

During the three or four months following the tiane celebration, the final counts of animals for the prestation are collected. Those members who have too many animals give some to others who need more—especially to the ayasilo, who, ritually constrained to sleep in the bau a every night, cannot make the trips to hunt the best grounds and so usually do not find enough to make all the prestations they have planned.

There follows the sogono celebration, which marks the end of the period of full-time hunting. The sogono is similar in many ways to the sibulu and tiane celebrations. The bau a members carry back their bundles of smoked game from the side bau a and chase the married men out of the clearing of the mother bau a with bull-roarers. In the afternoon the names of the people who are to receive bau a mado are announced, and the bau a members are permitted for the first time to smoke tobacco openly in the sight of men from the surrounding longhouse communities.

In the evening, the older bachelors play a prank on the youngsters. When the hunting magic is spoken and the animals are enclosed in the cooking packet to steam, the trailbreaker ayasilo creeps under a sheet of bark and snuffs out the torch that supplies the light. As the bau a is plunged into darkness, the bachelors suddenly scoop up ashes from the fire pits and fling them into the faces of the boys, yelling words of growth magic as if they were war cries.

The boys, coughing and sneezing, their mouths and eyes stinging from the ashes, frightened and confused by the hullaballoo, try to flee the bau a, but the married men waiting outside grab them and throw them back in. After they are sufficiently terrified, the trailbreaker emerges with a lit torch from under his bark sheet and the prank ends. Amid the smoke and settling ashes, he is the only person who looks normal; everyone else is covered white with ashes and "looks like a witch." The bachelors comfort the frightened boys and give them all the animals in the cooking packet to eat that night. Later that night, ordinary members are permitted to attend the longhouse ceremony celebrating the sogono, as long as they stay outside on the back veranda out of the sight of women.

The Final Ceremonies

The three months following the sogono are given over to preparations for the final celebration of the coming out of seclusion.

The members gather and stack an immense pile of firewood, cut sago and *wayo* palms to incubate grubs (for women and children who cannot receive mado), aid their relatives in catching crayfish and trapping and smoking animals, and make expeditions to the lower slopes of Mount Bosavi to gather gigantic cooking leaves. In spare moments they prepare new clothing and decorations. Five days before the final ceremony, the ayasilo lead the membership to a nearby stream and, with much exuberant whooping and hollering, bring over a hundred of the largest stones they can carry (some of them weighing 22.5 to 34 kilograms) back to the bau a.

At dawn of the day after they have collected the stones, the bau a members go hunting. While they are separated in the forest, the adz leader and the trailbreaker clandestinely go to the waterfall where the stone bride is designated to appear. For Wɔgɔle this was a lovely spot not far from the bau a. A small creek fell 4.5 meters over two cascades into an oval pool about 9 by 12 meters enclosed in cliffs and steep, forested banks, the stream flowing out through a narrow opening at the lower end. There the two ayasilo braced a tree trunk upright on the bottom of the pool, in the spray of the falls. Then they cleaned all the stones from the bottom of the pool and went back to the hunt. Everyone returned from the hunt in the late afternoon and immediately entered the bau a to perform the ritual cleaning and cooking of the game for the smoking rack. This time, however, the adz leader opened the cooking packet before it was done. "Look at this!" he said. "The meat is raw! We cooked this to divine for a witch. It's old Bɔbane [a man known not to be a witch]! Come on, we're going to get him!" With that he got up and led the membership determinedly out into the forest as if they really were going to kill someone. Arrived at a cleared area on a ridge near the pool, they all sat down to wait. Not everyone among the membership knew what was happening, and they were left to figure it out for themselves.

Everyone sat in silence while the dusk deepened and evening fell. They awaited the appearance of a small fruit bat that represents the presence of the mɛmul and indicates that the bride has arrived. When the bat was seen (or thought to be seen) to fly by in the darkness, the bau a members all rose and crept toward the pool. The mood was somewhat tense and mysterious.

My favorite informant recalled, "As we approached the place of the waterfall, lo! we saw there were many, many fireflies moving over the surface of the water pool. I said to myself, 'That doesn't happen every day!' " In this strange atmosphere the bau a members quietly took up positions around the pool under the direction of the ayasilo so as not to disturb the fireflies. The adz leader and the bachelor-end ayasilo stood above the waterfall, while the child-end ayasilo and the members sat in two rows blocking the exit channel of the stream at the lower end of the pool.

The mɛmul bride is believed to have come down the stream during the day, and to be resting at the foot of the tree trunk on the bottom of the pool. The members block the exit and sit ready to catch her if she tries to escape. At the signal, the trailbreaker leaps down the tree trunk, stopping halfway on a ledge. The adz leader follows immediately, passing to the bottom and grabs at the foot of the trunk for the stone. He shouts, "I take [her]!" Immediately everyone yells, "Buwɔɔɔ !"(the sound of warriors breaking from ambush), shattering the tension, and all plunge splashing into the pool.

Of course, at Wɔgɔle, there was no stone bride at the bottom of the pool, but amidst the splashing and confusion in the darkness, the shouts of "She's gotten away!" "She's over here!" "I've got her!" and "There she goes again!" (shouted by those members who had picked up and hidden the stone some months before), it was not at all clear that many people, even the adz leader, really knew this. As the excitement died down, the married men who had accompanied the expedition to watch lit torches at the sidelines. The members caught crayfish and put them in a sago bag intended for the stone bride and then marched triumphantly back to the bau a singing and calling out in celebration of the waterfall, the splashing, the capture, and the stone bride—while the women at the longhouse over the ridge answered their shouts with distant female calls. During the trip back, the actual stone bride was quietly slipped into the sago bag by the regular members who had found it. Amid the excitement, few people were aware that it was not actually taken in the waterfall.

Back at the bau a, the clearing is alive with torches and bonfires. The married men assemble to view the stone bride and congratulate the bau a members. The adz leader and the rest of the ayasilo may now speak freely with them for the first time since seclusion.

The stone bride is then hung in her sago bag on the fɛfɔleg post. Water brought back from the pool is splashed over those bau a members who had not gone to the pool (to make their skins beautiful), and the rest is saved for the final cooking.

During the time the bau a members are off at the pool, the married men and the few members of the bau a who remain behind are busy preparing a huge log-crib fire from the firewood that had been previously set aside and from the materials of the nage a, which they dismantle and burn as well. Others go inside the bau a and begin digging out a great pit, 3.5 meters wide and at least 2 to 2.5 meters deep, at the child end. This work continues until late at night by the light of torches and bonfires. All night long the bau a members bring down, sort, and wash the game from the smoking rack.

In the early dawn hours the bachelors load the boulders they have collected onto the fire crib. When all is ready, a little after dawn, the bau a members thrust burning brands into the crib. In a short time the fire is roaring to treetop height, at which point it becomes visible to the women at the longhouse. Unseasoned cooking boulders explode with great bangs, and the bau a members leap around in tremendous excitement, yelling magic spells to celebrate the fire and to make it burn still higher. Finally, when the stones are red-hot, someone pulls a crucial prop out from in front of the crib, and it collapses forward, spilling the smoking boulders across the bau a clearing. (At Wɔgɔle, it was considered a particularly good omen that one of the two largest boulders rolled directly into the bau a.) Yelling war cries, the bau a youths and bachelors rush to carry the red-hot stones by hand (protected only by a single cooking leaf) and dump them into the stone pit in the bau a. (An ordinary man would burn the skin off his hands, I was told, but these men were ''hardened'' by the bau a and so went unharmed.) When the pit is filled with hot stones, married men are chased out, and the bachelors prepare the cooking packet. Big leaves are laid over the stones, and the game is piled in a great heap on top. The whole is wet down with water and sealed with a further cover of large leaves. The stone bride is taken from her sago bag and placed beside the packet to ensure that the mado will be properly cooked. The packet is closed to cook all afternoon and all night while the bau a members keep a vigil. Anyone who begins to fall asleep is slapped in the face with stinging nettles to keep him awake. As the packet cooks down it settles; the settling is said to be caused by the feet of the mɛmul, who tread upon it as they make the customary public statement of marriage duties (*ga man salab*)—normally delivered by in-laws—which every groom must endure on his wedding day. The little boys are warned that they must remain awake, or the mɛmul will also tread on them and stunt their growth.

Very early the next morning, the bau a members troop down to the stream and wash thoroughly, oil themselves with animal fat, and put on the coming-out finery they have prepared. Back at the bau a, they seal the entrances and open the cooking packet, enveloping themselves in clouds of steam. They work in this atmosphere for several hours, piling the soft, cooked animals onto bark trays for presentation, and in the process, I was told, their skin is transformed to become beautifully smooth, light colored, and handsome.

When all is ready, the bau a members make a tremendous noise inside the bau a, banging on the walls and shouting at the top of their lungs. The sound notifies the people who have been gathering at the longhouse that the time of the distribution is at hand. At Wɔgɔle, people from at least sixteen communities, men and women and children, gathered in the clearing in front of the bau a—it must have been an impressive crowd of about 700 people. This is the only time that women and children see the bau a lodge, and it is the first time in about fifteen months that they see their sons and brothers who are members.

When everyone has arrived at the clearing, the bau a members, still sealed inside the bau a, let out another celebratory shout, banging on the walls of the bau a and vigorously bouncing a big spray of red cordyline that has been stuck through the peak of the roof, where it can be manipulated from inside.

The door of the bau a then opens, and the trailbreaker emerges, holding a cassowary-bone knife on the top of his head. He trots around the bau a once and disappears inside again. This ritual action is repeated three times by the rest of the ayasilo, who come out two by two holding strips of magically prepared sago on the tops of their heads. Then the full membership files out, each carrying a tray of mado covered with grass to hide its contents from the women.

They line up across the front of the bau a and shout the names of the men for whom it is intended, who then come forward to receive it. The distribution continues all morning, community by community, as bau a members return again and again into the bau a for more mado.

In the afternoon, the bau a members, dressed in their fullest finery, parade back to the longhouse, where they are greeted tumultuously. They attend a ceremony staged in the evening and gorge themselves on grubs and crayfish that have been presented to them and to the members of the sponsoring community as return gifts for the mado received (see fig. 4.1).

The bau a is formally closed down a few days later, after everyone has returned home from the distribution. The ayasilo from the sponsoring community (ayasilo from other communities already have returned to their homes) go back to the abandoned bau a and there cook and eat a yɛsi (sugar glider). After finishing, they close up the bau a and leave it for good. The structure is left to decay, visited only by some of the dogs who started their hunting careers there as pups—and who return, as one of my informants said, to howl for their former home.

Afterward

The social reverberations of the bau a, once its members have come out of seclusion, and if there are no immediate disputes or fights, wind down fairly quickly.

In the days or weeks following the coming-out-of-seclusion ceremony, the bau a bachelors and some of the older youths get together and visit the various surrounding longhouse communities, displaying themselves in their ceremonial finery before the young women and pros-

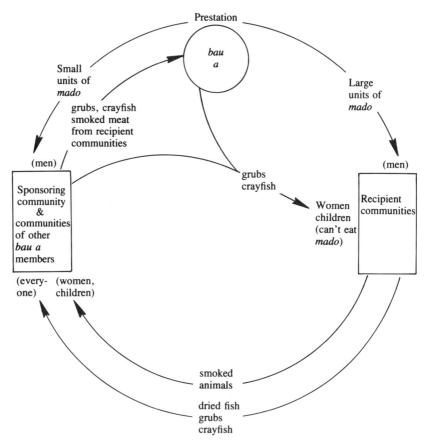

FIGURE 4.1   Scheme of prestations and countergifts at the Bau a final distributions

pective in-laws. As a result, some are offered wives. So many bachelors seem to get married within a short time after a bau a that a bau a is conventionally thought of as being followed in about half a year by a pork presentation, in which newly married bau a graduates make their first prestations to their affines.

In the meantime, without the social focus provided by the bau a, the frequency of visitation among longhouse communities falls off, people's interests turn in other directions, and disputes are allowed a fuller range of expression.

Aside from a certain renown, no special status or membership in a special group accrues to former members of the bau a. Once the stone bride is taken and placed by the cooking packet, her function is fulfilled.

The adz leader remains the custodian of the stone after the bau a and hides it somewhere near the longhouse, where it is preserved as a valued object, but it does not confer upon him any enduring ritual status or relation with the spirit world, and it is never used for any further purpose.

The mado prestations at the bau a, although they are made between friends and relatives and may coincide with particular strategic social purposes, do not by themselves create formal relationships or initiate a series of exchanges between donor and recipient—except insofar as they may stimulate the holding of another bau a.

When the excitement of the final ceremony has finally faded, then, the bau a has produced no enduring changes in the social order, and, except for vivid memories and the force of personal friendships formed within it, no enduring changes in the lives of the participants beyond expectation of mado some time in the future. Despite its many resemblances to an initiation program, the bau a cannot be said to be one.

THE BAU A IN COSMOLOGICAL PERSPECTIVE

How, then, shall we understand the significance of the bau a? In the world of everyday Kaluli understandings, people normally assume a rough division of the world into three domains: the domain of human sociality, the domain of the animals in the forest, and the invisible domain of the spirits. Now, the bau a is situated at precisely the juncture of these three domains. The young men move into the forest, where they live unwashed and nearly naked "like wild pigs" in close association with the spirits. The bau a does not represent a simple mediation of these three domains of Kaluli experience, however.

In everyday circumstances, Kaluli are most aware of and familiar with the ane mama spirits. These are spirits of the locality, and many are familiar characters, because they speak frequently through spirit mediums. They manifest themselves daily in the visible world through the songs of birds. The mɛmul spirits, on the other hand, live far way on Mount Bosavi. They are remote and peripheral to everyday awareness.

In the bau a this situation is reversed. The mɛmul spirits become the center of awareness and concern, and the ane mama are not mentioned at all. This not only amounts to the concentration of the bau a members on a neglected class of spirits, it also involves such a thoroughgoing inversion of human perspective on the spirit world, and of relations with it, that the bau a members could almost be said to be dealing with an alternative spirit place.

In everyday life, there is no communication with the ane mama spirits until a man (or, rather, his soul) passes on to the invisible side of reality and marries a spirit woman. Subsequently, he becomes a medium and acts as a channel of communication with the ane mama.

In the bau a, communication with the mɛmul also involves a spirit marriage, but the purpose of the bau a is to *bring about* the marriage, and it is the bau a *context* that makes possible communication with the mɛmul. The marriage is made, not by having a human soul move to the invisible, but by having a spirit woman move into the visible side (as a stone). Once this is established, however, communication with the mɛmul spirits ceases, and the bau a comes to an end. Thus, communication with the mɛmul spirits through the bau a is an inversion of the normal manner of relationship between human and spirit realms.

In day-to-day life, relations with the ane mama spirits are maintained primarily for the purpose of curing the sick. Humans ask the ane mama to gather up the scattered parts of the sick man (invisibly dismembered by a witch) and put them back together to heal him.

In the bau a, relations with the mɛmul spirits involve causing their deaths. Humans invoke mɛmul witches to dismember mɛmul invisibly so that their body parts may become game for the hunters.

The result of these transformations is to situate the bau a members in a relation to the spirits which is quite different from that which people inhabit in everyday life. In daily life, relations with the ane mama are principally harmonious and affectionate. In the bau a, relations with the mɛmul are intrinsically ambiguous.

Moreover, this ambiguity is not situated in the context of ordinary Kaluli understandings about relations to the spirit world but is embedded in the special perspective that obtains only in the bau a. The conflicting terms in which this ambivalence is focused in the bau a are, of course, the desire for marriage and the causing of death. Preoccupation with marriage and death, however, is hardly restricted to the bau a; it is a preoccupation that runs through all levels of everyday Kaluli social concern. Marriage and death are ordered as contrasting terms with the same scenario of social reciprocity. Prestation (consequent upon marriage) and retaliation (consequent upon death) are but two alternative modalities of the underlying social process of reciprocity that structures much of Kaluli social life. While these modalities are important in any case, they are particularly poignant to a young man who, unmarried and with limited connections, is trying to make his way into the adult world of more established married people. Here it is a matter of becoming known, or being taken seriously, through the assertion of personal dynamism and the appeal of engaging personality and appearance. And this effort, insofar as it may lead young men to seduce or elope with young women, to lend a too vigorous and violent support to disputes that elder married men may wish to contain and control, or to look for trouble and excitement on their own, is a potentially disruptive force in Kaluli society. For youths and bachelors, on the other hand, their situation is potentially frustrating. These youths are structurally positioned—as they are in many societies—in such a way that their aims, efforts, and energies to make their way come across as disruptive to the already established members of the society. As I have pointed out earlier, the elder members of Kaluli society seem to be well aware of this dilemma. The bau a takes up and reorders this dilemma. The two fundamentally problematic kinds of activities of the young men, namely violence and involvement with women, are strictly forbidden as the basic ritual conditions for bau a membership; but they immediately reappear in more acceptable forms in the relation to the mɛmul, that is, through the hunt and the seeking of the stone bride. The potential problems, frustrations, and ambivalences of the young men's situations on the everyday social plane are thus transformed and recast in the relation between the bau a members and the mɛmul. The mɛmul spirits stand in much the same relation to the members that married adults do to youths and bachelors in day-to-day life: they are benefactors, yet authorities; they have what the young men aspire to (women, marriage, and manly recognition), but also control and withhold it. Thus, on the surface, the bau a provides a social space where problems implicit in the young men's ordinary relations to their elders may be projected and played out in their relations to the mɛmul. Beyond merely channeling the young men's disruptive energies safely into the spirit world, though, the bau a raises the ambiguity of their situation into conscious recognition and presents it for reflection every time they observe ceremonial decorum and speak their hunting spells. In so doing it reveals a profound insight to them, as well as to their elders, who observe the bau a proceedings appreciatively. In the bau a the ambiguity concerning the youths' and young men's societal situation is not mediated or resolved. On the contrary, it is revealed as basic to the significance and operation of the bau a even as it is intrinsic, on reflection, to Kaluli life itself.

Indeed, it is precisely by embracing the contradiction between the desire for marriage and the causing of death that the members of the bau a are able to achieve success. Their success in turn reveals that the ''disruptive'' energy of young men is also profoundly creative and productive. At the same time, the possibility of living productively within ambiguity and contradiction is demonstrated, with the bau a as an exemplary model.

In revealing the creative side of the young men's energy, the bau a transforms and reorders it into an integrative force in Kaluli society, one that focuses social attention and motivates cooperative activity and suspension of local hostilities. For the young men, the bau a removes them from the margins of social attention and thrusts them to its center: they emerge from seclusion in their best and most appealing cultural image.

All this underlies why Kaluli men found the bau a experience to be exciting, productive, and rewarding. Amid their reminiscences of hunting and a vigorous manly life, their glee at mystifying the women, their embarrassed humor about homosexual activity, their impressive talk about taboo and secrecy, and their potentially dangerous (hence rather thrilling) relations to the mɛmul spirits, one senses a feeling that the bau a realized, for them, something deeply important about what they believed themselves and their world to be. It stood for and revealed to them the best strengths of their lives: its manliness, drama, generosity, and goodwill, expressed in marriage and in ceremonial gifts of meat.

THE BAU A AND INITIATION

The questions before us are these: If the bau a isn't an initiation program, then why isn't it? How does it differ from initiation? And how does it contribute to our understanding of the ritual process? It should be clear that the bau a is not to be differentiated from initiation on the basis of contents of the rituals. Indeed, here they exhibit so many common elements (in the period of seclusion, the rituals of male growth and identity enhancement, and the transmission of cultural lore) that one might legitimately wonder whether it is really worth distinguishing them.[2] The important differences are to be found on formal grounds: in

---

[2]Basically the issue here is whether one would include the bau a in a broader "genus" of initiation on the basis of its socialization and cultural transmission functions. To do so, however, opens the door to calling any kind of ritualized transmission of cultural knowledge "initiation" without regard for whether it also represents a process of recognized social *transition* from one group or status to another within the society. We then run the risk of destroying the analytic value of initiation as a sociological concept. On the other hand, remaining with a characterization of initiation based on the transition structure of the rite (following Van Gennep 1909, Turner 1969, and Keesing, this volume) enables comparison with other types of ritual strategy—which is the subject of this section.

differences in the structure and strategy of the ritual processes themselves, and in the type of social outcome in which they eventuate.

For our purposes there are three defining characteristics of the ritual process of initiation which are relevant here. The first is that of formal status change. From the time of Van Gennep (1909), anthropologists have understood initiation as a *rite de passage* that is aimed at separating a youth or youngster (both socially and psychologically) from his former childhood status and admitting him (sometimes by graded steps) into a new social status or stage in the life cycle. As I have noted, the absence of much status advancement is one of the conspicuous points at which the bau a differs from initiation.[3]

A second striking difference between initiation and the bau a is in the ritual posture the novices must take in relation to the rest of society. In initiation, novices are made to adopt a dependent and submissive posture toward those representatives of society who sponsor or initiate them. The message underlying initiation, as Turner (1969) has pointed out, is that the initiates become social adults, not by their own efforts, but, rather, because society makes them so. In contrast, the bau a members display no such submissive attitude; they assert a posture something like "separate but equal" or "equal but special" in relation to the rest of Kaluli society during the period of seclusion. Once the basic lore and ritual procedure have been taught to the ayasilo in the first days or weeks of the bau a, they run the bau a themselves without significant outside direction. Married men and all those not of the membership are barred from the bau a and on important ritual occasions are chased temporarily out of the bau a clearing.

This curious inversion of the posture we normally associate with initiation is connected with the third and most important difference between the bau a and initiation: the relationship each establishes between the novices (or members) and the rest of society. This point is made clear in the symbolism of the closing events of the ritual process. During the closing events in initiation, when the initiates are returned to society, there is a public display of the marks of their new status,

---

[3]The status of a bau a member after coming out of seclusion may be compared with that of an ordinary American citizen after being discharged from the armed services. Both the bau a graduate and the ex-serviceman have been through an extended period of separation from the mainstream of society. Both have been living in a disciplined all-male community with a strictly enforced order of its own. Both receive special training, some of which is relevant to ordinary life, and both share the experience with comrades. On coming out of seclusion, however, neither receives any special social status for having been in the service (or bau a) for which the service was intended to prepare him.

indicating openly that they are reincorporated in the society in a new structural position. With the bau a, the members also return to society, but there are no marks of new status. Indeed, the significance of the closing events (a spirit marriage followed by a worldly prestation) is puzzling. Normally in Kaluli society the marriage of a man to a spirit woman inaugurates the career of a medium and opens a new avenue to the invisible. The adz leader, though, does not become a medium, and his relationship to the spirit world *ends* when he receives the stone bride. Moreover, the final prestation is not presented by the elders or sponsors of the bau a in celebration of the membership coming out of seclusion, as normally happens in initiation. It is made by the members themselves, from the fruits of fifteen months of their own hunting efforts. It is as if, instead of acknowledging dependence on society and submitting to the bestowal of its marks of status, the bau a members force the surrounding communities to take account of them by placing them all in their debt through gifts of mado. In this respect, the bau a rather inverts the initiation process.

Now, however, if we treat the spirit marriage and mado prestation as a single ritual sequence, something interesting emerges. Kaluli marriages are normally followed by prestations, since a new husband is supposed to make gifts of pigs or smoked game to his in-laws. From this fact, it is possible to construct the underlying cultural logic that the bau a seems to be working out.

We have already shown that there is within the liminal world of the bau a an ambiguity implicit in the relationship between its members and the mɛmul spirits and, further, that this situation is analogous to the ambiguity of the situation of youths and bachelors vis-à-vis their established elders in everyday life. When the adz leader receives the stone bride, the ambiguous relation toward the mɛmul is resolved (even as it would be toward one's elders if one were to marry in real life). But, as the tension of the ambiguity evaporates, so does the relation that was formed within it between the bau a members and the spirit world. The resolution of the spirit relationship is then immediately (but symbolically) transformed into an assertion of human relationship when the bau a members make (what corresponds to) their first marriage prestation to the human analogues of their spirit in-laws and resume normal relations with society.

In other words, a spirit marriage becomes transmuted into a human relationship at the moment the bau a members emerge from their seclusion. The acceptance of the membership by the mɛmul spirits (via the marriage) is transformed into acceptance by society as the members of the surrounding communities accept the prestation.

Now, no Kaluli informant explained things to me in this way; this interpretation is the product of symbolic analysis. Nevertheless, without further elaboration it seems plain enough that the bau a strives to establish a relation between the youths and the elder members of Kaluli society on the model of *alliance*. The underlying logic of the bau a implies the assertion from the beginning that the older youths and bachelors, at least, intend to be considered on equal footing with the rest of adult society. Rather than submitting to socially formative ordeals they attempt to wrest recognition from society by placing themselves, implicitly and symbolically, in the position of marriage allies through the making of the grand prestation. The success of the effort rests upon the success of their relations with the mɛmul spirits, who are the original givers of the moral order and of the ways of marriage and prestation.

This acceptance of the youths as symbolic allies is clearly a very different sort of relationship from that of being incorporated into the society as an adult through initiation. To my knowledge, it is unique among ceremonial means by which youths and bachelors gain acceptance from adults short of marriage itself.

The contrast between the outcomes of initiation and the bau a strikingly illustrates the different structural consequences of alternative ritual procedures. Both modes represent attempts to enhance maleness and to gain youths and young men acceptance as adults, but they resolve the situation in different social ways and through different symbolic models. Through initiation, a society bestows novices with the signs of new status, incorporating them clearly and explicitly within its established structural order. In the bau a, on the other hand, the youths bestow a prestation upon society—whose acceptance of them on adult terms (that is, based on the model of allies) is implied in adult acceptance of their prestation. Acceptance as an ally is quite a different matter, structurally, than being incorporated into the membership of a group, for an ally always tacitly remains an outsider. To complicate matters further, for the members of the bau a, the structural significance of their acceptance remains implicit: the implied structural relations are never explicitly spelled out. Indeed, that the youths and bachelors are striving to establish a symbolic alliance with society is by no means clear to the Kaluli themselves. This opaqueness results primarily because the idea is hidden in various symbolic transformations between spirit bride and real prestations which made up the coming-out-of-seclusion ceremonies. But if the "alliance" is largely out of Kaluli awareness, it remains as a kind of massive implication lodged within the multiple analogies laid down in the symbolic process.

To reiterate, the bau a did not accomplish any formal social result; the youths and bachelors did not become "allies of society" in the sense that initiates become social adults. Rather, in the bau a, the youths *represent* themselves as allies—but only implicitly; the relationship is modeled rather than established. It contains the implications, not the substance, of alliance. In the Kaluli the force of that (alliance) model did not lie (as it might for us) in the possibility of their explicating or revealing it as a social commentary on their situation. Rather, its force lay in the implicit obligation for return laid down by the prestation in which the "alliance" was created.

When they left the bau a the youths and bachelors reentered the world of ambiguous relations with their elders; but the alliance they asserted and the renown they had attained reduced that ambiguity for a while through the sense, if not the substance, of the alliance relations implied.

In contrast to the stability of relations established by New Guinea initiation, what the bau a established was always veiled and attenuated with time. If the assertion of the alliance relation was only implicit, though, the prestation in which it was embodied was real and ensured that it would be answered, reasserted, and perpetuated, for the prestation produced a general obligation for its recipients to make a return, which could be done only by holding another bau a. Thus, though it is not mandated by the structural requirements of Kaluli society, the bau a was perpetuated by the repetitions of exchange.

Looking at the bau a, then, as a kind of exchange, we can close this section with a speculation about its symbolic implications on a higher structural level which follow upon that exchange. The mɛmul marriage and (human) prestation followed by another mɛmul marriage and (human) prestation look rather like a kind of spiritual marriage exchange (although, again, Kaluli do not say so). If implicit in the logic of the situation, the relationship so depicted between the bau a and the surrounding communities (by way of the mɛmul spirits) models, through a glass darkly, a sister exchange, the strongest relationship of social alliance possible in Kaluli society. The bau a therefore reaches beyond the significance of relationships between youths and adults to represent—but not formally create—potential alliance relations among the communities that sponsored and received meat from it.

198

THE DEMISE OF THE BAU A

Despite its dramatic appeal and positive ritual and social character, and despite the great nostalgic and affectionate regard in which it was held by men, the bau a was a fragile institution. With virtually no enduring roots in the structural arrangements of the society (such as initiation into an age grade or politically important cult groups, or the gaining of politically important ritual knowledge), there was no strong societally generated motivation for the bau a.

It depended for continuance not on imperatives derived from social structure but on the establishment of community consensus about a number of disparate motivating circumstances and enabling conditions, including pressure from others for reciprocation of previous bau a. Equally important, the existence of the bau a depended on a delicate balance of mutual understandings and agreements among the various communities about maintaining its ritual inviolability and providing social support.

When this balance was disturbed, the bau a collapsed.

In 1958, the Australian colonial administration began conducting a series of regular patrols to the Bosavi area once every two years, with the aim of solidly establishing administrative influence in the region.

When fighting and cannibalism had been suppressed, the Unevangelised Fields Mission moved in. In 1964 two European missionaries arrived in the Bosavi area with a party of workmen to build an airstrip and mission station. At this time two Kaluli communities were sponsoring bau a, and their youths were in seclusion hunting. Believing that the missionaries were another government patrol, the Kaluli found themselves in a vulnerable position. Since the bau a was a secret, quasi-sacred institution, for a ''government patrol'' to walk in on it would be a disastrous violation of its inherent nature. For instance, had the members been called for census or to work on the airstrip, they would have been exposed to the eyes of women, thus spoiling the bau a. There was additional fear that the ''government'' might disapprove of the bau a, as it had of fighting and cannibalism, and jail the people associated with it. Worst of all, they feared that carriers and police would appropriate for themselves the growing pile of smoked meat in the bau a itself. (Similar liberties had been taken by government carriers who had stolen from gardens and clandestinely killed and cooked local pigs during earlier government patrols.)

The Kaluli hurriedly terminated the bau a and distributed the meat.

The youths, now out of seclusion, went to work on the airstrip. In this way, the Kaluli themselves quietly discontinued their most dramatic ritual institution. The event marked an acknowledgment that their political autonomy was gone. With the building of the airstrip came the permanent presence of outsiders in their country, which meant that the delicate balance of internal forces upon which the bau a depended would no longer exist. Another bau a will never be built in Bosavi.

REFERENCES

ERNST, T.
N.d. Stealing another man's wife among the Onabasulu of the Great Papuan Plateau.
FELD, S.
1979 Sound and sentiment: birds, weeping, poetics, and song in Bosavi expression. Ph.D. dissertation, Indiana University.
KELLY, R. C.
1976 Witchcraft and sexual relations: an exploration in the social and semantic implications of the structure of belief. In *Man and Woman in the New Guinea Highlands*, ed. P. Brown and G. Buchbinder, pp. 36−53. Washington, D.C.: American Anthropological Association.
1977 *Etoro Social Structure: A Study in Structural Contradiction*. Ann Arbor: University of Michigan Press.
SCHIEFFELIN, E. L.
1975 Felling the trees on top of the crop. *Oceania* 46 (2):25−39.
1976 *The Sorrow of the Lonely and the Burning of the Dancers*. New York: St. Martin's Press.
TURNER, V. W.
1969 *The Ritual Process: Structure and Anti-structure*. Chicago: Aldine Publishing Co.
VAN GENNEP, A.
1909 *Les Rites de Passage*. Paris: Émile Nourry.

5 OPPOSITION AND COMPLEMENTARITY OF THE SEXES IN NDUMBA INITIATION

Terence E. Hays and Patricia H. Hays

The Authors

Terence E. Hays is Associate Professor of Anthropology at Rhode Island College. He was born in Iowa in 1942 and educated there. Dr. Hays began university work in sociology and later conducted postgraduate training in anthropology at the University of Colorado, where he earned an M.A. In 1969 he went to the University of Washington and began focused research on ethnosemantics and New Guinea studies with J. B. Watson, K. E. Read, and John Atkins. Between 1971 and 1972, Dr. Hays conducted intensive fieldwork on individual variation in plant and animal knowledge among the Ndumba, a Tairora-speaking community of the Eastern Highlands, Papua New Guinea. He received his Ph.D. in 1974 for the first detailed analysis of a New Guinea people's ethnobotany. He has taught at Rhode Island College since 1973.

Professor Hays has published several articles in *American Ethnologist*, *Ethnology*, and elsewhere, and he is the author of *Anthropology in the New Guinea Highlands* (1976), which has become a standard reference work in the field. His teaching and research interests include cultural anthropology, cultural ecology, language and culture, and medical anthropology. He is currently engaged in a comparative study of oral literature in the New Guinea Highlands.

Patricia H. Hays is Instructor of Anthropology at Rhode Island College. She was born in San Francisco in 1945 and received her undergraduate education in history at the University of North Carolina, Greensboro. Her graduate training in anthropology began at the University of Colorado, where she received an M.A. and conducted field research on folk medicine among the Hispanic population of Denver. Working as a research assistant to Robert Hackenberg on

201

the Pima-Papago population study, she developed a strong interest in the demographic analysis of social structure. With Terence E. Hays, she conducted field research in 1971 and 1972 among the Ndumba. She is currently completing her doctoral dissertation, a demographic analysis of Ndumba genealogies. Patricia Hays has taught anthropology in Colorado and Washington and currently lectures on general anthropology, social change, and computer applications in social science research.

INTRODUCTION

The people we refer to as Ndumba form a community of about 360 Tairora speakers, living in a cluster of six hamlets on the northern slopes of Mount Piora in the extreme southeastern corner of the Eastern Highlands Province. Despite some influences from the Sambia and the Baruya Anga (cf. Herdt, this volume, chap. 2) to the south and from the lower-elevation Waffa speakers to the east, Ndumba possess many sociocultural traits that have come to be recognized as characteristic of a general Highlands configuration. Among these are primary dependence on sweet potato cultivation, pig husbandry and pork prestations (but not large-scale pig exchanges), patrilineal-descent ideology, nonhereditary big-man political leadership, endemic warfare, and male domination of public affairs.

Doubtless related to this last trait is the widely reported Highlands cultural theme of sexual opposition, which is rooted in beliefs about contrasting male and female natures or essences. Manifestations of this theme, as in a social emphasis on physical separation of the sexes, are ubiquitous in Ndumba, and some of the clearest and most dramatic expressions of it may be seen in the ceremonies described in this chapter. The *'ummanra* ceremony, a mandatory initiation rite held for boys aged ten to twelve, is permeated with both implicit and explicit expressions of opposition between the sexes. Our first task here, following a general characterization of Ndumba male-female relations and their underlying rationales, is to describe this ceremony in some detail. We then offer a partial analysis, emphasizing those ways in which the theme of sexual opposition is encoded in and transmitted through structure and content of the ceremony.

We shall then shift our focus to a description and partial analysis of the *kwaasi* ceremony among women, which is held at a girl's first menstruation. The introduction of this material into an examination of male initiation advances the discussion in two ways. First, it reveals that the theme of sexual opposition is prominent in *both* ceremonies and, accordingly, may be seen as an aspect of the wider "Ndumba culture," rather than simpy a preoccupation of males. Second, in the *kwaasi* ceremony we see a second theme—that of *complementarity* of the sexes—clearly emerge, in contrast with the *'ummanra* rite, in which it is present but understated. By thus expanding the ethnographic context in which we analyze a male initiation ceremony, we are led to the conclusion that Ndumba consider men and women to be opposed by their very natures, yet interdependent. This viewpoint, in turn, makes more understandable the character and perpetuation of Ndumba social relations between the sexes, which are clearly defined, yet replete with undertones of ambivalence.

Stated another way, the juxtaposition of the two ceremonies enables us to understand what the men are "saying" in the *'ummanra* rite as part of a "male-female conversation and not a male monologue" (Lindenbaum 1979). To do this requires that we turn our ears not only to the songs, stories, and speeches in the men's house but to those outside of it as well.

NDUMBA MALE-FEMALE RELATIONS

In Ndumba many women are assertive, undoubtedly exercise influence over particular men, and occupy some prestigious positions, for example, as curers. Men, however, dominate public life: it is they who orate, settle disputes, plan and wage both war and peace, organize and run public ceremonies, arrange marriages and economic exchanges, and kill women with material weapons. While individual women may verbally and physically attack individual men, or even kill them indirectly through the ethereal weapon of their very natures, the social role of women is to listen, watch, and participate in public events as they are directed to do so.

In addition to their distinctive dress, a division of labor based almost entirely on age and sex, and the allocation of primary responsibility to men for certain crops (bananas, sugarcane, taro, and yams), social distinctions between the sexes are ubiquitous and reinforced by a minimization of physical contact. It is important to note, however, that it is not simply males and females who are kept apart. Rather, the concern is with separating initiated males (those who have gone through the '*ummanra* ceremony, and thus all males over the age of about twelve) from other people, including young boys.

One of the major ways in which Ndumba reduce physical contact is through residential segregation. In 1971–1972, forty-eight of the ninety-two (52 percent) initiated males currently residing in Ndumba lived in traditional men's houses.[1] These structures, encircled by six- to eight-foot-high palisades, function as residences, gathering places, and ceremonial centers, with entry strictly forbidden to all females and young boys. Most of the remaining initiated males lived in small houses of two to five men each, while only five (three adults and two of their sons) lived in houses containing women and children during the field-work period. Even in those cases, partitions separated the sleeping quarters of the two sexes.

Women live in small houses with their children or in households composed of various combinations of consanguine or affinally related kinswomen. Within women's houses, initiated male visitors (including husbands) are segregated, sitting and placing their belongings on a "male" side of a pole placed horizontally across the earth floor. Only for the purpose of sexual intercourse would a man cross this divider, and such a choice for a liaison would be uncommon, since most sexual intercourse occurs in the forest.

A counterpart to the men's house is the women's seclusion house. Each hamlet possesses one or two such houses, located well outside of the hamlet fence, where women are required to reside temporarily during menstruation, childbirth, and the early postpartum period. These houses, in contrast to others, are built and dismantled only by women, strictly avoided by initiated males, and generally shunned by boys past the age of three. Besides allowing seclusion, the houses serve as refuges and gathering places for women, sites for various women's ceremonies, and "day-care centers" for infants and small children.[2]

On public occasions, initiated males generally sit apart from

[1]The field research reported here was generously supported by a Pre-Doctoral Fellowship (Terence E. Hays) and a Pre-Doctoral Traineeship (Patricia H. Hays), both awarded by the National Institutes of Health. We are grateful to that body and to James B. Watson and Robert A. Hackenberg for their help in obtaining this support. We are especially indebted to Gilbert Herdt, Lewis Langness, Shirley Lindenbaum, Fitz Poole, Michelle Rosaldo, Edward Schieffelin, Alice Schlegel, Donald Tuzin, Roy Wagner, and James Watson for their insightful and extremely helpful suggestions on earlier versions of this chapter.

[2]The communal houses are of recent origin, having replaced individual seclusion houses since first European contact in the 1950s.

women and children, and men and women form separate dance groups during ceremonies. While women cook food (except meat) for men, crops harvested from certain areas may be eaten only by females or uninitiated males. A special network of paths is also reserved for women who may unexpectedly discover that they are menstruating or beginning the labor of childbirth. Women are thus assured of passage to their seclusion houses without having to walk on the trails used by initiated males.

Numerous other avoidances could be mentioned—for instance, the handling or use of implements and belongings of the opposite sex is minimized, and great care is taken never to step over their bodies or possessions. Sexual activity poses the greatest avoidance problems, and informants' statements as well as genealogies indicate that Ndumba must and generally do follow various sexual prohibitions. (These will be discussed more fully below.)

The Ndumba concern with limiting physical contact may be understood in terms of a principle of "contagion" or "pollution." While informants seldom articulated these notions in great detail, we believe that the emphasis on sexual segregation and much of the ceremonies to be described are best understood and explained by imputing such a principle to both men and women.

In the expressed view of both sexes, the sexual division of labor is consistent with differences in men's and women's natures. Men and women are seen as having different, and largely complementary, mental and physical capabilities. In other respects, the natures of the sexes are in opposition, and their juxtaposition carries dangers, at least for males. Physical contact poses the greatest dangers, especially when the contact is intimate and involves that part of the body, namely, the genitals, most closely associated with menstruation and childbirth. Some researchers (such as Faithorn 1975, Meigs 1978) have recently argued that the mystical dangers men present to women in other Eastern Highland societies have been underestimated and underreported. Among Ndumba, at least, men can pose pollution or contagion threats to women only under special circumstances, and not by their very natures.[3] The

---

[3]For example, men may inadvertently become vectors of a powerful mystical substance thought to be deadly to women. This substance is acquired through direct contact with a particular tree fern that grows on the subalpine grassland summit of Mount Piora, an area from which women are absolutely excluded. Should a man accidentally touch this plant, he must thoroughly cleanse himself before returning to the company of women and children. This is one of several such dangers faced by women which derives from the high forest, rather than from male "essence," since the men are only vicarious agents of the plant's contaminating power.

cultural themes expressed in the ceremonies discussed below are to be understood as rooted in a concern, shared by both Ndumba men and women, with the dangers *to men* which are posed by women's natures, especially as manifested in menstrual blood.

Ndumba men report (and women concur) that frequent or prolonged contact with women can make men's bones dissolve, their breath grow short, and, generally, lead to debilitation and even death. Ndumba cite many examples, especially in the context of the ceremonies described below, of people's carelessness in these matters and its terrible consequences. Contact with menstrual blood is particularly dangerous, as instanced by a man or initiated youth approaching a seclusion house, a menstruating woman, or her personal effects. A sleeping mat, clothing, or—literally—the ground on which a menstruating woman walks may contain drops of this fluid and thus must be avoided.

A woman may also be suspected of having premeditatedly murdered a man by having placed menstrual blood in his food or by having given him food that came from a contaminated area. Such possibilities result in severe restrictions on the kinds of foods an initiated male should accept and on the range of women from whom he should accept it. Not only should he distrust food offered by women other than his mother, sisters (real or classificatory), or a wife of long standing, but he should avoid food offered by uninitiated children, who, simply because of their ignorance, may have obtained it from inappropriate places or people. For example, food that has been handled by a menstruating woman, has been in or near a seclusion house, or comes from a garden made near (but never on) the site of a former seclusion house, may not be eaten by an initiated male. Even the crops that grow in garden areas where women walk may become contaminated by their long skirts, which may brush against growing plants and thereby transmit a woman's "essence" into the underground tubers or roots.

Coresidence is to be avoided because of the dangers posed by women themselves and by those things that they frequently handle. Likewise, the men's house must be secure from intrusions by women or by boys, who lack the knowledge necessary to counteract the effects of their continual association with women.

Sexual intercourse is at once the most dangerous and the most inevitable form of physical contact between the sexes. For this and other reasons, Ndumba attitudes toward it could be characterized as ambivalent. If sexual norms are followed (and the birth spacing of children—on the average, three years—as well as other information, suggests that they probably are), sexual contact can at least be kept to a low frequency. Premarital intercourse is never approved, and we know of no instances of unmarried men engaging in sex. In six cases of premarital sex on the part of women over a period of fifteen months, all involved married men.

Sexual activity is not an immediate consequence of marriage. Wedding rites are brief, and they are preceded, sometimes by months or years, by a *nraase* ceremony for the bride (discussed below) and immediately followed by a day of seclusion of the groom in the men's house. On both occasions, married women and men, respectively, provide instruction in the mechanics of sexual intercourse, tell stories about the dangers of sexual intimacy, and subject the novices to physical ordeals. These events collectively convey the impression, repeatedly expressed by married informants, that sexual intercourse is at once painful, pleasant, and dangerous to men. Following instruction, the groom is expected to spend several months hunting and trapping in the high forest for game to be given later to his wife's kin, after which he prepares new gardens for his bride. Only after one garden has been harvested (this may occur as long as a year after the wedding) – a period during which the groom's mother closely observes the behavior of her son's wife, who has moved in with her or with one of her adult daughters—is sexual consummation of the marriage considered appropriate. Some couples reportedly waited for as long as four years for their first act of intercourse.

Several acts of coitus, each of which must be followed by a man's ritualized cleansing, are believed necessary for conception to occur. When pregnancy is discovered, a prohibition on further sexual activity begins for the women and lasts until the subsequent child has been weaned, which may be as long as two or three years. In addition to these prohibitions, for a man intercourse is absolutely forbidden with a menstruating woman or in connection with various other activities—for instance, prior to battles and hunting trips. Moreover, it is not uncommon for women, after giving birth to several children, to prevent additional pregnancies by denying their husbands further sexual access to themselves. Pregnancy and childbirth are viewed by women as painful, restricting, and generally negative. Significantly, while both verbal arguments and physical fights between husbands and wives were commonplace during our fieldwork, the fighting virtually never overtly concerned denied sexual rights, nor were charges or disputes regarding adultery or fornication common.

Ndumba ambivalence toward sex, we believe, is deeply rooted in the perceived dangers, yet undeniable attractions, of intimate contact with women. The dangers and fears derive from the postulated contrast between the natures or essences of the two sexes and, in turn, lead to an emphasis on separation and a view of the sexes as being opposited or in a state of antagonism.

NDUMBA AGE CATEGORIES

For both sexes the development of gender identity is a gradual process (cf. Herdt, this volume, and Poole, this volume, chap. 3), punctuated by parallel but largely unsynchronized category transitions.[4] Sex distinctions are noted from birth but not routinely encoded linguistically until the age of three or so, when the child is fully weaned and shows decreasing dependence on its mother. In referring to such children, the term *nraa'inra* ("baby"; cf. *'ora nraa'inra* and *nraase nraa'inra* for male and female children, respectively, when precision is needed) is gradually replaced with *nraammwa* ("boy") or *'iaatara* ("girl"). At about the age of five, both boys and girls have their nasal septa and, sometimes, ears pierced with a cassowary bone; this is a casual rite performed by the mother in the house she shares with the child. Later those holes will accommodate various ornaments for both sexes, including pig tusks for boys when they reach late adolescence.

The freedom allowed in early childhood is eventually modified along lines based on sex. Boys form play groups of age-mates and wander at will through hamlets and gardens but are confined to the lower fringes of the forest (as are all females of any age) and forbidden entry into the men's house compound. Girls are increasingly given garden tasks to perform and responsibility for the care of younger children.

A girl's life proceeds in this way until she becomes a kwaasi at menarche, usually around the age of seventeen to nineteen. A boy, by contrast, is eligible to be initiated as an 'ummanra when he is ten to twelve years old. Both of these transitions are marked by major ceremonies, after which both sexes begin periods of extensive instruction and preparation for adult roles.

Full adult status does not come until marriage, which is preceded by another ceremonially marked transition. When a sufficient number of males (usually between five and twelve) have reached the age of sixteen to twenty, the *'ia'vaati* ceremony is held in a men's house. Following

---

[4]This account of the life cycle supersedes and differs in some details from that given in Hays (1974:81−91).

this event, a man is eligible for marriage (although this usually will not occur for some years) and for full participation in adult male activities, including warfare. A woman becomes marriageable after passing from kwaasi to nraase status at the age of twenty-one to twenty-five. The nraase ceremony, held in a women's seclusion house, involves primarily instruction about sexual matters and male-female interpersonal relations. In recent years there has been a tendency to incorporate the nraase ceremony and weddings into the final day of the 'ummanra rite.

While a number of de facto distinctions exist among newly married individuals, those with children, and senior adults, the only remaining transition to a named social category comes when one is too infirm, through disabilities or advanced age, to attend to one's own needs. A man then becomes a *naambai* and a woman a *sona*. Little is expected from them, and their welfare is a variable function of the attention of others.

Each age category has many behavioral expectations, violations of which evoke referential demotions in discussion by others; thus, for instance, a kwaasi might be referred to as a 'iaatara, or an 'ummanra as a nraammwa, as a means of public shaming. While all of these categories merit further attention, the nraammwa-'ummanra and 'iaatara-kwaasi transitions may be seen as pivotal. Boys leave their mothers' houses and enter, for life, the restricted company of males. To do so they must receive the knowledge that will protect them from the dangers of the women's world they leave behind. This, we contend, is a primary function of the 'ummanra ceremony and the extended period leading to the 'ia'vaati status. Girls reaching menarche are now in possession of a power they must learn to control, and the relevant instruction is, we suggest, a central concern of the kwaasi ceremony. Only after the kwaasi "novitiate" and the more narrowly focused learning contained in the nraase ceremony is a young woman ready for the intimate contact with a man following marriage. Having passed through a comparable learning period as an 'ummanra, and also having undergone the more specialized 'ia'vaati and bridegroom instruction, her husband will be prepared for her.

THE 'UMMANRA CEREMONY

During our fieldwork, two 'ummanra ceremonies were held, approximately one year apart. This double opportunity for firsthand observation was especially fortunate since, rather than being calendrically based, the decision to stage the three-day event depends not only on the availability of eligible nraammwa but on the mobilization of the entire community and the coordination of complex social and economic interests (see Gewertz, this volume, chap. 7, for a discussion of such factors in Chambri initiation).

According to our own observations and informants' recollections, the novices may number from one to eighteen, with five or six being usual. They represent a mixture of patriclan and hamlet affiliations, although it is common for the majority of boys to be from a single hamlet. The activities, however, center on one men's house. (Sometimes, in the past, boys from nearby "enemy" hamlet clusters would be initiated together with Ndumba boys, but we lack clear information about that.) Men of all Ndumba hamlets and clans take part, and the structure of role allocations is not simply a function of kinship, residence, or any other single social relationship. One firm rule, however, is that a boy may not be sponsored by a member of his own patriclan. The stated ideal is that the sponsor be the boy's mother's brother, but this is not always feasible, such as, for instance, when the mother is from a distant group currently accorded "enemy" status.[5]

The First Day

Early in the morning an earth oven is prepared in the hamlet that will be the focal point of the ceremony. As women prepare food and the men decorate themselves in their respective men's house compounds, the mothers and close matrilateral kinswomen of the novices decorate the boys outside of their houses. After applying a coating of pig grease to the boy's whole body, the mother clothes him in a new sporran and bark cape; in addition, a new (empty) arrow bag is looped over his neck to hang down his back. After a vertical smear of grey mud is rubbed on his bare chest, he is fed ginger root and *do'a* leaves (*Cyanotis* sp.) by a senior woman of his clan "to give him strength."

By midmorning the earth oven has been opened and the food distributed to all but the novices. Later, at the sound of a horn (made of bamboo and hollowed-out cucumber), groups of men begin arriving from various hamlets. They approach shouting, chanting, beating

---

[5]Hamlet clusters do not permanently become enemies or allies, but alternate from one to the other as periods of warfare are interrupted by truces, which may result in shifting alliances or simply an absence of fighting for the time being.

drums, waving their plume headdresses, twanging bows, and thumping battle shields, as other men burst out of the nearby men's house compound, greeting them in a similar manner.

Women join in the excitement, some of them twanging bows and clutching arrows as well as being elaborately decorated with ferns, leaves, and flowers. As groups dance in circles—and eventually nearly the whole of the Ndumba population gathers—it is hardly noticed that some men have surrounded the novices, leading them out through the hamlet fence and up the hillside toward the forest above. Discovering this, the women turn their attention to the procession, which now includes scores of men completely surrounding the boys. The women, especially the boys' mothers, shout in apparent surprise and threaten the men with their bows and sticks as they try to reach through to their sons. This threat occasions derisive laughter and resistance from the men, and the procession continues.

The mothers follow the men up the path, shooting arrows at the ground beneath them, until they are stopped near the forest edge by a human barrier of older initiated boys. A few older women advance to join the mothers, while younger women and children belatedly set out from the lower hamlet. The first to ascend are married women with children, who form small groups of two to five, singing and beating drums as they take up scattered positions on the hillside. Finally, a large group of young married and unmarried women arrive, intermingled with children of both sexes.

Having paused at the edge of the forest, the procession of men and novices now disappears into the trees, while the women and children remain behind, watched over by a man dressed in women's garments who ensures that none of them intrudes upon the secrecy of the forest activities. For the next hour or so, groups of women sporadically sing and dance while others watch or crouch in the grass, alert for the first signs of the procession's return. Hidden in this way, they evoke an image of enemy raiders awaiting an opportune moment to strike.

As the procession enters the forest, its mass narrows to accommodate the path. The boys are hoisted onto the backs of their sponsors and carried the rest of the way. Suddenly, there is an attack by men who have secreted themselves in trees, behind boulders, and on the ridge slopes. Amid bow twanging, shouting, and chanting, the line of men with their wide-eyed passengers slowly makes its way through these men and arrives at the bank of a stream.

The mock attack ends as the boys are lowered to their feet, stripped, and led down into a shallow pool. There they are told to bathe

211

under a small waterfall or in the rapids, while men and older initiated boys crowd the stream bank to watch. The novices are then lined up in the pool, with sponsors in front of and behind each boy. The man standing behind pulls the boy's arms and head back, while the one in front produces two bundles of sharp-edged, stiff sedge (*Cyperus* spp.), which he shoves up the boy's nostrils. The sedge leaves are repeatedly thrust and withdrawn with a sawing motion, while the boy arches his back and the stream bank erupts with shouts and drum pounding. A copious flow of blood pours into the stream as the novices cry out for their mothers. They are then released, and as they stand with heads bent, boys who became 'ummanra at the previous ceremony are brought into the pool to have their noses bled. This augmented group of boys is then lined up, and stinging nettles (*Laportea* spp.) covered with chewed ginger root and salt are shoved up their nostrils, reportedly to help staunch the flow of blood. While the boys sob and shouts continue from the stream bank, stinging nettles are rubbed over their entire bodies, after which they are told to bathe.

After the "old" 'ummanra are sent out of the stream, the line of novices is told to collect wild duck eggs from a small brush shelter on the opposite bank. Instead, however, they find men who jump out and lash them with more branches of nettle leaves. Directed to a second shelter, they are greeted by a chanting man holding a tiny bow and arrow with which he threatens the boys' genitals.

Then the boys are lined up again and a long (six to eight feet) stalk of sugarcane is held parallel against them with their penes placed across it. As a big man cautions them against taking sugarcane that does not belong to them, their sponsors present them with their first fighting arrows. They are admonished not to steal arrows or anything else they may hereafter see left unattended in their new residence, the men's house.

After a final bathing, the boys are led out of the stream. They are dressed again in their new garments and are given leafy branches with which to obscure their faces and small vertical bamboo flutes to blow. The male procession lines up on the path as before; as they set out, another mock attack is staged by the men (including those of the boys' own patriclans) who have been observers. The line, closing ranks around the boys walking in the middle, is not deterred, however, and all continue out onto the open, grassy hillside where the women and children have been waiting.

As the procession emerges, the men who had been the "attackers" join the front line of women, and together they threaten the protectors (especially the initiation sponsors) of the boys. Bows twang, shouts fill the air, and all move down the hill toward the hamlet, with almost the whole of the Ndumba population now involved. As they breach the hamlet fence and approach the men's house compound, the novices' mothers and other senior women rush ahead and present a wall of resistance. The line bursts through them, however, and passes through the entrance of the men's house palisade, leaving all women and children behind.

The women turn their energies toward dancing, from which the unmarried girls soon withdraw. The older women stage displays of mock antagonism as sisters-in-law pair off, threatening, chasing, and briefly confining each other. Amid the dancing also there are sporadic acts of what might be mock childbirth, as one woman forces another to the ground and covers her captive with her own skirts. The latter escapes through the surrounding concentric circles of dancers and disappears into the crowd of onlooking women and children. These interruptions and the dancing itself gradually lose their momentum until the groups disband and all of the women sit down to eat. The mood is festive throughout these events.

Inside the men's house compound, a more serious tone prevails. After dancing around the circular men's house several times, singing and shouting, the whole procession enters the house. At a signal, the men touch their bow tips over their heads to the sacred center pole and sing several brief songs, reportedly to give strength to the bows and magical powers to their owners. With a final shout, they go back out of the house as the men encircle it, forming a corridor of two concentric rings. The novices are led through the corridor around the house, each ending up before the man who held him while his nose was bled. The fight leader, who had presided over the sugarcane ritual, now passes in front of the boys, holding a nose ornament and bespelled leaf under the nose of each in turn, while all of the surrounding men chant.

The corridor then disperses as some men form two rows toward the rear of the compound. The novices' sponsors lead them between these rows, which now become a shouting, blow-inflicting gauntlet. Arriving at the back fence, they reveal the secret (traditional) deep-pit latrine, which henceforth the boys are always to use, rather than urinating and defecating in the forest as they have previously done. Having passed through the gauntlet again, the novices huddle under the house eaves as all of the men dance, chanting, around the men's house.

After circling several times, most of the men leave the compound, while the boys whose noses had been bled for the second time are led

213

back into the men's house. There they find several piles of leaves on the floor. The leaves, turned up to disclose sandpaper-like undersides, have been covered with ginger and salt, which the boys are told to lick. As they do so, their tongues begin to bleed, and shortly thereafter they are told to stop as the novices are brought inside. The latter are shown the bloody leaves and ordered to lick off the remainder of the ginger and salt. This they do, and soon their tongues are bloody, too. As the leaves are taken away, the new 'ummanra are told to lie down and take a nap on the sleeping-platform areas reserved for them. They are admonished to leave the men's house only to use the latrine, and at such times they will be accompanied by a man so they will not "lose their way." Except for this posted guard, the men leave to sleep in other men's houses for the remainder of the afternoon.

At dusk, blasts from a horn (or, in the past, bamboo flutes) are clearly audible throughout all hamlets, emanating from the men's house where the boys have been secluded. Scores of men and youths gradually arrive until the house is filled.

As the evening wears on, casual conversation is supplanted with songs, freely initiated by many men, and stories directed specifically at the novices are told. The songs vary in content, from paeans to favorite birds or marsupials to dirges about men who have been slain. The stories, however, have a more consistent theme. Nearly all tell of incidents— mythical, legendary, and historical — in which 'ummanra or older initiated males violated various taboos, with tragic consequences. Urinating in a place that is accessible to the public, accepting food from a strange woman, having sexual intercourse "too often," using a bow after a woman had stepped over it — all of these are said to have resulted in serious illness, abnormal growth, or death. Many stories deal with sexual behavior and its dangers. For example, stories tell of 'ummanra who died following their seduction by women under various circumstances. Sex is generally presented as an activity in which only grown men may participate and still live. It is dangerous even for them, though, according to the stories; thus, old men, still living but no longer "strong," are held up as examples of the weakness and debilitation that result from long-term contact with women. The fact that 'ummanra have little knowledge of sex at their young age may suggest that such stories constitute warnings that are meaningful to them mainly in terms of their severity.

Beginning late in the evening, the story telling and singing are periodically interrupted by the sound of bamboo flutes being played outside the men's house. This sound provokes no special behavior inside, but the novices are told they they are hearing the voice of Mokure, a forest spirit who is lurking about to observe the proceedings and harm any intrusive women or children.

Other interruptions occur almost hourly as groups of men stage dramatic entrances. On some visits they do nothing more than rub the boys' bodies with stinging nettles; at other times they bring ginger, salt, and special leaves for the boys to eat, or sugarcane for all. Each time the boys eat, they are admonished not to take food from gardens other than those of their parents and reminded of the many categories of people (mostly female) from whom they should not accept food. The most frequent visits, however, are devoted to nettle rubdowns, which are concentrated particularly on the boys' penes, "to make them grow long and have hair."

The night passes with this alternating pattern of songs, stories, and visitations. Toward dawn the songs take a decided turn, telling of the deaths of specific males (sometimes, but not always, due to the actions of women), which leads to weeping and chanting by all of the men. As dawn breaks, the bamboo flutes are heard again. Suddenly the file of night visitors enters the men's house, blowing the flutes in a simple high-low pattern, and the true source of the ghostly night sound is revealed to the novices. After rushing outside to circle the men's house a few times, the flutists reenter, surround the house center pole, and crouch down around its base. At a signal, a shout of *Tai'eso* ("It's over!") erupts, and men gradually begin to filter out of the house.

As men leave the men's house compound, they find that during the night leaves, branches, and ferns have been strewn all over the outside of the compound palisade. They speculate loudly that some "pigs" must have made the mess and that it will have to be cleaned up. Some men linger for that purpose; the others set out for their respective homes to sleep.

The men's house compound palisade has, in fact, been despoiled by women, who have been up all night singing and dancing in the hamlet courtyard. During the night, as the men were gathering in the men's house, women from various hamlets were converging outside. Dress is deceptive, as some kwaasi wear the full skirts of nraase, and other women, both nraase and kwaasi, have abandoned their usual attire for shirts and shorts borrowed from various men. Joining the circle of dancing women who greet them, these transvestite "men" twang bows, beat drums, and adopt men's dance steps (side-to-side movements and occasional twirls), while the rest dance in the women's style (front-to-back movements with no twirling). By late evening, nearly all women

215

are dancing in one large circle but in separate clusters of "men" or women, thus visually presenting the arrangement that is normal during singsings. The only male acknowledgment of these festivities is a brief visit by a man from inside the compound, who tells them that their singing is good. In response, the women shout, "Yes!" and the man slips back into the men's house.

The women's dancing goes on all night until, as dawn approaches, they set out for the stream where the novices were taken the previous morning. There they bathe in the same pool and collect ferns, leaves, and branches. Decorated with this foliage, they leave the forest in a procession, led by the women dressed in men's clothing. In their midst are young girls, who carry branches in front of their faces. As they move down the hill, the women sing, "*Nraammwa*, don't cry." Arriving back in the hamlet, some women resume their dancing, while those dressed as men approach the men's house compound palisade. Their shouts evoke no response from inside the men's house, so, in apparent disgust, the women throw the leaves and other stream-bank foliage at the palisade. By the time the men emerge and discover what the women have done, those in men's clothing have changed back into their traditional skirts. The men thus find the courtyard thronged with women and children, and soon all disperse to their homes to sleep.

The Second Day

After sleeping and resting all day, the men are again summoned to the men's house by the sound of the horn (or flutes) at dusk. The evening proceeds in much the same way as the previous one, with singing and storytelling in the men's house. A few women gather to sit and sing outside of the houses near the men's house compound. Their songs are addressed to the 'ummanra inside, both new and seasoned. There are informal, personalized messages to individual boys, as well as generalized warnings for all, such as "Don't eat rats" (referring to one of the many foods now prohibited to them as 'ummanra).

Inside the men's house, too, the emphasis is on warnings and instruction. Occasionally the boys' attention is renewed with nettle rubdowns, but the frequent, stylized visitations of the night before are not repeated. Instead, songs and stories like those of the previous night are sung and told until dawn approaches. Dawn is greeted with a brief ritual as burning brands of bamboo and handfuls of dirt are thrown over the back of the men's house palisade. At sunrise, most of the men disperse to their hamlets.

The Third Day

Early-morning activities are varied. Women and children begin to gather in the hamlet and prepare food for earth ovens. Some men clean the cooling pits and heat the oven stones, while others take their bows and arrows and kill the pigs that their donors have tethered nearby. Usually several pigs will be donated for each initiate by both patrilateral and matrilateral kin. Other men remain in the focal men's house courtyard and decorate the new 'ummanra.

Each initiate is dressed in a new sporran, a narrow coiled bark girdle traditionally worn by all initiated males, armbands, wristlets, leg bands, bark cape, and arrow bag. His sideburns and hair are cut, and the remaining hair, shaped like an even skullcap, is then brushed. New shell necklaces, bandoliers, headbands, and special bamboo-tube decorations, all donated by various kin, complete the ornamentation, and the boys are given the new fighting arrows they had previously received at the stream. As the boys are being decorated, other men gather in the men's house courtyard; when the dressing is finished, all circle the men's house several times, chanting and twanging bowstrings. Then, forming a procession, they move toward the men's house compound palisade.

As the procession, including the novices, emerges into the hamlet, a great cry goes up from the waiting mothers and other women, and the males move to an open area within the hamlet fence. The boys stand in a line as men and women dance in circles around them, singing, beating drums, and twanging bows. After a brief period, the crowd backs off, and women approach the new initiates with gifts: new sporrans, pandanus sleeping mats, and arrow bags. Carrying heaps of these gifts in their outstretched arms, the boys are then led back into the men's house, where they store them in their assigned sleeping compartments.

Meanwhile, others turn their attention to the earth ovens that will contain the pigs freshly butchered earlier. The initiates are free to move about, and they return outside to watch the opening of the ovens and food distribution, following which the crowd disperses.

At this time the boys may walk around at will, but they will hereafter sleep, eat most of their meals, and keep their personal belongings in the men's house. In fact, for the first month as 'ummanra, they may not eat any food that has been cooked outside of the men's house. In addition, numerous food taboos are now placed on them, some of which will be lifted after a month; when they are ceremonially given these foods in the men's house, their special decorations are removed, and everyday clothing is adopted. During this month, informants say, the boys will "frequently" be beaten with nettles, especially by their fathers and other males of their own clans, though matrilateral male relatives and other initiation sponsors help protect them.

SEXUAL OPPOSITION IN THE 'UMMANRA CEREMONY

In several particulars and in its general configuration, the 'ummanra ceremony resembles initiations that have been described for other Eastern Highlands societies. Although a point-by-point comparison with them might prove illuminating, our focus here—to examine the theme of sexual opposition as it is expressed on this occasion—is much more limited. Other aspects of the ceremony, such as its role in inducting boys into the Ndumba warfare complex, merit analysis and discussion. When the ceremony is viewed in the context of the whole male life cycle, moreover, it reflects a general Ndumba concern with growth and maturation (cf. Lindenbaum 1976). In Ndumba, male growth is not an automatic consequence of aging, but a process that requires monitoring and stimulation through ritual (cf. Herdt, Poole, this volume). One of the greatest obstacles to male growth and maturation, in Ndumba men's eyes, is the existence of women and of the forces they possess. For a growing boy to protect himself against these forces, his physical maturation must be accompanied by intellectual or ideological maturation as well. Our focus here is on the part played by the 'ummanra ceremony in these latter types of growth. We see the ceremony as at once manifesting and transmitting to boys a particular view of the world of human relationships and especially those relationships between the sexes. It is a dramatic part of a long-term process by which male gender identity is acquired and core Ndumba values and concepts are perpetuated.

It is important to bear in mind that the decision to initiate a given boy is also a decision to sponsor such an initiation; thus it must be seen as an act with social, economic, and political motivations and ramifications (cf. Gewertz, this volume). Unlike the kwaasi ceremony, to be described below, the 'ummanra rite is neither triggered by nor accorded the urgency due to specific physiological changes or processes. In this sense it is an example of action rather than reaction, and the timing can be deliberately manipulated. Thus, for example, the second ceremony we observed was performed for a single boy who was chronologically "overdue" but whose initiation had been delayed, and it was finally prompted by economic concerns (mainly involving the availability of pigs). Moreover, some boys have reportedly become 'ummanra in the recent past at younger ages than was traditional because of concern over their imminent departure for mission school in the nearby To'okena hamlet cluster.

This is not to say that 'ummanra candidates may be of any age or state of physical maturity. It appears that the age range of novices is fairly narrow, with a mode of ten to twelve years old. Physical growth and maturation are processes that are, after all, dependent on certain parts of the rite, as when boys are rubbed with stinging nettles "to make them grow," when their penes are given special attention "to make them grow long and have hair," or when special foods are consumed and others prohibited on the basis of explicit beliefs about their imputed effects on growth.

Nevertheless, the fact that boys can be initiated "prematurely" (as in the case of the schoolboys), just as later they can go through the 'ia'vaati ceremony "ahead of schedule" (as has happened recently because young men are departing for extended periods of wage labor), directs our attention to the other kinds of growth and maturation which are our primary concern here. The 'ummanra ceremony—whatever else it does—accelerates a process by which boys acquire knowledge and a view of the world which will, in the end, "make men of them." It is concerned with *education*, not only in the sense of transmitting informa-tion but, as Roy Wagner has suggested,* with the molding of a youth's character.

This view of the world—centering on the theme of opposition between the sexes—is not, of course, completely inculcated in a single ceremony. Rather, the 'ummanra rite accelerates a learning process that began in early childhood but is now made more explicit and deliberate, to be continued during the long period of residence in the men's house, intensified with the 'ia'vaati ceremony, and given final formal expres-sion at marriage. The pedagogical function of initiation can be seen in many particulars of the ceremony, with the central ideas encoded in both the structure and content of the performance.

The social emphasis on the physical separation of initiated males from all other people is manifest in those events of the ceremony which not only exclude women and children from direct participation but even prohibit them from observing. These events take place mainly in the highly exclusive men's house compound, but others, namely, the events

*Wagner 1979: personal communication.

in the mountain stream, are staged just inside the forest—not ordinarily a restricted area. There the required privacy is secured by the posting of a "guard" against trespass by the uninitiated. Even in the "public" events, segregation is maintained. Not only do men and women prepare their body decorations and, generally, eat apart, but when they do come together, as on the first and final mornings, they sing and dance as separate groups.

In addition to being presented as separate, men and women repeatedly appear as mutual antagonists. The male procession sweeps up the boys and takes them away from the world of women and children, of which they have always been a part. Unsuccessfully, the women "attack" the procession again and again, seemingly trying to regain their boys. Female rescue attempts and walls of resistance cannot succeed, of course, in a society that is publicly dominated by men, any more than can floral assaults on the men's house compound palisade, which are dismissed in the end as nothing more than the results of the insignificant rooting of pigs.

If the opposition between males and females is implicit in the structure of the ceremony, it is made explicit in the instruction received by novices in the men's house, not only during the ceremony but for years afterward as well. The men's stories stress, in their recurring central moral, the dangers women and children pose to initiated males. The boys are given many examples of the dire consequences of not maintaining the desired separation, and patterns of avoidance behavior which cannot have gone unnoticed during the boys' childhood are now linked to general principles that are directly expressed and ritually reinforced in a context in which the power of senior males is forcefully asserted. Thus we see the structure of differential male and female participation in the 'ummanra ceremony; the revealed secrets, which initiated males must never disclose to "the enemy" (including their younger brothers); and the rules of everyday behavior which redundantly express a central message: We "real males" are distinct and *vulnerable*; only together, sharing our knowledge and our strength, can we prevail against the forces that by their very nature can destroy us.

The locus of these feared "forces" is clear enough: women, their domain, and anything that contains their essence, especially their blood. Given Ndumba males' anxieties about menstrual blood in particular, it is tempting to see the nosebleeding rite as not only related to but somehow encapsulating the entire message of the initiation ceremony. Indeed, it is the "secret" that men appear to be most concerned with keeping (as evidenced by their admonitions to the boys and the attempts to conceal their blood-streaked faces with branches on the return from the forest stream); and the ceremony was always referred to in Tok Pisin as *sutim nus* (''nose piercing''). To an outsider's eyes at least, it is certainly the most dramatic of the various events.

Nosebleeding (and also bleeding of the tongue and/or urethra) may be universal in the Eastern Highlands. Some observers (such as Berndt 1962, Read 1965, Lindenbaum 1976) have suggested that it is an imitation of menstruation, but we have no evidence to indicate that Ndumba men or women view it in this way. It was referred to only as a way to make boys ''strong'' and to rid them of their ''mothers' blood.'' The latter claim would appear to suggest that bleeding is a ritual cleansing, as Langness (1967:165) proposes for the BenaBena. If this be so, the nose may be chosen as a focus in Ndumba (in addition to the tongue) because a boy has been ''inhaling'' and ingesting the essence of women for ten years or so, or simply because it is a relatively safe way to produce an abundant, dramatic, but short-lived flow of blood. In either case, nosebleeding can be viewed as a necessary ''purificatory'' act that must be performed before a boy may enter the men's house (as its position in the initiatory sequence would also suggest), learn the men's secrets, and participate in their affairs. While never articulated as such by informants, this interpretation would place the nosebleeding rite as a crucial link in the process by which ''polluted'' boys are transformed into pollution-avoiding initiates, who can now become full males and not endanger others of their newly obtained gender category in the bargain.

One difficulty with this interpretation, however, is that nosebleeding is also performed on girls in the kwaasi ceremony as they reach menarche. Surely there can be no concern with ''cleansing'' a girl of what is her true essence. Moreover, in the first 'ummanra ceremony held during the fieldwork period, one of the five novices was exempted from the nosebleeding portion, but not from the rest. He was a schoolboy at the nearby To'okena mission, and there was great concern that upon his return to school he could not be properly ''watched out for'' by men and would thus be in great danger if his nose were bled. Whatever may have been the root of this particular concern (perhaps fear of hemorrhaging or vulnerability to sorcery), the significant point is that the nosebleeding was considered a dispensable part of the ceremony. The ceremony itself, however, was *not* dispensable, even for a schoolboy who was rapidly moving into a highly uncertain future. Presumably, what the 'ummanra ceremony is ''really about'' was also indispensable, and clearly that significance must be sought in what occurs *after* the nosebleeding, that is, the enculturation of an initiated male.

221

We turn now to the kwaasi ceremony, which is important to the present argument in three ways. First, its inclusion of nosebleeding forces us to examine more critically the meaning of that act, which may have, in this context, different significance from that suggested by its occurrence in the male ceremony. Second, the significance of the theme of sexual opposition in a women's ceremony in addition to that of the men makes more understandable the support Ndumba women give to a male ceremony that, on the surface at least, appears to cast them in a wholly negative light. We suggest that a view of men and women as being fundamentally different, with those differences posing real dangers to men, is one that is shared by Ndumba men and women alike. The 'ummanra ceremony thus becomes intelligible in terms of concerns for all Ndumba, and not just Ndumba males. Third, the clear emergence of a theme of sexual complementarity in the women's ceremony leads us to reexamine the men's initiation rite, the multiple messages and cultural themes that are encoded in it, and the implications that the differences between the ceremonies have for a more thorough understanding of Ndumba relations between the sexes, which are never as simple as might be suggested by the content of the 'ummanra ceremony alone.

THE KWAASI CEREMONY

Because of the demographic factors, only one Ndumba girl reached menarche during our fieldwork, and the following description is based primarily on our observations at that time. Reports from several women and men informants, however, indicate that the observed ceremony followed the usual pattern and that our description may be considered generalizable.

Unlike most naraammwa-'ummanra transition ceremonies, the ritual change from 'iaatara to kwaasi is focused on a single individual following her first menstruation, an event that occurs for most Ndumba girls between the ages of seventeen and nineteen. Women informants claim that 'iaatara are ignorant of menstruation and must seek explanation from their mothers at the sight of their first menses. When a mother learns that her daughter has discovered inexplicable bleeding, she ushers the girl away to the seclusion house, saying that the time for her kwaasi ceremony has arrived.

Once secluded in the house, the girl removes all clothing except the short skirt modesty requires. Receiving provisions of sweet potato, taro, and edible greens from her mother, she eats and rests until evening, her menstrual flow absorbed in a pad of skirt material or moss. At night her mother will return with other senior women and share stories and explanations through the hours of darkness. The following day is one for the bestowal of gifts, visible markers of the girl's changed status. Her mother and "sisters" give her *saamma (Eleocharis dulcis)* to be fashioned into the skirts she will wear on the final day of the ceremony. The task of making these skirts is assigned to the girl herself. Working alone, she strips and then dries the skirt material on the roof of the seclusion house. Later she will tie the strands together to create the thick, rustling layers that turn the bodies of women into musical instruments as they swish and shake on the dance ground.

During the first five days of her seclusion period, occasional visitors drop by to chat, but nights are reserved for sleep. As the girl's menstrual flow wanes, then ceases, the active phase of the ritual begins. During the events of a single evening, social recognition of her altered status shifts from individualized to communal expression. The news that the night will be a time for dancing swiftly travels from garden to garden, woman to woman. Thus, on the sixth evening after she entered the seclusion house, the girl is joined by more than fifty kwaasi and nraase, a cross section of Ndumba women representing every hamlet, clan, and adult age category. Well past dark, after children have fallen asleep in their houses and all men have retired to the men's house for the night, the women slip away to the seclusion house to share the secrets that are the source of their strength and that must never be shared with men.

As the women enter to choose seats, their choices follow a simple but obligatory pattern. In the middle of the circular one-room house, seated behind a hearth, the girl occupies the central position, wearing an old bark skirt and tattered blanket. To her right, her mother sits alone, warming herself beside the low fire. On her left, three noted curers, one of whom is a half sister (mother's daughter) to the girl's mother, await the cue to start their performance. The area behind the mother is designated for women who are members of her clan and whom she calls *daasa* (mother's sister). The space in back of the curers must accommodate all others.

Laughter and chatter fill the air as spirits heighten. Movement in the crowded house is nearly impossible as more and more women squeeze in to find places in the rear. Suddenly the noise abates, and the three curers rise to sing. Always performing in pairs, but alternating in each of the possible permutations, the curers move their bodies as they sing. Bending slowly at the knee while leaning forward with hands extended toward the fire, they seem to draw out the heat of the smoldering logs. They sing of cultivated crops—the wing bean, native asparagus, and others.

A sound is heard at the door, and all eyes turn to see the first dancers come bursting in. A mother-and-daughter pair enter and repeatedly circle the fire in a mock chase. The daughter wears the characteristic kwaasi bark skirt; leaves decorate the skirt back, and a garland of flowers hides her hair. Giving chase with exaggerated male dance steps, her mother twangs the string of the arrowless bow that she holds. Her attire, like her mannerisms, is that of a male (from which she borrowed it). A song accompanies their charade, an unusual melody that will be repeated for each new set of dancers as the evening progresses. Introducing one chorus, a solo voice wails, ''Men are the enemy.'' Again and again the mother and daughter circle the fire before finally disappearing outside.

New lyrics arise spontaneously from the spectators while some of the initiate's kinswomen prepare fish and rice for distribution. Songs are united by a common theme as they speak of the fertility of fruits, flowers, birds, and marsupials. Soon the food that has been provided by the initiate's mother is presented to the guests. Junior women of the maternal clan first serve the senior women of the girl's patriclan, then others are served. Singing gives way to eating and chatting until all have finished. Then, on a cue from the curers, the songs resume, supplemented by a pantomime of the curers depicting the growing and cultivation cycles of crops.

Perhaps intentionally upstaging the singers, another group of dancers make a noisy entrance. Their leader, a nraase wearing men's clothes, is followed by five kwaasi dressed in the garb of neither sex but rather in skirts made of leaves and flower garlands. No weapons are carried, nor is pursuit implicit in their steps as they circle the fire. They leave shortly, and native asparagus is placed on the fire to bake while one of the curers sketches, through gesture and voice, the plant's cycle of growth. Steaming asparagus stalks are then passed through the crowd, and the initiate is lectured about her new responsibilities by her own mother. The rhetoric begins with a warning: now that she has become a kwaasi, she must watch where she steps lest her gardens, food, pigs, and especially men succumb to the contaminating power of her womanhood. She must always take care not to inadvertently harm men, for her father and brothers will take food from her hands, entrusting her to be mindful of their vulnerability.

When the mother's teaching ends, her half sister (a curer) stands solemnly and addresses her sister's child, saying simply, ''Your mother is right." Then she sits down as more dancers force their way into the house. All of the intruders are young nraase or kwaasi, dressed, like the previous group, in genderless foliage. Unlike their predecessors, however, they do not perform in unison. Instead, they move atomistically, sometimes colliding with spectators as they work themselves into a frenzy, following which they make an abrupt exit. A potpourri of songs follows their visit, telling of eels, marsupials, birds, and various crops. While women in the crowd initiate other songs, those about specific crops are the domain of the curers, who usually cook a sample of the food as they sing about it.

At about 3 A.M., a fourth group of dancers bursts into the house. Their costumes range from the simple to the elaborate, from improvised cotton loincloths to thick leaf skirts ornamented with feathers and flowers. As the fire is stoked, its heat becomes so intense that an older woman removes a bamboo tube of water from the house wall and circulates it among the audience. Each woman fills her mouth with water from the vessel and spits it out in a fine spray over the dancers. Again the dancing escalates into a frenzy, with some performers leaping across the blazing hearth. Then, abruptly, the costumed figures disappear into the night.

Songs resume, commemorating things in nature. Having no other common theme, they are strung together haphazardly until the yam is introduced as a focus. Again the curers command the stage as one rises, waving a smoldering log over the heads of the initiate and her matrilateral kin seated behind her and showering them all with sparks. The girl's daasa respond by blowing pipe smoke into the fire, while the curer, having given the log to someone else to hold, stretches out her hands, pretending to draw the smoke from the fire toward her before casting it back. A second curer rises and pantomimes grief, wiping her eyes and tearing wildly at the bark strands of her skirt. Next she places a yam between her legs and dances with an ''erect penis.''

The drama ends as more communal singing precedes the entry of another set of dancers. This time four nraase, one in men's shorts and the others draped with leaves from waist to knees, seek the attention of the crowd. They are older women (thirty-eight to forty-five), but no other significant element unites them. Seeming oblivious to the paths chosen by others, they gyrate around the fire. One flails her arms as she sings, moving in so closely to the fire that she could easily be burned. Although she seems fully aware of her position, she is restrained by the first curer, who carries her away from the circle. Again the excitement builds as self-control slips away from the dancers. Another is affected, losing her balance and tottering between her audience and the rising flames; she, too, must be removed.

By 5 A.M., activities have wound down to a slower pace. Group songs and pantomimes by the curers are followed by the final dance. The strange melody heard at some point during all of the previous performances does not accompany the last group as it revolves around the now-dying fire. Their dress is deceptive: four wear the full bark skirts of nraase, while one has donned the side-slitted bark kwaasi skirt. In reality, the first four are kwaasi disguised as nraase, while the lone nraase in their midst masquerades as a kwaasi. The kwaasi and nraase have exchanged places for a brief interlude, trading the symbols of differential status. Their movements, carefully coordinated, deliberate, and feminine, are in striking contrast to the frantic pace set by earlier dancers. When they, too, finally disappear into the darkness, they take with them the festive atmosphere that had settled over the room while they danced.

New songs strike out at unsuspecting targets and affect the emotions of everyone present. They are songs of lament and shame. Sobbing, but not otherwise responding, a woman buries her head in her hands as she hears how the carelessness of her young daughter resulted in the death of a piglet. Weeping becomes widespread as the women remember someone they admired, a prominent female curer, who had died several months before. At the doorway, a woman sits watching for the new day as these songs continue. As first light silhouettes her figure, she whispers, *Izara* ("the dawn"). Then, in silence, the women file out, heading for their homes and sleep. The seclusion house is left to the initiate, a few of her maternal kin, and her mother.

Doubtless drained of energy and emotion, the women and the new kwaasi spend the day in sleep, as they do the following evening and night. The morning after this rest period, the girl is brought out of the seclusion house for a public reception. An earth oven is prepared, pigs are killed and butchered, and large numbers of people (especially those representing her mother's clan) gather in the hamlet courtyard. While the food is steam cooking in the oven, the girl is summoned by men of her matriclan and led to a nearby stream, where she is escorted into a shallow pool. There she is seized by a man of her mother's clan and her mother's brother forces bundles of sedge leaves up her nostrils, exactly as is done in the 'ummanra ceremony. After repeated insertions and withdrawals, she bends her head to let the blood drip into the stream while other closely related kwaasi have their noses bled. Following the nose piercing, all of the girls are switched and rubbed with stinging nettle leaves. The crowd of adults who have been watching from the stream bank (with children excluded from observing this part of the ceremony) add their shouts to a general hubbub of frivolity, in marked contrast to the solemnity and relative secrecy of the nosebleeding in the 'ummanra rite.

The crowd then leaves the stream and returns in a procession to the hamlet feast site. While the kwaasi sit by a fire soothing their noses with warmed aromatic leaves, a dozen arrows are stuck into the ground in two parallel rows, forming a corridor. Both men and women urge the girls to crawl through the corridor on all fours, plucking the arrows out as they go. When the earth oven has been opened, the new kwaasi is given sugarcane to chew by her mother's brother, who, standing over her, spits water and sugarcane into her face, making a short speech about her new responsibilities.

A group of men gathered around a blanket-covered heap on the ground shout to the girl that she should come look at the "dead dog" they have under the blanket. Chanting, they suddenly remove the blanket, revealing piles of pork and other food, which is now distributed to the crowd. After obtaining their portions, the spectators gradually leave to eat in the privacy of their own homes, the main participants slowly disperse, and the new kwaasi retires to her mother's house and her new life.

SEXUAL OPPOSITION IN THE KWAASI CEREMONY

The kwaasi ritual signals a major turning point in a girl's life. She must intensify her preparations for the general roles and responsibilities of an adult Ndumba woman by taking seriously the gardening and other tasks she will have to perform and by acquiring the knowledge necessary to execute them properly. More particularly, the kwaasi ceremony— precipitated by the event of menarche—calls attention to her special responsibility as one who is now endowed with the dangerous potentials characteristic of her gender but is not yet in possession of the knowledge needed to control their potency. The kwaasi phase of life may be seen as a novitiate, a time for learning what every woman must know in order to ensure the fertility of the land and to protect the lives and well-being of its inhabitants.

It is only when a girl becomes a kwaasi that she discovers the extent of men's vulnerability and, because of it, the threat she represents to all.

227

In the seclusion house and in subsequent life, a maturing woman learns that no man is immune to the forces she possesses. From the moment her menstrual blood begins to flow, the new responsibilities attendant upon being the custodian of a lethal weapon are placed squarely on the initiate's shoulders. She must learn to exercise the power inherent in her body with the expertise and caution of a surgeon. Just as his carelessness may result in the loss of his patient and occasion a suit for malpractice, her negligence not only endangers men but ultimately threatens her own life and those of others of her sex. Unwilling to accept their own vulnerability passively, men can be expected to defend themselves actively against the treachery and imprudence of women. Routine prophylactic measures, imparted to 'ummanra and 'ia'vaati at initiation, are the first line of male defense. If the death of a man can be traced to a woman, however, that woman may pay with her life. Ndumba genealogical data indicate that pollution by women is frequently cited as a cause of male deaths. In most cases, the exact identity of the offender is not determined, so suspicion falls on several women, all of whom deny their culpability. In the past, at least some women are said to have been killed, usually by their husbands or his relatives, for such offenses. During our fieldwork, for example, one woman was severely ostracized by her husband and other men because she was believed to be responsible for her brother's death by having stepped over his bow.

Menarche, then, is not an event in a girl's life which can be treated casually, either by her or by the community at large. Just as men bond together to defend themselves against women, women must also come together to share their knowledge. Through the kwaasi and, later, nrasse ceremonies, women unite to emphasize their common duties and define their collective dangers.

Some of the motives for the kwaasi ceremony are thus similar to those that inspire the 'ummanra rite, springing from a basic premise of contrasting male and female natures and from the hazards inherent in such differences. In structure and content, both ceremonies reveal additional similarities, especially as they incorporate the themes of separation and opposition between the sexes. The isolation of a menstruating female is pro forma in Ndumba, but the gathering of women in the seclusion house for a night of singing, dancing, and dramatic instruction is a direct, if attenuated, counterpart of the men's house activities for 'ummanra. When men join in the kwaasi ceremony, their roles are clearly distinct from those of the women; indeed, women are little more than observers in the final "public" events. Opposition between the sexes is manifest in the songs and stories performed in both ceremonies, but it is even more dramatically expressed in the women's rite. While the public acts of antagonism which characterize the 'ummanra ceremony are absent, there could hardly be a clearer expression of the theme than in the drama of a ''man'' chasing a nubile woman (actually a mother-daughter pair) around the fire in the seclusion house. When a song states, ''Men are the enemy,'' the women achieve a degree of verbal explicitness unparalleled in the 'ummanra songs and stories.

SEXUAL COMPLEMENTARITY IN THE CEREMONIES

Several points of contrast between the two ceremonies deserve noting. First, the kwaasi ceremony is held for a single girl; for two or more to reach menarche at precisely the same time would be unlikely. The 'ummanra ceremony may focus on only one boy (as in the second performance we witnessed), but this is considered extraordinary. Second, the timing of an 'ummanra rite is manipulable, as already discussed, whereas the kwaasi ceremony is a response to an unpredictable and uncontrollable physiological event. In recent years, however, several prepubescent girls reportedly have gone through the kwaasi ceremony before being allowed to leave Ndumba for the mission school in To'okena (see the discussion of ''early'' 'ummanra and 'ia'vaati above). This change is significant, and it supports our contention that a principal function of the kwaasi rite (as with the 'ummanra ceremony) is to transmit an awareness of the dangers of menstruation and ways to control them. Even though schoolchildren return to Ndumba on weekends and school holidays, there was concern, people said, that a girl might experience her first menstruation while away and would need the knowledge imparted in the kwaasi ceremony to manage it without endangering others. Third, participation in the kwaasi ceremony is based much more on kinship ties than is the case with 'ummanra initiations. In the male rites, certain structural arrangements do derive from clan affiliation (as in the designation of sponsors); within the context of the kwaasi ceremony, behavioral roles of individuals are more accurately predicted on the basis of kin category membership.

A second set of differences between the two ceremonies are especially intriguing, as they appear to represent cultural inversions or reversals. First of all, in the 'ummanra ceremony, nosebleeding is followed by instruction in the men's house; in the kwaasi rite, on the other hand, instruction in the seclusion house precedes nosebleeding.

Second, in the boys' initiation, ornamentation and group dancing are conspicuous in public, while none occur inside the men's house; but with the girls' ceremony, ornamentation (of women only) and dancing take place in the seclusion house, but not in public. Third, the 'ummanra ceremony spurs physical maturation of young boys, while the kwaasi ceremony acknowledges the maturation that has already occurred. Finally, gifts (from women) are presented to 'ummanra at the conclusion of their initiation, while gifts (again from women) are given to a new kwaasi at the very beginning, with none at the end.

Although these reversals are analytically tantalizing, for present purposes we wish to focus on another point of contrast: the clear emergence of the theme of complementarity of the sexes in the kwaasi ceremony. Examination of this theme illuminates at least three questions that arise from our study of the 'ummanra ceremony: (1) Why is nosebleeding, often interpreted in the literature as a "cleansing" or "purificatory" rite, also practiced on females? (2) Why do women not only cooperate in but appear to "connive" in the maintenance of men's secrets and the inculcation of misogynistic values and beliefs (cf. Gourlay 1975)? (3) To what extent are the themes of sexual opposition and complementarity actually internalized by men and women alike?

We mentioned earlier that within the sexual division of labor, men and women are seen as enacting interdependent roles, employing their "natural" complementary abilities and inclinations. The 'ummanra ceremony, with its overt emphasis on the theme of separation and opposition between the sexes, would not appear to extend these notions of interdependence beyond the economic domain. Indeed, it may well be that from the novice's vantage point, women are little involved in what is overwhelmingly a male rite, except as they are glimpsed crouching in the grass, clutching at the boys, "attacking" the men, or wailing in the background. Nonetheless, women are constantly involved, if only covertly, and in such ways that the basic interdependence of men and women is affirmed.

In recognition of their biological limitations, men must leave to women the task of bearing a child, just as they can only but acknowledge women's vital contribution to the child's physical being through the provision of the child's red, "soft" parts and through the milk with which children are nourished. So, too, do men depend on women throughout their lives as provisioners of food, garments, and various commodities (as illustrated in the gifts bestowed upon new 'ummanra). Men themselves contribute the white, "hard" parts of the fetus; they also safeguard and maintain the institutions that make social life possible. Women produce children, as men cannot; it remains for men to create society, and to make of children the adults that society needs (Ortner 1974).

Perhaps appropriately in terms of this view of things, women prepare nraammwa on the morning of their transition to the world of 'ummanra and men, and they officially acknowledge this change with gifts at the ceremony's conclusion. The ritual contexts that effect this transition (i.e., the forest-stream and men's house events) are exclusively male domains, with the concurrent women's activities peripheral to, rather than integrated with, those of the men.[6] While "men" may join the women (through transvestism on the parts of some women) in their dances and on the dawn trip to the forest, women never intrude on the men's activities, either in reality or through male masquerade. Women are omnipresent in the abstract, of course, as characters in the songs and stories that tell of the forces against which men are rallying, and visual images of them "attacking" and challenging the men may linger in the minds of the novices, but actually they are, and must be, "offstage."

If we attend, then, primarily to the rhetoric and most conspicuous messages of the 'ummanra ceremony, the separation and opposition of the sexes overwhelms the acknowledgment of sexual complementarity that is, in fact, there. On the surface, we see men antagonistically take boys away from women and begin to "make men of them." Probing deeper, we find that women lay the foundations and prepare the boys for their eventual fate, leaving it to the men themselves to complete the task. It is significant, we believe, that Ndumba themselves appear concerned with the surface view in the 'ummanra ceremony, whereas "the making of a kwaasi" involves explicit and unambiguous representation of the theme of complementarity.

In the kwaasi ceremony, the surface view differs, as both men and women play major and interdependent roles. Even in the seclusion-house activities, which men cannot witness, "men" are made to be present, through female transvestism and the sporting of a yam "penis." Men may be presented as antagonists, as in the chase scene, but the central fact is that they are symbolically represented. Nothing of the sort occurs in the men's house 'ummanra activities: women remain "offstage" with their dances and charades (which, interestingly, again include "men").

[6]It was never suggested in any way that the women's activities on the first night were essential to, or even a "real" part of, the 'ummanra ceremony.

An even more evident contrast between the two ceremonies' surface structures may be seen in the differential involvement of men and women at various stages. The nraammwa-'ummanra transition occurs by three steps: a public preparatory stage, with women playing a central role; a private stage of nosebleeding and instruction in the men's house, performed exclusively by men; and the public social recognition of the new initiates. An 'iaatara becomes a kwaasi in three stages as well: a private period of instruction in the seclusion house, carried out by women but with female transvestite "men" playing important roles; the semiprivate nosebleeding, closed only to children, with men in charge; and public feasting, with additional rituals performed by men.

The contrast is clear. While women prepare boys and publicly acknowledge their new status, the core of boys' social transformation is an exclusively male prerogative and responsibility. A girl "becomes a woman," on the other hand, in the presence of, and through the representation and acts of, both women and men. The instructions and secrets she receives from women cannot be equated simply with the mothers' preparation of their sons for initiation, but in both instances it is left in the hands of men to *complete* these important social transformations. Men instruct boys and lead them out of childhood; women instruct girls, but for them to move beyond the status of child requires the participation of men.

We must ask at this point just what it is that men contribute to the molding of a kwaasi and why they play such a crucial role. After all, if a major aim of the ceremony is to transmit women's secrets and knowledge (and we believe that it is), the men would seem to have little relevance. Apart from the arrow-corridor rite and other rituals connected with the kwaasi feast, men are most conspicuously in charge at the nosebleeding stage. Women agree that this bloodletting marks the end of the transition; after it occurs, and only then, is a girl really a kwaasi.

MALE DOMINATION AND WOMEN'S POWERS IN NDUMBA INITIATION

Earlier, we discussed the bloodletting associated with the 'ummanra ceremony and suggested that conventional interpretations (that is, for example, imitative menstruation or a cleansing of mother's blood as purification) are problematic in the Ndumba case for two reasons. First, bloodletting is nowadays dispensable for certain boys, as demonstrated in the exemption of one novice in the first performance we witnessed.

Second, and perhaps more important, it is also performed on girls in the kwaasi ceremony. It is not necessary to speculate here as to whether one ceremony provided an original model for the other or whether, indeed, the nosebleeding within the two contexts is, in all respects, really "the same thing." We do submit, however, that in both instances the men's forceful bleeding of initiates' noses may be seen as an assertion of men's power.

Women's power, by contrast, needs no special ritual context for its assertion. Perceived as arising from women's very natures, it continually manifests itself in menstruation and procreation, and its physical products—menstrual blood and children—represent ever-present dangers for Ndumba men. As Langness (1974) and Lindenbaum (1976) have insightfully pointed out, not only do menstruation and reproduction present a consciously perceived threat involving mystical forces, but, perhaps more importantly, they represent a major challenge to the men's domination of women and society. Menstrual and reproductive cycles are ordered in ways that are outside of men's direct control. Ndumba men are themselves uncertain as to whether women, with their secrets, can in fact control these bodily processes; but of one thing they are sure—men cannot, at least directly, control them.

As possessors of forces that men cannot harness, then, women represent a threat to men in Ndumba. In addition, they pose other dangers. Ndumba men fit the pattern Langness (1974:205) has attributed more generally to New Guinea Highlanders in believing that women are, by their very natures, more sexually motivated and active than are men: women are continually trying to seduce men and thereby weaken them, and their appetites are frequently at the bottom of young boys' and men's problems in myths and legends. Women's sexual and natural promiscuity are therefore constant hazards to the maintenance of the health and well-being of males and of the social order itself.

Besides their sexual appetites, women's potential for rebellion or simply their lack of cooperation is a constant threat, dependent as men are on women in the division of labor. As producers as well as reproducers, women must be reliable: "They must do what is required of them—and when it is required. . . . If women do not [perform their tasks] well, or refuse to do them at all, not only is the prestige of the males involved, but also the reputation and well-being of the group, thus the necessity to control the activities of women" (Langness 1974:205).

Finally, men must solve the problems inherent in entrusting their children's, and especially their sons', early nurturance to women. Not only are boys thus constantly exposed to women's dangerous mystical forces, but the boys' very identification and loyalty to men may be in jeopardy. If men and warriors are to replenish the men's houses and maintain society, there can be no ambiguity as to where lies the allegiance of men and boys:

Boys are naturally attracted to their mothers and must be removed from them by the community of males. Young men are naturally attracted to females and must be forcibly kept in line lest their loyalties stray. If a man, in the depths of his passion, or even in his everyday routine, came to favor his mother or wife and wanted to please her more than he wanted to please and help his fellows, the foundation of the New Guinea social order would collapse. . . . Given the necessity for strength and cooperation among males [in the context of chronic warfare], it would be an intolerable situation. (Langness 1974:208)

The above considerations are all relevant for understanding not only Ndumba bloodletting but the entirety of the 'ummanra and kwaasi ceremonies. These concerns pose serious problems for Ndumba men, whose ceremonies—whatever else they may do—are attempts to express and resolve these problems. The theme of sexual opposition inculcated by these rites rationalizes, creates, and maintains the structural arrangements and institutions that men have devised for the operation of society and for placing the public control of society in the hands of men. Bloodletting ceremonies are, then, a dramatic and graphic representation of male domination and the assertion of male power. It is especially important that such displays be made in the context of two ceremonies that are "about" the power women possess.[7]

For men to control public affairs in Ndumba, they must contend with two realities, which are represented by novices in the 'ummanra and kwaasi ceremonies. Only in boys can men find the raw material that they will slowly, carefully, and painfully mold into replications of themselves. While the task of effecting the social transformation from being a boy to being an initiated male may be exclusively that of the men, the

---

[7]We would agree, of course, that the ceremonies under discussion are "about" other concerns as well and that they are surely multifunctional. One line of investigation which we hope to pursue elsewhere concerns the possible effects of the belief system and ceremonies reported here on the suppression, and thus control, of male sexuality. It is likely that the central theme of sexual opposition which is inculcated in boys during the 'ummanra ceremony makes it considerably easier for older males to control marriage and reproduction through the instillation of fear of women in prepubescent youths. The relevance of such a possibility to Ndumba politics and to such concepts as paternity certainty seems clear.

preparatory acts of creating and nurturing male children must fall to women. Herein lies the dilemma underlying the sexual opposition in the 'ummanra ceremony. Men need boys, but to have them they must acknowledge the procreative and nurturing powers of women. To establish their claims over boys legitimately, they use ritual to challenge and proclaim socially a victory over female powers. In the sexual antagonism dramatized in the first hours of male initiation and in its forcible bloodletting, we see formal expressions of the passing of control over the lives of boys from women to men. The task is made more complicated by the possible presence, in the boys' bodies, of "female pollution" and, more importantly, by their primary identification in childhood with women and their world. Bloodletting, nettle rubdowns, various deprivations, and forced isolation from women not only assert the primacy of men's aims and power but also give men the opportunity to persuade the boys, through revealed secrets and intensive instruction, that in the end the transformation is for their own good.

In the kwaasi ceremony, men are faced with a different situation—not a boy whose social identity is ambiguous, but with a girl whose social identity is all too clear. She embodies, with menstruation, the mystical forces and dangers with which men constantly live. Not only must action be taken to establish who is "really" in charge, but it must be a social, collective, and unopposed effort.

The most tangible symbol and evidence of a woman's identity and powers is, of course, the menstrual blood that will now flow periodically and that is, inevitably, uncontrolled by men. By forcibly bleeding her nose, men assert their dominant position in society and also produce bleeding that *is* controlled. Perhaps this is also the way to understand the bleeding of boys' noses. Informants did refer to it as "ridding the boy of his mother's blood." Rather than interpreting this merely as a "cleansing," however, we might see "mother's blood" as "women's blood," in other words, "women's power." If we view nosebleeding as a symbolic statement of control over society instead of as a merely physical purification, the exemption of a single boy from this part of the ceremony would still be consistent with the message of the act as long as it is performed on other boys at the same time.

Given this interpretation of bloodletting—as an expression of the supremacy of men's power over women in the social world—it is more understandable that all nosebleeding must be performed by men. The sequential placement of the kwaasi nosebleeding—following rather than preceding instruction and revelation of secrets—also takes on new meaning when seen in this light. Considering men's anxieties about the extent of women's control over their own mystical forces and their general suspicion of women's conspiracies, to follow the men's activities with instruction and closed women's rituals would raise the question of women's capacities to counteract the men's efforts. Instead, following the women's secret ceremony with male ritual action allows the men to "have the last word." This interpretation is, of course, yet another phrasing of the central message concerning power distribution in Ndumba society.

Why do Ndumba women thus actively cooperate in the performance of ceremonies whose central meanings consign them to subservient positions in society and whose main theme appears to be misogynistic? If the 'ummanra and kwaasi ceremonies have at their core the assertion of men's power, they also imply women's acceptance of that social imbalance.

To suppose simply that Ndumba women fear the brute force that men might employ against them is, we think, inadequate. Certainly they are not cowed by such fear as individuals, as any fight between a husband and wife will attest. In the seclusion house, during kwaasi and nraase ceremonies, women have the opportunity, after all, to spoil the men's game, if game it is. They could devote their instructional lessons to training girls to exploit men's anxieties and develop wily strategems for coping with an unfortunate and groundless male chauvinism.

Instead, women enthusiastically play their part in the 'ummanra ceremony even when it means, in several important senses, that they lose their sons in the process. Moreover, in the privacy of the seclusion house, at the same time that they acknowledge that "men are our enemies," not only do they not undermine the men's insistence on separation and opposition of the sexes, but they incorporate these very themes into their own rituals. When they also stress complementarity of the sexes, it is in acquiescence to men's ultimate control of society, not as a way of qualifying that social dominance.

We suggest that Ndumba women believe in their mystical powers and the dangers they pose to males as fully as do the men and that they also see the need to control these powers if men and society are to survive. For the common good, women must educate girls and remind each other that they possess forces that are so powerful that men cannot, working alone, safeguard themselves. Nor do men trust women to exert such controls as might exist, so they do not leave the matter entirely in women's hands. The theme of complementarity which becomes explicit in the cooperative male and female performances of the kwaasi ceremony underscores this important point. While the 'ummanra ceremony may be seen as one in which males come together to share their strategies for coping with women, the kwaasi ceremony is not simply the converse. Women do express, in their ceremony, solidarity against males, but they also acknowledge that, *by the nature of things*, society—men and women—has a problem that must be approached through combined efforts.

In their participation in the 'ummanra ceremony, women acknowledge men's anxieties as legitimate and release their sons to the world of men. When they prepare the boys, they know what they are doing, and when they acknowledge the secret nature of the lessons to be given by the men, they also support the enterprise of which the secrets and their revelation to initiates are such an important part. While women are barred from observing the 'ummanra nosebleeding, under the reported threat of death, one cannot believe that they are completely ignorant of its nature. Women might well extrapolate from what they witness at the kwaasi nosebleeding, and some Ndumba men admitted to us that they have described the bloodletting to their wives. Nevertheless, we have no reason to believe that women pass on what knowledge they have of the men's ceremony to girls or to nraammwa. Discussions with uninitiated boys on several occasions led to persuasive pleas of ignorance on their part, and older boys assured us that their fear of men's retribution was too great for them ever to reveal the secrets to anyone.

Thus, women's cooperation in the 'ummanra ceremony and the nature of the kwaasi ceremony both establish sexual opposition and its derivatives in Ndumba as something more than an androcentric obsession: they emerge as basic tenets of Ndumba *culture*. Far from being simply a misogynistic male belief, the postulation of fundamental male-female differences that are dangerous to men and thus problematic for society may be seen as a contention shared by men and women alike. The need to exert control over women's powers is acknowledged by both sexes; the institutional mechanisms for doing so are firmly grounded. To possess such awesome forces is a heavy responsibility and, perhaps, one that carries its own satisfactions. When a Ndumba woman prepares her son for initiation or instructs her daughter in the new powers of her body, "it would seem that, as a conscious human and member of culture, she has followed out the logic of culture's arguments and has reached culture's conclusions along with the men" (Ortner 1974:76). As she does so, her knowing wink may not even be noticed by the men.

237

REFERENCES

BERNDT, R. M.
1962 *Excess and Restraint: Social Control among a New Guinea Mountain People.* Chicago: University of Chicago Press.

FAITHORN, E. D.
1975 The concept of pollution among the Kafe of the Papua New Guinea Highlands. In *Toward an Anthropology of Women*, ed. R. R. Reiter, pp. 127–140. New York: Monthly Review Press.

GOURLAY, K. A.
1975 *Sound-Producing Instruments in Traditional Society: A Study of Esoteric Instruments and Their Role in Male-Female Relations.* New Guinea Research Bulletin no. 60. Port Moresby and Canberra: Australian National University Press.

HAYS, T. E.
1974 Mauna: explorations in Ndumba ethnobotany. Ph.D. dissertation, University of Washington.

LANGNESS, L. L.
1967 Sexual antagonism in the New Guinea Highlands: a Bena Bena example. *Oceania* 37 (3):161–177.
1974 Ritual power and male domination in the New Guinea Highlands. *Ethos* 2 (3):189–212.

LINDENBAUM, S.
1976 A wife is the hand of man. In *Man and Woman in the New Guinea Highlands*, ed. P. Brown and G. Buchbinder, pp. 54–62. Washington, D.C.: American Anthropological Association.
1979 Comments on ''New Guinea Male Initiation,'' a symposium held at the Annual Meetings of the Association for Social Anthropology in Oceania, Clearwater, Florida, March 2.

MEIGS, A. S.
1978 A Papuan perspective on pollution. *Man* 13:304–318.

ORTNER, S.
1974 Is female to male as nature is to culture? In *Woman, Culture, and Society*, ed. M. Z. Rosaldo and L. Lamphere, pp. 67–87. Stanford: Stanford University Press.

READ, K. E.
1965 *The High Valley.* New York: Charles Scribner's Sons.

238

6

THE MAKING
OF MEN:
Ritual and Meaning in Awa
Male Initiation

Philip L. Newman and David J. Boyd

The Authors

Philip L. Newman is Associate Professor of Anthropology at the
University of California, Los Angeles. He was born in Eugene,
Oregon, in 1931. After completing undergraduate work in anthropology in Oregon, he went to the University of Washington for
graduate training. Studies with K. E. Read and J. B. Watson led him
to undertake New Guinea fieldwork among the Gururumba, a previously unstudied Eastern Highlands people, from 1959 to 1960. The
dissertation for which he received the Ph.D. in 1962 from the
University of Washington was among the first detailed analyses of an
indigenous system of supernaturalism and ritual in a Highlands
group. Since 1961 he has taught at UCLA, where he also served as
chairman of the anthropology department from 1969 to 1973.

Professor Newman has continued his New Guinea research and
teaching, and the following coauthored paper is based on later
fieldwork among the Awa tribe, another Eastern Highlands group.
He worked with the Awa in 1964–1965 and in 1970, when he
conducted investigations on ritual and social change. Dr. Newman,
who has published papers in the *American Anthropologist* and has
authored a widely read case study, *Knowing the Gururumba* (1965),
presently teaches courses on Melanesian ethnology, comparative
religion and symbolism, and—a subject in which he has a long-
standing interest—the interpretive construction of ethnographies.

David J. Boyd is Assistant Professor of Anthropology at the
University of California, Davis. He was born in Iowa in 1942 and
received his secondary and undergraduate schooling there. Between
1964 and 1966 he served as a Peace Corps volunteer in rural Peru,
and he has also conducted summer fieldwork among the Alaskan
Eskimo. His graduate work was done at the University of California,

Los Angeles, beginning in the late 1960s. In 1970, with Professor Newman, and in 1971–1972 he conducted research concerning subsistence production and economic exchange in the context of recent social change in the Awa village of Ilakia. For the resulting dissertation he was awarded the Ph.D. in 1975.

Professor Boyd brings a deep interest in cultural ecology to his New Guinea work and university teaching. He has published and delivered papers on resource management, behavioral strategies of economic production, agricultural intensification, labor migration, and social change. In addition to teaching anthropological theory, ecological anthropology, adaptation and development planning, and agricultural systems, he is presently completing a book on domestic household ecology and social change among the Awa.

INTRODUCTION

A key perspective for understanding Awa male initiation is to view it as a human activity aimed at manipulating cosmic forces that are manifest in the human body.[1] If the notion of cosmology is understood to mean a conception of the most general or fundamental forces operant in reality, then important cosmic processes for the Awa are growth and procreation. Awa male initiation attempts to control and manipulate bodily substances and generative processes to achieve physical growth, general physical well-being, and procreative success. The performance of ritual events is embedded in a system of knowledge that has ramifications for many cultural domains beyond the initiation cycle itself. The ritual sequence commences with the expression of a few basic ideas that, as the initiation process progresses, gradually acquire many layers of meaning. The purpose of this chapter is to describe the performance of Awa initiation rituals within the context of an unfolding system of knowledge. The understanding of operant cosmic forces and the acquisition of techniques to control bodily substance are essential aspects of life for adult Awa men, and these are forcefully communicated during the ceremonial making of men.

[1]The authors wish to thank the following institutions for their support of the field research on which this chapter is based: National Science Foundation, National Institute of Mental Health, and the Department of Anthropology, UCLA. We are also grateful to K. L. Ito, T. E. Hays, G. H. Herdt, and E. L. Schieffelin for reading and commenting on earlier versions of this chapter.

The term *Awa* refers to a linguistic unit of some 1,500 people occupying seventy-eight square miles of territory in the southeastern part of the Eastern Highlands Province. The Awa language belongs to the Eastern family of the East New Guinea Highland stock, a classification it shares with Auyana, Gadsup, Tairora, and several other smaller nearby groups (McKaughan 1973:3).[2] Awa speakers are distributed among eight largely autonomous nucleated villages located in this rugged region of the Kratke Mountain Range.[3] Forested hilltops rise above 7,000 feet, and grassland valleys descend to about 3,000 feet along the banks of the Lamari River, which bisects Awa territory east to west.[4]

The general patterns of Awa life are similar to those of their Eastern Highland neighbors, including a rather extensive form of swidden agriculture, small-scale pig husbandry, exogamous, putatively patrilineal clans, residential separation of adult men and women, and endemic warfare between neighboring villages.[5] Communal men's houses and the rituals of initiation associated with them are also present. These Awa initiation rituals are marked by such commonly reported features as various physical ordeals, bodily purging by bleeding and vomiting, the imposition of food taboos, restrictions on contact with women, and the revelation of profound knowledge.

Many anthropological investigations of initiation have added to our understanding of these rites of passage in other Highlands groups by exploring their relationships to other aspects of social life, such as the development of male solidarity and its role in maintaining the security and viability of the local group, ritual performances as contexts for exchange activities, the social-structural configurations of the ritual events, and the manner in which rituals shape and maintain the behavior of men and women toward one another (see, for example, Allen 1967;

---

[2]For linguistic analyses of the Awa language, see the several articles by A. Loving, R. Loving, and H. McKaughan in McKaughan (1973).

[3]Almost all of our fieldwork was carried out in the Awa village of Irahqkiah-Poqna. Brief surveys of other Awa communities, conversations with visitors from other villages, and questioning of locals about the customs of other communities make it clear that the fundamental pattern of male initiation is the same across all Awa communities, although details may differ. We also have benefited from access to the personal field records of David M. Hayano, who, while a doctoral candidate at UCLA, conducted eighteen months of fieldwork among the Tauna Awa. Several of the myth texts appearing in this paper are transcriptions of tape recordings made by Hayano, and we thank him for permission to use this material.

[4]For more information on the physical environment and settlement patterns in this region, see Pataki(1968).

[5]For details of Awa subsistence patterns, social organization, and warfare practices, see Boyd (1975) and Hayano (1972).

Berndt 1962; Langness 1974; Meggitt 1964; Newman 1965; Read 1952, 1965; Strathern 1970). The investigation of Awa male initiation to be presented here will view the sequence of rites as a ritual setting in which young men are taught the nature of cosmic forces influencing growth and procreation and the techniques used by men to manipulate and control these processes. The forces that dominate the processes of physical growth, the maintenance of physical well-being, and the achievement of reproductive success are manipulated by the exertion of control over the growth-inducing, generative processes and bodily substances associated with the procreative powers of both men and women.

Providing an account of the major ritual events comprising Awa male initiation entails certain ethnographic problems that warrant comment at this point. One of these problems concerns the data on which the account is based. The rituals occur over a period of several years, and it was not possible for us to observe the entire sequence. Our presentation of the ritual sequence, therefore, is necessarily based on diverse sources of information. These include field observation of several rituals in the sequence, accounts solicited from men who participated in some or all of the rituals, voluntary commentaries comparing the way the rituals were performed in the remembered past to the way they were performed at the time of the field studies, and examination of mythic texts that ostensibly explain how things came to be as they are. In addition, it is clear from accounts of the rituals, provided by older men who had gone through the entire sequence, that various circumstances, both individual and communal, can result in the shortening or lengthening of the sequence in time and also can result in the exclusion of some segments or the merging of segments that under other conditions would be separate. Finally, these rituals, like other aspects of Awa culture, have been changing since the time of Western contact (if not before), as well as between the time of initial fieldwork in 1964 – 1965 and two subsequent periods of fieldwork in 1970 and 1971 – 1972.[6] The account we present is, therefore, a composite portrayal of Awa male initiation as it might occur in its most elaborate and lengthy form. This is done to maximize the amount of data available for interpreting the meaning of key events and symbols within the ritual sequence.

---

[6]Initial Western contact occurred in 1947 and intensified in the late 1950s. The total fieldwork period was thirty months. The initial period of twelve months, when Newman was in the field during 1964 – 1965, was followed by a three-month period in 1970, when Newman, Boyd, and Donald Rundstrum (a Ph.D. candidate in anthropology at UCLA at the time) were in the field together. Boyd then returned for another fifteen-month period in 1971 – 1972.

A second problem in providing an account of Awa male initiation lies in establishing what set of rituals to include in the sequence. Male initiation, as generally discussed in anthropological literature, is identified with the onset of puberty and the end of sexual latency. Published materials on male initiation in the Highlands of Papua New Guinea tend to present it as beginning with the separation of young boys from their mothers, followed by incorporation of the youths into the men's house, and ending some months later when the initiates emerge as junior .nembers of the adult male group. The initiatory phase of their lives is usually considered concluded at this point. While it may be useful for various analytical purposes to restrict attention to rituals that occur within this limited period, we feel that an understanding of the relation between such rituals and Awa ideas about growth and procreation is better served by our considering a series of five rituals covering a period of ten to fifteen years. This series begins when boys, in their early teens, are (1) inducted into the men's house, and continues through (2) their first bodily purging and (3) their achievement of "finished" *mahbi* (young unmarried male) status; the sequence ends with the (4) sweat ceremony and (5) severe penis-cutting rituals associated with betrothal, after which a man and woman begin the routines of married life. This view may seem to extend the referent of "initiation" beyond reasonable limits, but the Awa themselves conceive of this set of rituals as a single unit. Such is indicated, for example, in a myth that brackets the ritual cycle in just this way.[7] The myth, told to initiates after they have undergone the second of the five rituals mentioned above, is conveyed to them as an ancestral act that set the pattern of the events they have recently experienced.

The myth begins with two boys living with their mother. She is knotting a string net bag and accidentally drops her bone netting awl through a crack in the house floor. When the boys are sent under the house to retrieve the awl, they inadvertently catch sight of their mother's genitalia. Thinking that what they see is something to eat, perhaps a fuzzy rodent or marsupial, they repeatedly call out to her to give it to them. The mother, greatly disturbed by this impropriety, decides to leave her children and hide in another village. She arranges a subterfuge so the boys will not immediately discover her absence, but they eventu-

---

[7]The Awa have a category of oral narrative called *mani*, which is what we gloss by the term *myth*. Mani refers both to the type of narrative and to the humanlike beings whose actions are depicted in the narrative. These beings lived in the distant past, and their actions are presented as setting many of the patterns of Awa life.

ally realize she is gone and are greatly dismayed.

The boys try to determine where their mother has gone by using a divination technique that involves shooting grass-stem arrows in various directions. If an arrow is fired in the direction traveled by the person being sought, it flies in a straight line; but when an arrow is shot in any other direction, it circles back and strikes the archer in the genitalia. After shooting many arrows and receiving an equal number of blows to their genitalia, the boys fire off the last remaining arrow. Fortunately, it does not return, indicating the boys have found the direction in which their mother has gone, so they set off in search of her. By nightfall they still have not found their mother, so they decide to sleep in the ground nest of a large bird.[8] The next day, they are discovered asleep in the nest by an old man who has come into the forest to collect the eggs of this bird. He pulls the boys out of the nest, dusts them off, and takes them back to his village. There he puts them into the men's house, but he does not inform his wife, who is, in fact, the mother of the boys. He does, however, tell her to make the various kinds of arm and leg ornaments that are worn by initiated men. The old man wants to make the boys strong young men, so he does all the things involved in the second ritual, decorates them with the new ornaments, and finally brings them out of the men's house to show his wife, declaring them to be his sons. Although the ritual has transformed them from boys to young men, they are recognized by their surprised mother, and the four of them dance together, singing a song composed by her.

In the final segment of the myth, the young men are working in the garden of the old couple, cutting branches from a large tree. Unknown to them, two sisters see them in the tree, and, finding them attractive, each selects one for a husband. They mark their choice by placing bone awls in the ground at the base of the tree. When the young men climb down, they step on the awls, driving them deeply into their legs and causing much pain and bleeding. This painful bleeding induces further growth in the young men. Eventually, they recognize the young women as possible mates, and the myth concludes with their marriages.

This myth can be regarded as an Awa paradigm for male initiation which places the ritual with which it is associated in the broader context of a sequence of events. The mythic sequence begins with the boys' separation from their mother, continues through their incorporation into

---

[8]The bird here referred to belongs to the genus *Megapodius*. It gathers rotting plant material and builds a mound several feet in diameter, which acts as an incubator for its eggs.

the men's house, and includes their consequent transformation into young men. It continues with a painful bloodletting event connected with the identification of their mates and ends with marriage. While the myth does not mention details of any of the five rituals that occur during the period bounded by the myth, it alludes to all but one of them and demonstrates their continuity by placing them in a single developmental sequence.

No Awa term or phrase that can be glossed as "male initiation" represents the five rituals of the sequence identified above. The Awa refer to the first three of these rituals as "mahbi making." The term *mahbi* is applied to a male from the time he is first inducted into the men's house until arrangements for his betrothal have been completed and his future wife has been transferred from her natal group to his. The Awa recognize three major phases in the making of a mahbi, and these correspond to passages through each of the first three rituals. Completion of every phase is marked terminologically by the addition of a descriptive modifier to the word *mahbi*. These modifiers refer to degrees of maturity (or "ripeness") and can be applied to plants or animals as well as to people. In the context of ritualized mahbi making, they refer both to physiological maturity and to the assumption of increasingly adult social responsibilities, but the emphasis is clearly on the former. These references to growth and development are more than simple analogies. In Awa thought, the rituals accompanying these initiation phases do not only mark the passage from one phase to another, but actually bring about the discernable and desirable physical transformations.

The first initiation ritual occurs when boys of twelve to fourteen are inducted into the men's house.[9] Boys at this stage are referred to as *pehgeri* mahbi, indicating they are physically developed enough to begin the growth that will eventuate in manhood. They are said to be like plants that have sprouted but not yet put out leaves. The second ritual, which includes purging by bleeding and vomiting, occurs about a year later, when the boys are thirteen to fifteen. Boys who have gone through this ritual are referred to as *akahtaq* mahbi and are likened to a growing, but not mature, plant or animal. The third ritual occurs three to five years later, when the youths are eighteen to twenty. At that point they participate in a ritual that involves eating wing beans; afterward they are referred to as *anotah* mahbi, indicating they are fully grown but not yet

---

[9]These ages, and others given below, are necessarily approximations, since the Awa do not age themselves in terms of absolute years. Also, numerous factors can alter the actual duration of the intervals between the rituals discussed in this chapter.

ready for procreative activities. It is only then that the process of mahbi making is complete, and the Awa speak of these youths as fully "finished" mahbi.

The two remaining rituals occur some five years after full mahbi status has been achieved and the youths have become young men in their early to mid-twenties. The first of these rituals is referred to as *auq*, meaning "to sweat." The central component in the ritual is a lengthy period of seclusion in the men's house during which the young men fast and sweat. This event takes place just before the future wives of the young men participating in the ritual are transferred from their natal group to their prospective husbands' groups. The second ritual, called *ahpwi tari eqe*, or "severe penis cutting," occurs a few days after the sweat ritual, when the transfer of the women has been completed. The two rituals accomplish a transition from the status of mahbi (young, unmarried male) to that of *menahwe* (young, married male). At this point the initiatory period can be considered concluded. The rituals that have occurred up to this time involve the inducement of physical maturity and strength thought necessary for the accomplishment of adult tasks and the preparation of the initiates for adult reproductive activity. Adult married men will continue to follow certain of the ritual practices and restrictions introduced to them as initiates, but they will do so to protect and maintain their physical well-being and capacity for procreation rather than to bring these into being.

The sections to follow will be ordered by the sequence in which the five rituals occur. Insofar as possible, the ideas about growth, physical well-being, and procreation incorporated in these rituals will be presented in the order in which they are made known to the initiates. We feel it is important to proceed in this way because many of the key ritual elements have different meanings and purposes at different points in the sequence. The initiates' understanding of the cultural significance of ritual elements is developed by the careful unveiling of Awa knowledge.

INDUCTION INTO THE MEN'S HOUSE

Prior to induction into the men's house, boys in their early teens usually reside with other boys of roughly the same age in small makeshift huts of their own construction within the village. They are relatively free of responsibility, and although they no longer sleep in their mothers' houses, the boys still rely on their mothers to supply most of their food.

The sequence of male initiation begins when these boys are forcefully removed from this setting and taken away to the men's house, which has been strictly off limits to them until this time. The boys are surprised by this abduction, because parental preparations for the event, such as the accumulation of food and firewood and the making of ornaments associated with the event, have been carefully hidden from them. Adult men asked to recall their experiences of the induction affirm that they knew little of what was to happen to them. They describe their feelings as fearfully apprehensive and freely reveal that they cried and shook when taken away to the men's ground.

The boys are taken one by one across the open space surrounding the men's house through parallel lines of adult men blowing reed whistles (*pempiah*).[10] These whistles are not hidden from women or children, and they are used in a number of ritual contexts involving spatial passages. Bull-roarers (*tehbu*) also are sounded, but this is done in the brush nearby and out of sight of the uninitiated.[11] When the boys have been assembled in the men's house, they are told what is expected of them in terms of changes in their behavior and are given a broad understanding of the relationship between ritual separation from their mothers, the progress of their own physical development, and such distant concerns as their eventual marriage. The following statement by an adult man recounting his own experience provides a summary of this instruction: "They said to us, 'You are just small boys and still sleep near your mothers. Now we will take you to sleep with us in the men's house. Now that this is done, you can't go back to stay with your mothers. If you stay with your mothers you will not grow quickly. If you stay there you will be like the little ones that still suckle. You won't become grown. You must come into the men's house, you must hear what your fathers have to say, you must grow rapidly, and you must become married.' Then they said, 'If you disobey your fathers and you go down to where your mother is cooking food and you eat, you won't grow, you will remain thin, and you will stay that way forever. So remain in the men's house and eat with us. While here you must listen to what your fathers have to say, things that people from the past have told us. When you have heard, when you have raised your own food and cooked it in the men's

---

[10] These whistles are in the form of small, end-blown reed tubes. There are six in a set, each tuned to the others and each blown individually by men standing in a double line facing one another.

[11] Bull-roarers were not observed in use during our field studies, but their use was described and their construction demonstrated to us by older men.

house, when you have remained here until you are fully grown, then you can go eat in your mother's house.' That is what they told us.''

Following this instruction, the boys are placed in the small sleeping cubicles that line the inner wall of the men's house, one boy to each cubicle. There is a small fire pit in each cubicle, in addition to the large one in the open center of the house, and the boys are enjoined to sit close to their fires while preparations are made for their first physical ordeal.

The adult men have been harvesting sugarcane for some days prior to this time. The cane is cut into lengths of about five feet, tied into bundles of ten to fifteen stalks each, and stored out of sight near the men's house. While the boys are in the sleeping cubicles, the bundles are brought inside, and what happens next is described in this man's account: "The men say, 'Come out of the cubicles, we want to tell you something.' We all came out and gathered in the center of the house. Then they said, 'We don't want to tell you anything, we want you to have some sugarcane. All of you get down on the floor in a line.' Our arms were underneath us against our stomachs, and they threw the sugarcane onto our backs. They didn't just lay them down on us, they threw them down hard! They kept on piling on the bundles until there was a big heap. Then the men said, 'Try to throw the sugarcane off. We want to see if you can throw it off and toss it about, or if the cane can keep you down.' We tried with all our strength and threw off the cane bundles in all directions. They said, 'Oh, it looks like you are really strong.' Then they said, 'It is our custom to plant sugarcane for all to eat, but it is hard work and gives us pain. Now you have felt the pain of sugarcane.' '' This ordeal not only emphasizes the responsibilities of adulthood but is also regarded by the adults as a general test to see whether the boys are physically strong enough to withstand the rigors of subsequent parts of the ritual.

During the next several days, the boys are offered small pieces of sugarcane to chew but are not allowed to eat solid food or to drink water. They are told that this restriction on food and drink is to inure them to the pangs of hunger and thirst they will experience in the future when doing difficult garden work, hunting pigs, traveling long distances, or participating in warfare. They are reminded that adults have undergone these hardships in the past to provide sustenance and protection for their dependents and that the initiates must also be self-sacrificing as they grow and take on adult responsibilities.

The prohibition against drinking water also has additional meanings. Growth and development of the human body, in Awa thought, involve not only the building up of flesh and bone but also the increasing substantiality of physical form through drying out. This drying process contributes to individual growth and strength until middle age, when it reaches a stable plateau, but after which it results in the desiccation of old age. To facilitate this process, the boys not only abstain from drinking water but also spend much of the time they are confined inside the men's house sitting next to the fire to induce sweating. The connection between growth and driving liquid out of the body by sweating is explicated for boys, as indicated in another man's remembrance: "We sat there and soon began to sweat. They [the adult men] said, 'You are young, and you have eaten all kinds of things, and the liquids from these things are in you. This fire will make all that liquid come out of your body. After it has all come out, your bodies will begin to grow. Then you will have the body of mahbi.' They said that and put us by the fire. Plenty of sweat came out, from the legs, arms, all parts of the body."

The "things" referred to in the above statement are the various kinds of marsupials, rodents, birds, fish, reptiles, and amphibians found in the region. Women consume these creatures throughout their lives, but males may eat them only prior to the time they are inducted into the men's house and again after they are mature married men with children of their own (see Barth 1975; Meigs 1976). During the interim period, however, men may not eat such animals. The association in Awa thought among these creatures, liquid substances, and the control of growth is important, but it is not made explicit to the initiates at this time.

During this period of fasting and sweating, the boys also undergo two other ordeals. First, they are periodically taken outside the men's house and beaten and stung with stinging nettles. Several nettle stalks are formed into a bundle and bound together with a vine to make a large switch. The swelling and stinging occasioned by this act are said to induce and hasten the bodily development associated with the mature mahbi. Next, and again outside the men's house, the boys are made to straddle a vine, about one inch in diameter and several feet long, that has been wrapped with various kinds of brittle leaves and smaller, rough-textured vines. Two adult men stand at either end of the vine and pull it back and forth vigorously in such a manner that it scrapes the inner thighs of the boys until they are raw. The stated object is not to draw blood per se but to make the boys experience the pain, and thereby lose the fear, of climbing vines or trees in the course of hunting and gardening activities they will undertake when they become older. An adult man described the rationale as follows: "It is just to instruct us about the vine. It is to teach us not to be afraid of climbing trees when looking for marsupials, or of other things like cutting branches out of trees while making a garden. If we are afraid of climbing trees, we won't be able to do these things. They [the adult men] think we are afraid of climbing vines because these might break or scrape our skins, so they show us this, and we aren't afraid.''

The sweating, fasting, and physical ordeals of induction into the men's house occur over several days. They are accompanied by a lack of sleep and an abundance of verbal abuse concerning the lack of past helpfulness and the boys' general ineptitude. Finally, the initiates are ''shown the garden.'' Uncooked yams, taro, sweet potatoes, bananas, edible greens, edible pitpit, and sugarcane are brought into the men's house and displayed in a large pile. Speeches containing two basic themes are made. First, men say that this food was produced by men and women's hard work and that the boys will now be expected to help produce. They can no longer play about the gardens in a childish manner. Second, elders make it clear that the foods displayed before the boys are the only foods they will be allowed to eat until instructed otherwise. The rationale behind this directive is not explained at the time, and the boys are not given any instruction about the foods they may not eat. They are told simply that the permissible food will stimulate the firming of their flesh and the hardening of their bones. After this instruction, the food is cooked in the men's house, and the newly inducted boys eat with the men for the first time.

The boys are then fitted with the first of several sets of body ornamentation they will receive in their progress toward manhood. Each of these sets is distinctive and marks passage through one of the major initiation rituals. The outfit they now receive contrasts dramatically with the simple string pubic covering and makeshift ornaments they have worn up to this time. It consists principally of bark strings woven into the hair, which hang to the shoulders; a vegetable-fiber headband; seed or twisted rope waistbands; a grass sporran that is trimmed to a point just short of the knees; narrow, woven bands for the upper arms and lower legs; and new net carrying bags, worn at the side. Thus adorned they are instructed in the proper comportment of a pehgeri mahbi: basically, this includes maintaining a quiet, dignified demeanor rather than running about like children, staying with men rather than following their mothers to the garden, accepting cooked food from men only, and doing what men command.

On the following morning, when all is ready, the boys are taken to a stream below the village which is the site for many important initiatory events. There they are washed, and final adjustments are made in their outfits.[12] Amid the dancing and singing men, they return to the men's house ground to be paraded before the assembled women and children of the village, who see them for the first time in their new status.

The Awa, like many other Highland peoples (see Gourlay 1975), utilize pairs of large bamboo flutes (*purereta*) in various ritual contexts. They are kept out of the sight of women and children, and the secret revelation that the sound they make is not the sound of spirit beings is an important component of male initiation. The flutes are sounded at various times during the period described above, but the boys do not see them, and the fact that the sound is produced by men is not revealed to them at this time. Boys are aware of this sound prior to induction into the men's house, but they have been told by their parents and other elders that the sound is made by an ominous, black spirit bird (*kumpehpeh*) that they must avoid seeing when they hear its call lest it attack them and cause illness or even death (see Read 1952). This frightening image is sustained throughout the induction period, and when the flutes are blown inside the men's house with the boys present, the boys are either made to stay in their sleeping cubicles with their eyes turned away or made to lie on the floor with their heads covered. Furthermore, if there occurs some event requiring the extended use of the flutes in the men's house before their secret has been revealed, the boys will be moved to other men's houses in the vicinity until the event has been concluded.

This first phase in the initiation sequence most obviously concerns effecting a separation of the initiates from the pursuits and relationships of childhood and directing their attention to the importance of achieving the physical growth, the strength, and the social commitment toward men deemed necessary in adult life. These matters are mostly a background in the consciousness of the boys, who experience the ritual primarily as frightening and painful and who are full of uncertainty about what may happen to them. Nevertheless, the ritual does introduce them in dramatic fashion to fundamental ideas. In the period between their

---

[12]Another ordeal an initiate is likely to undergo during this visit to the stream consists of having his nasal septum punctured with a bone awl and then having a small cylindrical piece of dried reed fitted in the opening. All Awa males do have their nasal septa pierced, but informants' accounts differ as to the exact timing of this ordeal in the initiation-ritual sequence and the location of the site where the piercing is conducted. It is clear, however, that this ordeal is performed on all men prior to the conclusion of the third ritual in the sequence and that it usually is done at the stream site, although one informant said it was done to him inside the men's house. The primary reason for piercing the nasal septum is to provide a hole for the attachment of various nose ornaments, and it does not seem to be connected with the central symbolism of mahbi making.

induction and the next major ritual, they eat the solid garden foods that build firm bodies, draw away from the attachments of childhood, and begin participating in the work activities of adult males, if only in small ways. The ritual also sets a pattern for later rituals in the sequence, and as the initiates pass through the whole process, the adult meaning of many of the elements in this rite are brought more fully into their awareness.

FIRST PURGING

The next ritual in the initiation sequence, which we call the "first purging," may occur anytime from several weeks to a year or more after induction, depending on a variety of circumstances ranging from the availability of food, which, if in short supply, will lengthen the time, to the existence of warfare hostilities with surrounding communities, which may shorten the period. Ideally, it should be deferred until the boys have begun to show signs of pubescence, such as the appearance of axillary or facial hair.

The beginning of this ritual, like the preceding one, is marked by the assembly of the initiates in front of the men's house and their being led inside, one by one, to the sound of whistles and bull-roarers. They are seated around a fire in the central area of the men's house and, amid the shouts of the adult men, are intermittently beaten with sticks, firebrands, and a cudgel made from the burl of a hardwood tree. Although it is their matrikinsmen who lead them into the men's house, it is their patrikinsmen who administer the beatings with the cudgel (which is not, incidentally, used in any other context, and is called *ahku*—the word for patriclan). This beating, unlike the beating with nettles administered in the preceding ritual, is not connected with inducing physical growth, but is instead linked to ideas of social responsibility within the patriclan. The emotional atmosphere in the men's house is highly charged at this point as individual kinsmen of the initiates (frequently elder brothers) sporadically begin recounting misdeeds that a particular boy has committed in the past, such as stealing or causing a fight. These harangues rise in crescendos of anger as the older men push to the center of the house and thrash the youths in retaliation for their transgressions. It is not only transgressors who are beaten, however, for blows are also administered in the name of men killed in warfare or as retribution for wounds inflicted on the living while they protected the initiates when the latter were too small to aid the group in its own defense. Thus, all initiates are beaten, whether they have been transgressors or not. In this manner they are

252

forcefully instructed regarding both their obligation to act responsibly toward clan members in the future and their duty to become strong enough to help defend the group against attack from outside.

The brunt of the beating is borne during the first night of this period, but further beatings may occur over the next day or two while the initiates are in the men's house, sweating and fasting. They are told that they will soon be taken to the stream to wash, as in the previous phase, and that they will then be given a new set of body ornaments. This is a partial deception that initiates do not soon forget, as exemplified in this statement by an adult man: "We slept one or two nights, and then we were told we would go to the stream and wash. We thought that and slept well, but in the morning that isn't what happened. Indeed, what happened was something altogether different! The men had been gathering pitpit for nosebleeding, small vines for vomiting, and bamboo knives for penis cutting. All these preparations had been made in secret, and we didn't know it. We thought we were going to wash and that after washing we would go back to the house. This is what we thought, but that isn't what happened. We finished washing and were standing at the edge of the stream. Then we were told that there was something at the edge of the stream we must look at and that there was something else besides washing. We heard that, and we all started to shake."

The initiates are indeed taken to the stream—more particularly, to a spot several hundred feet down the steep ridge on which the village is located. The substantial forest growth along the edge of the stream contrasts with the brush and grass characteristic of the upper reaches of the ridge. There are several natural springs in the area and upstream from them a waterfall of some twenty-five or thirty feet with a pool beneath it. The trip down to the stream is not marked by any special occurrences. The party of men and initiates is followed by a group of married women and older unmarried girls related to the initiates; this group is ostensibly going along to collect water at the springs and help in bathing the youths. The initiates are stripped, except for a small string pubic covering, and are washed by the women and some of the men near the springs. Other men bathe themselves further upstream at the waterfall. When the washing is finished, the women begin to fill their bamboo water tubes at the spring. They are very slow about it, and although the men keep trying to hurry them up, they continue to dally about in obvious hesitation until the men finally separate them from the initiates and drive them off with threatening gestures. The initiates are then run upstream to a spot near the waterfall, where they see what appears to be the body of a man riddled with arrows and partially covered with leaves and branches (see

Hays and Hays, this volume, chap. 5). They are directed to go look at it, and as they come near, the leaves stir, and a man leaps out from under the branches with pitpit nosebleeders protruding from each nostril and blood running down his face and chest. The men begin to chant as he attacks the initiates, beating them with branches and exclaiming that now they will understand the purpose of the pitpit they saw floating in the pool beneath the falls. Each initiate, in turn, is held fast by several men while one of them jabs a pair of nosebleeders into his nostrils, pulling them in and out several times until severe bleeding occurs. Each youth is then released into the stream and the blood is carried away by the water. When the flow of blood has partially stopped, the same action is repeated again, and it is mockingly threatened a third time, although this threat is seldom carried out. While an initiate is slumped, bleeding, in the stream, he may be given one or more heavy whacks across the back with a large piece of dried bamboo or a heavy stick.

As the last initiate is completing this ordeal, a group of men who have been off in the nearby forest approach the pool from above the waterfall. They have been preparing a certain kind of narrow, flexible vine that, when stripped of its outer covering, has a smooth, slippery surface. A length of the vine about five feet long is doubled, and the looped end is forced deep into the throat of each youth. It is vigorously pulled back and forth several times before the initiate is released into the stream, gagging and vomiting.

After this, the glans penis of each initiate is cut. This bleeding is accomplished by several men lifting the youth off his feet and firmly holding him stomach up with his legs spread wide apart. The foreskin is held back with a split stick, and an incision is made on each side of the glans with a bamboo knife. He is then released to bleed into the stream. One or more men may approach him, jeer at him for struggling or crying out in pain, and poke at his wounded genitalia with a long stick.

While the bleeding is subsiding and the boys are trying to regain their composure, the men form two parallel lines along the sides of the stream and arm themselves with branches, pieces of bamboo, and stalks of stinging nettles. The initiates are then made to run down the rocky, slippery stream bed, the men striking at them as they pass and mocking their awkward, painful progress. At the end of the gauntlet, the initiates are reassembled to dry off and warm themselves by a small fire. They dress, adjust their ornamentation, and finally set off with the men to return to the men's house.

During these events, the women linger about the vicinity for a time, and the men, mindful of their presence, send up shouts and chants to

PLATE 6.1   An older man bleeds an initiate's nose during the first purging ritual.

mask the cries of the initiates. The women have not been idle, however, for while the men are busy with the initiates, the women have been preparing sticks, bundles of cane, and nettle switches with which to attack the men as they return with the initiates to the village. The women lie in wait in the brush near the point where the trail emerges onto the ridge top. When the male group approaches, with men in front and back and the initiates in the middle, the women move in and begin striking at the men, shouting at them, and, in general, berating them for the pain and anguish they have caused their sons and brothers. The women openly display their anger, and although the men respond primarily in a defensive manner, it can happen that a man and woman become so embroiled that they have to be separated to prevent them from inflicting serious damage on each other. Eventually, some of the men round up the initiates and run them off to the men's house ground. (The following excerpt from field notes describes the final scene of this confrontation:)

All the men finally gathered around the men's house, and the women collected just outside the tabooed area. There was some further skirmishing, particularly at the point when the initiates were carried into the men's house on the backs of

PLATE 6.2   A male group counters a woman's "attack" following the first purging ritual.

their male relatives, but the women were eventually driven away. The men feigned indifference to the belligerent women by turning their backs on them or, in a more defiant gesture, exposing their buttocks to them. Finally, the men rushed the women, and another large fight broke out. There was some buffoonery in the attack as one man ran through the middle of the village with a stick about fifteen feet long in a mock assault on a very old woman. For most people, however, it was all quite serious. The women then counterattacked just as the boys were being carried into the men's house on the backs of their male relatives. The fight boiled up for the last time with another round of whacking, and the women were driven off. The women continued to shout at the men, however, and several of them came onto the men's ground and threw down their bundles of switches in disgust in front of the men's house.

When the men and initiates have gathered in the men's house, crowding around the center post in a closely compacted group with the

256

boys in the center, they set up a chant while touching their hands and pressing their bodies to the post (see Hays and Hays, this volume, and Schieffelin, this volume, chap. 4). The center post of the men's house, as well as the physical structure it supports, is imbued with powerful, vital qualities. There is no dwelling spirit in the men's house, but it is thought to have *ahweh*, which living people also have and which is identified with the animating life-force of the body. Some illnesses, for example, are seen by the Awa as resulting from ahweh leaving the body temporarily, and death occurs when it is gone permanently. When a men's house needs to be replaced, it is not burned, destroyed, or allowed to rot away, because such actions would drive away its ahweh. Instead, the old house is carefully taken apart, pieces of it are incorporated into a new structure, and rituals are performed to ensure the transfer of ahweh from the old house to the new. Ahweh accumulates in a house as a result of men living in it, so when the men and initiates gather at the center post, they are quite literally imparting some of their ahweh into the structure by pressing against it. Moreover, this act simultaneously puts the initiates in contact with the accumulated ahweh of the house. This contact is regarded as beneficial to them, for it helps stimulate their growth and protects them from maladies that result from loss of ahweh.

The initiates remain in the men's house for the next two or three days. While recuperating from their ordeals, they are given (1) an explanation of purging, (2) an expanded knowledge of how to control growth and strength through food, and (3) a more benign image of the flutes. We shall briefly describe each matter in turn.

First, purging by nosebleeding is explained in a manner analogous to the explanation given for sweating. Sweating is thought to remove liquid from the body so that one's flesh will become firm. The Awa think of physical growth as, in part, a process of drying out, one that involves a transformation of the body from being amorphous and watery to being well formed and firm. Sweating thereby contributes to the development of muscle and overall strength, prerequisites for an effective adult male. Blood, in the Awa view, is composed of a liquid and a fiber-forming or fiber-hardening substance. Bleeding gets rid of the liquid part but leaves the fiber-forming part, which builds flesh. Bleeding, then, directly stimulates the drying, strengthening processes of tissue growth. Bleeding the penis is explained to the initiates as similar, in this respect, to bleeding the nose but as contributing specifically to the strengthening and development of male reproductive organs. The penis, scrotum, and testes are thought of as a bodylike unit, with the glans being the "head" and the testes the "innards." The two incisions made on the glans are analogues of the two nostrils penetrated by nosebleeders. Bleeding the penis is like bleeding the nose, but the latter relates to the whole body, while the former relates just to its genital parts. Purging by vomiting also is explained as a way of removing liquid from the body, but specifically the liquid associated with certain kinds of food (see below). This point is exemplified in the following statement by an adult man: "It [the vomiting vine] is put down the throat, and vomiting occurs. If it is done to a new mahbi, many kinds of things, such as rats, marsupials, and birds, all the kinds of things he has eaten as a child, all these things come out. When they all have been gotten out, then a mahbi can become large. If the liquid from these things stays inside, the mahbi will not grow large. If you put the cane down this throat, turn it and turn it in the stomach so the liquid of all these things comes out, then doing that, along with the bleeding, will make a mahbi grow."

Other statements we collected stress the additional point that ritual vomiting in initiates, at this point in their development, is beneficial because it not only gets rid of old food but also enlarges the stomach, and thereby enables them to eat copiously. This increased capacity, in turn, will contribute to their growth.

Second, the initiates' understanding of the relationship between food and bodily development is also extended. During the induction phase of initiation, the initiates were enjoined to eat only certain foods, which were shown them in the men's house. Now, however, specific food taboos are introduced along with reasons for their prohibition. These food taboos are initially quite extensive, and although their number gradually decreases over the years, some are retained well into mature adult life.

Knowledge about these taboos is organized by a division of edible animals and plants into those that are wild and those that are domesticated (see Lindenbaum 1976). Taboo restricts initiates from eating any wild varieties of animals or plants: marsupials, rats, birds, snakes, frogs, fish, eels, insects, and feral pigs may not be consumed. Similarly, nuts, seeds, fungi, various greens, and several kinds of leaves and bark used as condiments are all forbidden. An explanation of these restrictions is not given to the initiates at this time beyond the injunction that such foods are too "strong" for them and would impede their growth. Animal flesh that may be eaten includes only domesticated pig and nowadays chicken. Taboos on domesticated plant foods are organized by another set of categories based on color discriminations. All domesticated plant foods are classified as either white, red, or black. Those in the white category are associated with the building of bone and the firming of flesh, and all such foods may be eaten. Those classified as red must be avoided, since they are associated with the liquid portion of blood, and ingesting them would impede the drying/firming process essential for growth. Those in the black category must also be avoided. It is said that black foods, like the wild foods mentioned above, are too "strong" for the only partially formed initiates at this stage and that eating them would cause their internal organs to turn black and decay. It should be noted that not all varieties of a given type of plant fall exclusively within one color category. For example, yams, taro, plantains, and sugarcane each have many varieties; some varieties of these food plants are distinguishably white, while others are red or black. On the other hand, all varieties of sweet potato are viewed as light colored, and all are classified as white, whereas all varieties of wing beans are dark colored and considered black. Initiates, then, can freely consume all types of sweet potato, but must carefully avoid eating any wing beans or the various red and black varieties of other domesticated food plants.

Third, at various times during this phase of mahbi making, such as around the men's house at night or above the waterfall when the initiates are at the stream, the bamboo flutes are blown. Although they are still kept out of sight, a somewhat more benign image of them is transmitted to the initiates after their ordeal at the stream. Initiates are told not to fear the sound, for it is not really a destructive spirit bird, but rather a male and female spirit couple who live in the high forest (see Herdt, this volume, chap. 2, and Lindenbaum 1972). The abode of the couple is said to be in the top of a large tree. It is obscured from view by many vines hanging down from the forest canopy, and the initiates are told that they are not to try to find it.[13] This old spirit couple is depicted as coming down from the forest to help the adult men in mahbi making by exhorting the men to remember the many things that must be done and spurring them on in the physical labors of collecting firewood and food associated with the rituals. The sounds the initiates hear are said to be the voices of the couple emanating from holes under their arms, which open and close like mouths as they raise and lower their limbs.

Finally, as this period of seclusion in the men's house draws to a close, a new set of body ornamentation is prepared and fitted to the initiates. The principal items are a netted cape, a decorative girdle, a penis cover, and a new bow with finely made arrows. The girdle (kamoka) is formed of narrow strips of bast twisted together and tightly

---

[13]Despite this caution, we were told by one young man that he and his age-mates used to sneak away from adult supervision to search in the forest for this hidden place.

259

wrapped with wider bast strips to form a hoop that fits around the hips. The penis cover, held in place by a length of bast between the legs, is cup shaped and made from pounded bast stretched over a framework of sticks or from a carved piece of wood. Another strip of bast, four to five inches wide and cut long enough to hang to the ground, extends down the back of the kamoka. It is painted with decorative motifs and enhanced with tassels. This strip and the netted cape, which hangs down the back to about the knees, cover the buttocks.

When the necessary preparations have been completed, the initiates remove their grass sporrans and tie them to the base of the center post in the men's house, where they remain and gradually decompose, an act that once more imparts some of the boys' life-force into the structure and thus contributes to its protective properties. Newly ornamented and carrying their new bows and finest arrows, the initiates—now known as akahtaq mahbi—descend from the men's ground to walk single file through the village. They are greeted by their mothers and older sisters, who, in a show of admiration, hold the tails of their kamoka girdles and walk with them to a display of cooked food containing the first pork the initiates will have eaten since their induction into the men's house many months before.

THE FINISHED MAHBI

The transformation of an akahtaq mahbi to an anotah mahbi is marked by a ritual that reduplicates some elements of the previous phase but that also contains elements indicating the end of a state of what might be called transient "mahbi-hood" and full emergence into the status of mahbi. Men refer to this ritual by a phrase that means "give them wing beans," and it occurs when the initiates are in their late teens or early twenties. Its major components include a second purging, an extension of knowledge concerning the flutes, the removal of certain food restrictions, the reinforcement of other food taboos, and an emphasis on the importance of controlling sexual behavior.

The beginning of this ritual—in contrast to the two previous rituals, when the initiates were led into the men's house to the accompaniment of pempiah whistles—is not marked in any dramatic way. These whistles are sounded when certain kinds of spatial passage occur, as, for example, when groups of invited guests enter or leave the village or when young women move from their natal residence to that of their husbands-to-be. In the two previous rituals, the sound of the whistles marks the passage of the initiates from the dwelling place of women and children to that of men, but they are not sounded during this ritual, or during subsequent rituals in the initiation sequence, since that passage is now considered complete. The wing bean ritual occurs when a general consensus that the initiates are sufficiently grown is reached. It is timed to coincide with the availability of appropriate food resources.

When the time is right, the boys are taken to the same pond and waterfall of their first purging ritual. There they undergo a second purging involving the same elements of nosebleeding, forced vomiting, and penis cutting. These acts are carried out with no less vigor than before, and the pain is just as intense, but the initiates are not beaten and ridiculed as they were in the earlier event.

Although this chapter does not deal with the way these rituals are structured by kinship or other social relations, it should be noted that in the first purging ritual it was the older, married matrikinsmen of the initiates who carried out the operations. They bear responsibility for overseeing the general welfare of their sisters' and daughters' children, and as they bleed the initiates they are taking an active role in the physical development of such offspring. The second purging, however, is done by young men who most likely are in the same patriclan as the initiates. These young men are either betrothed or newly married, and are called "menahwe," a term designating the next major phase in the male life cycle after mahbi. This second purging marks the first time these young men have acted as initiators, and their efforts are carefully supervised by older, more experienced men. In acting as initiators they are assuming important adult responsibilities, but their participation is also related to the fact that they are, as adults, also expected to purge themselves on various occasions. Having someone else bleed your nose or incise your penis is painful enough. As one can easily imagine, bleeding oneself involves a great deal of fortitude, as well as a certain amount of skill, and the Awa view this menahwe participation as a preparation for purging themselves. The initiates, too, are encouraged by the older men to try purging themselves, but few muster more than feeble attempts, and the operation is quickly taken over by the more enthusiastic menahwe.

As the initiates are recuperating from the purging ordeals and eating from an earth oven alongside the stream, the flutes are heard from the forest above the waterfall. Here the human origin of the sound is revealed to the initiates for the first time (see Hays and Hays, this volume). One young married man recalled his own experience this way: "They told us to look upstream above the waterfall, as something would be heard and if we looked we could see it. We turned around and looked

PLATE 6.3   A man forces the vomiting cane down an initiate's throat during the
second purging ritual.

and saw people coming down blowing the flutes. They kept on coming down until they came right up to us. They said, 'What did you think before when you were a child and you heard that sound? Did you think it was a spirit being talking, or what?' We answered that we didn't understand what it was. Then they said, 'Now you see that it isn't a spirit being talking, but that it is the sound of flutes blown by men.' They said that to us and then hit us with the flutes so we would know what they really were.''

The flutes are made of green bamboo, usually three nodes long, with the blowing hole in the center section. They are played in pairs by two men who face each other and move slowly back and forth across the stream as they advance toward the initiates. Here, the flutes are decorated with cordyline leaves, red ones at one end and black ones at the other end of each flute. It is said that these leaves represent the red and black categories of domesticated vegetable foods which have been forbidden to the initiates since their induction into the men's house— taboos that will be lifted at the conclusion of this ritual.

Except for learning that the flutes are sounded by men rather than spirit-being voices, the initiates are not told much more about them at the time. A very strong injunction is placed, however, on revealing their nature or exposing them to women or the uninitiated. This injunction was paraphrased by an adult male thus: "They said, 'Concerning these flutes, you must never play around with them in the village. If some other mahbi suggests that the two of you play the flutes in front of the children and you do it, you will be killed. This is a taboo found everywhere. It isn't a taboo that is found only here. If you show them to women or to children, the men will hear of it, and they will want to kill you. Now, even if someone comes and warns you that you are about to be killed, and you are thinking of running away to another place, you won't be able to get away with it. The men in other places will have heard what you have done, and they will kill you.' That is what they told us.''

In other explanations of this injunction it is clear that "everywhere" includes not only all Awa-speaking communities but any community known to use such flutes as part of male initiation. Older men, who were initiated before Western contact, specifically mentioned Fore and Auyana communities, and younger men initiated later included such distant parts of their expanded world as the Gimi, the people living around Kainantu and Goroka, and the Chimbu. In other words, there would be no escape from breaking this injunction, as it was a matter of grave concern to all men, irrespective of place.

The revelation that the flutes are objects made and manipulated by men should not be taken to mean that the initiates now view them as some kind of meaningless hoax perpetrated by the adult men. The strength of the injunction itself clearly communicates that the flutes are connected with extremely important matters: as children, the initiates associated the sound of the flutes with something powerful and frightening which had to be avoided; as mahbi, they come to associate them with the painful purgings and controlled food abstinences said to be essential to their physical growth. Furthermore, a complex of associations between the flutes, the purging rites, food taboos, physical well-being, and female procreative powers begins to be fostered at this time, as will be demonstrated later. Understanding of these associations is strengthened in the period between attainment of full mahbi status at the conclusion of this rite and the next major transition of manhood.

After the flutes have been revealed, the initiates return to the men's house, where the final event in the ritual will be performed. During the events at the stream, the older men and women of the community have been preparing food in the village. Some food is cooked in earth ovens and is intended for a general distribution that accompanies the rite. Other food is specially prepared in the men's house by an older man and is only for the initiates. This special food is cooked in bamboo tubes over an open fire (a common Awa cooking method) and consists of two classes of vegetable foods which have been taboo to the initiates since their induction into the men's house: the wild plant foods, primarily bitter nuts, seeds, and fungi; and the dark-colored domesticated plant foods, including the red and black varieties of yams, taro, and unripe plantains as well as the exclusively black wing beans. Dark varieties of sugarcane also are eaten. (These foods were all represented previously by the red and black cordyline leaves tied to the ends of the flutes that the initiates have just seen.)

For the final act of this ritual, the initiates are assembled in the men's house, seated on the floor, and restrained by adult men who hold the youths' arms behind their backs. Handfuls of the specially prepared food are stuffed into their mouths, and they are expected to swallow it quickly without much chewing. The food, being only partially cooked and containing bitter nuts and seeds that are usually eaten only by birds, is quite unpalatable. If the initiates gag or spit out the food, they are slapped and beaten; their lips are frequently cut as the food being shoved into their mouths mashes their lips against their teeth. The intent of this abusive treatment is not simply to convey that these foods *may* be eaten, but to communicate forcefully that they *must* be eaten, and eaten in large quantities. Songs and shouts accompany this forced feeding and exhort the initiates to eat plentifully of all the foods that they are now allowed to consume. Subsequently, men explain that the dark-colored vegetable foods are very ''strong'' and that young initiates have had to avoid them because they were potentially harmful, inducing, as they do, very rapid growth—too rapid for the undeveloped bodies of the young initiates. Through sweating, purging, and restricting their diet to white, ''bone-building'' vegetable foods and the muscle-building flesh of domesticated animals, their bodies have partially cast off the watery substances of youth, becoming firm and strong enough to ready them for the additional growth these foods will now stimulate. Wild animal foods, however, remain tabooed.

Afterward, the initiates, now called anotah mahbi, are taken out of the men's house to join in a general food distribution. No special actions or body ornamentation mark their emergence as finished mahbi, although they wear newly made ornaments of the same types they acquired after the first purging ritual.

In the period between the bean-eating ritual and the next set of rituals in the initiation sequence (which occurs about five years hence), the mahbi are expected to begin taking an active part in gardening. Soon they will clear and plant their own section of a larger garden belonging to their parents and guardians. During this time their instruction gradually shifts away from a strict emphasis on growth and the development of manly traits and toward a concern with reproductive processes. They are taught more about the nature of female procreative powers and the relationship of these forces to the development and maintenance of their own physical well-being. Specifically, they learn about the reasons for maintaining spatial separation between men and women, they become aware that sexual intercourse can be dangerous to themselves (and all adult men), and they come to associate the flutes with contexts in which they are used as energizing and growth-inducing instruments. These understandings come to the initiates, not in ritual settings but by participation in certain events that occur in the natural course of everyday life and by conversation and discussion stimulated by these events.

Since their induction into the men's house, the initiates have been restricted in their interaction with women, not only by sleeping, eating, and spending much of their time in or around the men's house, but by observing other spatial separations from women as well. For example, the interior of a woman's house is divided into two sections by lengths of bamboo or sticks attached to the floor; one section is for initiated men, the other for women and children. There are also separate trails for men and women which must be followed by all when entering or leaving the village, as well as the general prescription that men should remain on the uphill side of women whenever possible. In addition, the section of the village where food is prepared for public distribution is divided by small logs pegged into the ground, which function to separate women and uncooked food on one side from men and cooked food on the other. As the initiates mature in the status of finished mahbi, their understanding of these separations is expanded, and the importance of observing them is reinforced. As young initiates, removal to the men's house and injunctions to avoid women were connected ideationally and emotionally with moving away from the places and activities associated with mother and childhood, and toward those associated with father and adulthood. Now they begin to understand this separation, and others mentioned above, in relation to the inherent danger of substances associated with female procreative powers, especially menstrual blood. They know by this time that women menstruate, and they now learn that the reason women seclude themselves in special huts below the village during their menses is to protect men from this dangerous female discharge. By avoiding direct contact with women, especially during the transfer of food, the initiates avoid touching the residue of this discharge, which may still adhere to women's hands. Moreover, initiates also begin to understand that menstrual blood is dangerous because it is part of the powerful, generative, growth-inducing substances that women have in their reproductive organs. For anotah mahbi initiates, the danger of these substances is that they will trigger an *over*acceleration of the physical maturation they are undergoing. Their own maturation can become so overstimulated by these female substances that it advances directly into physical decay. Thus, initiates not only must avoid general physical contact with women but must specifically refrain from sexual intercourse, since this is of course much more dangerous than simply touching or ingesting the remnants of these substances (cf. Lindenbaum 1972). The latter could make them ill, but the former could turn them into old men and cause premature death.

These consequences are explained to the initiates in a straightforward way, but they are also embodied in a myth they are told at this time. In the myth, a finished mahbi sees the young woman to whom he is betrothed dancing with her age-mates. He is erotically aroused and that night sneaks into her house, where they have sexual intercourse. In the days that follow, he grows ill; his muscles wither, becoming slack like those of an old man; and his skin begins to slough off. Various attempts are made to cure him, but to no avail. Realizing the inevitable result of his transgression, he covers himself with ashes of mourning and sets out to kill himself by hanging. His bride-to-be discovers his disappearance and, noticing the trail of ashes he has left, follows it. She finds him but cannot prevent his suicide. In her grief she hangs herself as well, and the pair are then transformed into two kinds of vines commonly used in making woven body ornaments.

The young man in this myth is identified as a full anotah mahbi and as such has not yet undergone the two final rituals in the initiation sequence. The message is clear: no matter how strong the feelings of attraction and attachment between the mythical pair were, the effect of their untimely union was unavoidably disastrous. Likewise, even though such young men have had their bodies developed and strengthened through sweating, purging, and the controlled intake of food, they are not yet ready to cope with the power of female substances inherent in sexual unions.

The idea that the power of female procreative substances is potentially harmful to males is also reinforced for the full mahbi, who, unlike younger initiates, are allowed to participate in a curing ritual dealing with an affliction that may befall married men. The affliction has been called "male pregnancy" (see Hayano 1974, Meigs 1976, Robbins 1970). This condition is thought to occur in married men as the result of having sexual intercourse too frequently, having sexual intercourse with a menstruating woman, or penetrating the vagina too deeply during intercourse so that the penis contacts the blood and water thought to be contained in the womb. The condition is thus produced by womb blood traveling up the male urethra and mixing with semen. The "cure" involves bleeding the "impregnated" man at several points over the surface of his body, including the penis, with a small, stone-tipped arrow. Bleeding removes female blood from the male body and halts the reproductive process its presence induces. Male pregnancy is not a condition that is apt to afflict the initiates since, in the usual course of events, they are not sexually active, and also because their semen is not considered to be fertile enough for pregnancy to occur. Participation in this ritual does make it clear to them, however, that males remain vulnerable to female substances well into adult life.

Most of what the initiates have learned about the powerful, growth-inducing substances women have in their bodies has emphasized the dangers they represent to males and has focused on controlling their effects through abstinence, avoidance, and strengthening the male body in ways that are frequently very painful. As the initiates progress toward betrothal and marriage, they are made aware that males have another,

267

more benign way of diffusely controlling the power of female substances and using it in a beneficial way. This control is exercised through the use of the flutes. The initiates learn that in the mythic past these flutes were the exclusive property of women, who kept them in the menstrual huts (see Lindenbaum 1976). They were embodiments of female generative power and were blown during pregnancy to ensure proper fetal growth and also during birth to ease the pain of delivery. Men are said to have come into possession of the flutes by a kind of trick. A man, hearing the sounds, went down to the menstrual huts and convinced a woman to turn the flutes over to him with the argument that he could blow the flutes more vigorously than she and would therefore be more successful in producing their desired effects. (This man and woman are now the spirit pair who live in the forest and whose presence is summoned when the flutes are blown during the rituals previously described.) As a result of this duplicity, the men gained control of the flutes, using them to aid in the physical transformation of boys into young men, and women now experience pain in childbirth. Men also use the flutes, however, to aid women experiencing particularly difficult deliveries.[14] In such instances, the flutes are blown in the brush around the house where the delivery is occurring, but still out of sight of the women. Water is poured through the flutes, collected in a container, and then passed to attending women, who rub it over the body of the afflicted woman and give it to her to drink. The use of water in this context is efficacious, and its meaning will be discussed in the next section of the chapter.

It is relevant here to insert a note. In 1972, the Awa of Irahqkiah-Poqna village began using the flutes in a new context, but in a way that is clearly compatible with their older usage and that illustrates the nature of their efficacy. The Awa, unlike their neighbors to the west, did not have very elaborately developed techniques of pig husbandry. They did not, for example, tether pigs, feed them frequently, or provide any shelter. As a result, the pig/human ratio was rather low compared to those of neighboring groups, such as the Fore or Auyana. In 1972, however, the people in Irahqkiah-Poqna decided, for economic and other reasons, to intensify their pig production.[15] As part of this effort, they engaged in certain ritual activities that involved frequent sounding of the flutes. The flute playing was thought to have an effect on both the pigs and the

---

[14]Two cases of this use of the flutes were observed in the field: one involved a lengthy delivery culminating in a stillbirth; the other involved a breech birth in which both the mother and the child eventually died.

[15]For details of this attempt to intensify pig husbandry, see Boyd (1974).

people tending them: it would induce the pigs to eat copiously, grow rapidly, and copulate frequently, and it would induce people to be vigorous in activities associated with pig tending, such as producing food for the pigs. It also was thought to summon up the spirit pair associated with the flutes. This pair would help protect the pigs when foraging in the forest, where the animals are wont to stray and frequently get lost. The use of the flutes in this changing context is instructive because it clearly identifies them as general instruments of control over energizing, growth-inducing powers in both humans and animals.

In summary, then, the image of female procreative power available to the initiates at this transition point is one in which female substances are potentially dangerous to the physical well-being of males but which is also identified with generative forces that can be controlled by males through the use of the flutes. In the rituals to follow, the initiates will learn more about the role these substances play in conception and the practices they must follow to ensure successful reproduction.

AUQ, THE SWEAT CEREMONY

The sweat ceremony begins when the initiates, now in their early to mid-twenties, are taken into the men's house, where they will remain for a week or more. During this period they are made to sit close to the fire, so they sweat almost constantly. The perspiration that accumulates on the skin is scraped off with a pair of small bamboo sticks (decorated for the initiates with incised designs) that they will wear in their bark girdles when they emerge from the men's house at the end of this ritual.

During seclusion, the initiates are again forbidden to drink water, and their diet is restricted to sugarcane and small amounts of white tubers. They are encouraged, however, to eat red pandanus fruit (cf. Meigs 1976). Red pandanus is cooked and eaten only in the men's house and only by males who have passed through this ritual. Its consumption is a carefully guarded secret, and men hold that women do not know it is edible. Women may not eat any cultivated plants grown on land near the sites of abandoned men's houses where cobs of red pandanus fruit have been thrown in the remembered past, a prohibition publicly sanctioned by the general restrictions on women's access to grounds occupied exclusively by men.

While the young men eat and sweat, they are instructed about the responsibilities of marriage, particularly with respect to marital fidelity and the obligations of fatherhood. They are reminded that it is time for

269

them to take wives and have children and that families must be looked after carefully. Initiates are told specifically that having sex with women other than their wives will produce unfortunate consequences. For example, the wives and children of an adulterer will abandon him, and another man will thus be able to find wives for his male children—a circumstance that should be avoided, it is said, because it will eventuate in a loss of social support in his old age. Moreover, adultery can lead to premature death, for reasons that are explained to them later.

In addition to instruction concerning the proprieties of sexual conduct, which takes place in lecturelike situations, the initiates' understanding of other aspects of sexuality is deepened as they pass the time listening to older men talk informally about matters related to procreative processes. These matters emerge in conversation on such topics as how conception occurs and also through the recounting of mythic events considered appropriate for the initiates to hear at this time. There are many important ideas and images in these oral traditions, but we shall restrict attention to those aspects dealing with the nature of female procreative power because it is related to the meaning of several ritual practices and food taboos central to male initiation. Space does not permit an extended presentation of this material, so synopses of a few of the myths must serve as a basis for discussing general themes.

Myth One

There was once a woman living alone in Irahqkiah. A man from Tauna [village] saw the smoke from her fire and, wondering who it might be, went to investigate. He arrived but became fearful of her when he discovered she was living alone and was covered with sores. She, on the other hand, was enamored of him and begged him to take her back with him. He tried various subterfuges to get rid of her, but she followed him anyway. On returning, and shaking with fright, he sought the advice of an older clansman. The clansman inspected the woman and found that she had no vaginal opening, so he got a stone scraper and made one by cutting her. Copious amounts of blood flowed out, forming two of the existing major streams in the region. Also, many marsupials and rodents came outside of her. That stone is still said to be inside the vagina making blood.

Myth Two

A married couple had a daughter who was not yet married. She wondered whom she would marry. One day she discovered a tree kangaroo and enticed it down from its tree with food. She thought she

270

would continue to feed it until it got big enough to serve as her husband. Her mother discovered what she was doing and killed the animal. When the daughter found out what her mother had done, she killed her and ran away.

While running away, the girl dug ditches in the ground with a cassowary bone and called out for water to flow through them in order to cover her tracks. She was eventually discovered by a man, who took her to his village. The two were married, and she became pregnant. When it was time to give birth, she delivered many kinds of dark-colored yams and taro, as well as a child.

Myth Three

A wife ate the contents of a food packet that her husband had given her to cook but that he intended to eat himself. When he discovered what had happened, he threatened to beat his wife, who then ran away with her children to a garden near the edge of the forest. Fearing he might find them and harm the children, she lay down and called her children into her vagina. When her husband arrived, she was swollen and unrecognizable. She was also in a good deal of pain and asked him to cut her open, saying she was bloated from eating too many ripe bananas. When he did so, all kinds of wild creatures came out of her: birds, cassowaries, feral pigs, rodents, and various kinds of marsupials. Before this time, these creatures did not exist, and if they had come into existence by themselves, instead of from a human, they would be plentiful instead of scarce.

Myth Four

A man noticed that the fruits of a tree were being eaten and, suspecting it might be a marsupial, set watch one night to catch it. He saw what appeared to be a large marsupial with its offspring on its back approach the tree and begin gathering the fruit. He then realized it was a woman and her child. Seeing she was an attractive woman, he grabbed hold of her, thinking to take her home. The woman resisted and changed form, becoming in succession a tree, a stone, a rodent, a marsupial, muddy earth, and water, but the man hung onto her. Finally she changed back into the form of a woman, and he took her home.

One day the wife left her child with the husband while she went gardening. The child cried for food, but when the husband offered it garden tubers, it refused them, wanting to eat only wild tree fruits. The husband admonished the child for its odd behavior but succeeded only in making it cry louder. The wife overheard the ruckus, became angry at

271

the man for mistreating her child this way, and determined to run away. She left that night with her child and traveled into the forest, where there was a large stone. Her husband, who had followed them, saw the mother and child standing in front of the stone and calling to the woman's mother, who was inside, to open it and let them inside. The stone opened, but as they were going in, the man came up and grabbed at them. He caught hold of the child's foot, and although the mother and child were turning into marsupials, he kept pulling until he yanked off the child's toe, allowing them to slip inside. Today it can be seen that marsupials have one toe that is short and stubby as a result of this.

Images in the Myths

The first image in these myths we wish to discuss involves the association between women and water. This mythological association is important to our understanding of the relationship among the sweat ritual, taboos against eating creatures that live in the water, and ideas about conception and fetal development. In the mythic texts, women cause flowing water to come into existence, either by willing it to flow or by transforming their vaginal blood. (There are still other myths in which women are created from tadpoles or water-dwelling frogs, as well as one in which dead children are resurrected because their bones are placed in a stream among tadpoles.) In addition to these mythic associations, Awa ideas about conception and birth, revealed to the initiates during the sweat ritual, identify water as the medium of fetal development. The initiates are reminded that pig fetuses, which they have seen while helping in the butchering of pigs, are encased in a water-filled sack. They are told that human fetuses are similar in this respect, as is evidenced by the fact that human birth is preceded by a rush of water. When men pour water through the flutes to aid women experiencing difficult deliveries, it is an act intended to manipulate this water of birth. Finally, they learn that conception occurs when male semen and female blood mix together in womb water: fetal development is a coalescing of the semen-blood mixture out of the watery medium. Water, then, appears as an inherent part of female nature; women are represented as creating water or being created from creatures that live within it, and human life-forms are represented as developing out of the water in a woman's womb. Water is not considered an inherent part of male nature, however, and males must rid their bodies of as much of it as possible in order to achieve the firmness of flesh associated with manly strength. The long period of sweating the initiates endure in this ritual sequence is seen as the

272

culmination of a strengthening, energizing, growth-inducing procedure that began when they were first made to sweat on induction into the men's house. This process was also aided by removal of the watery portion of youthful blood through nosebleeding and the liquid portion of wild animal food through vomiting. Although the sweat ritual represents a developmental culmination, in the sense that the initiates' bodies are now thought to be sufficiently purged of the watery substances of youth, the young men know they must continue to protect the firmness of their bodies for several years to come by following the taboos on eating fish, eels, frogs, and other creatures of the water.

A second mythic image involves an association between women and various kinds of wild, land-dwelling creatures (see Lindenbaum 1976 and Meigs 1976). To begin with, the myths make identifications between women and marsupials: a woman seeks to marry one; they emerge from women's reproductive organs; a woman and her child are first mistaken for marsupials, then act like marsupials by eating wild fruit at night, and finally become transformed into marsupials. It is relevant to note that when males are transformed in Awa myths, they never change into an animal form but always into some sturdy plant form, such as a tree or vine, or some permanent feature of the landscape, like a large, rocky outcropping. Further, in three of the myths cited, the vagina is represented as containing various kinds of wild creatures and, in one instance, dark-colored tubers—the kind that are too "strong" for young initiates to eat (see Buchbinder and Rappaport 1976). (This narrative image is also found in another myth, in which a man inadvertently peers into a woman's exposed vagina, which he describes as "full of all kinds of small things, strewn about like items in an ill-kept sleeping room.") A similar image is presented ritually to young men in the final rite of the initiation sequence (see below) in the form of a fabricated vulva fashioned from a fruit and used during instruction about sexual intercourse. The young men are thus taught that deep penetration during intercourse is to be avoided because the female organ is full of "small red things and dark things," all of which will come out if care is not exercised.

These texts also suggest an identification between the major types of wild, land-dwelling creatures (marsupials, rodents, amphibians, reptiles, and birds) and the human fetus. All of these creatures are represented as inherent parts of the female being; either they are inside of female reproductive organs, or they came into existence by way of such. There is also an identification based on similarity of shape, as with, for example, marsupials, whose stubby limbs and general body configuration are said to be fetuslike and in whose pouch fetal forms are near the

273

surface of the body. Rodents are considered to be of similar shape, and one way of referring to a newborn child's throbbing fontanel is to call it "the infant's rat" (the rat is "in the child," and the throbbing is its movement). Amphibians, such as frogs, newts, and salamanders, are said to be like a fetus because of the mucus covering their bodies. This idea is even extended to a certain cultivated plant the leaves of which, when cooked, have a slimy texture and are, incidentally, forbidden to initiates or married men whose wives are pregnant. None of these items can be eaten by males after induction into the men's house and onward, well into adulthood; they must especially abstain from eating fetal items like insect grubs and bird eggs.

In general, earlier explanations of such food taboos—during the first purging ritual—simply involved telling initiates that such foods were too "strong" for them and that their ingestion would result in an internal rot that would destroy their bodies or at least impede their growth. Now they understand that these foods are dangerous because they are, in shape, substance, and origin, essentially female and therefore antithetical to males, involving generative powers that the male body cannot handle.

To conclude about the sweat ritual: after several days of sweating, singing, instruction, and conversation involving the above matters, the young men are readied to emerge from the men's house. After days by the fire, their skins have become sooty, and this effect is enhanced when their bodies are rubbed with a mixture of charred leaves and pig oil until they have a black, shiny appearance. They are given a new bark girdle (*tahtare* kamoka: literally, "second bark girdle") that is similar to their first one except that it is fitted with a belt, about four inches wide, made from the inner linings of bamboo and decorated with geometrical motifs. The incised sweat-scraping sticks are thrust through this belt. New feather and shell ornaments are provided, and bundles of decorative leaves are tied at the elbows, wrists, knees, and ankles. The young men also receive a prime symbol of adult male status in the form of a nose ornament made from two boar tusks and worn in their nasal septum with its points up. They emerge from the men's house carrying new bows and fine arrows over their right shoulders, holding onto the sweat-scraping sticks protruding from their bamboo belts with their left hands, and bracing their elbows stiffly to their sides. After displaying themselves to the admiring community, several other events, these connected with betrothal, occur. It is at this time, for example, that the prospective brides are transferred from their natal hamlets to that of their future husbands. The final ritual in the initiation sequence remains, however, and it takes place within the next few days.

AHPWI TARI EQE, OR SEVERE PENIS CUTTING

The severe-penis-cutting ritual is alluded to in the paradigmatic myth of the two boys who lose their mother when, at its conclusion, the youths are caused much pain and bleeding by stepping on bone awls left at the base of a tree by the two young women they will marry. The ritual begins with seclusion of the initiates in the men's house for a day or two, accompanied, as before, by fasting and abstinence from water. They are given a special food consisting of singed nettle leaves cooked in bamboo with small amounts of pork fat. Eating this mixture causes very painful stinging and swelling in the throat, and a day or two are allowed to elapse before the initiates are subjected to the next ritual phase.

The main part of the ritual is carried out at the same stream that was used for previous events in the initiation sequence; only married men may attend. It includes bathing, flute playing, nosebleeding, and penis cutting, but not vomiting or beating. The bleeding, however, is accomplished in a more severe manner than the first time. Now the instruments used for bleeding the nose are not simply jabbed into the nostrils, but are driven in deeply with a stone or wooden pounder to cause very profuse bleeding. Similarly, the glans penis is not simply incised, but small wedges of flesh are removed from either side, producing deep, half-inch-long gashes that occasionally penetrate the urethra. The lacerated glans then is struck sharply and repeatedly with the blade of the bamboo knife used in the cutting and also is rubbed vigorously with salt or nettles.

This violent bleeding of the nose and penis may appear to be a reduplication or intensification of what has been done in rituals throughout the initiation sequence; and, indeed, the Awa say that these practices, as in their previous performances, are done to "strengthen" the initiates. Nevertheless, these acts, along with the eating of nettles and the irritation of the glans, are not done in the service of facilitating physical growth. Rather, the intense pain is thought to stimulate the movement of one's ahweh, or life-force, within the body. For example, the stimulating or energizing effect of pain is commonly relied on by adult men to prepare themselves for difficult or dangerous undertakings of various kinds, such as going into battle. (Older Awa men state that the fiercest warriors often would lead an attack with nosebleeders left jammed into their nostrils or the ends of vomiting canes protruding from their mouths. Such preparations were said to increase the men's strength and to terrorize on sight their less hardened opponents.) In the context of initiation ritual, the pain experienced by the initiates is again thought to strengthen them against the dangers of imminent contact with powerful female substances inherent in approaching sexual intercourse with their new wives. Finally, inflicting pain on the penis at this juncture is specifically thought to induce the production of semen, making it "boil up" in the genitals and thereby contributing to their procreative success as adults.

After ritual surgery on the initiates has been completed, all the men present at the ritual line up to have their own penes bled. One by one, they stand in front of an experienced practitioner and hold their penes forward to receive two small puncture wounds in the glans from a small, stone-tipped arrow fired from a miniature bow, the same instrument used in treating male pregnancy. Such penis "shooting" is a common occurrence in the lives of most adult Awa men, who routinely resort to it several times each year to combat simple lethargy and to prevent or treat more serious illness.[16] Regular penis bleeding is said not only to energize and strengthen a man but also to promote general physical well-being by draining off any harmful female substances, especially residual menstrual blood, that may have inadvertently entered the penis during sexual intercourse. This group penis bleeding, during this fifth ritual of initiation, revitalizes all adult men just prior to the critical commencement of the initiates' sexual contact with their new wives.

After eating and resting at the stream, the initiates and attendant party return to the village and assemble in a secluded area on the men's house ground (not in the men's house itself). There they are given explicit instruction about certain cautions that must be observed during sexual intercourse to protect their physical well-being. A wild fruit fashioned to represent a vulva and a piece of edible pitpit representing the penis are used to instruct the initiates, graphically, in exactly how intercourse should take place in order to minimize contact with the dangerous substances in the female reproductive organ. Here is an older married man's summary of this lecture: "An old man holds up the fruit and the pitpit and says, 'A woman's vagina looks good on the outside, but inside there are other things; red things, water, and blood, which is deep inside.' The old man marks on the pitpit just how far a young man's penis should penetrate the vagina. He tells them that putting the penis too deeply into the vagina is not good because it will cause all of these things to come out. If they come out and go into a man, he will become like a pregnant woman. Women have a womb and can have a baby, but where

---

[16]Awa men who had returned from tours of labor migration reported that they occasionally bled their penes while employed on lowland, coastal plantations. Again, the stated purpose was to energize and strengthen their bodies, which were weakened by the hot weather and different life-style.

is a man's womb? The child will just grow inside him, and its teeth will develop and bite him, and he will die."

The failure to take proper care during sexual intercourse does not inevitably result in male pregnancy, although this is the most serious possible consequence and is therefore emphasized in the above statement. The adverse effects range from general feelings of malaise or listlessness to various protracted, debilitating maladies that cause weight loss and gradual wasting away. Moreover when warfare was still a reality in Awa life, being wounded in a fight was sometimes attributed to vulnerability caused by such carelessness in sexual activities. All of these misfortunes can be caused by other errors in sexual conduct besides excessive penetration. Proper restraint must be exercised in all sexual encounters, and the initiates are thus carefully instructed about appropriate times, places, and frequencies for coitus, as well as cleansing procedures to be followed afterward.

Following this instruction, the initiates are taken into the men's house, where they are further lectured about the social consequences of marital infidelity. In the men's house they are shown a display of bows, arrows, axes, and fighting sticks. These, they are told, are the instruments of reprisal which will be used against them by enraged husbands should they be discovered seducing other men's wives. The consequences of such a transgression are not only social, however, and the initiates are told that if they have sexual intercourse with another woman and then with their wives, the "fluids of these two vaginas will strike one another inside you," causing illness or even death.

After these teachings, the initiates are finally allowed to rest and recuperate from the ordeal at the stream. They are in a great deal of pain, and the penis must be carefully bound and tended to facilitate healing of the deep gashes in the glans. After a few days, when they are sufficiently healed, the young men parade out of the men's house in full adult male body ornamentation. The boar-tusk nose ornament is now worn with the points down rather than up, thus marking the assumption of their new status as menahwe—young adult males—and their preparedness to be sexually active in marriage.

THE RITUAL PREPARATION OF WOMEN

During the time young men are undergoing the fourth and fifth rituals of their initiation, which change their status from mahbi to menahwe, the young, unmarried women, called *arahisi*, who have been chosen to be

277

their wives, also are ritually prepared to assume their new social positions as *ipaini*, young married women. Space does not permit a detailed description of these rituals here, but a brief consideration of the major events, which in many ways parallel those described for males, will help emphasize important similarities in the performance and symbolism of these ritual acts.

These rituals occur when the young women are in their late teens or early twenties and the arrangements for their betrothal have been completed. By this age, their bodies are well developed and they have passed menarche, an event not marked by any special ritual in most Awa groups.[17] Unlike males, whose growth and physical development must be induced and carefully controlled by direct human intervention, the physical maturation and procreative capability of women occur as a natural process without human assistance. The physical well-being of women, however, is not so assured. In order for this desired end to be promoted and maintained, the forces within their bodies must be manipulated through ritual means.

The first ritual begins when the young women are taken from their mothers' houses by female matrilateral relatives and, accompanied by other married women of the village, are led to a location slightly downstream of the site used for male purging rituals. There they are joined by the young women's male patrikin and mother's brothers, who have collected and prepared the implements to be used in the ritual. The only persons prohibited from viewing this event are younger unmarried women and males who have not yet undergone their first purging. After the older women, who will assist with the ritual, have bathed themselves and their own body coverings, the young women are brought to stand in the shallow water clad only in a narrow bark-string apron that covers the pubic region and another that sparingly covers the buttocks. Each is quickly restrained by her male patrikin while her mother's brother inserts a nosebleeding instrument into each nostril (see Berndt 1962; Hayano 1972; Hays and Hays, this volume; Lindenbaum 1976). These nosebleeders and the manner in which they are manipulated are identical to those used in the purging events performed during the second and third rituals of male initiation. After her nose is vigorously jabbed several times, she is released to bleed into the stream. When the bleeding has

---

[17]Hayano (1972:88–89), however, describes a ritual of first menstruation for the Tauna Awa. It is likely that the performance of this ritual, like that of several other rituals reported for the Tauna Awa, is due in large part to their proximity to and influences from Auyana peoples. For a description of first menstruation rituals among the Auyana, see Robbins (1970:99–101).

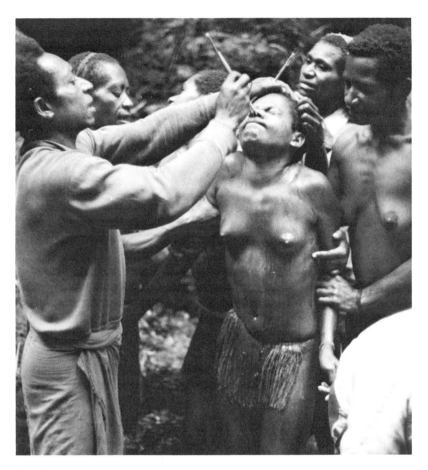

PLATE 6.4 A young woman is nosebled during preparations for her marriage.

subsided a bit, the procedure is repeated. On one occasion we observed, the two young women initiates each had their noses bled four times, with several of their mother's brothers taking a turn wielding the nose-bleeders. When the blood flow finally slows, the young women are bathed, and the older women clothe them with a new bark-string pubic apron in front and cordyline leaves hanging from the waist string in back. Still standing in the water, the young women are beaten with nettle switches by the men. The older women finally intervene, wrap the young women in bark capes, and move them off toward the village, where each young woman is secluded in the house of her mother.

279

While in seclusion, the young women are told by their mothers and other married women that the ritual they have just experienced will increase their strength and promote their well-being by stimulating the life-force within their bodies. This energizing effect will make them strong and healthy, able to perform the arduous tasks and fulfill the many responsibilities of being adult women. These responsibilities are made more explicit by the older women present, who give them instructions on three major topics. First and foremost, they are informed of the potent powers of female reproductive organs. All vaginal secretions are a potential threat to the well-being of a husband and his male patrikin, and the woman has a responsibility to behave in a manner that will protect these men from possible harm. They are warned to watch where they walk and sit and to be particularly careful in the handling and preparation of food. Menstrual blood is especially dangerous, they are told, and when the signs of a menstrual period appear, they must immediately go to the menstrual hut, remain there until the flow stops, and then go to the stream, where they can dispose of the leaves and moss used to catch their fluids and wash themselves before resuming normal activity. They also are warned that failure in these matters not only will be disgraceful but also will be severely punished by both women and men, especially their own fathers and brothers.

In addition, the young women are informed of their sexual obligations and responsibilities. A woman must follow the sexual initiative of her husband and have sexual relations with him only. They must never have intercourse in the village, in their gardens, or in any other location that could potentially harm other people or contaminate foodstuffs. They both must wash after sexual activity, and it is the responsibility of the woman to see that semen and other fluids do not dribble from her vagina to be collected by sorcerers or eaten by earthworms, both of which may jeopardize her own and her husband's health. They must not have intercourse during the period of particular events when such contact is proscribed for everyone—for example, during garden planting, mortuary rituals, postpartum periods, or fight preparations. Finally, the young women are told of their responsibility to work hard at making gardens, raising pigs, and carrying out other domestic duties. If a woman is lazy about these tasks, she will anger her husband and shame her brothers.

After a few days in seclusion, the young women are prepared for transfer from their own residences to those of their intended husbands, who have just emerged from the men's house after undergoing the fourth ritual of initiation, the sweat ceremony. The skins of the young women are lavishly rubbed with pig oil, their faces are painted with red ocher, and many new bast skirts and aprons are tied to their waists. Decorated with valuable shells and various woven ornaments and carrying a bundle of arrows in one hand and several large cooked taro in the other arm, they set off for their new residences accompanied by singing and the sounding of whistles. They move along a path strewn with leaves of all the major cultivated food plants, signs of the abundance they will find and the responsibility to feed others they will assume. Upon arrival at their destinations, each woman presents the arrows and feeds the taro to the father or male guardian of her husband-to-be. Each of the young women is led into her respective house by her future mate's mother or other close female relative. These older women will closely supervise the activities of the young wives. The intended brides remain inside the houses until their future husbands complete the fifth ritual of their initiation and emerge from the men's house as menahwe, wearing their tusk nose ornaments pointed down.

The appearance of the new couples in public, marked by an exchange of food between the patrikin of each couple, shortly precedes the final ritual, which prepares the young women for their new role as married women. The young women are taken at night to a special place near the edge of the forest by a group consisting of several older male patrikin of their respective grooms and some of the older women married to these men. The ritual site, which is not used for any other purpose and must be avoided at all other times, is cleaned up by the older women. They then separate and seat the younger women at some distance from each other and tell them that they each must prepare to have sexual intercourse with the several patrikinsmen of their future husbands. The older women may begin the proceedings by pulling their own husbands down on top of themselves to show the young women exactly what is intended. Eventually, each young woman submits to as many of her future male affines as wish to copulate with her. When one man finishes, another takes his place, and each man may copulate with the young woman as frequently as he desires. When the men's energies begin to wane, the older women, who have been carefully monitoring the conduct of these activities, intercede to wrap the young women in bark capes and lead them back to the village. The men walk to the stream and wash their bodies before returning to the men's house.

The purpose of this prolonged, serial copulation, in terms of our present discussion, is to ready the young women for procreative activities by "opening" the vagina and forcing out any bloody fluids that would harm their husbands and thereby impair successful reproduction. The older men who engage in this ritualized sexual intercourse have already fathered several children, and it is thought that their susceptibility to the dangers posed by contact with such potent female substances is therefore relatively low. These senior patrikinsmen of the prospective grooms believe that they are, in effect, protecting the well-being of their younger male kin and promoting the successful reproduction of their group. This experience is, of course, quite painful for the young women involved; but the severe pain is rationalized as necessary to invigorate the life-force in their bodies.[18] Inflicting pain on the genitalia of young women, as on those of young men, is said to strengthen reproductive organs and stimulate the production of bodily substances associated with procreation.

When the new menahwe and ipaini have sufficiently recovered, a period that may last from a few days to several weeks, each newlywed couple shares a private meal and begins the activities of adult married life.

CONCLUSION

Awa male initiation is composed of a sequence of five ritual transitions thought essential to the making of men. These rituals influence the expression of important cosmic processes of growth and procreation in males by manipulating and controlling bodily substances and generative processes. Fasting, sweating, ingesting specific foods, and suffering various physical traumas serve to induce physical growth, establish general physical well-being, and develop procreative capability.

The Awa understanding of the relationships between bodily substances and the processes of growth and procreation is couched in a system of hidden knowledge, gradually revealed to initiates, that posits several fundamental oppositions between men and women. First, the growth, maturation, and procreative ability of women are natural aspects of being female and occur, therefore, without any human intervention. For males, however, these processes do not occur naturally. Adult men have the responsibility to take specific action to induce and stimulate

---

[18]We recognize that this experience has many other important psychological and social implications, but these cannot be dealt with here. We hasten to add, however, that the serial intercourse event described here is not the same as that called "gang rape." Although coercion is certainly present, from both the older men and the older women, the ostensive purpose is not to punish or degrade the young women, but to complete ritual preparations thought essential for successful marriage and procreation.

growth and procreative capacity in younger males. They begin to fulfill this responsibility by separating the young boys from their mothers and younger playmates and secluding them in the men's house. There the young boys are promptly and forcefully informed that adult men are different from women and from uninitiated boys in basic and important ways. This knowledge is initially underscored by the disgust and indignation with which the newly inducted boys, who are considered closely associated with females, are treated. During the first and second rituals, while being viciously berated and brutally punished, they are warned that they must sever their ties with women and uninitiated boys: they must conform to the disciplined life of men and accept adult social responsibilities. Furthermore, they must submit to the behavioral restrictions and ritual acts that will induce their physical growth. The patriclansmen of each boy are especially aggressive during these initial proceedings. So great is their hostility toward the boys that they are not allowed to be directly involved in the purging ritual lest they handle a nosebleeder, vomiting cane, or bamboo blade in such a manner as to inflict serious injury on their young relatives. Before the third ritual stage of initiation, however, the attitude of all adult men to the young initiates dramatically changes. Instead of being viewed as irresponsible, troublesome youths closely allied with women, they are treated as growing, maturing, neophyte clansmen requiring and deserving ritual assistance of their elders. This change in the status of the initiates is marked by the active participation of their elder clansmen in the formal instruction and ritual performances. Although the rituals are still very painful, they lack the punitive aspects of previous events. The elders' attention has turned to broadening and deepening the initiates' understanding of the processes of growth and physical development, and to teaching the techniques required to manipulate bodily substances.

By the time of the fourth and fifth stages of male initiation, the emphasis has shifted from nearly exclusive preoccupation with growth, physical development, and social responsibility to a concern with procreation. A second fundamental opposition between men and women is introduced at this time. Not only does the procreative ability of women develop naturally, but the generative force of female procreative powers is considerably greater than that of men and therefore poses serious dangers to men. Men must therefore undergo ritual treatment that activates their own generative powers and induces the production of bodily substances necessary for successful reproduction. The initiates are simultaneously taught to perform specific techniques that will inure them to the dangers posed by their imminent contact with female generative substances. The procedures learned at this time will be performed periodically throughout the remainder of a man's sexually active life so that his physical strength and well-being may be maintained.

Women, too, are prepared for adulthood at this time. According to male dogma, however, the painful rituals in which they participate are not designed to induce growth or procreative ability, both of which are already well developed in them. Rather, bleeding of the nose stimulates the life-force and increases the physical stamina necessary to perform the arduous labors of adult women. Again, the pain inflicted on a woman and her genitalia energizes the bodily substances associated with procreation and strengthens the reproductive organs to withstand the trauma of childbirth.

The final rituals of male initiation convey an important understanding of the nature of procreation and inform initiates of their responsibility to transcend the fundamental oppositions of men and women. They are warned of the hazards of contact with female generative substances but are told also of their responsibility to engage in sexual intercourse and produce offspring. The techniques they have learned to manipulate their bodily substances will, if properly performed, immunize them against the dangers of procreative activity and allow them to establish the necessary complementary relationships of married life. Transcending the "natural opposition" of men and women is the great imperative of Awa adulthood, and this fundamental integration is accomplished by the polarized preparation of women and making of men.

REFERENCES

ALLEN, M. R.
1967 *Male Cults and Secret Initiations in Melanesia*. Melbourne: Melbourne University Press.

BARTH, F.
1975 *Ritual and Knowledge among the Baktaman of New Guinea*. New Haven: Yale University Press.

BERNDT, R. M.
1962 *Excess and Restraint*. Chicago: University of Chicago Press.

BOYD, D. J.
1974 "We must follow the Fore": pig husbandry intensification among the Ilakia Awa of Papua New Guinea. Paper read at the Annual Meeting of the American Anthropological Association, Mexico City.

1975 Crops, kiaps, and currency: flexible behavioral strategies among the Ilakia Awa of Papua New Guinea. Ph.D. dissertation, University of California, Los Angeles.

BUCHBINDER, G., and R. A. RAPPAPORT
1976 Fertility and death among the Maring. In *Man and Woman in the New Guinea Highlands*, ed. P. Brown and G. Buchbinder, pp. 13–35. Washington, D.C.: American Anthropological Association.

GOURLAY, K. A.
1975 *Sound-Producing Instruments in Traditional Society*. New Guinea Research Bulletin, no. 60. Port Moresby: Australian National University Press.

HAYANO, D. M.
1972 Marriage, alliance, and warfare: the Tauna Awa of New Guinea. Ph.D. dissertation, University of California, Los Angeles.

1974 Misfortune and traditional political leadership among the Tauna Awa of New Guinea. *Oceania* 45:18–26.

LANGNESS, L. L.
1974 Ritual power and male domination in the New Guinea Highlands. *Ethos* 2:189–212.

LINDENBAUM, S.
1972 Sorcerers, ghosts, and polluting women. *Ethnology* 11:241–253.

1976 A wife is the hand of man. In *Man and Woman in the New Guinea Highlands*, ed. P. Brown and G. Buchbinder, pp. 54–62. Washington, D.C.: American Anthropological Association.

MCKAUGHAN, H. (ed.)
1973 *The Languages of the Eastern Family of the East New Guinea Highland Stock*. Seattle: University of Washington Press.

MEGGITT, M. J.
1964 Male-female relationships in the Highlands of Australian New Guinea. In *New Guinea: The Central Highlands*, ed. J. B. Watson, *American Anthropologist* 166, pt. 2(4):204–224.

MEIGS, A. S.
1976 Male pregnancy and the reduction of sexual opposition in a New Guinea Highlands society. *Ethnology* 15:393–407.

NEWMAN, P.
1965 *Knowing the Gururumba*. New York: Holt, Rinehart and Winston.

PATAKI, K. J.
1968 Time, space, and human community. Ph.D. dissertation, University of Washington.

READ, K. E.
1952 Nama cult of the Central Highlands, New Guinea. *Oceania* 23:1–25.

1965 *The High Valley*. New York: Charles Scribner's Sons.

ROBBINS, S. G.
1970 Warfare, marriage, and the distribution of goods in Auyana. Ph.D. dissertation, University of Washington.

STRATHERN, A. J.
1970 Male initiation in the New Guinea Highlands societies. *Ethnology* 9:373–379.

7 THE FATHER WHO BORE ME:
The Role of Tsambunwuro during Chambri Initiation Ceremonies

Deborah B. Gewertz

The Author

Deborah B. Gewertz is Assistant Professor of Anthropology at Amherst College. She was born in New York City. After completing undergraduate work in English literature at Queens College, City University of New York, and Princeton University, she attended the Graduate School of the City University of New York, where she studied social organization, economic anthropology, and Melanesia with Mervyn Meggitt and Robert Glasse. Her fieldwork was conducted from 1974 through 1975 among the lake-dwelling Chambri tribe, whom Margaret Mead first studied in the 1930s and wrote about (most notably in *Sex and Temperament in Three Primitive Societies* [1935]). Dr. Gewertz's dissertation research concerned a socioeconomic analysis of exchange spheres among the Chambri; she received her Ph.D. in 1977. Her articles have appeared in several journals, including *Oceania, The Journal of Polynesian Society, Ethnology, Anthropological Quarterly*, and *The Journal of Anthropological Research*. Most recently, she has published "An Historical Reconsideration of Female Dominance among the Chambri of Papua New Guinea" in *The American Ethnologist*.

Professor Gewertz has taught at Amherst since 1977, and she remains committed to research. Her teaching has encompassed general anthropology, economic theory, social processes, history of anthropology, and egalitarian societies. She returned to the Chambri in 1979 for further research on recent environmental and social changes. She is currently completing *A Confluence of Powers: An Historical Ethnography of the Chambri and their Neighbors*, a book that addresses the question of how different groups of people have integrated sociocultural elements of one another within their relatively autonomous social systems.

INTRODUCTION

In the initiation ceremonies of the Chambri of the East Sepik Province of Papua New Guinea one participant, the *tsambunwuro*, by virtue of his special relationship with the initiate, can have the boy's blood spill on him without suffering ill effects. During ritual scarification, the first phase of Chambri initiation, the tsambunwuro lies face down on an overturned canoe and the initiate lies face down on his tsambunwuro's back. While observing male initiation during 1974,[1] I was especially interested in the tsambunwuro relationship because, although the Chambri have adopted most other aspects of Iatmul initiation (Bateson 1958), this particular relationship is absent from Iatmul ceremonies. Among the Iatmul the *wau*, or mother's brother, acts in place of the tsambunwuro. In both societies the scarifiers, specialists chosen from the initiation moiety opposite to that of the initiate, finish the operation within ten minutes, making hundreds of half-inch vertical cuts in rows down the initiates's back, buttocks, and upper thighs. The fact that during scarification the Chambri substitute the tsambunwuro for the Iatmul wau suggests that the tsambunwuro relationship is particularly significant to them. In this chapter I shall explain why this is so. Specifically, I will unravel the meaning and significance of the tsambunwuro within Chambri initiation ceremonies and within the larger sociopolitical context of these ceremonies, demonstrating that tsambunwuro perpetuate the relationships upon which Chambri society depends.

THE CHAMBRI

The Chambri, a tribe of sedentary hunters and gatherers, numbered 1,300 in 1974. Their three villages, Indingai, Kilimbit, and Wombun, are located south of the Sepik River along the shore of Chambri Lake. Surrounding Chambri Mountain, which rises to a height of some 500 feet, this lake is little more than two tributaries of the Sepik River which yearly overflow their banks. Although Chambri Lake is shallow, ranging in depth from 3 to 20 feet, it contains many fish. The Chambri subsist on these, together with sago, a carbohydrate produced from the pith of the

[1]My research among the Chambri from 1974 through 1975 was funded by the East West Center Population Institute, the National Geographic Society, and the graduate school of the City University of New York. I am grateful to all three institutions and also to Mervyn Meggitt, Donald Pitkin, Krystyna Starker, Kenneth Gewertz, and the other contributors to this volume, whose assistance in formulating my ideas and editing my words has proved invaluable.

287

sago palm, *Metroxylum rumphii*. Chambri women acquire sago at barter markets in the Sepik Hills, where they exchange one fish for one small chunk of sago.[2]

There are fifteen spirit houses in the three Chambri villages, some owned jointly by up to six patriclans. The Chambri consider all patriclans, which are landowning, residential, and ceremonial groups, to be equal. Each is affiliated with one of two patri-moieties, *Nyaui-nimba* or *Nyemi-nimba*, which are in theory exogamous. In fact, only 60 percent of the people marry into the opposite moiety. When a spirit house is owned by only two clans, the members of one belong to Nyaui-nimba and sit in the western half of the house, and the members of the other belong to Nyemi-nimba and sit in the eastern half.

Two other pairs of ceremonial moieties structure Chambri society. The first, *Pombiantimeri/Yambuntimeri*, functions only during initiation ceremonies. The second, *Ilasone/Pangasone*, apparently used to function during war ceremonies involving the awakening of powerful ancestors in the form of crocodiles. The Ilasone/Pangasone ceremonies have not been performed for about fifty years, and the information I collected about them is vague and contradictory.

The spirit houses are located along the shore of Chambri Mountain, and the member clans own strips of land extending from the shoreline through the rocky, wooded mountainside to the mountaintop. The women's houses are built on the mountainside up to 200 feet above the shore. Postmarital residence is viripatrilocal, and, although each married man prefers to build a separate house for his wife (or wives) and children, frequently a father and his married sons establish their families in one large house. In most circumstances, females are forbidden to enter or even to approach spirit houses, for the men fear the weakening influences of menstrual blood. Two roads run parallel to the shoreline through the three villages; when women pass a spirit house, they must take the road further from the sacred ground. Men visit their wives at night for sexual intercourse, and they may return to the spirit house in the morning only after they have washed all female pollutants from their bodies. A constant complaint of the older men is that their sons spend an inordinate amount of time with their wives in the women's houses instead of profiting from the discussion of their elders in the spirit house. The older men blame the women for coercing the young men away from the spirit house. They believe that women need sexual intercourse, while men

[2]Today the Chambri acquire most of their sago at money markets (Gewertz 1977).

would be happier without it. Indeed, they argue that women need sex in order to remain healthy, while men are depleted each time they succumb to their partner's desires.

The Chambri believe that a man should marry into his mother's clan and that a woman should return in marriage to her mother's clan in repayment for her mother. In no case is marriage with either the biological mother's brother's daughter or father's sister's daughter permitted or practiced, for it is believed that if a man marries a woman who shares his blood their children will not survive. Thirty percent of the people do find mates in their mother's brother's clan, while only 2 percent marry a member of their father's sister's husband's clan.

The rate of village endogamy is high (73 percent in Indingai, 78 percent in Kilimbit, and 83 percent in Wombun), surpassed only by that for intra-island marriages (over 91 percent in all). Affinal exchanges link clans, and a mother's brother's (wau) obligations to his sister's sons (*psambǝn*) culminate in a major initiation ceremony that ideally takes place over three to four months.

FIRST PRINCIPLES

Tsambunwuro figure significantly in initiation ceremonies. The Chambri translate the term tsambunwuro from their own language into the neo-Melanesian word *poroman*, meaning friend, or "a partner or pair to any object, of a pair of pig's tusks, one is poroman to the other" (Bateson 1932:266). The translation is not, however, completely accurate, for although many things are poroman, and every individual may have numerous friends, each male has only one tsambunwuro. Specifically, a tsambunwuro is acquired in the following manner: the man under whom your father lay will become your tsambunwuro, upon whom you will lie during your initiation. You, in turn, will lie underneath your tsambunwuro's son, who will call you tsambunwuro and will become tsambunwuro to your son.

Tsambunwuro, Chambri say, assist one another by exchanging all kinds of goods and services. The exchanges must be absolutely equal. If a tsambunwuro gives his partner a leg of a pig, for example, then the partner must reciprocate with precisely a leg of a pig. To inflate a return gift, or to fall short, is to break the rules that define the relationship.

This reciprocity spans generations, for within the context of initiation, one repays a tsambunwuro by assisting his son. At each initiation a young man incurs a debt to the older man who lies beneath him.

PLATE 7.1   An initiate lies on top of his tsambunwuro.

Although this debt cancels the identical obligation incurred by the older man to the younger man's father, it can itself be canceled only during the initiation of the older man's son. Over time, then, tsambunwuro participate in a system of alternating asymmetries we may call reciprocity. Moreover, their reciprocal relationship is underwritten by the strictly upheld prohibition against engaging in competitive exchange with one another.

I do not mean to give the impression that competitive exchange characterizes most other intermale relationships among the Chambri. Indeed, Chambri play the "status game" by rules very different from those followed by men in the Highlands of New Guinea. Highlanders establish and maintain status differentials between individuals and groups through competitive equalizing exchanges. One individual gives a number of goods to his trading partner, who reciprocates with more goods and forces the first donor to give even more goods in return. Certain individuals and groups are indebted to other individuals and groups at any point in time, and "the only way they can maintain their alliance is by continuing positive ceremonial exchanges of valuables. . . . The ceremonial exchange system is one in which reciprocative transactions prevail and the relationship between partners is relatively egalitarian'' (Strathern 1971:214−215).

Among the Chambri, too, clans are potentially equal, but the Chambri do not engage in competitive equal exchange. Instead, enterprising big men achieve status and power on behalf of their patriclans by assisting unrelated clans to meet their affinal debts. The relationship between affines is an unequal one; wife givers are considered superior to wife takers. Their superiority is institutionalized in asymmetrical affinal exchange, and valuables move from wife takers to wife givers during initiation and other rites of passage celebrated for sisters' sons. When an individual and his clan comembers cannot amass sufficient valuables to compensate their wife givers, they seek assistance from an unrelated clan. The unrelated clan, by helping, gains power over its clients. While one's own affinal relationship is a source of inequality, the affinal relationships of others provide unrelated men with the opportunity of achieving power. Thus, competition between equal clans is played out within the context of unequal affinal exchange.

It is important to recognize that the Chambri accept the de facto nature of affinal inequality, particularly given their preference for mother's brother's daughter's marriage. As Fortune points out, this marriage preference ideally creates ''a lien in perpetuity upon the male line [that a married woman] comes from in favor of [her husband's] male descendants. The women who are sisters of a male line are in entail, so to speak, to a vis-à-vis line'' (1933:3). Thus, the stability of affinal inequality makes the affinal exchange relationship the perfect non-repercussive arena for extravagant display.

The tsambunwuro relationship is also enduring, and in one sense it recapitulates affinal inequality, with younger men perpetually in debt to the older men who lay beneath them during their initiation. The tsambunwuro relationship does not, however, create a lien in perpetuity in favor of one or another group of kinsmen. Rather, the system of alternating asymmetries which operates between tsambunwuro transfers indebtedness from one group to another with each new generation.

Tsambunwuro, therefore, are both equals and unequals simultaneously, which is to say that tsambunwuro articulate the structural properties of two distinct categories of people within Chambri society: the category comprising asymmetrical, intergenerational, agnatic, and affinal relations, and the category comprising symmetrical, interclan, and intervillage coordinate groups.

The two categories, whose structures are articulated through the person of the tsambunwuro, are analytically distinct throughout Chambri initiation ceremonies. For example, it is the wau, or mother's brother, who inaugurates the scarification of his sister's son, thereby producing an adult male member of his in-law's patriclan. On the other hand, members of all three Chambri villages divide into two competing initiation moieties, Pombiantimeri and Yambuntimeri, which crosscut both affinal and agnatic connections and exist only during the ceremonies.[3] I shall elaborate upon the distinctiveness of these categories while providing a brief description of the four phases within the initiation procedure.

Although the mother's brother makes the first cut on the back of his sister's son, he leaves the enclosure immediately afterward, for it is said that he cannot see his nephew's blood spill without crying, and to cry aloud would be to alert his wives and sisters that something is amiss. The scarifiers who finish the job work together as members of the initiation moiety opposite to that of the initiate.

Frequently, when two of the initiates belong to different initiation moieties, they are scarified simultaneously, each by specialists belonging to the opposite moiety. Whenever possible, an equal number of initiates from each moiety should be scarified, for only then will each moiety's ancestral crocodile, who is understood to be responsible for "eating the backs of the initiates," return to a peaceful sleep after the ceremonies are completed.

After each initiate is cut, the scarifiers lead him into the spirit house, where they lift him onto one of the platforms that flank both sides of the interior. As he lies there, his mother's brother uses a chicken feather to paint his cuts with tree sap. The sap causes the cuts to heal as keloids, a much admired result of the initiation. Meanwhile, two of the scarifiers, who have remained in the enclosure, whirl bull-roarers that contain the spirits of the initiate-eating crocodiles. Inside the men's house, representatives of both initiation moieties face each other to play sacred ancestral bamboo flutes.

The playing of the bamboo flutes marks the beginning of the second phase in the initiation of Chambri males, their acquisition of the manly arts, excluding warfare. During this phase, members of the opposite initiation moiety pretend to instruct the initiates in the knowledge and skills they will need to become effective members of their spirit houses. Since initiates from both moieties are commonly present, representatives of each generally teach all the initiates together. Actually, the real

---

[3] I suspect that the initiation moieties of the Chambri are residual wards that were once rooted in ties of kinship and marriage. Now, as among the Iatmul, these dual structures emerge only in the domain of ceremonialism. Readers interested in dual organizations throughout the Middle Sepik should consult Tuzin (1976).

instruction is negligible, and the "instructors" merely taunt the initiates under the guise of imparting knowledge.

This phase has always varied greatly in duration, although in modern times there has been a trend toward abbreviating it. The substance of the taunting and the mode of its presentation have always varied as well, but certain elements remain constant. The important prerequisites include mock instruction in playing bamboo flutes, in producing and wearing penis sheaths made of the pelts of fruit bats and wigs made of the skins of cassowaries and tree kangaroos, in preparing and smoking cigarettes, in paddling canoes, in preparing and chewing betel nut, in cutting the grass around the spirit house, in making brooms from coconut fronds and sweeping the inside of the spirit house, and in knotting cordyline leaves for use in sending messages. "Instructors" have occasionally "taught" dance steps, food preparation, carving, the weaving of ceremonial decorations, and drumming, but they consider these skills to be relatively inconsequential.

Most initiates have already long since mastered the skills their teachers mockingly demonstrate. As "children," however, they are not allowed to display their ability publicly. The teachers' mode of instruction is, in this sense, sarcastic, for it ridicules the very behavior toward which the initiates strive. A favorite pedagogic device is to make a giant broom, which a man will then wield, pretending that the initiates are debris to be swept away.

During the hazing phase the initiates are not allowed to eat or to smoke with their fingers, but must hold their food and cigarettes in tongs made of rattan. They cannot eat fish, but must subsist on pork, sago, and rice—foods provided by their mothers' brothers, who must also bring them drinking water in a coconut shell. When the initiates must defecate, their mothers' brothers carry them to the nearest outhouse.

Frequently, particularly at night, the initiates are told stories of the ancestors, not by their teachers, but by their fathers and mothers' brothers. These stories include genealogical and totemic information, but never anything truly magical or esoteric, for, although told in whispers, they are overheard by everyone in the spirit house.

Meanwhile, the initiates' cuts are healing. Their mothers' brothers continue to apply tree sap to the scabs. When the scabs have formed, but before the initiates are sufficiently healed to be able to stretch their skin by standing straight, the third phase of the major initiation ceremony takes place. This is instruction in warfare.

Most Chambri enjoy participating in this portion of the initiation ceremony, which involves a mock battle between both male and female

PLATE 7.2   Mothers' brothers lead initiates to learn the art of warfare.

members of Pombiantimeri and Yambuntimeri. The battle is not in the least dangerous, for members of one moiety merely hit the legs and arms of members of the other moiety with brooms, sticks, and leaves. The number of people whom a given individual can beat is limited. A Yambuntimeri who is also a member of the crosscutting marriage moiety Nyaui-nimba can attack only Pombiantimeri who are also members of Nyaui-nimba (see table 7.1). A Pombiantimeri who is a member of Nyemi-nimba can only wallop Yambuntimeri who are also members of Nyemi-nimba, and so on. Chambri express this rule by warning all participants to avoid beating their affines. They refer, however, not to actual affines but rather to potential wives and in-laws in the opposite marriage moiety.

The warfare phase proceeds in an orderly fashion. All relatives of the initiates—affines and agnates, males and females—who are mem-

294

TABLE 7.1 Crosscutting Relationships Among Initiation and Marriage Moieties

	INDINGAI		
	Yambuntimeri	*Pombiantimeri*	*Yambuntimeri and Pombiantimeri**
Nyemi-nimba	10	19	2
Nyaui-nimba	24	13	0
Nyemi- and Nyaui-nimba*	23	14	2
Total	57	46	4
	WOMBUN		
Nyemi-nimba	35	51	2
Nyaui-nimba	41	26	4
Nyemi- and Nyaui-nimba	22	5	0
Total	98	82	6
	KILIMBIT		
Nyemi-nimba	31	30	2
Nyaui-nimba	24	42	2
Nyemi- and Nyaui-nimba	0	15	3
Total	55	87	7
	THE THREE CHAMBRI VILLAGES		
Nyemi-nimba	76	100	6
Nyaui-nimba	89	81	6
Nyemi- and Nyaui-nimba	45	34	5
Total	210	215	17

Note: Data were collected by the author in 1974 and include all adult men and women whose affiliations I am sure of, approximately 75 percent of the adult population, above the age of eighteen.

*A few Chambri claim dual moiety membership.

bers of the opposite initiation moiety, line up in two rows inside the spirit house. Members of that moiety who are not related to the initiate continue the two rows outside the spirit house. Before the entrance are two stakes, frequently lashed to form an inverted V, with the apex about three feet from the ground. Participants who belong to the initiates' moiety must file into one end of the spirit house, through the lines formed by the initiates' relatives, out the other end of the spirit house, through the inverted V, and, finally, through the two lines formed by their remaining antagonists waiting outside. As they march, they receive blows on their arms and legs from those standing in line. The initiates are either led or carried by their mothers' brothers. They know that their backs are safe from blows, but they experience pain nonetheless from mere movement. If there are no initiates from the opposite moiety, the warfare phase of the initiation ceremony is now over. If, however, there are representatives of both moieties, as is more commonly the case, the beaters and the beaten trade places and repeat the process.

This phase in the initiation ceremony is the least solemn. Most participants try to distinguish themselves as they march through the lines of antagonists. Men, dressed in feather headdresses and shell valuables, strut and swagger, some displaying violent contempt for their antagonists by fighting with the air or by feigning total aloofness. Women generally behave less obtrusively. Most are content simply to wear their best native or European clothes, while others prefer to dance through the lines of antagonists. Those Chambri who remain spectators respond with appreciative cheers as each participant emerges from the spirit house through the inverted V. The participants respond to this attention by spreading their arms.

After each moiety has been beaten by the other, all participants return to their houses. The initiates return to the spirit house, where hazing continues. Meanwhile, members of Pombiantimeri and Yambuntimeri participate in elaborations of the warfare and taunting phases. These activities are optional, and their inclusion depends chiefly on the persuasiveness and organizational ability of the initiates' mothers' brothers and fathers, although there are others who may initiate these activities. Any enterprising and charismatic Pombiantimeri or Yambuntimeri, whether or not he is related to the initiates or is even a member of the initiates' village, may organize one or several intermoiety competitions.

At one such competitive elaboration, twenty inhabitants of Wombun and Kilimbit boarded two large canoes, ten Yambuntimeri in one canoe and ten Pombiantimeri in the other. They paddled out into Chambri Lake until they were about 200 yards from shore, positioning their canoes so that the prows—carved crocodile heads—faced one another, about 20 feet apart. Each crew threw war spears at the other, but with only enough force for them to land in the water near the opposing canoe. Then they paddled back to shore, where they embraced their moiety comembers, who had been observing the mock fight.

Next day twenty-six members of Yambuntimeri from Wombun carried a man of Pombiantimeri on a mattress to Indingai, where they threw him into Chambri Lake under the pretense of giving him a bath.

PLATE 7.3   A man enters the men's house after being beaten by members of the opposite moiety.

All concerned, even the man from Kilimbit, were laughing and singing and generally having a clowning good time.

The Pombiantimeri, however, would not be surpassed. Nearly forty members from all three Chambri villages, although primarily from Kilimbit and Wombun, tied a Wombun of the Yambuntimeri moiety to a chair and then carried him from Wombun to Kilimbit and marched him three times around the largest of Kilimbit's men's houses. Releasing the man, they returned to Wombun, where they donned ceremonial accoutrements. They then went back to Kilimbit and danced through the night. Refreshments in the form of coconuts and beer were periodically provided by the wealthy father of three Kilimbit initiates, who was also a member of Pombiantimeri.

The Yambuntimeri decided to join the dancing, and on the next day a large contingent arrived from Wombun and was joined by comoiety

297

members from Kilimbit. Then, much to everyone's delight, although their intentions had already been announced, nearly forty Indingai arrived at Kilimbit to join in the festivities. Marching in two lines, Yambuntimeri and Pombiantimeri, the Indingai were accepting a challenge that had been implicit in all the festivities up to this point.

Indingai was the only Chambri village not scarifying its young men. Its members had held a large initiation ceremony the year before, when neither Wombun nor Kilimbit wished to do so. By now they were clearly peripheral to most of the proceedings; only those who held kin ties to the initiates of Wombun and Kilimbit participated in the various phases of the ceremony. Nevertheless, when most of the Yambuntimeri and Pombiantimeri from Wombun and Kilimbit converged on Kilimbit's largest men's house, many Indingai also decided to participate.

They decided to outdo—to "win"—everyone else and therefore came dressed completely traditionally. Even a former catechist to the Catholic mission came *as nating*, as he put it, without anything on but the traditional penis sheath, shell necklaces, and body paint. They came as Indingai, but they merged with their moiety comembers, first Yambuntimeri then Pombiantimeri, to dance around the men's house.

The fourth and final phase of initiation begins early in the morning, when the mothers' brothers decorate their nephews with body paint made from mud and white rock and then lead them to the lakeshore. There wait the initiates' mothers, mothers' sisters, and sisters, who will carry out the washing, and their fathers, fathers' brothers, and brothers, who will repay their wives' brothers for having cared for their sons.

Many other people have arrived to watch the proceedings, but their view is partially obscured by a fence made of coconut fronds. Between the fence and water stand men dressed as ancestral crocodiles, the eaters of male backs. Each initiate must crawl between the legs of the opposite moiety's crocodile in order to enter the water. Their female relatives, who are exempt from doing this, simply jump into the water, exhibiting great pleasure and abandon. After their sons, nephews, and brothers have braved the crocodiles and are in the water, the women jump on top of them, splash them, and generally engage their male relatives in boisterous water play.

After the body paint is thoroughly removed, the initiates leave the water. They are met by their mothers' brothers, who wrap them in towels, sprinkle them with powder, and provide them with new clothes, an elaborately decorated lime gourd, and a woven basket containing tobacco, a comb, and betel nuts—insignia of adult male status.

Meanwhile, the initiates' fathers construct what may be called "money trees." They attach many low-denomination bank notes, often

PLATE 7.4   A woman carries section of money tree to her husband's house.

numbering in the hundreds, to sticks, which are then thrust into the fibrous spine of a sago palm frond. The fathers display their money trees side by side, next to the spirit house in which their sons have been sequestered. Each tree is decorated with a string bag—the kind of bag used by Chambri women to carry their newborns—which contains additional money or occasionally shell and feather valuables. Frequently a father will specify how much money he and his fellow clansmen wish to give to each member of his brother-in-law's clan by pinning a note listing names and amounts to this string bag.

The last events in the initiation ceremony occur after the mothers' brothers help their nephews dress in the new clothes. Each then uproots the money tree he earned by sponsoring this sister's son's initiation and marches with it to his house, accompanied by his nephew and by fellow clansmen. There his wives have prepared a feast in honor of the initiate and his agnates. The feast generally consists of pork, sago, rice, and coconuts, frequently supplemented by such nontraditional items as beef, tinned mackerel, and packaged biscuits. If the feast is a very generous one, the initiate's clan comembers may feel compelled to provide their affines with additional valuables, but this is a rare occurrence.

GROUP DYNAMICS

Structure

It should now be clear that Chambri male initiation mobilizes two distinct categories of people, the initiate, his agnates, and their affines, on the one hand, and the intervillage and interclan initiation moieties, Pombiantimeri/Yambuntimeri, on the other.

It is also accurate to describe initiation as an enactment of two separate dramas, one about marriage relationships and the other about male interaction. Generally speaking, the dramatis personae are sharply defined: the initiate's affines and agnates play out the drama of marriage, while the initiation moieties, with their emphasis on equal competition, enact the drama of male interaction. The tsambunwuro link these two dramas in space and time. Specifically, they introduce equality where there is intergenerational inequality between fathers and sons and between mothers' brothers and sisters' sons. Furthermore, they provide continuity through alternate generations because alternate tsambunwuro are of the same agnatic line.

The dramas themselves are interrelated elsewhere in Chambri society. I refer to the ongoing politics of affinal exchange, which also

300

unites equals and unequals but in a way that has profound social and economic consequences. As I have already mentioned, among the Chambri prestige is achieved through affinal exchange. Potentially equal individuals and groups indirectly compete through their unequal affinal exchange relationships. A headman is successful if he can pay his affines large bride prices, overcompensate his brothers-in-law for their contribution of foodstuffs during rites of passage celebrated for his sons, and assist nonrelated clans to do the same. In fact, it is by patronizing unrelated individuals and clans and helping them to meet their affinal debts that individuals achieve power over others.

Patron-client relationships were both originated and verified during the initiation ceremonies that I observed. In fact, five of the eight initiates at Wombun and Kilimbit were not sponsored by their actual mothers' brothers, nor by members of their mothers' brothers' clans, but by patrons who had achieved power over these clans.

The ex-catechist from Indingai, for example, forced the agnates of an initiate from Wombun to provide him with affinal recompense by sponsoring the young man's initiation. This was an unusual incident because the initiate to whom the catechist acted as wau was actually his father's father's father's father's brother's son's son's son's son. The ex-catechist had acquired the recognized "wauship" after the initiate's actual mother's brother had repeatedly requested and accepted his financial assistance in meeting affinal obligations. The ex-catechist, who had become the actual mother's brother's patron, now received all affinal recompense due his client. It was his practice to use whatever money he received in this manner to extend or to strengthen his web of patron-client relationships. When I knew him, he was acting as wau to nineteen individuals originating from ten different clans within both Wombun and Indingai. Only five of these individuals were related to him as patrilateral kinsmen, six were related as distant matrilateral kinsmen, and eight were not related at all.

More patron-client relationships are established during initiation ceremonies than at any other time. This is so because the affinal recompense during initiation is usually quite large and therefore difficult to accumulate from the contributions of clan comembers alone. (Of the eight money trees that I observed at Kilimbit and Wombun, each contained between 70 and 230 Australian dollars, a total of 860 dollars in all.) More important, though, it is the mother's brother who puts the ceremonial events into motion. The initiate's fellow clansmen may, at the time, be unprepared to recompense him sufficiently. Therefore, unlike the payment of bride price, which can be avoided by the groom's temporarily refusing to marry, initiation payments are due upon the demand of one's wife givers.

It is crucial to recognize that although status differentials are established within the context of male initiation ceremonies, these ceremonies are not the only contexts in which patron-client relationships are formed and verified. There are many other occasions—bride price transaction, a haircutting ceremony, a house opening—in which exchange relationships are established between affinally linked groups and within which unrelated individuals gain power by controlling the affinal prestations of unequals. In order for us to understand male initiations fully, it is necessary to determine why the Chambri choose to initiate rather than engaging in some other activity that would involve affinal exchange and would therefore allow for the formation of patron-client relationships and status differentials.

To put the question another way: What informs the Chambri decision to initiate young men at one time rather than another? We can best approach this problem by considering the end product of the ceremony, that is, initiated males. Why are these individuals significant in Chambri society?

Social Process

Clearly, it is through initiation that older men socially reproduce themselves. They transform young men—who have no access to their ceremonial houses nor knowledge of the sacred accoutrements that are stored there—into adult males with adult rights and duties. By initiating young men, Chambri adults grant them the privileges of adult status, while they expect the newly initiated, in turn, to fulfill appropriate adult obligations.

Essentially, initiated males no longer participate passively in affinal exchange but become active exchangers themselves. They can marry, thus obligating themselves to their wife givers, while they must also assist their coclansmen in meeting the group's affinal debts. Initiation thus allows for the reproduction of two interrelated relationships. As marriage partners, young men indebt themselves and their coclansmen to their affines. As productive clansmen, on the other hand, the newly initiated help pay off the debts that they and their agnates incur through marriage. It seems logical to assume, therefore, that initiation takes place when there is a systemic need for additional marriage partners and/or for productive exchangers.

I cannot here detail the social processes that result in the reproduction of adult male productive exchangers. To summarize, the initiation of Chambri males is triggered by those patriclans—approximately one-third of the total number in Chambri—that have become locked into the mother's brother's daughter's marriage system. These clans (I am speaking about the time prior to the introduction of steel tools, before 1900) have no easy access to the six quarries that provide the stone from which Chambri males shape their primary commodity, stone adzes and axes for sale to Iatmul and other native purchasers. It is through the production and sale of stone tools that adult males can expand their revenues for use in affinal transactions of all kinds. Those clans that cannot easily expand production are those that either become clients of larger clans or are locked into the mother's brother's daughter's marriage system.

As we have seen, within a mother's brother's daughter's marriage system it "is impossible for a man to marry a woman without his creating a lien in perpetuity upon the male line she comes from in favor of his male descendants" (Fortune 1933:3). This perpetual lien, though, is only a theoretical construct. Wife givers frequently prefer to marry their daughters to successful clansmen who will pay large bride prices and maintain a high level of affinal exchange. Wife takers, on the other hand, depending on their relative wealth and power, may try either to acquire inexpensive women or to display their success by marrying "high-priced" women. Members of nearly 30 percent of Chambri patriclans do, however, marry women of their mother's brother's clans, and these men tend to belong to clans whose sufficient but not excessive resources are equally committed in both the wife-giving and wife-taking directions.[4] Only among these men's clans are perpetual liens advantageously maintained, and the organization of male initiation ceremonies is the mechanism through which these clansmen maintain their advantage.

To work properly, a mother's brother's daughter's marriage system must involve a minimum of three clans. Women move from clan A to B, from clan B to C, and from clan C to A, while valuables move, in repayment for these women and their future children, in the opposite direction, from A to C, from C to B, and from B to A. Thus the relationships among A, B, and C are equitable, with all three clans both giving and receiving women and affinal recompense. Wife givers ac-

[4] I am suggesting that the 30 percent of the Chambri who marry mother's brother's daughters are in clans distinct from those of which the other 70 percent are members. I know this claim may seem odd to ethnographers familiar with the egalitarian social systems of New Guinea Highlands societies, but I have become increasingly convinced that incipient stratification characterizes the complex totemic societies of the Middle Sepik region.

quire necessary valuables from wife takers, and the marriage system is, at least temporarily, self-contained and closed.

The system works very well until one of the clans is forced to increase its outlay of ceremonial valuables, generally when its wife givers' daughters achieve maturity and become marriageable. Each time wife takers (who practice mother's brother's daughter's marriage) must give bride prices to acquire wives for their sons, they have difficulty amassing the necessary valuables. Those valuables they periodically receive from the clans of their own daughters' husbands are used to pay for their present wives and children. There is little, if anything, to spare; certainly not enough to acquire new brides.

They cannot remedy this situation by increasing their production and sale of stone tools. The genealogies I collected among the Chambri indicate that those who systematically practice mother's brother's daughter's marriage are never themselves custodians of stone quarries. They do not have direct access to the stone resource and thus cannot increase production without an initial outlay of valuables to pay the quarries' custodians.

The only way for clans practicing mother's brother's daughter's marriage to contribute more to their wife givers is to receive more from their wife takers. And each mother's brother has the power to do this by arranging for the initiation of his sister's son. He thereby acquires the valuables he needs to amass bride price, while also increasing the number of potentially productive males among his wife takers. His wife takers may later be able to pay him a larger amount of valuables because there is a greater number of producers of stone tools among them. More important, though, initiated men marry and thereby acquire wives who produce mosquito bags, the other primary commodity sold by Chambri men to acquire ceremonial valuables.[5] Moreover, these men marry their uncles' classificatory daughters, thereby obligating themselves to main-

---

[5]Chambri women also earned valuables by manufacturing the cylindrical, ten- to fifteen-foot-long mosquito bags (*arənk*), made of plaited sago shoots or bast, which were used throughout the Middle Sepik. Before the European introduction of cotton and nylon mosquito netting, these bags were the people's only protection from the ferocious mosquitoes that infest the area, particularly during the transitional periods from wet to dry season and from dry to wet.

According to Mead,

the people of the Middle Sepik purchase these mosquito bags, in fact they are so much in demand that purchasers take option on them long before they are finished. And women control the proceeds in kina and talibun. It is true that they permit the men to do the . . . trading [in] mosquito bags. The men make a gala occasion of these shopping trips; when a man has the final negotiations for one of his wives' mosquito bags in hand, he goes off resplendent in feathers and shell ornaments to spend a delightful few days over the transaction. . . . But only with tain affinal exchange relationships and so triggering another round of initiations.

In other words, when maternal uncles initiate their nephews in order to acquire valuables, the nephews must acquire women who make it possible for them to meet their affinal obligations. To acquire these women they must pay bride price, and to do so they, in turn, initiate their own sisters' sons. Thus initiations, marriages, and affinal exchanges maintain the mother's brother's daughter's marriage system, which impedes, at least for a time, the designs of large clans practicing the politics of affinal exchange.

Once one man arranges the initiation of his sister's son, other initiations—provoked, not by imbalances in the ratio of available wives to available valuables, but by one or several political contingencies that generally involve interclan competition—are likely to be arranged as well.

The Kilimbit initiations provide an interesting example of these contingencies, for all of the initiates there are related to Wanipak,[6] the biological father of the initiates labeled A and B in table 7.2. His relationships to the three other initiates were established in the following manner:

1. The mother of initiate C married Wanipak after divorcing her first husband, C's actual father.

2. Initiate D, a schoolteacher from the village of Biwat working for the Catholic mission, felt that initiation scars were extremely attractive and wished to possess them. Bamak (G) volunteered to act as his mother's brother, which forced Wanipak to become D's "father."

---

his wife's approval can he spend the talibun and kina and the strings of conus rings that he brings back from his holiday. He has wheedled a good price from the purchaser; he has still to wheedle the items of the price from his wife. (1963:254)

As I have discussed elsewhere (Gewertz 1977), Mead here confuses control of the means of production with control of the relations of production. Although Chambri women never had any real decision-making power, they were nonetheless producers of a commodity that brought "more kina and talibun into circulation, and it [was] by the presence of kina and talibun that the ceremonial life [was] kept moving, each ceremony [i.e., affinal exchange] necessitating the expenditure of food and valuables" (Mead 1963:266).

The men practicing mother's brother's daughters marriage had already committed the valuables earned by their wives to maintaining existing affinal relations. The wives were rarely willing to increase their production of mosquito bags, for they had no personal stake in working harder.

[6]All personal names have been changed.

TABLE 7.2 Genealogical Relationships and Moiety Memberships of Major Participants in Eight Scarifications at Kilimbit and Wombun

	INITIATORS				INITIATES		
	Relationship to Initiate	Marriage Moiety	Initiation Moiety		Relationship to Initiate	Marriage Moiety	Initiation Moiety
F	M B S	Nyaui-nimba	Yambuntimeri	A	M F B S S	Nyemi-nimba	Yambuntimeri
G	No relationship	Nyemi-nimba	Yambuntimeri	B	No relationship	Nyemi-nimba	Yambuntimeri
G	No relationship	Nyemi-nimba	Yambuntimeri	D	No relationship	Nyemi-nimba	Yambuntimeri
H	M F F F B S S S S	Nyaui-nimba	Pombiantimeri	C	F F F F B S S D S	Nyemi-nimba	Yambuntimeri
I	M F B S	Nyaui-nimba	Pombiantimeri and Yambuntimeri	E	F Z D S	Nyemi-nimba	Yambuntimeri
J	F F F F B S S S S	Nyaui-nimba	Yambuntimeri	M	F F F F F B S S S S S	Nyemi-nimba	Pombiantimeri
K	No relationship	Nyemi-nimba	Pombiantimeri	N	No relationship	Nyaui-nimba	Pombiantimeri
L	No relationship	Nyemi-nimba	Pombiantimeri	O	No relationship	Nyaui-nimba	Pombiantimeri

3. E is Wanipak's actual brother's daughter's son, and I is a member of the clan.

Bamak figures significantly in the events at Kilimbit. He is the older brother of Toan, a man who had achieved considerable prominence within his village and had, in fact, nearly won the ''big-manship'' from the aged Wanipak, whose limited participation in political events no longer matched his reputation.[7] Bamak, for many years a migrant laborer in Wewak, had contributed much money to his brother's campaign for prominence. Upon returning to Kilimbit, he wished to be recognized as the leader of his clan, a position he believed his age and wealth merited. His covillagers had become accustomed to acknowledging Toan's priority, and Bamak correctly reasoned that by sponsoring Wanipak's sons' initiations he would achieve a reputation to match his younger brother's. Since Toan had used Bamak's money to establish a patron-client relationship with B's mother's clan—wife givers to Wanipak—and since F had already decided to sponsor the initiation of Wanipak's other son, A, it was not difficult for Bamak to arrange to act as B's wau.

Bamak's reputation would not be made, however, by sponsoring only one initiation, and he was pleased when D expressed interest in scarification. Bamak essentially forced Wanipak to accept D as a son, by letting it be known throughout Kilimbit that Wanipak's reputation far surpassed his wealth.

Wanipak countered Bamak's assertion not only by adopting D but also by informing H that he would welcome his decision to sponsor the initiation of C. Wanipak could not bring direct pressure to bear upon H, for he was Wanipak's wife giver. Once it was known that Wanipak wished C to be initiated, though, Bamak publicly challenged H—who was a member of a small but moderately successful clan—by questioning his capacity to mount adequate feasts.

H accepted Bamak's challenge, which is precisely what Bamak hoped he would do, for Bamak had planned a huge initiation feast to outdo anything H or F could arrange. As it happened, he had calculated correctly and thus gained a considerable reputation throughout the three Chambri villages as a wealthy and clever man.

He did not, however, supersede Wanipak. While paying affinal recompense to F and to H and to Bamak himself, Wanipak was also,

---

[7]Although in theory there are as many status positions as there are individuals to hold them, in fact each Chambri village generally supports only one, or perhaps two, big men.

through his coclansman I, sponsoring E's initiation. The feast held by Wanipak far surpassed those held by the other waus. In fact, he invited many nonrelated members of all three Chambri villages, distributed *manjan* (a ceremonial bread made of coconut milk and sago flour) to everyone he met, whether they had been invited or not, and, most impressive of all, he arranged for his *tumban* (an ancestral figure representing one of his clan's most important ancestors) to dance for the assembled guests outside his spirit house.

I am less familiar with the actors at the Wombun initiations than with those at Kilimbit and therefore will not speculate about the political connections that were established, reaffirmed, broken, or transformed during the ceremony there. I am certain, however, that, as in Kilimbit, many crosscutting allegiances and antagonisms—based upon agnatic, affinal, and patron-client connections—activated the proceedings.

It should not be forgotten that these political challenges, each resulting in the formation of status differentials in Chambri society, do not themselves stimulate the performance of initiation ceremonies. Rather, initiation occurs because the equitability of the mother's brother's daughter's marriage system cannot be maintained through time unless its participants coordinate their marriages, birth payments, initiations, and funerals so as to accommodate their wife givers and be accommodated by their wife takers simultaneously. This balancing of input and outlay is nearly impossible to accomplish, and the mother's brother's daughter's marriage system is therefore inherently unstable.[8]

---

[8] I suspect that the link between male initiation and mother's brother's daughter's marriage has been attenuated because many young men today leave the three Chambri villages to attend school or to seek employment.

In order for mother's brothers to be assured of receiving part of these young men's earnings, they must initiate them before they leave Chambri. Once initiated, the young men are obliged to contribute to their agnates' affinal prestations, or else they lose recognition as full clan members. Although only a few migrants regularly provide a portion of their earnings to their fathers and brothers, very few fail to contribute altogether. Since many Chambri migrants work as artifact sellers in the towns of Wewak and Madang, rather than in more permanent positions in factories or for the government, it is in their interest to maintain amicable relationships with their relatives in the village and thus preserve the option of coming home again. Even those who take permanent jobs are rarely allowed to forget their relatives at home. They are reminded by the many Chambri males who practice short-term circular migration, visiting the towns when they wish to earn money for a bride price or to engage in other clan business. These individuals maintain town-village interaction by relaying messages of importance to the more permanent migrants, who return periodically to Chambri for native cures, to marry, for a mother's funeral, or for some other pressing reason.

By initiating young migrants before they leave Chambri, men claim a portion of their sisters' sons' earnings in the form of future affinal payments. If the migrants leave suddenly—perhaps to

We can now understand the significance of the tsambunwuro, who engage in the most reciprocal relationship within Chambri society. This relationship represents, I believe, the structural resolution of the dilemma that triggers male initiation ceremonies. It does not create a lien in perpetuity on women or valuables in favor of one or another group of kinsmen, but rather transfers indebtedness from one group to another with each new generation.

The relationship between tsambunwuro is characterized, not by simple hierarchy, wherein the older man dominates the younger man, but essentially by what Burke calls the "hierarchic principle":

The hierarchic principle is complete only insofar as it works both ways at once. It is not merely the relation of higher to lower, or of lower to higher, or before to after, or after to before. The hierarchic principle is not complete in the social realm, for instance, in the mere arrangement whereby each rank is overlord to its underlings and underling to its overlords. It is complete only when each rank accepts the principle of gradation itself, and in thus "universalizing" the principle, makes a spiritual reversal of the ranks just as meaningful as their actual material arrangement. (1969:138)

Tsambunwuro, it seems, are neither competing equals nor noncompeting unequals. In a sense, they compete unequally by accepting the hierarchic principle and by knowing that those now on top will, by the next generation, be quite literally underneath. They therefore represent an ideal—one that male initiation strives but inevitably fails to accomplish because of the instability of the practice of mother's brother's daughter's marriage and the mutability of social groups involved in the politics of affinal exchange.

---

avoid the assumption of adult responsibilities—they are initiated as soon as they return home, generally during Christmas, when factories, schools, and the civil administration provide their workers and students with at least a two-week vacation. Thus, Chambri social, political, and economic organization has not been bifurcated into town and village sectors. Rather, by initiating their sisters' sons, men assure themselves that money will be extracted from the towns for introduction into intratribal sociopolitical life.

What traditional and modern initiation practices have in common is that in both forms initiation serves as a mechanism for introducing new sources of wealth into the affinal exchange system. The difference is that the source of wealth has moved from the village (mosquito bags, stone tools) to the town (wage earning, artifact sales). In neither case is the desire to commemorate the passing of a milestone in the life cycle the primary determinant of the ceremony.

OPPOSITION AND REGULATION

Thus, the tsambunwuro relationship is ideally balanced, which means that tsambunwuro are exempt from interacting within either the drama about marriage or the drama about male interaction. The tsambunwuro relationship does much more, however, than provide an ideal structural resolution of the dilemma that triggers male initiation ceremonies. Within the context of these ceremonies, the hierarchic principle operates to link an initiate's father and uncle. These two men are members of the same generation and are in this sense equals. They cannot compete, however, because they are united through marriage. The elder tsambunwuro is also a member of their generation. He, too, is a non-competitor, but not because he is their affine. Rather, the elder tsambunwuro is an equal noncompetitor and as such becomes the perpetuator of the system of competition and dependence between the clans which the other two men represent. In doing so he establishes his central position in Chambri initiation ceremonies and within the larger context of Chambri society.

Before I can explain these last points further, I must provide some new information and reinforce several of the points I have already made. Specifically, I must emphasize the fact that although the Chambri accept the de facto nature of affinal inequality and recognize that affines of the same generation cannot compete, they explicitly blame the existence of this inequality upon women who do, in fact, link men together as unequals (see Forge 1972). The ambivalent attitude with which Chambri men regard marriage can best be illustrated by an examination of a Chambri myth in which an attempt is made to escape from the social relationship that marriage normally implies.

Tsambali Kanusaraman, an ancestor who lived by himself on an island in Chambri Lake, decided to create two large wooden carvings (*chambən*) in the image of women. He named the carvings Wobunprendu and Kabunprendu, and upon doing so he enlivened them. He called them daughters and instructed them in sago preparation and other domestic chores. The three lived happily together for many years, the only people on their island.

One day, as the two sisters were preparing sago, two hawks fell from the sky and landed next to their sago baskets. The girls hid the birds underneath their baskets after placing a feather from each through the holes in their earlobes. They returned to their work but were interrupted when two brothers, Wundan and Pumbun, arrived in search of the hawks. The two men knew by the feathers in the girls' ears that they had come to the right place, but the sisters denied having seen the birds. When Wundan found them underneath the sago baskets, he demanded that he and his brother be taken to the girls' father.

Tsambali Kanusaraman welcomed his visitors and instructed his daughters to prepare the hawks for a feast. Meanwhile, the two brothers asked Kanusaraman for his daughters in marriage, suggesting that he accept the hawks as bride price. Kanusaraman agreed to the marriages and to the bride price. He told the brothers that he was accepting such a small bride price only because his daughters were nothing more than carvings; they had no blood and had been carved without sexual organs. The brothers, not disappointed by this news, assured Kanusaraman that they were interested in the girls only as housekeepers and cooks.

Upon arriving home, Wundan and Pumbun were met by their mother's brother, Owibuni. Seeing the girls they had brought, he warned his nephews that nothing good would come of stealing other people's women. Wundan and Pumbun assured him that they had paid for the girls and asked him to help open up their wives' vulvas. Owibuni, after building a fence to ensure privacy from onlookers, put the sisters to sleep with a magic spell and then carved a vagina for each of them with a sharp piece of bamboo. Blood gushed from their wounds, but Owibuni stopped the bleeding by bandaging them with leaves. The women rested for six weeks and then were able to assume normal sexual duties. Both immediately conceived children.

They lived happily until Wundan and Pumbun decided to hold a ceremonial sacrifice to their ancestors. In the past, they had offered a chicken or a pig, but this time, they decided to sacrifice a man. The brothers persuaded Owibuni to help them collect water lilies from Chambri Lake. While he was in the water, they stabbed him with a fishing spear and then severed his head with a bush knife.

All would have been well if Tsangirapan, the mother of Wundan and Pumbun and the elder sister of Owibuni, had not been pulling in her fish basket at the time. In her basket she found pieces of her brother's flesh, and when she saw her sons place his head on top of their ceremonial house, she knew what had happened. She prepared a soup from the excrement of dogs and chickens, and presented it to her sons and their wives. They drank it, as she did herself, and the five of them immediately turned into boulders, which can still be seen today on the top of Mount Karundui. (See fig. 1 for the cast of characters.)

I do not wish to analyze the symbolism of the myth, but merely to identify and discuss its major themes. First, the myth tells of a man who creates his own daughters but unfortunately cannot guarantee himself grandchildren, for his daughters are bloodless and infertile. Their infer-

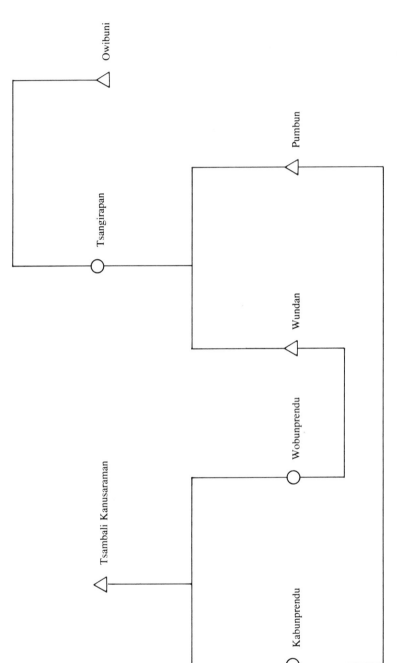

FIGURE 7.1   Cast of characters in the myth

tility and bloodlessness are predictable, given the Chambri belief that a child's bones are the product of its father's semen, whereas its blood comes from its mother. Wobunprendu and Kabunprendu have no mother and hence have no blood.

Second, the myth describes the girls' exogamous marriages to two brothers who pay bride price with foodstuffs. Such marriages would be unsatisfactory to the Chambri, who generally practice intraisland and intraphratry endogamy. Moreover, the Chambri insist that ceremonial valuables and not foodstuffs be the items of bride price. Because of the girl's infertility, the bride prices for Wobunprendu and Kabunprendu could reasonably have been reduced, but they certainly would never have consisted exclusively of edibles, and a Chambri father would sooner eat crow than accept hawk as bride price.

Third, we learn that the brothers do care about procreation and that they ask their mother's brother to complete their wives by endowing them with sexual organs. Again, the appearance of a mother's brother is intelligible given the Chambri preference for mother's brother's daughter's marriage. The girls become reproductively functioning women—they are blooded, so to speak—at the hands of their husbands' mother's brother. By performing the operation, he, I would argue, assumes his rightful role as father to his nephews' wives.

Fourth, the two brothers kill their mother's brother, thus severing the affinal connection they acquired after their wives' operation. And finally, in the style of grand tragedy, the remaining protagonists are destroyed by the mother, who also kills herself.

The myth deals, in effect, with three different attempts to avoid the affinal bond, the first by creating one's own children, the second by practicing what might be called "terminal exogamy"—marrying women from such distant villages that the affinal relationship is nearly irrelevant, and the third by murdering one's mother's brother, who is, in Chambri terms, one's most important wife giver. The myth also shows us (or rather the five boulders atop Mount Karundui show us), that these attempts were to no avail.

The most interesting fact about the myth, from my perspective, is that the interactions it portrays contrast so absolutely with the formally polite and stable relationship between Chambri wife givers and wife takers. In fact, Chambri affinal links are stronger than patrilineal ties, in that the explicitly unequal relationships between affines, with wife takers indebted to wife givers, are generally immune from the aggressive competitiveness that characterizes the relationship between equals. As Forge points out, "to be equal and stay equal is an extremely onerous task requiring continual vigilence and effort. Keeping up with the Joneses may be hard work, but keeping up with all other adult males of a community is incomparably harder'' (1972:533-534). Since men linked through women cannot be equal to each other, they cannot therefore compete for status and prestige.

Nonetheless, the myth indicates that the Chambri find the affinal relationship to be problematic—so problematic, in fact, that the husbands prefer to murder their mother's brother rather than engage in it.

I can best explain the levels on which the Chambri experience difficulty with the affinal relationship by returning to the myth, specifically to the episode in which Tsangirapan pulls in her fish trap to find that her catch consists of pieces of her brother's flesh. My Chambri informants were always particularly amused when relating this element, for, as they explained, Tsangirapan should have been pulling in pieces of her husband and not of her brother. Clearly, among Chambri the fish trap represents Tsangirapan's vulva, for they explicitly recognize the symbolism, and Chambri men fear their wives' capacity to entrap, literally, their patrilineal substance during sexual intercourse. Thus, the sexual act (which Chambri men state they engage in begrudgingly, only because they pity their wives, who would die without it), creates new members of the patriclan while it depletes the strength and very substance of living adult members. Moreover, the children born of women must be periodically bought back from their matrilineal kin, who have the power to co-opt their young relatives' hearts. Affinal exchange, therefore, both pays for women and buys back children.[9]

---

[9]Wobunprendu and Kabunprendu, the myth's wooden women, became living examples of the danger inherent in females. The Chambri describe them as chambən, carved wooden hooks, generally representative of particularly significant patrilineal ancestors.

The Chambri recognize two types of chambən by their respective functions. The first is hung by every married or initiated man from the ceiling of his wife's or mother's house. This type of chambən is carved by its owner to represent personally significant patrilineal ancestors, perhaps the ancestor for whom the man is named or one who is thought to dwell in the house. A man's wife or mother is responsible for keeping the woven reed bag that hangs from her husband's or son's chambən filled with sago and fish, so that he can eat whenever he returns from his spirit house. Women do not own chambən, for, I was told, ''they prepare their own food whenever they like.''

The second type of chambən resembles the first in construction but is suspended from the ceiling of a man's spirit house. These chambən are passed down from generation to generation and represent apical ancestors. Their baskets are filled with ceremonial accoutrements—human bones, shell valuables, or feather decorations. These objects are used during the various ceremonies in which the particular ancestor plays a significant part. Thus, when the ancestor Saungai is due to ensure that the ''white water'' of the Sepik River will return to Chambri Lake after the dry season, the leader of the Saungai clan places his Saungai chambən and ceremonial basket close to the area where the ceremony is performed. Chambən, therefore, are repositories of patrilineal power. They are extremely important in both the secular and the sacred lives of Chambri males, and they are never used by women nor carved to represent female ancestors.

The women who link men together as unequals are thus also capable of stealing away the essence of patrilineality, so Chambri men are in a classic double bind, for they can neither live with nor live without the social relationships established through women. They are committed to reproducing themselves through women and are therefore forever condemned to affinal inequality—to buying themselves and their children back from their potentially entrapping matrilateral kinsmen.

Bateson defines a double bind as "a situation in which no matter what a person does he can't win" (1972:201). He uses an illustration from Zen Buddhism, an instance when the Zen master "attempts to bring about enlightenment in his pupil in various ways. One of the things he does is to hold a stick over the pupil's head and say fiercely, "If you say this stick is real, I will strike you with it. If you say this stick is not real, I will strike you with it. If you don't say anything, I will strike you with it" (1972:208). The initiate has no way out unless he cares nothing for his relationship with the master, in which case he may decide to take the stick away from him.

The Chambri, too, have no easy way out. If they refuse to marry, they cannot reproduce themselves. When they do marry, they are in continual danger of losing their patrilineal substance to their matrilateral kin. Even in myth there is no escape, for Wundan and Pumbun do not disavow their mother, while she is obviously quite capable of dispatching them.

In such an impossible situation, escape can be found by shifting to a metaphorical order of response. Thus, one can defend oneself metaphor-

---

Wobunprendu and Kabunprendu are female chambən, a dangerous contradiction in terms. Women are safe, or at least controllable, when relegated to the position of mediators between patrilines. Through marriage they move from one male group to another, to reproduce their husbands' partrilines. Wobunprendu and Kabunprendu, however, represent to Chambri males their greatest fears about the reproduction and continuity of their patrilines. The Chambri are one of the many peoples who believe that women once owned cultural traditions but were tricked out of their sacred accoutrements—including spirit houses, bamboo flutes, and chambən—by devious males. If women are not carefully controlled, they are capable of winning these cultural traditions back again.

Wobunprendu and Kabunprendu represent such a possibility. Not only are they female chambən and thus partake of the cultural realm, but also they try to steal Wundan and Pumdun's hawks by hiding them underneath their sago baskets. Hawks figure prominently in Chambri mythology as representatives of male ancestors or of living men who magically assume the likeness of the birds. Sago, on the other hand, symbolizes female sexuality, a fact I discuss in n. 10 below. Wobunprendu and Kabunprendu, by hiding the hawks underneath their sago baskets, were attempting to steal away the essence of patrilineality. This theft is precisely what Chambri males fear will happen during sexual intercourse. Wundan and Pumbun were not, however, deceived by the girls' ploy, but instead coerced them into marriage, the Chambri means of controlling female sexuality. As we have seen, though, marriage is only the lesser of two evils, for although it allows for the control of females, it necessitates arduous affinal transactions.

ically by becoming someone else, or by insisting that one is somewhere else, or by transforming the very nature of the interaction; "then the double bind cannot work on the victim, because it isn't he and besides he is in a different place" (Bateson 1972:210). Bateson argues that schizophrenics defend themselves by shifting to a metaphorical order of message and that "the pathology enters when the victim does not know that his responses are metaphorical or cannot say so. To recognize that he was speaking metaphorically he would have to be aware that he was defending himself and therefore was afraid of the other person" (1972:210).

Chambri men are well aware that they fear their wife givers. They are particularly afraid of embarrassing themselves in front of them, for fathers must pay recompense to their brothers-in-law for the inappropriate behavior of their sons. They cannot confront their fear directly by, for example, refusing to pay the affinal recompense. Such a refusal would sever the affinal relationship, and Chambri men cannot live without the social relations established through women. Their double bind therefore forces them to defend themselves metaphorically. They do as much by denying the inequality of the affinal relationship through a symbolic transformation of matrilateral cross-cousin marriage into sister exchange. This point brings me back to the male initiation ceremony.

I have already described how the separate affinal reimbursements to mothers' brothers are displayed side by side in the form of money trees made of sago-palm fronds. Although I cannot discuss here the elaborate tree symbolism used by the Chambri (which rivals in complexity that found by Gell [1975] among the Umeda), suffice it to say that sago palms are frequently used in Chambri mythology to symbolize women, in contrast to the essentially masculine coconut palm. [10] In fact, each money

---

[10]This association of the sago palm with women, and with female sexuality in particular, is widespread throughout Papua New Guinea. Ruddle et al., in their comprehensive survey of the use and meaning of palm sago throughout the marginal lowlands, write that

> in a society where sago is the staple and sago work almost exclusively women's responsibility . . . sago is equated with sexual intercourse, hence its role in . . . marriage ceremon[ies] and . . . incest taboo[s]. These themes are common to . . . sago-using societies. For example, in southern Irian Jaya on the Mappi River, the public giving of the marriage sago by the women to the man is the decisive act in the marriage proceedings . . ., and among the Arapesh, parents may not eat sago worked by their children, a taboo which protects the parents from the child's developing sexuality. . . .
> Although the supporting data are unevenly available, it seems possible to make the general statement that where sago work is women's work, sago is a symbol of female sexuality in myth and ritual. [1978:92–92]

The Chambri situation is somewhat more complex than the majority of cases discussed by Ruddle et al., for neither Chambri men nor women themselves produce sago. Rather, Chambri women barter for the carbohydrate with sago-producing bush women from the Sepik Hills.

tree is decorated with a *bilum*, a net bag used by Chambri women to carry their infants. Thus, wife takers are returning symbolic representations of women to their wife givers when they pay them their affinal recompense during initiation. They thereby transform asymmetrical cross-cousin marriage into sister exchange and reestablish, albeit metaphorically, their status as equal men among men. They thus negate the significance of their double-bind situation by providing their wife givers with an equivalent dilemma. Since they are, in the realm of affinal relations, unequal wife takers, men cannot express their essentially equal maleness through either actions or objects. They remain deferent recompensers, the payers of ceremonial valuables. By switching communicational pathways though, they enter the domain of symbolic imagery, where their assertions of equivalence come through.

When all is said and done, however, the giving of a money tree is not the same as the giving of a flesh-and-blood woman, and the asymmetry between wife givers and wife takers remains socially intact. It is significant that while the Chambri express their discomfort with the asymmetry of the affinal relationship in a variety of ways, they take pains to ensure that this relationship is not disturbed in any real sense. One of the ways in which asymmetry is preserved is through the participation of the tsambunwuro in initiation.

The Chambri believe that a child's bones are the product of the father's semen, whereas its blood and flesh come from its mother. When a boy is initiated into his father's patriclan, the scarification ceremony is explicitly intended to rid the initiate of the weakening influence of his

---

Chambri men and women view all sago-producing bush people as weak, dirty, and submissive, as essentially "feminine." They describe the barter relationship as a marriage between fish and sago and believe that they, as fish suppliers, act at the market as "wife takers," acquiring feminine sago from the bush people.

As "sago takers," however, Chambri fish suppliers do not recapitulate the affinal relationship. As I have already suggested, wife takers are perpetually in debt to their wife givers. Sago takers, on the other hand, dominate the political scene. At barter markets, Chambri fishwives seat themselves on the ground, and the bush women pass among them holding small chunks of sago, which they obsequiously offer for inspection. The fishwives invariably deprecate the offerings of the bush women, frequently screaming that their sago is of inferior quality, barely edible, in fact. Moreover, until recently this ritualized interaction at barter markets duplicated the wider political situation, for the sago producers lived in their hill hamlets to avoid the possibility of attack by the larger and better organized populations of Chambri and Iatmul fish-supplying headhunters.

Thus, while the Chambri "marry" female sago, they do not act like wife takers within the barter relationship. Instead of submitting to the inevitability of affinal inequality, the Chambri, as fish suppliers, both marry their sago and dominate it.

mother's blood.[11] Everyone but the tsambunwuro would be polluted by contact with his weakening blood, which the Chambri feel can essentially transfer the blood debt. To bleed upon an individual is to become like his mother and therefore to establish an asymmetrical relationship as if between wife givers and wife takers. Tsambunwuro can bleed upon one another without suffering pollution because the apparent asymmetry of the relationship works itself out to absolute equality over the generations.

This equality is unique among the Chambri, at least on an intra-tribal level, and its occurrence during the initiation ceremony is an indication that some other relationship is specifically being avoided. What are the alternatives to the tsambunwuro relationship? The initiate could lie on the bare canoe so that his blood would fall on no one, but this would be unacceptable since, as the Chambri state, a "comforter" is essential while the initiate is undergoing this great mental and physical stress. A second alternative would be to have the initiate lie on his father or on a member of his father's clan. This too would be unacceptable, for, to allow the mother's blood to all on a member of his father's clan would defeat the entire purpose of the ceremony, which is to rid the initiate of the weakening influence of the blood and enable him to join his father's clan as an adult member. Finally, the initiate might lie on his mother's brother. This alternative has been adopted among the neighboring Iatmul (Bateson 1958). The Iatmul rationale for this interaction is unknown to me, but among the Chambri, at least, it would be no more acceptable than the first two. To allow the initiate's blood to fall on his mother's brother would be to reverse the relationship between them, making the initiate "mother" to a member of his mother's clan. Such a reversal would confuse the de facto stability of affinal inequality, a stability that, as I have shown, is necessary to the process of an orderly sociopolitical life.

There is another important dimension to the tsambunwuro's capacity to have the initiate's maternal blood spill upon him. As I have already mentioned, an initiate's tsambunwuro is, in an intergenerational sense, his father's parthenogenetic brother. Thus, a tsambunwuro's social link is through the initiate's father. With the maternal blood, though, the tsambunwuro also incorporates the affinal relationship. He

[11]Initiation is not the only ceremony designed to rid young men of the weakening influences of their mothers. The hair with which they emerge from their mothers' wombs must be ceremonially "finished," for example, if they are to grow into strong members of their father's patriclans.

therefore, becomes, both father and mother to the initiate and is thus the only individual who is capable of "giving birth," during initiation ceremonies, to a fully developed man—a man who is no longer limited by his possession of mother's blood.

I have already discussed several of the consequences of the tsambunwuro's "delivery." First, by producing a man, he assures his own son of a tsambunwuro with whom he, as an older man, has an equal relationship and with whom his son will have an identical relationship, though in the opposite age direction. Consequently, each tsambunwuro produces men who will provide intergenerational agnatic continuity.

Second, by delivering a man a tsambunwuro provides both the wau and the initiate's father with a valuable resource. The mother's brother has a marriage partner for his clanswomen, and the initiate's father has an active producer and exchanger who may gain status for his clan by overpaying for his mother's brother's daughters.

Tsambunwuro, then, are essential to the perpetration of the long-range relationships among agnates and between wife givers and wife takers. It is they who maintain the Chambri sociopolitical system by reproducing its crucial relationships, regardless of personal changes within clans and the political manipulations of adoptive mother's brothers.

REFERENCES

BATESON, G.
1932 Social structure of the Iatmul People. *Oceania* 1:245−291, 401−453.
1958 *Naven.* 2d ed. Stanford: Stanford University Press. 1st ed. 1936.
1972 *Steps to an Ecology of the Mind.* New York: Ballantine.
BURKE, K.
1969 *A Rhetoric of Motives.* Berkeley and Los Angeles: University of California Press.
FORGE, A.
1972 The golden fleece, *Man* 7:527−540.
FORTUNE, R.
1933 A note on some forms of kinship structures. *Oceania* 4:1−9.
GELL, A.
1975 *Metamorphosis of the Cassowaries.* London: Athlone Press.
GEWERTZ, D.
1977 From sago suppliers to entrepreneurs: markening and migration in the Middle Sepik. *Oceania* 48:126−140.

MEAD, M.
1963 *Sex and Temperament in Three Primitive Societies*. New York: William Morrow and Co.

RUDDLE, K., et al.
1978 *Palm Sago*. Honolulu: University of Hawaii Press.

STRATHERN, A. J.
1971 *The Rope of Moka*. Cambridge: Cambridge University Press.

TUZIN, D. F.
1976 *The Ilahita Arapesh*. Berkeley, Los Angeles, and London: University of California Press.

8 ▰▰▰▰▰▰▰▰▰▰▰▰▰▰▰ RITUAL VIOLENCE AMONG THE ILAHITA ARAPESH:

The Dynamics of Moral and Religious Uncertainty

Donald F. Tuzin

The Author

Donald F. Tuzin is Professor of Anthropology at the University of California, San Diego. Born in 1945 in Chicago, his early education was in Minnesota and Chicago. He did undergraduate and graduate work in Ohio, spending six months in an Appalachian farm community for an M.A. in anthropology. In the late 1960s he took up postgraduate studies at University College, London, and was influenced by Phyllis Kaberry, who urged him to study a Plains Arapesh people of the Sepik River area in Papua New Guinea. In 1969 he received a university scholarship to the Department of Anthropology, Research School of Pacific Studies, Australian National University, and while there he worked with Derek Freeman. From 1969 to 1972 he conducted fieldwork on social and ritual organization, among the Ilahita Arapesh—the first anthropologist to study an Arapesh group since Margaret Mead did her Mountain Arapesh studies in the 1930s. He received his Ph.D. from ANU in 1973 and has since taught at San Diego.

Over the past several years Professor Tuzin has actively engaged in research and has advised students in general anthropology, religion and symbolism, psychological methods, Melanesia, and the history of anthropology. His papers have appeared in numerous journals, including *Southwestern Journal of Anthropology* and *Ethos*, and in several books. He is the author of two major monographs dealing with his fieldwork; *The Ilahita Arapesh* (1976) and *The Voice of the Tambaran: Truth and Illusion in Ilahita Arapesh Religion* (1980), which are among the most significant and detailed studies ever to appear on a Sepik society. He is currently writing on Arapesh symbolism and planning new research in Indonesia.

321

INTRODUCTION

The essays in this volume confirm once again that violence is a central component of ritual life in many New Guinea societies. Violence in any form is, of course, startling to behold; but when it is imbued with religious necessity it becomes for many Westerners, whose experience with ritual violence is limited to sublimations such as the Holy Eucharist, an object of extreme and exotic fascination. The image of Sir James Frazer's ill-fated priest of Nemi brooded over a period during which anthropologists openly shared the layman's interest in such practices. Since the early years of this century, however, anthropologists have found ways of their own for sublimating this sort of violence: nowadays, it is typically reported as background noise, rather than as a primary object of ethnographic attention. This condition largely reflects the established ascendancy of empirical models that make no provision for affect. Initially, however, the quest for a more objective approach to ritual phenomena was equally a reaction against the harsh, ethnocentric, and even racist conclusions that were often drawn from the spectacle of ritually sanctioned violence. For example, we now see how superficial and uncharitable was the opinion of Hutton Webster when in 1907 he denounced the "fraud and intimidation" practiced by Melanesian secret societies as being "the source of wholesale oppression and almost unmitigated evil" (1968:61).

If Webster, among others, erred in taking the aggressive component too much at face value, the modern tendency errs in the opposite direction: after the symbolism and structural-functionalism of the broader ritual context have been exhausted, there still remains the unanalyzed fact of the violence itself. Between these two epistemological poles lies a fertile ground bounded by an ancient question: Why do good people do bad things to one another?

Anthropologists rarely address this question directly, though it is implied in many of their studies. Scholars in the tradition of Marx and Weber, adhering to an optimistic view of human nature, are disposed to regard such violence as an instance—perhaps the purest instance—of man's being set against himself, dehumanized by institutions alien to his nature. Others, Freudians especially, conceive that acts of aggression reveal a lethal urge in human nature, a dark proclivity that in the absence of social institutions would cast us back into the Hobbesian nightmare of violence. According to this view, *ritual* violence is a culturally constituted, relatively harmless outlet for the discharge of psychologically primitive aggression (Sagan 1974; cf. Girard 1977).

In various ways, then, the study of ritual violence has been highly tendentious. One result is that the actors' own evaluation of this curious form of behavior has not received the analytic attention it deserves. With this deficiency in mind, I propose in this chapter to consider ritual violence as a source of moral and ethical disquiet on the part of its practitioners. The question of why good people do bad things to one another, although distinctively elaborated in the Western philosophic tradition, is not unique to ourselves, but occurs in various forms—and with various consequences—in other traditions as well. Among the Ilahita Arapesh, the question scarcely if ever arises in response to secular conduct: nonritual violence is easily accounted for by (1) the inherent wickedness of the perpetrator; (2) acute or chronic insanity; or (3) the exigencies of war. In ritual, however, ostensibly stable, peace-loving men are called upon to perform acts of actual or implied violence against women and children; hence the problem.

It is perhaps surprising to find this ethical problem in the domain of ritual. Does not the ritual "bracketing" of such violence specifically exempt it from any moral or ethical indictment? After all, in their own eyes the men are merely enforcing a religious prescription—one for which they are not personally or even collectively accountable, one that originates in a superhuman authority. Where, then, is the problem? The problem, I suggest, arises wherever the ritual justification scrapes against recurring elements of religious skepticism. To the extent that the religious rationale is undermined, the men assume responsibility for their violence, thereby evoking the painful realization that what they are doing egregiously offends against a domestic ethic that prescribes an attitude of nurturance and affection toward those who are their ritual victims. Whatever its merits may be as an analytic device, the ritual "bracket" is imperfect as a partition separating different areas of experience. Thus, what is noticeable to the outsider as a logical contradiction between ritual and domestic values is reified by the actors as an ethical dilemma embracing and confounding two of life's most important areas.

THE PROBLEM

Male initiation among the Ilahita Arapesh is centered on an elaborate men's cult, the implications of which pertain to the general problem just discussed.[1] The issue may be stated simply: How can the cruel and

[1]Fieldwork lasting twenty-one months was carried out in Ilahita village during the period 1969–1972. Major funding was provided by the Research School of Pacific Studies of the Australian National University, with a supplemental grant in aid from the Wenner-Gren Foundation for

323

horrific images of the men's cult, and the sometimes brutal practices mandated by the cult, be reconciled with the relatively benign tenor of domestic life and ideology? Surveying the grim array of ritual prescriptions—the sadistic hazing and genital mutilation of youthful novices; the cynical exploitation of young men by cult elders; the terrorism directed against women, even including ritual and judicial murder—one is left wondering how a society could exist with such predicates. A short stay in the village, on the other hand, shows that this pessimistic view profoundly neglects the concern and tenderness frequently demonstrated between persons of antithetical ritual categories. Needless to say, quarrels and beatings do occur; but these are also occasions when third parties counsel the principals to remember that husbands and wives, parents and children, should be loving and loyal to one another. Such admonitions rarely fail to have an ameliorative effect. In general, the nurturant and protective attitudes expressed in the domestic sphere are reminiscent of the temperamental qualities ascribed by Mead (1935) to the Mountain Arapesh—who, it should be noted, appear to lack the ritually ordained ferocity of their linguistic cousins, the Ilahita Arapesh.

There is, then, a significant and abiding conflict between a man's positive attachment to his wife and children and the antagonism toward these others which is ritually enjoined upon him. Each side of the contradiction has both emotional and ideological aspects. Moreover, just as positive sentiment is an ambient quality of nuclear-family relationships, so the aggressive component of the ritual sphere diffuses beyond moments of overt violence. Cult images and rhetoric are charged throughout with hostile significances, and an intimidating secrecy excludes noninitiates from virtually all cult activities—especially pork feasts, which are ostensibly presented to the cult spirits in return for human and natural fertility, war success, and other benefactions. Moreover, because villages are locally engaged in a network of ritual collaboration, the immanence of these values is more or less constant; thus, during intervals when a village is not sponsoring its own cult rites, it is likely to be participating in such activities elsewhere in the region. Of equal constancy, however, are the sentiments that recoil at these harshnesses.

Anthropological Research. I am grateful to those bodies for their generous support and also to the following scholars for their critical comments on earlier versions of this paper: Terence E. Hays, Bruce Heitman, Gilbert H. Herdt, Fitz John Porter Poole, Edward L. Schieffelin, Melford E. Spiro, and Marc J. Swartz.

The reader will notice that I have used strong language in describing the Arapesh ritual ethos. This requires some justification, inasmuch as such words as *cruel*, *brutal*, and *sadistic* might seem to imply a reversion to the kind of ethnocentrism for which I criticized Webster. Without wishing to defend ethnocentrism, I would suggest that the abhorrence felt against this bias has produced a climate hostile to the legitimate study of ethical values in other, especially nonliterate, societies. The difficulty is compounded by the paucity of terms and concepts available for this type of study and by the need for extraordinary delicacy in distinguishing between one's own judgments and those of the people whom one is studying. While the observer's own sense of propriety usefully alerts him or her to ethnographic problems of a moral or ethical kind, the same subjectivity becomes ethnocentrically distorting when it enters into the analytic task.[2] Viewed in these terms, it is an entirely empirical matter whether, for example, "cruel" is a valid epithet for some ritual practice. Western society has no monopoly on such concepts; and in discussing these matters with Arapesh informants I was often struck by the negative valuation that they themselves placed on certain of their ritual customs: the act was "cruel," though the intention frequently was not. That the men were capable of such self-scrutiny is an extremely important datum, for without it there would be no grounds for asserting, let alone analyzing, the presence of a moral dilemma with respect to ritual conduct.

Although my purpose is not to seek historical origins, it is worthwhile for us to consider for a moment, as a final orientation to this study, how the Arapesh might have come to be in this predicament. To begin with, the ambivalence that the men express toward cult violence is almost certainly influenced by Christian values. Nevertheless, it must be stressed that the village in which I worked was only lightly missionized, and most of my informants were conspicuously proud of their pagan-

---

[2] Two recent examples show how easy it is for "honest reporting" to slip into something very close to ethnocentrism. In their respective studies of the Ik and the Goilala, Turnbull (1972) and Hallpike (1977) did not shrink from speaking plainly about the unsavory aspects of life in those societies. If applied carefully, such candor can be the basis for valuable insights. Unfortunately, however, the gratuitously insulting and contemptuous manner of both of these authors vitiated their efforts, undermined their credibility, and led some critics (e.g., Barth 1974; Strathern 1978) to charge, justly, that their studies lacked professional tact and detachment. Both authors felt that these criticisms had been unfair and misguided (Turnbull 1974; Hallpike 1978).

One senses a cross-purposiveness in these angry exchanges, a mutual indignation that suggests the need for further discussion on the relative limitations of honest reporting and "value-free" anthropology.

ism.[3] A more likely source is to be found in the last century, when the forebears of today's Ilahita Arapesh imported many cult elements—notably the more grisly ones—from the warlike Abelam and Kwanga who moved into the area from their homeland near the Sepik River. This is a large topic, one about which I have written elsewhere (Tuzin 1976). Suffice it to say that contact with these Middle Sepik peoples wrought tremendous changes in village social organization and created an unsettled external situation favoring a village cult of war and violence (cf. Herdt, this volume, chap. 2). In the light of the contradiction we are discussing, it would appear that some of the attitudes associated with the new martial spirit were never fully integrated into the preexisting cultural system. While this interpretation is obviously speculative, it is nicely supported by certain Mountain Arapesh data that I will have cause to adduce in the final section of this chapter.

In what follows, my plan is to depict the paradoxical relation between religious and domestic cultural domains, verifying that this paradox is apparent and morally disturbing to some (and perhaps many) of the actors. This will lead me to argue that the *behavioral* content of cult rituals is partly intelligible as a response by members to the exigencies of their dilemma; in particular, I will examine the role of guilt and its accompaniments under these circumstances. While space considerations force me to limit my descriptions to those aspects most relevant to my theme, extensive background information on Ilahita Arapesh kinship and religion is available elsewhere (Tuzin 1976, 1980).

THE DOMESTIC SPHERE

The Ilahita Arapesh, numbering about 5,000 souls, occupy seven large, sedentary villages situated in a hilly region of the East Sepik Province, some twenty-five kilometers west of the local administrative headquarters at Maprik. Dialectically and culturally distinctive, they take their name from the largest village of their number: Ilahita, a sprawling community of 1,490 inhabitants. Subsistence is based on the lowland staples of yam, taro, and sago; hunting is less important for the incidental

---

[3]At the time of fieldwork, only about 15 percent of the residents of Ilahita village were even nominal Christians, despite the fact that the South Sea Evangelical Mission had been established there since the early 1950s. There are several reasons for this nonresponsiveness, some of which are discussed in Tuzin (1976:33 ff.).

protein it supplies than for the fact that meat (pig, cassowary, various marsupials) is the prime menu item in the secret feasts of the men's cult.

Village social structure is based on a highly complex dual organization (Tuzin 1976) through which ritual, residential, and descent groups are functionally integrated. Descent ideology is patrilineal; patriclans are localized within the ward (the major residential subunit, of which there are six in Ilahita village), while their constituent patrifilial segments are domiciled in the congeries of hamlets making up the ward. Although residence is patrivirilocal, its significance for relations within the nuclear family and between affines is fairly minimal because of the high rate of village and ward endogamy—92 percent in the former case, a range of 38 to 79 percent in the latter (Tuzin 1976:93). Thus, the behavioral problems that reportedly arise when wives are customarily obtained from stranger—perhaps enemy—groups (see, for example, Meggitt 1964) are generally absent in Ilahita. Instead, men seek wives for themselves or for their sons from families that are nearby, familiar, and friendly. Sister-exchange marriage and infant betrothal are the preferred means by which friends or political allies may wittingly cement their relationship and ensure common cause on into the next generation. Of course, over time relations may sour, and there are special problems associated with affines living in close proximity to one another (Tuzin 1976:104). Nonetheless, though ambiguities may inform the wife's brother/sister's husband tie, these do not disfigure the extraordinary warmth and affection that, in interpersonal relations and in ideology, surround the relation between a man and his mother's brother. Whatever opinion a man may hold of his sister's husband, regard for his sister—combined with his own inclinations and a ritually elaborated sentimentality—invariably ensure that he will be indulgent toward his sister's son. In a large corpus of dispute histories assembled during fieldwork, not one case involved a mother's brother in direct conflict with a sister's son. I stress this point because the mother's brother/sister's son tie is specifically exempted from the ethical contradiction discussed earlier. During initiation rites, a man is not obliged to participate in hazing a sister's son who is among the novices. Indeed, the role of the mother's brother is to protect and shelter his nephew and, in some proceedings, to suffer the ordeal with him.

With the preceding as background, we may briefly consider the narrower circle of nuclear-family relations, which, as noted earlier, are generally quite felicitous. Despite occasional discord and philandering, especially in the early years of marriage, divorce is rare; from middle age onward, it is unthinkable.

LIVING ARRANGEMENTS

A married woman is entitled to a house of her own. This is where she keeps all her utensils and personal belongings, and she has the right to sulk there in privacy when and if the need arises. It is also the family hearth, the center of domestic activities, for it is shared as sleeping and living quarters by her husband and their preadolescent children, and all family members gather there for communal meals. The sanctity of the abode is indicated by the fact that while simple theft and simple adultery are reprehensible enough, when they involve housebreaking and invasion of the nuptial abode, these crimes become heinous, for they add insult to injury.

The exclusive coresidence of members is modified in standard ways according to the developmental status of the nuclear-family unit. Just as, in some senses, a wife is "lady of her castle," so a husband's special rights are focused on his yam house. There are usually one or two yam houses near or adjacent to the family dwelling house. A wife is permitted to enter the front of the house to fetch yams for cooking, but the rear is strictly off limits to her, because there are stored male implements and secret ritual paraphernalia. As the family grows up and children start entering adolescence, more and more of a man's time (eating, waking, and sleeping) is spent in and around his yam house. This is the period of a man's political and ritual prime. Magical and ritual enterprises command much of his attention, and for long intervals he lives in his yam house to avoid the polluting influences of femininity and sexuality which pervade the family dwelling. The need for avoidance is most stringently felt toward an adolescent daughter, for it is thought that her unrelieved sexual energies constitute the greatest threat to his ritual (and, indeed, physical) well-being.[4] To a lesser extent, adolescent sons are also avoided as possible sources of contamination, since they cannot be depended upon to maintain disciplined contact with members of the opposite sex. A father in such circumstances may still eat "with" his family, though he is seated apart from the others, a few meters away in front of his yam house. After a man's children are grown and married

---

[4]Men say that this problem has become more troublesome in recent years, as there is a modern tendency for daughters to marry at a later age. (Formerly, marriage for girls occurred soon after menarche.) On the other hand, this perception may actually be a response to an earlier onset of menstruation resulting from improved nutritional conditions rather than to any factual change in marriage age. Whatever the reason, sexually mature daughters are around longer than they used to be.

and both his wife's sexuality and his own ritual activities are on the wane, he is likely to resume residence in the family house (Tuzin 1978).

The possibility of ritual pollution, and also the (universal?) tendency for teenagers to maintain rather odd hours and opinions, are part of the reason why parents condone the practice of adolescents banding together with others of their sex and age to build boys' and girls' clubhouses, usually with four to six residents. From these dormitories, groups of boys make nightly sorties to girls' clubhouses in their own or (more likely) other wards, spending the wee hours in gay banter and light sexual play. The girls' houses are loosely termed *haus blut* ("menstrual house") in Pidgin English, but the vernacular term *gamba* is more accurately glossed as a house that is "secret" or "private"; similarly, the green room used by cult initiates to don their costumes is called "gamba."

The latter contrast is worth stressing, because the Arapesh do not have "menstrual houses" in the usual sense of the term. To be sure, menstrual blood is thought to be inimical to male substance and activity; but one should not overstate the intensity of this opinion nor infer from it an inordinately stark male-female division or antagonism. When a man's wife has her period, he will move his sleeping mat to the other side of the house and will ask some other kinswoman to prepare his food. There is no necessity for the wife to vacate her house. When, as often happens, a young wife does remove herself to a local gamba, she does so mainly for the purpose of enjoying a brief reunion with friends of her sex. Moreover, if Arapesh men felt that same horror of female sexuality which is reported for many other Melanesian societies, it would be extremely difficult to fathom the testimony of several male informants that cunnilingus is a common and enjoyable form of lovemaking.

THE SPIRITUALITY OF MARRIAGE

Marital harmony is judged to be dependent on a corresponding spiritual harmony between the spouses. This spirituality implies one advantage to early betrothal. Years before actual marriage and cohabitation, a boy and girl can become acquainted with each other and with their prospective in-laws. The cultivation of a behavioral relationship is paralleled on the spiritual plane through the process of eating each other's family's yams. As described elsewhere (Tuzin 1972), the Arapesh belief that yams possess spirits entails, inter alia, the notion that eating these tubers is a sacramental act. By ingesting yams that are the descendents (through vegetative propagation) of the yams eaten by one's ancestors, one partakes of a spiritual essence whose lineage goes back to the beginning of time. Before puberty, a girl actually takes up residence with her fiance's family, both to finalize this spiritual incorporation and to ensure that her activities hereafter will be chaperoned by the people who care most about her virtue. By the time the marriage occurs, the basis of lifelong harmony ought to be fully established.

The wedding itself is a simple affair, but it does contain certain elements that contribute to my theme. First, both families give the newlyweds a supply of yams; some of these will be used to start the couple's own gardens, while the others will be eaten during the months before their first harvest. For various reasons that need not concern us here (but see Tuzin 1972), the bilateral distinction between yam "lines" is maintained. This bilaterality is a sign that the spiritual union is less than perfect, though it is progressively enhanced as husband and wife continue to eat each other's ancestral yams. From the time their children have all married, however, this distinction is no longer observed; the yams are allowed to mingle freely, for it is assumed—with ample justification—that the spirits of the old couple have finally and completely fused.

To return to the wedding itself: After a matrimonial feast involving both families and other well-wishers, the newlyweds retire to their new house for a honeymoon seclusion lasting several days, the object of which needs no comment. Responding only to nature's calls, they emerge, much to the delight of any onlookers, holding their hands over each other's genitalia. At the end of this period, the couple descends to a nearby stream, there to bathe and to conduct a moving little ceremony that sanctifies their union. The bride begins by damming part of the stream with a small bundle of twigs and other debris. Then, for the first and last time in her presence, her new husband lets blood from his penis into the pool collected behind the dam. When the flow has stopped, man and wife kneel and, brushing away the dam, swish the blood on its way downstream, pledging to each other their eternal love and fidelity and praying to the ancestral spirits in the stream to grant their marriage fruitfulness and permanence.

AFFECT AND DEFECT IN MARRIAGE

The preceding section has provided part of the sociocultural context relevant to my contention that ties within the nuclear family contain a good deal of warmth and affection; what has been said regarding the

PLATE 8.1   A father tenderly comforts his son after the boy has swooned during a cult ceremony.

marital relationship could be extended, *mutatis mutandis*, to the nurturant and otherwise positive bond between parents and children. This impression is based on a great number of casual observations, any of which—a meaningful touch or gesture—might seem trivial and inconclusive; but in attempting to characterize something so qualitative as a feeling tone, we must turn to this information as the best we have. As an illustration, let me cite one brief incident that captures the essence of what I am characterizing. Whether or not the protagonist's behavior typified what others would have done in similar circumstances, it is noteworthy that none of the several persons with whom I discussed the incident considered his actions to be odd or surprising.

Returning home from the garden, Kwambwean fell into an argument with Akotan, a man who was her distant cousin and with whom she was usually on excellent terms. The issue was trivial; but both parties were hot-tempered, and

331

the match quickly degenerated into an exchange of very ugly insults. Finally, Kwambwean broke away and went weeping to her husband, Falipen, to tell him what had happened. His instant reaction was to leap up, rush to Akotan's hamlet, and engage him in a fistfight. Falipen's greater fury made up for his slight disadvantage in size and strength, and in the end the two men emerged about equally bloodied.

On the face of it, this was simply a matter of a man defending his *own* honor by attacking his wife's assailant. Nevertheless, prompted by the circumstances and personalities involved, I asked Falipen why he had fought Akotan. "I would not have done it," he replied, his voice and lips quivering, "but *he made her cry.*" However much his own pride had been involved, it was Falipen's feeling for his wife that had precipitated his action.

Such emotion, and the ideology approving it, squares badly with a ritual system that insists that men feel and express only a contemptuous hostility toward women and a bullying superiority over youthful novices. Cult symbolism is crowded with images grotesque, devouring, and weirdly preternatural—all of which are pressed into the service of intimidating cult outsiders. One analytic response to this situation would be to deny that there is any necessary contradiction: by definition, the ritual context segregates cult behavior from all other domains. The implication would be that men go about their brutalities and hazings, if not merrily, at least content in the knowledge that their deeds are ritually sanctioned and required. Indeed, most of the time the men rationalize their conduct in precisely these terms. Nevertheless, a residual element exists which neither their rationalizations nor the anthropologist's (formally equivalent) reification can accommodate: namely, the guilt that the men, by their admission and in accord with my own observations, occasionally experience in these settings. These are moments when the worldly character of many of these rules is admitted and when the reflective individual is faced with the painful fact of his own moral responsibility.

It is not surprising that such guilt would be a troubling factor in the otherwise benign circle of family emotions. Its influence is shown in many ad hoc manifestations and also in certain conventions involving the nuclear family. Of the latter, the most striking example occurs when someone in the family dies. At dusk on the evening of the funeral, the surviving members of the immediate family gather in the hamlet of the deceased, nervously seeking to determine whether the ghost holds one of them responsible for his or her death. Conch shells are blown in an eerie chorus to attract the shade's attention, and then the name of the deceased is called into each quadrant of the surrounding forest. This is repeated until the ghost is heard to answer, *Mein?* (''What?''), signifying that no resentment is felt and that the survivors are reasonably safe from deadly reprisal. If after many attempts no response is heard, the grim implication is that retribution is surely on its way. In every case I observed, the level of motivation was high enough to induce one of the listeners to hear (or think he or she could hear) the desired response.

Significantly, the urgency of this exercise is greatest when it is a surviving husband who is attempting to divine the inclinations of his deceased wife. Indeed, in other circumstances the living often dispense with this consultation. Although the ghost of a man is assumed to be dangerous and unpredictable, practically speaking his wife and preadult children have little to fear, for a man who has violent intentions toward his family does not have to wait until he is dead to activate them: the power and the opportunity are there all along. In addition, women and children do not practice sorcery, and therefore the ghost would not judge them to be blameworthy in this respect. In the case of a deceased wife, on the contrary, the surviving widower has every reason to feel threatened and to beg reassurances from the recently departed that all is well in her feelings toward him. This threat holds true whether or not he is directly innocent of her death. Why? Because the wife now has two things she never had in life: unlimited power and unlimited awareness. Beyond the petty resentments that have accumulated over her married life, as a ghost she now possesses the supremely aggravating realization that she has been systematically duped by the fraud and intimidation of the men's cult. Little wonder that in addition to normal grief, men express (in dreams, in divinatory actions, in conversation) a morbid anxiety on the occasion of their wives' deaths.[5] As we shall see, this syndrome of guilt and fear of retribution is bound up with preemptive violence in the cult context.

A final note: Attributing ''guilt'' to the men in this context depends on the assumption that they have internalized the values elaborated within the domestic sphere. That is to say, their disquiet stems not only from the prospect of being discovered in their deception but also, more importantly, from the punishing voice of their own consciences. While my understanding of these people leaves me in no doubt that this assumption is valid, the evidence of anecdotes, general observations,

---

[5]This pattern is consistent with the notion that the most dreaded curses are those of one's mother, wife, and father's sister—not only because they are inherently more powerful but also because a woman does not have the mystical ability to lift the curse once she has pronounced it.

and isolated statements by informants—although impressive in aggregate—is not of the psychologically definitive sort that would be preferred. With this proviso, I will trust to my intuition and continue using the notion of "guilt" in this essay.

THE TAMBARAN CULT

The Arapesh practice a cult that is found in many versions throughout the Sepik River basin (see Mead 1938:169 ff.). Known generically by the Pidgin English term *tambaran*, the cult is rigidly exclusive to males, internally graded according to degrees of ritual advancement, and focused on ritual communication with spirits (ancestral or other) whose benevolence is thought to be the source of all life's necessities. The spirits of the cult also have a terrible power for destruction, which men are able to contain only by providing them with regular sacrificial feasts of pork, long yams, and other delicacies. Such banquets are exclusive to males who have achieved that grade, while the spirits being honored are supposedly present as invisible guests, eating the invisible essences of the feast food.

In Ilahita, the Tambaran cult contains a series of five grades roughly paralleling the succession of important stages of social and physical maturation during a man's life. Thus: (1) *Falanga* has to do with sundering the nurturant and affectual bonds uniting a young boy with his mother and, by implication, others of her sex; (2) *Lefin* certifies an older boy's membership in male society by bringing him into intimate contact with beings of another order, who inhabit a world that men regard as their spiritual homeland; (3) *Maolimu* celebrates the adolescent's dawning sexuality and imminent social majority, signifying the gravity of this transformation with the radical image of species metamorphosis; (4) *Nggwal Bunafunei* toasts the achievement of full social and physical prowess while allowing men to gloat over the raw dominance they enjoy in relation to women; (5) *Nggwal Walipeine* confers on the small group of surviving old men supreme ritual knowledge and authority, thus redeeming their unenviable position of social, physical, and ritual morbidity.[6] Admission to these grades occurs during successive ritual

---

[6]To the best of my knowledge, based on a survey of all Ilahita Arapesh villages and on a reading of the literature dealing with other Sepik groups, Ilahita village is unique in providing the oldest males with a grade of their own. The historical and functional issues surrounding this singularity are treated at length in my study of the Ilahita Tambaran cult (Tuzin 1980).

''seasons'' lasting one to three years, separated by quiet intervals whose lengths vary according to internal and external political relations, availability of feast foods, and other factors technically independent of ritual considerations.[7] Through a variety of ceremonies, ordeals, feasts, and seclusions, novices assume custody of the knowledge and paraphernalia associated with a given grade, retaining these until it is time for them, as initiators, to transmit the secrets to the sons of their own initiators. (This will be discussed below.) It is important to emphasize that the correspondence between ritual and sociophysical maturation is only approximate: while these existential significances are overtly expressed in Tambaran symbolism, the actual age of novices to a particular grade may vary considerably.[8] An entire ritual cycle takes about fifty years—about the span of an Arapesh lifetime.

Cult activities are organized around a complex series of dualistically opposed structures (Tuzin 1976), the most important for our purposes being the initiation classes *Sahopwas-Owapwas*. Put simply, these are the groups that initiate one another; but this relationship must be understood in several ways at once. First, the words themselves may be translated ''older brother'' and ''younger brother,'' respectively, signifying with a kinship metaphor the superior ritual status of Sahopwas (Tuzin 1977a). Second, the initiation-class division is isomorphic with that obtaining between the two constituent subclans of each clan. More precisely, the actual parties who initiate one another are individuals or patrifilial segments belonging to complementary subclans. These partnerships descend patrilineally, as do the specific cult spirits and paraphernalia (flutes, drums, paintings, statues, and the like) that are shared by (and exchanged between) the hereditary partnerships (see fig. 8.1). Third, at the opposite extreme Sahopwas and Owapwas are society-wide ritual categories cutting across all the clans. In the great rituals, the multitude of operating units merge with others of like status to perform as members of these all-inclusive categories. At the regional

---

[7]Note, however, that a village may anticipate a ritual season by stepping up its garden operations, restricting hunting, and initiating truces with current enemies.

[8]I do not know whether this ''roughness of fit'' is at all common among societies practicing male initiation. I suspect, however, that terms such as *initiation rite* and *puberty rite* have fostered undue ethnographic attention toward the *novices* in these proceedings, thus encouraging the neglect of two aspects that, in Ilahita at least, are crucial to an understanding of the general phenomenon: (1) the fact that a male's initiation into one of these grades is truly complete only after he himself has served as an initiator; and (2) the sense in which the rite is serving the expressive purposes of all participants—including, indeed, the ''nonparticipating'' audience. See Gewertz (this volume, chap. 7) for a similar point drawn from her Chambri data.

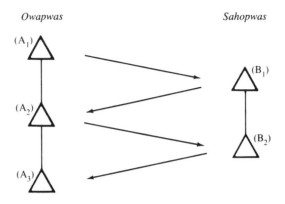

FIGURE 8.1   Initiation-class reciprocity

level, the ubiquity of this division permits orderly participation by different villages in each others' rituals. Fourth, these initiation statuses reverse themselves semicyclically. Those who are, say, Sahopwas at this point in time will be Owapwas a half cycle later. Sahopwas status is assigned to the group currently in charge of Nggwal Bunafunei, the penultimate tambaran; thus, advancement to this grade implies that one's entire initiation class, previously Owapwas, has ascended to Sahopwas status.

A further refinement in this scheme is brought about by the fact that each class contains two ritually active generations. While fathers and sons belong to the same class, they differ greatly in their degrees of advancement through the cult. It is necessary, therefore, to distinguish initiation *subclasses* within the larger units. In the absence of a vernacular term, I have simply designated these "Sahopwas Senior," "Sahopwas Junior," and so on. Thus, referring again to figure 8.1, the individual/group labeled A_1 is Owapwas Senior; B_1 is Sahopwas Senior; A_2 is Owapwas Junior, and so forth.[9]

Without our entering into more baroque complexities (but see Tuzin 1980), the preceding is sufficient to indicate that the initiation structure is characterized by pervasive reversals of rights and duties. Not

[9]Note that although B_1 is in possession of Nggwal Bunafunei and is nominally the most senior group on the chart, their own senior partners (A_1) control the higher authority of Nggwal Walipeine. The disparity between nominal and actual authority is bound up with circumstances surrounding the superaddition, late in the last century, of Nggwal Walipeine to the Ilahita cult. See Tuzin (1980).

only does the entire status system reverse itself every half cycle, it is also the case that each initiation class is simultaneously initia*tor* and initia*ted* with respect to different tambarans. These features confer on the system a strongly bilateral character, even though at any particular moment ritual supremacy is given to one group over the other. More to the point of this analysis, the cult is structured in such a way that fathers do not directly initiate their own sons; rather, their junior partners perform this service on their (the fathers') behalf. While this arrangement certainly blunts the fathers' moral dilemma—amounting to a kind of structural accommodation to the fact that they would prefer not to abuse their own sons—there are other reasons, yet to be considered, why the problem of ritual violence is not fully resolved by the conventions of initiation reciprocity.

INITIATION RITES

In keeping with the line of my argument, I have omitted from the following descriptions many details (magical and symbolic elements, mythic exigeses, feasting patterns, and so forth) in order to concentrate on the violent aspects of cult ideology and practice. What cannot be conveyed in a short space is the full emotional force of this violence: it is one thing to be thumped on the head or to have your penis lacerated, but when these attacks are staged in a dramatic atmosphere of weird costumery, unearthly sounds, and frenzied stomping, screaming, and singing by scores, perhaps hundreds, of armed warriors, each of whom seems madly intent on your destruction, the experience is transformed into one of nightmarish horror. Let it be remembered, then, that the horrific element looms large in nearly all the following initiatory rites.

Falanga

Admission to the lowest grade Falanga occurs in early childhood, after about the age of three. The initiation is calculated first to sever a boy's close, confidential attachment to his mother and other female kin by entrusting him with a set of ritual secrets all his own, and second, to orient him along the path of male development and association by ridding him of the pollution of his mother's milk and physical presence. Weaning is therefore a prerequisite. Toilet training is also essential: an adult male avoids unnecessary contact with a baby, who might soil him, as it is thought that the urine and feces, being constituted of breast milk, are agents of female pollution. Thus, the welfare of both novice and initiator are taken into account in the timing of Falanga.

As in many societies, the mechanism of sexual purification is an assault on the genital organs. The climax of the Falanga initiation occurs when the boys are taken down to a nearby stream. The true nature of the ordeal is dissembled with a metaphor: they (and their mothers and sisters) are told that the Tambaran will force them to slide down the spiked trunk of a falanga sago palm, and thus rip open their bellies. Upon arriving at the water, the novices are divided into two groups according to age. While the younger ones look on in fear and distress, the older boys are subjected to an attack by three or four men hideously attired as "pigs." The boys' penes are lacerated with bamboo razors, and the blood is collected in leaves, which are then tucked under the bark of large, nearby trees. As the tree grows strong and great, so will the novice who is now spiritually affiliated with it. Then the incisors turn on the younger boys, who are held down while their penes and scrota are vigorously rubbed with stinging nettles. When this operation is concluded, both age groups are seized and thrown headlong into the pool, which has been filled with stinging nettles. An attentive mother's brother is one who would join his nephew in this ordeal; and because of the high density of kinship ties in this relatively endogamous village, it happens that a good many of the men immerse themselves.

The major revelation of Falanga concerns the true nature of a class of masked figures known as *hangamu'w* (pl. *hangahiwa*). A variant of the widespread Bismarck Archipelago form known in Neo-Melanesian as *tumbuan*, the hangamu'w is a full-body costume consisting of a woven helmet mask, a shoulder area fashioned from coiled strands of bright orange fruits, and a concealing body curtain of yellow sago fibers (Tuzin 1980:41). The women are told the half-truth (see below) that these are spirits incarnate, rather than being merely men disguised as such. To guard this deception, the figures are mute at all times, and the wearer may even go the the length of strapping coconut husks to his feet so as not to leave human footprints. Mead describes the Mountain Arapesh tumbuan as "gay and laughter-giving" (1934:245). To some extent, this is true also of their Ilahita cousins: in silent, comic fashion, they roam about the village begging treats of food for later enjoyment in the privacy of their spirit house. There is also, however, a more sinister side to this institution, one involving ritual murder (*laf*).

Of the 214 hangahiwa recorded in Ilahita village, about 10 percent have a reputation for murder. Their trappings include crimped cordyline leaves as homicide badges and (until the Australian authorities suppressed the custom) the skulls of their victims hung in grisly display around their necks. By donning one of the hangamu'w masks, it is said, the wearer becomes possessed of the in-dwelling spirits of its victims; wild with their passion of revenge, he is likely to kill any living thing that crosses his path. Upon doing so, he supposedly recovers his senses, returns the mask to its place among the others in the spirit house, and, concealing his guilt, joins in the general distress that is agitated when the victim's body is discovered. Moral responsibility is deflected onto the Tambaran itself, which is credited with another killing as evidence of its insatiable appetite. The identity of the human agent is judged to be irrelevant, for even though it may be suspected that selfish motives have entered into the choice of victim, the success of the deed proves that the Tambaran was accomplice to it. Moreover, because the victim is nearly always a woman or a child, the event is usually taken to be a simple expression of the Tambaran's customary balefulness toward those whom he considers repugnant or dispensable.

Ritual murder is by no means restricted to the capricious violence of the hangamu'w masks. As we shall see in the case of Nggwal-sanctioned homicide, the correlated themes of anonymity and absolution from moral responsibility will appear again.

Lefin

Entry into the Lefin grade comes in late childhood. The event is seen to be the final purgation of female influences, corresponding to which the novice's male identity is affirmed through the mingling of his essences with those of the ancestral and cult spirits. The "voice" of this tambaran is a bull-roarer, its eerie sound represented to the uninitiated as the gigantic voice of a dwarf with red hair and beard and a huge mouth with great teeth, which he uses to carve drums and slit gongs. Piercing this image, the revelations of Lefin include, first, the truth about the bull-roarer, and, second, the secret techniques and devices used to carve drums and slit gongs.

For their ordeal, the novices are once again led down to the stream, this time to a portion of it which is believed to be inhabited by cult and ancestral spirits, along with other creatures of that realm. A roofless house has been built out over the water, in which, exposed to the elements, the novices spend two to three weeks in seclusion—long enough, that is, for their genital wounds to heal. The ordeal begins with the novices being seated in the house. A tumultuous singing and stamping starts up from the initiates on the bank in concert with those who are crowded into the house with the novices. At the peak of intensity, another sound is heard: the unmistakable call used to summon a pig. From a concealed chamber under the house floor, two pig incisors emerge and move down the line of novices. While initiators hold the boys and peel back their foreskins, the incisors slash at each glans penis with bamboo razors. Then the novices are ordered to lie down with their penes placed between the floorboards, so that the blood may flow freely into the water below.

The object of this last detail is revealed to the boys a few days later. While their attention is diverted, one of the initiators tosses a rock into the stream with an audible splash. Crying that his shell pendant has fallen into the stream, the man orders all the novices into the water to look for it. As the boys feel around in the mud and silt of the stream bed, they are (as they later learn) benignly contaminating themselves with the "oily" essences of their own penile blood—which, during intervening days, has mingled with the spiritual essences already there. Thus introduced to the other world, thus sanctified in their masculinity, they may proceed on the normal course of manly development.

The revelation of the bull-roarers occurs as part of a separate Lefin ceremony, during which we see for the first time the mock battling between initiation classes—specifically, between the initiators and the fathers of the novices—which is a repeating element in all subsequent Tambaran ritual. Apropos of later analysis, I should note that the initiators are often aided in their role by foreign villagers—who may indeed be real enemies and whose presence there is provided under a truce arrangement. This lends verisimilitude to the battle (in the eyes of the youthful novices), and it releases a number of home-place initiators to perform various behind-the-scenes roles connected with the initiation. In the present case, the Lefin novices are led or carried by their fathers into the ceremonial hamlet. There, they are corralled by their initiators with a length of lawyer vine and forced into a tightly crowded area in the center of the clearing. Many of the boys sob uncontrollably, alarmed as much by their fathers' apparent fear as by the series of lunges made at them by spear-wielding initiators. After several minutes, the boys and their fathers are dispersed to the sides of the clearing. A few initiators rush into the clearing and circle around, spraying the onlookers with rancid sago meal, said to be "feces." They are followed by two more initiators acting as armed escorts for a man who makes threatening gestures with a long-handled, specially hafted adz—the secret implement for carving slit gongs and hourglass drums. Finally, there starts a long succession of initiators wielding bull-roarers. One by one they enter the clearing, swinging their whirring devices in an aggressive, gladiatorial manner. Each time, two or three fathers step from the sidelines and challenge them. Staying just out of range of the flashing blade, they dodge about, waiting for an opening. When the initiator's arm tires, he lifts the thong high as a signal to his attackers that it is safe to rush in under the swinging bull-roarer. After pinioning him, the fathers lead him to one side to make room for the next bull-roarer that is just entering the precinct. When all the initiators have thus performed, the bull-roarers are individually presented to the novices, who eagerly set about practicing with them while the older men convene a small celebratory feast.

In sum, the two lowest grades of the cult revolve around images of growth—specifically, under the circumstances, masculine growth. "Lefin" and "falanga" are the names, respectively, for edible and inedible sago. Informants explain the symbolic connection by pointing out that sago palms are vigorous growers and that their habitat in the moist valley floors puts them into close contact with ancestral and cult spirits (Tuzin 1977*b*). On the other hand, sago palms exhibit a propagative exuberance patterned in a form that, to the Arapesh, is distinctly feminine. This paradox (or ambiguity) hints at an existential notion that will be fully elaborated in the symbolism of Maolimu, namely, that masculinity is apprehended as a *transcendence* of femininity, boasting powers of its own and yet retaining the fecundity of its opposite.

The bodily conditions for this growth are, according to the men, created through the bites of the pig incisor. We may grant that there is a type of logic in using the sexual organ to remove pollution of an essentially sexual kind. Given the importance of masculine purity, we might even allow that the ends justify the means. Neither of these rationales, however, accounts for the lurid violence of the genital operation. When the Jewish *mohel* circumcises his charge, he does not don a hideous costume, nor does he assemble a *minyan* of screaming, stomping accomplices. The terrorism embodied in the Arapesh practice derives, I suggest, from two interrelated sources: first, there is an intention to subdue the novices through an act of raw dominance, to impress upon them the life-and-death power of male society; second, the cut of the razor purifies because it is accompanied by a violent, *exorcistic* display against the offending spiritual substance. Combining these, we have the possibility that the boy novice is apprehended as a representation of the female principle, which is the latent object of aggression (cf. Bateson 1936:132). This view helps explain why it is felt that these boys need to be subdued at all, why, that is, a natural and unaided acquisition of male values and potencies is presumed to be impossible.

This interpretation is supported by the subsequent reorientation of Tambaran violence. Starting with Maolimu, the novice's masculine nature is no longer problematic; he has achieved puberty, thus proving the efficacy of Falanga and Lefin. Although some amount of hazing continues, the emphasis shifts markedly to a concern with ritual training, with consolidating male identity, and with refining the individual's understanding of his sexually ordained place in Arapesh society. Although the ritual hierarchy among males continues to depend on coercion and differential access to cult secrets, actual aggression—both physical and rhetorical—is increasingly directed at those whose absence is most conspicuous at the initiation rites: the women themselves.

Maolimu

The most striking feature of the Maolimu grade is that initiation into it requires a forest seclusion of several months' duration. In a secret village built for the purpose, the youths spend their time in gay camaraderie with the older men, singing, dancing, feasting, and learning such skills as formal oratory. The experience is designed to impress upon them the rules of proper conduct. A magical procedure ensures that the lesson "sticks" by making indelible whatever character they exhibit during the period of seclusion; therefore, only a fool or a moron would fail to behave in an exemplary manner. Beyond these practical considerations, Maolimu initiation strongly reinforces the misogynist ethos by presenting to the novice the image of a world complete in its masculinity.

The Maolimu seclusion is portrayed as the enactment of a myth. According to the tale, one day while the men are out hunting, the women maliciously burn down their spirit house. The women's guilt is revealed to the men by a bush demon, who offers them (in exchange for meat) a magic that will liberate them from the loathsome presence of these females. Using the magic, they are transformed into flying foxes and in that guise soar away to a distant refuge. The women are much alarmed at being abandoned, wondering who will care for and copulate with them. At this point, the bush demon reappears and offers them (in exchange for sex) the remains of the previous magic. They accept his proposition and, after changing into (smaller) flying foxes, take off in hot pursuit of their menfolk. They arrive at the place of refuge, only to be angrily rejected by their husbands, brothers, and sons: "Whom do you think we were running away from? You alone. It was your own fault for burning down our spirit house, so we ran away from you." Chastised, the women return to the village. That is why small flying foxes live near the village, while the large ones stay hidden deep in the forests and fields of grass.

Thus, one day, the Maolimu novices are unexpectedly informed that the following morning will begin their lives in the forest as flying foxes. Late that afternoon, they are taken to Maolimu's ceremonial hamlet in the village. Sitting there, wondering what will happen, they are suddenly accosted by a force of savagely attired warriors—strangers from another village—who, in turn, flee before the timely onslaught of a group of initiators. After the excitement dies down, there is held a solemn ceremony in which novices representing each ward in the village are presented with clay figurines, said to be "babies." Although nothing more is done with the dolls, they are the first indication that the experience upon which the youths are about to embark has a pseudoprocreative function (Hiatt 1971). When this segment is concluded, the novices are forced to run a gauntlet of two lines of initiators armed with clubs whose tips are wrapped with stinging nettles. After sharing in a small feast, the youths return home.

Later, after dark, a singsing is held in the ceremonial hamlet. Encouraged by their sponsors and initiators, the novices mock their mothers and sisters, singing that they (the women) will not see their faces again for a long time, that they will have to copulate with the dogs of the village. The women reply with sarcastic laments. In the predawn darkness, the initiators steal away, proceeding to the secret forest village to prepare for the arrival of the novices.

In the morning, the novices are led to the place of seclusion by their fathers. They arrive to find a curious tableau vivant. The actors do not seem to notice them. A funeral is under way, with a corpse laid out and men and "women" (transvestite initiators) gathered around in silent mourning. In the clearing one man is pretending to be a pig, another a chicken, another a pet cockatoo. Still another is pretending to weave a net bag. The fathers of the boys feign puzzlement and ask where the "trees" are, for the novices still believe they are to be turned into flying foxes. No response. The intruders feel as if they are invisible and noiseless spectators in a village complete in its masculinity.[10]

The fathers seat themselves and their sons under the porticoes of the bordering houses and watch the activity in the clearing. One initiator,

---

[10]With the exception of various body ornaments, the Arapesh traditionally went completely nude. Accordingly, ritual transvestism is necessarily a rather token affair, and it should not be thought that the presence of men "dressed up" as women does anything to conceal the essential and exclusive masculinity of the Maolimu proceedings.

who has been miming the motions of clearing grass, goes to throw away a handful of invisible cuttings. Having just disappeared from sight, he staggers back into the clearing, impaled with a spear through his chest. (The spear is actually only tucked under his arm.) Instantly, there is a massive attack on the camp. Armed and decorated warriors (the foreigners) pour into the clearing from all sides and terrify the novices, who, in the light of the abortive attack the previous day, are inclined to think that this one is genuine. After much confusion, the foreigners sit down amiably alongside their erstwhile victims. The pantomime ceases. Eventually, the youths are informed that this is to be their home for the period of seclusion.

The chief objective of Maolimu is to transform the novices into whole men by severing once and for all the ties of substance and affection which bind them to women, especially to their mothers. This process entails, among other things, gorging them on pork. It is in the nature of men to crave pig flesh; the unremitting pork diet distills this essence by effecting a consubstantial link between the novice's flesh and that of the pig itself, thus reminding us of the German proverb, *Man ist was Man isst*. Not only does the new man like pork, he requires it.[11] Nearly every day, pigs are carried to the forest village. Hearing the triumphal whoops and songs of the carriers, the women back in the village are told that these are ''women'' being taken to their sons and brothers for the purpose of copulating with them (Tuzin 1978). Replenishment of the wild-pig population in time for the next Maolimu initiation is provided for by a fertility rite held near the close of the seclusion period.

The significance of Maolimu is clear: in a society of men, women are not missed. Men may easily perform both sides of the division of labor, and surrogate women (i.e., pigs) are available in profusion. If women are absolutely needed to partner a marriage or to sing the high harmony of a song, a man simply plays the part. By their very nature, it is said, women are the source of nearly all discord and litigation within the community. Through their ceaseless enticements to adultery, their notorious insensitivity to the sensible commands of father, husband, and brother, and their mindless passion for gossip and intrigue—in these and countless other ways women are the bane of a peaceful society. As long as men never compromise their masculine unity, they will hold the secret

---

[11]Conversely, women, having never been fed pork ''by the Tambaran,'' supposedly neither like nor require this food. This is one of the justifications given for excluding them from all pig feasts.

to a paradisiacal world devoid of women and full of life's pleasures. Indeed, in this world women will not be required to produce babies, for men will have taken over this role as well—as symbolized in the curious baby presentation staged before the boys leave for the forest. A man's supreme loyalty must therefore be given to his sex group and to the important secrets they guard. No devotion to family can override this, and a man must be prepared to sacrifice—if necessary by his own hand—his mother, wife, or child at the behest of the Tambaran. The discipline is harsh and exacting, but in the ideology of the cult life depends on it.

Nggwal

The two highest grades, Nggwal Bunafunei and Nggwal Walipeine, are by far the most elaborate and time-consuming of the entire series; for the purposes of this analysis however, they may be treated together and briefly as extensions of themes that are already established. Again, we see an aggressive exclusion of women; more than this, Nggwal actually preys upon women to satisfy his appetite for human blood. Unlike the Mountain Arapesh, who swear to secrecy a woman who learns something that only men should know (Mead 1935:68), Ilahita cult members feel obliged to punish this transgression with death by strangulation. Such deaths may not be avenged, for they are regarded as ritual executions, or *laf*. Nowadays, these murders are outlawed by the government; but this means simply that women now consider themselves threatened by sorcery rather than by overt violence. Even if their knowledge or skepticism of cult secrets goes undetected by mortals, it is thought that Nggwal monitors their thoughts and will punish them directly. Not surprisingly, these circumstances make it all but impossible to discover what the women actually think about the men's secret activities. We can say with some certainty, however, that their fear of the Tambaran is quite genuine and that if private doubts do exist in the minds of some (or many) of the women, there is nothing approaching a conspiracy of acquiescence (cf. Hogbin 1970).

Two other forms of ritual murder (both classified as *laf*) are associated with Nggwal, in particular, with Nggwal Bunafunei. The first, an instance of outright human sacrifice, has been discontinued since the imposition of Pax Australiana in the early 1950s. The night before the two-day initiation ritual, two or three braves among the initiating group go about in search of a victim. The reputation of their group depends on them killing at least one person before dawn. The victim is preferably an

PLATE 8.2   During the Nggwal Bunafunei initiation, one of the initiators (right) runs about taking swipes at the assembled novices with an adz. Note the adult age of the novices. Note also that although some are breaking ranks, most of the novices do not show any apparent fear.

enemy villager—man, woman, or child. Apparently, however, the risk and difficulty of ambushing an enemy occasionally drives the assassins to seek a victim in their own village, perhaps even the unprotected wife or child of the killer himself. Word goes out that Nggwal has "swallowed" another victim; the killer remains technically anonymous, even though most Nggwal members know, or have a strong inkling of, his identity.

During the night following their initiation, the novice class must prove their mettle by providing a sacrifice equal to the one given by their initiators. Again Nggwal is credited with the killing, thereby reaffirming his sanguinary tendencies.

The second laf institution contains a species of judicial murder which, because of the fantasy on which it is based, continues to the present day. Virtually all deaths resulting from disease or accident are attributed by the Arapesh to sorcery. Various forms of divination are used to identify the culprit, which can lead to accusations and retaliatory actions. There is, however, an alternative procedure, one that appears to have been used with increasing frequency in recent years. Two types of

346

divination are capable of revealing that Nggwal is responsible for a death, either directly or by having guided the hand of the sorcerer. When this diagnosis is reached, the history of the victim is searched for an instance of religious misconduct. If the victim is a man, this search usually turns up a remembered act of defiance, crankiness, or simple error in a ritual context. If the victim is a woman, the crime is often that of having insulted her husband's manliness or of having blasphemed in some way against the Tambaran. Finally, a child's death is taken to be reprisal for a parental misdeed, and therefore the history of the parents becomes relevant. In any of these cases, it is wrong for the aggrieved to retaliate against a suspected sorcerer, and to do so would make him subject to further punishment by or in the name of Nggwal.

The notion of Nggwal-sanctioned sorcery discourages future anti-social conduct by causing the public to construe present deaths to be legitimate punishment for past offenses against the Tambaran. It also promotes village solidarity by palliating the disruptive effects arising from the idea that black magic may spring from entirely human (and therefore base) motives.[12] Nonetheless, the testimony of informants reveals that on any given occasion some members of the community privately recognize that the divinatory signs and interpretations are being manipulated to produce an outcome congenial to the majority interests in the case. Typically, these interest groups wish to see the matter resolved quickly and with minimum fuss; hence the preference for diagnoses implicating Nggwal. Even the immediate survivors of the victim may, depending on a variety of factors, welcome a solution that frees them of the obligation to initiate dangerous revenge actions. These pressures sufficiently prevent any skeptic from voicing his true opinion; for to do so would merely expose that individual to accusations of mischievous self-interest or, more ominously, blasphemy. Like Ibsen's tragic hero, he would become an enemy of the people.

This brief, selective account of Tambaran initiations and related practices should illustrate the themes of violence and aggression which pervade cult ideology and engender acts that are physically, emotionally, or, indeed, fantastically terroristic. There is no shortage of rationalizations: "We must beat and cut the boys so that they may

---

[12]Elsewhere, I have considered these beliefs and practices from legal and epistemological standpoints (Tuzin 1974, 1980). Malinowski (1926:88 et seq.) describes a strikingly homologous custom among the Trobrianders, whereby the authority behind alleged acts of judicial sorcery is that of the chief. See also Hau'ofa (1971) for an account of official sorcery practiced under the aegis of Mekeo chiefly authority.

grow!'' or, ''The women must be excluded because Nggwal will not tolerate their presence!'' We have just received hints, however, that such rationalizations may be flawed. Evidence confirming this interpretation will comprise the final element of my argument.

SKEPTICISM AND MORALITY

Skepticism over the status of Tambaran beliefs and recognition of the sometimes pragmatic nature of ritual acts are by no means limited to the context of Nggwal-sanctioned sorcery. Before I offer some additional instances, however, let me note that the persistence of these beliefs and practices requires something less than universal or unwavering adherence—*provided* that there are social conditions discouraging the publication and spread of doubt. In the case of the Tambaran such conditions regularly exist, and accordingly the ritual system is highly stable.[13] Still, there remains the fact that doubt is present somewhere in the cult system at all times, the implications of which must now be considered.

When the men hold their secret pig feasts, the story given to noninitiates is that the gigantic, devouring Nggwal is present in the flesh—hence the impossibility of outsiders joining the banquet. Initiates understand, of course, that this is a metaphor signifying real but *spiritual* attributes of the deity. Women are judged incapable of comprehending the metaphysical Nggwal; if told that Nggwal is invisibly present at the feast, they would not believe it and would insist on participating, thereby provoking wrath on a cosmic scale. For the men, Nggwal *is* present, eating the invisible essence of the food; when he ''devours'' his human victims, he does so either through a human agent—a sorcerer or laf executioner—or by striking directly, in which case the physical body displays no outward sign of having been ''eaten.'' The more senior and sophisticated initiates, however, especially those who have achieved Nggwal Walipeine, are privately cynical over the status of these convenient metaphors. More than once it was intimated to me that just as the fiction of a *physical* Nggwal enables men to dominate women, so the fiction of an *invisible* Nggwal enables the senior initiates to dominate their junior colleagues. The lie is itself a lie. Astonished upon first

[13]The maintenance of belief is, of course, necessary but not sufficient for the stability of the ritual system. See Tuzin (1980) for a comprehensive discussion of the wide range of social and power factors that also contribute to the viability of the Tambaran.

hearing this, I asked my informant, What, then, was the truth about Nggwal? to which he replied, "Nggwal is what men do."

Aware that much of what passes for religious "truth" is nothing but artifice, cult members are placed in the embarrassing position of having to confess to new initiates that they—the initiates—have been systematically deceived. The initiators themselves handle this in a jocular manner and are quick to point out to the novices the spiritual realities that are the true objects of revelation. If the novices are easily mollified, it is because they know that they are now beneficiaries of a system that formerly victimized them. The fathers of the novices, however, have none of these consolations. For years they have piously admonished their sons to grow or hunt food "for the Tambaran" in advance payment for their initiation. The feast is presented to the initiating class, but unknown to the novices, it is not the corporeal Nggwal but their own fathers who share in it. Whether or not the novices actually experience a sense of betrayal upon learning of their fathers' duplicity, the latter openly admit that they feel deeply shamed at having their true role revealed to their sons. Indeed, even after the young men have been formally initiated into Nggwal Bunafunei, their admission to the secret feasts is further delayed. It is at the behest of their fathers that this day is postponed in the hopes that if the news is leaked to the new initiates gently and judiciously, the blow of the discovery might be softened.

The attitude of the fathers reveals a flaw in the scheme of Tambaran rationalization. Cult ideology fully mandates their presence at these feasts, just as it insists on the need for secrecy regarding their participation. Why, then, should they be troubled over their role? I suggest that their guilty discomfiture springs from two converging sources: the intrusion into consciousness of secular filial sentiment, and the realization by some of the men, some of the time, that Nggwal is "what men do" and that in actuality, they alone bear responsibility for their actions. Thus, it often happens that a man will risk serious censure by surreptitiously taking a piece of pork to his wife. He explains to her that the (theoretically insatiable) Tambaran had eaten his fill and had kicked this remaining morsel aside, saying contemptuously that it may be given to the women. Of course, she is not to tell anyone that this occurred.

The men's moral dilemma is expressed in other ways as well. Consider, for example, the corpus of secret cult myths. The recurrent theme is that originally the Tambaran belonged to the women. In two of the stories, children and dogs, respectively, are given precedence. In those mythic days, it was the *men* who were terrorized by the audiovisual staging devices. When they discovered the true nature of the Tambaran, they were enraged at having been deceived. After murdering the rightful owners to silence them, the men usurped the Tambaran, proclaiming it as their own while concealing the fact of its true origin. Mindful of this history, men of today are uncomfortable in the knowledge that their ritual superiority lacks legitimacy. Senior cult members privately discuss their culpability, and in the symbolic realm the event of female vengeance is portrayed as a scene of primal destruction, overcast with images of castrative significance (Tuzin 1977*b*).[14] An urgency is thus added mythologically and psychodynamically to the preservation of cult secrecy. Instead of the leniency displayed in the preceding case, ritual brutality is intensified, taking on a punishing quality as the men attempt to dispel guilt that is colored with primary and secondary anxiety.[15]

Such maneuvers are, of course, futile and can only perpetuate the dilemma they seek to resolve, since the very acts taken to relieve the discomfort set the conditions for its future return. The result is a cultural addiction, in which the pain of continuing these ritual customs is exceeded only by the pain of relinquishing them. For an expression of the men's quandary. I can do no better than to quote the view of one informant who, when asked why the men do not admit women to the cult, had this to say: "It is true that sometimes men feel ashamed and guilty over eating good food while their wives go hungry. But if we told them now that for all these generations they had been deceived, they would make life unbearable for us. There is nothing we can do."

COMPARISON AND SUMMARY

If the contradiction examined in this chapter is ethnographically "real" and not simply an artifact of my method, we should expect to find some reference to it in the Mountain Arapesh researches of Mead—especially since her anthropology has the virtue of dealing more with the behavior of humans than with that of theoretical models. Indeed, she did notice the problem, and her observations are well worth considering for the light they shed on the Ilahita case. Noting that the Tambaran cult, as practiced

---

[14]In this regard, one should recall the male's special fear of his wife's ghost and also the myth that told of how the women once burned down the men's spirit house.

[15]Interestingly, in the myth recounting how the dogs formerly possessed Maolimu, the men acquire this tambaran peaceably and legitimately—by purchase rather than by violent usurpation. Thus, for whatever reason men of today are frequently cruel to their dogs, it is not because they are troubled by an image of canine revolt!

in many parts of New Guinea, enables the older men to sustain an aggressive authority over women and children, Mead writes:

In some tribes, a woman who accidentally sees the *tamberan* is killed. The young boys are threatened with dire things that will happen to them at their initiation, and initiation becomes a sort of vicious hazing in which the older men revenge themselves upon recalcitrant boys and for the indignities that they themselves once suffered. . . . Secrecy, age and sex-hostility, fear and hazing, have shaped its formal pattern. But the Arapesh, although they share part of the formal pattern with their neighbours, have changed all the emphases. In a community where there is no hostility between men and women, and where the old men, far from resenting the waxing strength of the young men, find in it their greatest source of happiness, *a cult that stresses hate and punishment is out of place*. And so the mountain people have revised most of the major points. Where other peoples kill a woman who chances on the secrets, and go to war against a community that does not keep its women sufficiently in the dark, the Arapesh merely swear the woman to secrecy, telling her that if she does not talk to others nothing will happen to her. (1935:67-68; emphasis added)

Their liberalism even extends to allowing uninitiated youths to participate in cult feasts; "but," Mead continues, "if critical and orthodox strangers . . . are present, the uninitiated boys are hustled out of sight, for the Arapesh are sensitive about their own happily muddled unorthodoxy" (1935:68).

The Ilahita Arapesh case instructs us that a cult stressing "hate and punishment" may, in fact, exist among a people whose temperamental inclinations are very like those that Mead describes.[16] Predictably, the Ilahita mismatch produces a muddled situation that is far from happy. The felicity of domestic relations must constantly contend with ritual prescriptions designed specifically to undermine marital and filial attachments; conversely, ritual orthodoxy is besieged by humane impulses that will not be denied. The stability of this contradictory situation suggests that an accommodation of sorts has been reached, one according to which opposed elements may carry on in troubled coexistence. The material presented in this chapter enables us, I think, to understand the

---

[16]It is likely that the Ilahita have diverged from what was formerly a common Arapesh pattern, the purest version of which has persisted among the mountain peoples. See Tuzin (1976) for an account of the dramatic shifts in Ilahita social structure and settlement patterns during the last century— events that, as noted earlier, are the probable sources of the value contradiction examined in this chapter.

nature of this accommodation and its behavioral implications.

To begin with, although Tambaran ideology insists that a man not differentiate between his hostilities toward noninitiates in general and those toward noninitiates belonging to his own family, the structure of ritual activities is such that overt physical aggression is rarely practiced against one's own wife and children. This tendency is especially true of the pattern of reciprocity between initation partners, whereby hazing is inflicted on *someone else's* son, and in the use of foreign villagers to enhance the terror of local initiation rites. It is easy to see that this convention would push the level of violence to the limits of permissibility, since filial solicitude favors returning punishment against those who would punish oneself and one's own. This granted, the fact remains that the men are, so to speak, "all in it together." The complicity of fathers in acts of violence, extortion, and deception against their sons is sufficient to induce feelings of guilt and embarrassment over the prospect of the latter discovering that the true state of affairs is a betrayal of filial trust and sentiment.

We see, then, that the accommodation spoken of earlier is only partly a function of the structure of ritual relationships. In addition, it depends on the willingness of actors to pay the emotional cost of living by two contradictory, affectively loaded codes of conduct. Although ideologically quite separable, in practice these codes have a ready tendency to invade each other's domain. In this chapter I have concentrated on the difficulty that actors sometimes experience in justifying, to themselves and to each other, the practice of ritual violence. Their problem is exacerbated by intermittent tremors of religious doubt. To the extent that the actor admits the contingency of his beliefs, he takes upon himself responsibility for deeds carried out in the name of those beliefs. This would not be emotionally taxing if his personal inclinations coincided with those prescribed by the belief system. And while some Arapesh men undoubtedly apprehend Nggwal and the other tambarans as agreeable and like-minded companions and therefore are morally untroubled as ritual executors, the great majority appear to subscribe to a domestic ethos that radically contradicts its ritual counterpart. For these men, when religious doubt asserts itself, domestic values are given momentary access to ritual consciousness; and when this happens, guilt results, impelling the actor either to mitigate or to intensify the severity of his conduct. Whichever way he responds, the respite is only temporary. The moral dilemma will continue as long as the individual is caught between two mutually abhorrent ethical doctrines.

CONCLUSION

The ritual violence described in this chapter is neither unusual nor extreme by New Guinea standards. Reports of such practices abound in the literature, and my fellow contributors to this volume provide additional examples. The question is, What is an appropriate anthropological response to ritual violence? One must, of course, attend to the ideological context, to the ethno-logic according to which such acts are deemed necessary. Surely, though, this task scarcely addresses the phenomenon's most interesting and anthropologically provocative aspect. Early observers may have been ethnocentric in their judgments and simplistic in their conclusions, but they were quite correct in their insistence that ritual violence be seen for what it is: a startling display of aggression carried out between persons who are not, by any normal stretch of the imagination, enemies. Restoring this sense of wonderment to our studies is, I suggest, an essential step in restoring the anthropology of ritual violence to the humanistic relevances with which it began.

In Ilahita, ritual violence evokes a problem in Arapesh ethics. The Tambaran requires men to perform acts that some of them, some of the time, regard with distressing ambivalence. Without analytic recognition of this ambivalence, without assessment of its various costs and rewards, it would have been impossible to account for the paradox of a cultural unity made up of major components that are logically irreconcilable. I do not know if the conflicts discussed here are unique to the Arapesh; but the fact that in many parts of New Guinea groups have been seen to abandon customs of ritual violence, suddenly and without apparent reluctance, at the first encouragement from missionaries and administrators, is a tantalizing hint that comparable problems may have existed elsewhere. In the Arapesh case, on the other hand, local European authorities have been hostile to the men's cult for over twenty years; and yet, with the exception of certain elements that are actually illegal, the people cling to the Tambaran with remarkable tenacity. This brings us to a question that looms large and unanswered at the close of this essay: Why do the Arapesh maintain—let alone why did they ever adopt!—an institution that, in its present form, engenders widespread mental and bodily pain? The relevance of this question is potentially far-reaching, for in their readiness to do bad things to one another and to punish themselves for doing it, these good people are not so very different from ourselves.

REFERENCE

BARTH, F.

1974 On responsibility and humanity: calling a colleague to account. *Current Anthropology* 15 (1):99–102.

BATESON, G.

1936 *Naven.* 2d ed. London: Cambridge University Press. 1st ed. 1936.

GIRARD, R.

1977 *Violence and the Sacred.* Baltimore: Johns Hopkins Press.

HALLPIKE, C. R.

1977 *Bloodshed and Vengeance in the Papuan Mountains: The Generation of Conflict in Tauade Society.* London: Oxford University Press.

1978 Accuracy, tact, and honesty. *Man* 13 (3):477.

HAU'OFA, E.

1971 Mekeo chieftainship. *Journal of the Polynesian Society* 80 (2):152–169.

HIATT, L. R.

1971 Secret pseudo-procreation rites among the Australian aborigines. In *Anthropology in Oceania: Essays Presented to Ian Hobgin,* ed. L. R. Hiatt and C. Jayawardena, pp. 77–78. Sydney: Angus and Robertson.

HOGBIN, I.

1970 *The Island of Menstruating Men: Religion in Wogeo, New Guinea.* Scranton, Pa.: Chandler Publishing Co.

MALINOWSKI, B.

1926 *Crime and Custom in Savage Society.* London: Routledge and Kegan Paul.

MEAD, M.

1934 Tamberans and Tumbuans in New Guinea. *Natural History* 34 (3):234–246.

1935 *Sex and Temperament in Three Primitive Societies.* London: George Routledge and Sons.

1938 The Mountain Arapesh: an importing culture. American Museum of Natural History, *Anthropological Papers* 36 (3):139–349.

MEGGITT, M. J.

1964 Male-Female Relationships in the Highlands of Australian New Guinea. In *New Guinea: The Central Highlands,* ed. J. B. Watson, *American Anthropologist* 66, pt. 2 (4):204–224.

SAGAN, E.

1974 *Cannibalism: Human Aggression and Cultural Form.* New York: Harper and Row.

STRATHERN, A. J.

1978 Review of *Bloodshed and Vengeance in the Papuan Mountains: The Generation of Conflict in Tauade Society,* by C. R. Hallpike. *Man* 13 (1):150–151.

TURNBULL, C. M.

1972 *The Mountain People.* New York: Simon and Schuster.

1974 Reply. *Current Anthropology* 15 (1):103.

TUZIN, D. F.

1972 Yam symbolism in the Sepik: an interpretative account. *Southwestern Journal of Anthropology* 28 (3):230–254.

1974 Social control and the Tambaran in the Sepik. In *Contention and Dispute: Aspects of Law and Social Control In Melanesia*, ed. A. L. Epstein, pp. 317-344. Canberra: Australian National University Press.

1976 *The Ilahita Arapesh: Dimensions of Unity*. Berkeley, Los Angeles, and London: University of California Press.

1977a Kinship terminology in a linguistic setting, In *New Guinea Area Languages and Language Study*, ed. S. A. Wurm. Vol. 3, *Pacific Linguistics*, series C, no. 40, pp. 101–129. Canberra: Australian National University Department of Linguistics.

1977b Reflections of being in Arapesh water symbolism. *Ethos* 5 (2):195–223.

1978 Sex and meat-eating in Ilahita: a symbolic study. *Canberra Anthropology* 1 (3):82-93.

1980 *The Voice of the Tambaran: Truth and Illusion in Ilahita Arapesh Religion*. Berkeley, Los Angeles, and London: University of California Press.

WEBSTER, HUTTON

1968 *Primitive Secret Societies: A Study in Early Politics and Religion*. Reprint. New York: Octagon Books. 1st ed. 1907.

INDEX

Abortion, 18
Adultery, 63, 207, 327; taboos on, 270, 277
Adz, 304; used in ritual, 170, 173, 180, 340
Afek, 116, 118, 120, 121, 125, 127, 128, 129, 131, 132, 133. *See also* Bimin-Kuskusmin
Age, of initiates, 12−13, 53, 107, 136, 157, 159, 175, 202, 204, 208, 209, 218−219, 222, 243, 245, 335, 337, 339
Aggregation, rites of, xiv
Ais am, 100−151; age groups in, 107−109; anger in, 144; dreams during, 114, 119, 145−146; and gender identity, 103, 104, 145−149; initiators in, 135−141; phases of, 104, 117−118, 120−134; physical problems during, 143−144; preparations for, 118−120; reactions to, 142−149; site of, 108−109, 117, 119, 132; social structure of, 116; trauma in, 138, 142−144, 150. *See also* Bimin-Kuskusmin
Amazon, 9, 11, 23
Androgyny, 114, 116, 127, 128, 129
Anteater, spiny, 104, 118, 124
Anthropology: and access to experience, 102 n.6; American, xiii; armchair studies of, ix-xiii, xvi, xix; British, xiii, xvi; symbolic, xviii, 2, 27−30, 38
Arapesh, Ilahita, xx, 4, 11, 12, 14, 16, 24, 111, 149, 322−353; beliefs on body fluids, 337−338, 340; bull-roarers used by, 339, 340−341; Christianized, 325; described, 326; divinations in, 333, 346−347; flutes used by, 335; kin in rituals of, 327, 335, 338; male initiation in, 323−324, 327, 328, 334−353; marriage in, 327, 328, 329−334, 351; moral dilemma of, 349−350, 352; mother/son separation in, 337, 344; myths of, 342−343; nuclear family in, 324, 327, 328−334; penis-cutting ritual of, 330, 337, 338,

340; pig feasts of, 324, 334, 348; ritual murder in, 324, 338−339, 345−347; sexual segregation in, 328; sorcery in, 345, 346−347, 348; spirit beliefs of, 332−333, 334, 338, 348; tambaran (male cult) of, 13, 14, 334−353; yams used by, 328, 329−330, 334
Arapesh, Mountain, 20, 324, 326, 338, 350−351
Auyana, 263, 268
Awa, xx, 6, 7, 12, 13, 14, 29, 240−284; age of initiates in, 245; beatings in rituals of, 249, 252−253, 254, 279; beliefs on body fluids of, 248−249, 252−253, 254, 257−258, 267, 279, 282; betrothal rites in, 274; bull-roarers used by, 247; childbirth in, 268, 272; described, 241; fasting in rituals of, 246, 248−249, 250, 253, 269, 275; female initiation rites of, 277−282, 284; flutes used by, 251, 257, 259, 260, 261−265, 268−269, 275; food taboos of, 241, 247−248, 258−259, 260, 263, 264−265, 269, 270, 273, 274; forced feeding in, 264−265; gardening by, 265; kin in rituals of, 252, 261, 278, 281−282, 283; male pregnancy in, 267, 276−277; male initiation rites of, 240−277, 282−284; men's houses of, 241, 245, 246, 247, 248−249, 255−257, 260, 269; mother/son separation in, 243, 244−245, 247, 283; myths of, 243−245, 270−274; nosebleeding by, 253, 254, 257, 261, 273, 275, 278−279, 283, 284; nose-piercing by, 251 n.12; ornamentation in, 250, 277, 280, 281; penis-cutting ritual of, 246, 253, 254, 257−258, 261, 275−277; pig-husbandry of, 268−269; on procreation, 240, 242, 243, 246, 272; purging in rituals of, 252−260, 261, 272−273, 274; seclusion by, 259; sex education of, 265, 266−267, 269−270, 272, 273, 276, 280, 281; sex taboos of, 265,

Manus Is.

NEW IRELAND

PAPUA
W GUINEA

NEW BRITAIN

5°

Madang

uku-Gama
BenaBena
Fore □
Ndumba
Markham R.
▲ Finschafen
Lae

□ Tauade

Popondetta ▲

Port Moresby ⊛

10°

Samarai

0   100   200

STATUTE MILES

150°